Quattro Pro 6 For Windows

COMPUTER BOOK SERIES FROM IDG

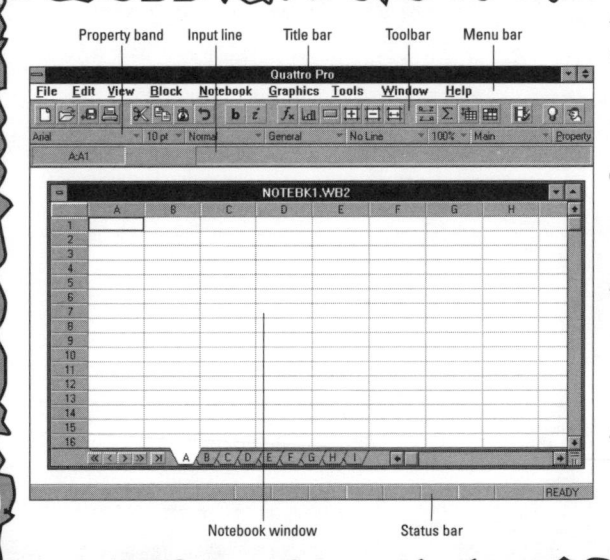

Labels: Property band, Input line, Title bar, Toolbar, Menu bar, Notebook window, Status bar

Formatting shortcut keys

Key Combination	Function
Ctrl+B	Boldface selected cells
Ctrl+E	Center selected cells
Ctrl+I	Italicize selected cells
Ctrl+L	Left align selected cells
Ctrl+R	Right align selected cells
Ctrl+U	Underline selected cells
Ctrl+Shift+S	Activate the Style pull-down on the Property Band
Alt+Right arrow	Display the SpeedFormat dialog box
Alt+P, Enter	Display the Object Inspector dialog box, which contains all the formatting options

Keyboard commands for dialog boxes

Key/Combination	Function
Alt+ *hot key*	Activate the control of the hot key (underlined letter) that you press
Tab	Activate the next control in the dialog box
Shift+Tab	Activate the previous control in the dialog box
Spacebar	Check or uncheck an option button or check box
Enter	Complete the command and close the dialog box (just like clicking the OK button)
Esc	Close the dialog box without completing the command (just like clicking the Cancel button)
Ctrl+PgDn	Display the next panel in an Object Inspector dialog box
Ctrl+PgUp	Display the preceding panel in an Object Inspector dialog box
Ctrl+Backspace	Clear an existing entry in a list or edit box
F1	Display help for the dialog box

The function keys

Key	Function
F1	Display on-line help that's usually relevant to what you're doing
F2	Switch the program into Edit mode so that you can change the contents of the current cell
F3	When prompted for a block or in Edit mode, displays a list of block names
F4	In Edit, Point or Value mode, cycles through all the possible cell references in formulas (absolute, mixed, relative)
F5	Move the cell pointer to a specific cell, named block or notebook page
F6	Move the cell pointer between panes in split windows
F7	Repeat the last data query command
F8	Repeat the last what-if table command
F9	In Ready mode, recalculates the worksheet. In Edit mode, converts a formula to its current value
F10	Activates the menu bar so you can select commands from the keyboard

... For Dummies: #1 Computer Book Series for Beginners

Quattro Pro 6 For Windows For Dummies

Cheat Sheet

Navigation keys

Key	Function
Left arrow	Move left one cell
Right arrow	Move right one cell
Up arrow	Move up one cell
Down arrow	Move down one cell
Ctrl+PgDn	Move to the next notebook page
Ctrl+PgUp	Move to the preceding notebook page
PgUp	Move up one screen
PgDn	Move down one screen
Home	Move to cell A1 of the current notebook page
Ctrl+Home	Move to cell A1 of the first page in the notebook
End, Home	Move to the last non-blank cell of the current notebook page
Ctrl+End, Home	Move to the last nonblank cell of the last page in the notebook
End, *arrow key*	Move in the direction of the arrow to the next non-blank cell before an empty one. If the current cell is empty, moves to the next filled cell in that direction
Ctrl+Left arrow	Move left one screen
Ctrl+Right arrow	Move right one screen

To change object settings or properties

Right-click an object and select the Properties command from the SpeedMenu to display its Object Inspector dialog box. You can change most settings from this dialog box.

To move a cell or block

Select a cell or block with your mouse and release the left mouse button. Left-click the selection and hold down the mouse button until the mouse pointer turns into a hand. Then drag the selected block to its new location.

To copy a block

Select a cell or block with your mouse and release the left mouse button. Press Ctrl while you left-click the selection and hold down the mouse button until the mouse pointer turns into a hand. Then drag the selected block to another location (the original cells remain).

Creating a graph

1. Select the cells that contain the data to be graphed (including labels).
2. Click the Graph tool.
   The mouse pointer turns into a miniature graph.
3. Click and drag in the notebook to specify the location and size of the chart.
4. When you release the mouse button, the chart will appear.
5. Double-click the graph if you want to change it in any way.
   After double-clicking a graph, the menus and toolbars change appropriately.

Mouse techniques

To select this	Do this
Cell	Click the cell
Block	Click a cell in one corner, hold down the left mouse button and drag to the opposite corner of the block. Or, click one corner, press Shift, and click the opposite corner
Noncontiguous block	Press Ctrl key while you drag blocks
Row	Click a row number in the border
Column	Click a column letter in the border
Page	Click the box at the intersection of the row and column borders
3-D block	First select the block in the first page, then press Shift while clicking the page tab for the last page in the 3-D block

Other useful shortcut keys

Key Combination	Function
Ctrl+C	Copy selection to Clipboard
Ctrl+N	Start a new notebook
Ctrl+O	Opens an existing notebook
Ctrl+P	Print the current notebook
Ctrl+Q	Exit Quattro Pro for Windows
Ctrl+S	Save the current notebook
Ctrl+V	Paste the contents of the Clipboard
Ctrl+W	Close the current notebook
Ctrl+X	Remove the selection and put it on the Clipboard
Ctrl+Z	Reverse the effect of the last command
Del	Erase the contents (but not formats) of the selected cells
Ctrl+Shift+T	Display the next Toolbar for the active window

Copyright © 1994 IDG Books Worldwide. All rights reserved.
Cheat Sheet $2.95 value. Item 174-4.
For more information about IDG Books, call 1-800-762-2974 or 415-312-0650

... For Dummies: #1 Computer Book Series for Beginners

References for the Rest of Us

COMPUTER BOOK SERIES FROM IDG

Are you intimidated and confused by computers? Do you find that traditional manuals are overloaded with technical details you'll never use? Do your friends and family always call you to fix simple problems on their PCs? Then the ... *For Dummies*™ computer book series from IDG is for you.

...*For Dummies* books are written for those frustrated computer users who know they aren't really dumb but find that PC hardware, software, and indeed the unique vocabulary of computing make them feel helpless. ...*For Dummies* books use a lighthearted approach, a down-to-earth style, and even cartoons and humorous icons to diffuse computer novices' fears and build their confidence. Lighthearted but not lightweight, these books are a perfect survival guide to anyone forced to use a computer.

> "I like my copy so much I told friends; now they bought copies."
> — Irene C., Orwell, Ohio

> "Quick, concise, nontechnical, and humorous."
> — Jay A., Elburn, IL

> "Thanks, I needed this book. Now I can sleep at night."
> — Robin F., British Columbia, Canada

Already, hundreds of thousands of satisfied readers agree. They have made ...*For Dummies* books the #1 introductory level computer book series and have written asking for more. So if you're looking for the most fun and easy way to learn about computers, look to ...*For Dummies* books to give you a helping hand.

QUATTRO PRO 6 FOR WINDOWS FOR DUMMIES™

QUATTRO PRO 6 FOR WINDOWS FOR DUMMIES™

by John Walkenbach

IDG Books Worldwide, Inc.
An International Data Group Company

Foster City, CA ♦ Chicago, IL ♦ Indianapolis, IN ♦ Braintree, MA ♦ Dallas, TX

Quattro Pro 6 For Windows For Dummies

Published by
IDG Books Worldwide, Inc.
An International Data Group Company
919 E. Hillsdale Blvd.
Suite 400
Foster City, CA 94404

Text copyright ©1994 by IDG Books Worldwide. Art copyright ©1994 by IDG Books Worldwide. All rights reserved. No part of this book may be reproduced or transmitted in any form, by any means (electronic, photocopying, recording, or otherwise) without the prior written permission of the publisher.

Library of Congress Catalog Card No.: 94-78910

ISBN: 1-56884-174-4

Printed in the United States of America

10 9 8 7 6 5 4 3 2

1A/QZ/RR/ZU

Distributed in the United States by IDG Books Worldwide, Inc.

Distributed in Canada by Macmillan of Canada, a Division of Canada Publishing Corporation; by Computer and Technical Books in Miami, Florida, for South America and the Caribbean; by Longman Singapore in Singapore, Malaysia, Thailand, and Korea; by Toppan Co. Ltd. in Japan; by Asia Computerworld in Hong Kong; by Woodslane Pty. Ltd. in Australia and New Zealand; and by Transworld Publishers Ltd. in the U.K. and Europe.

For general information on IDG Books in the U.S., including information on discounts and premiums, contact IDG Books at 800-434-3422 or 415-312-0650.

For information on where to purchase IDG Books outside the U.S., contact Christina Turner at 415-312-0650.

For information on translations, contact Marc Jeffrey Mikulich, Director Foreign & Subsidiary Rights, at IDG Books Worldwide; FAX NUMBER 415-286-0650.

For sales inquiries and special prices for bulk quantities, write to the address above or call IDG Books Worldwide at 415-312-0650.

For information using IDG Books in the classroom, or ordering examination copies, contact Jim Kelly at 800-434-2086

Trademarks: Quattro Pro is a trademark of Novell, Inc., and Windows is a trademark of Microsoft Corporation. All brand names and product names used in this book are trademarks, registered trademarks, or trade names of their respective holders. IDG Books Worldwide is not associated with any product or vendor mentioned in this book.

Limit of Liability/Disclaimer of Warranty: The author and publisher have used their best efforts in preparing this book. IDG Books Worldwide, Inc., International Data Group, Inc., and the author make no representation or warranties with respect to the accuracy or completeness of the contents of this book and specifically disclaim any implied warranties of merchantability or fitness for any particular purpose and shall in no event be liable for any loss of profit or any other commercial damage, including but not limited to special, incidental, consequential, or other damages.

 is a registered trademark of
IDG Books Worldwide, Inc.

About the Author

John Walkenbach is one of the country's leading spreadsheet authors and has published more than 250 articles and reviews for magazines such as *PC World, InfoWorld,* and *Windows*. He's also written a dozen or so books, all dealing with various spreadsheet topics. John holds a Ph.D. in experimental psychology from the University of Montana, and he has worked as an instructor, programmer, and market research manager for the largest S&L ever to fail (and he takes no responsibility for that). Currently he heads JWalk and Associates Inc., a consulting firm based in La Jolla, California. Besides spreadsheets, John is interested in Visual Basic programming and multimedia applications. He's an amateur musician and spends as much time as he can playing around in his MIDI studio trying to get his computer to help him compose decent music — but mostly just annoying his neighbors with weird synthesizer sounds.

ABOUT IDG BOOKS WORLDWIDE

Welcome to the world of IDG Books Worldwide.

IDG Books Worldwide, Inc. is a subsidiary of International Data Group, the world's largest publisher of business and computer-related information and the leading global provider of information services on information technology. IDG was founded more than 25 years ago and now employs more than 7,000 people worldwide. IDG publishes more than 220 computer publications in 65 countries (see listing below). More than fifty million people read one or more IDG publications each month.

Launched in 1990, IDG Books Worldwide is today the fastest-growing publisher of computer and business books in the United States. We are proud to have received 3 awards from the Computer Press Association in recognition of editorial excellence, and our best-selling ...*For Dummies*™ series has more than 12 million copies in print with translations in more than 24 languages. IDG Books, through a recent joint venture with IDG's Hi-Tech Beijing, became the first U.S. publisher to publish a computer book in the People's Republic of China. In record time, IDG Books has become the first choice for millions of readers around the world who want to learn how to better manage their businesses.

Our mission is simple: Every IDG book is designed to bring extra value and skill-building instructions to the reader. Our books are written by experts who understand and care about our readers. The knowledge base of our editorial staff comes from years of experience in publishing, education, and journalism — experience which we use to produce books for the '90s. In short, we care about books, so we attract the best people. We devote special attention to details such as audience, interior design, use of icons, and illustrations. And because we use an efficient process of authoring, editing, and desktop publishing our books electronically, we can spend more time ensuring superior content and spend less time on the technicalities of making books.

You can count on our commitment to deliver high-quality books at competitive prices on topics consumers want to read about. At IDG, we value quality, and we have been delivering quality for more than 25 years. You'll find no better book on a subject than an IDG book.

John Kilcullen
President and CEO
IDG Books Worldwide, Inc.

IDG Books Worldwide, Inc. is a subsidiary of International Data Group, the world's largest publisher of computer-related information and the leading global provider of information services on information technology. International Data Group publishes over 220 computer publications in 65 countries. More than fifty million people read one or more International Data Group publications each month. The officers are Patrick J. McGovern, Founder and Board Chairman; Kelly Conlin, President; Jim Casella, Chief Operating Officer. International Data Group's publications include: **ARGENTINA'S** Computerworld Argentina, Infoworld Argentina; **AUSTRALIA'S** Computerworld Australia, Computer Living, Australian PC World, Australian Macworld, Network World, Mobile Business Australia, Publish!, Reseller, IDG Sources; **AUSTRIA'S** Computerwelt Oesterreich, PC Test; **BELGIUM'S** Data News (CW); **BOLIVIA'S** Computerworld; **BRAZIL'S** Computerworld, Connections, Game Power, Mundo Unix, PC World, Publish, Super Game; **BULGARIA'S** Computerworld Bulgaria, PC & Mac World Bulgaria, Network World Bulgaria; **CANADA'S** CIO Canada, Computerworld Canada, InfoCanada, Network World Canada, Reseller; **CHILE'S** Computerworld Chile, Informatica; **COLOMBIA'S** Computerworld Colombia, PC World; **COSTA RICA'S** PC World; **CZECH REPUBLIC'S** Computerworld, Elektronika, PC World; **DENMARK'S** Communications World, Computerworld Danmark, Computerworld Focus, Macintosh Produktkatalog, Macworld Danmark, PC World Danmark, PC Produktguide, Tech World, Windows World; **ECUADOR'S** PC World Ecuador; **EGYPT'S** Computerworld (CW) Middle East, PC World Middle East; **FINLAND'S** MikroPC, Tietoviikko, Tietoverkko; **FRANCE'S** Distributique, GOLDEN MAC, InfoPC, Le Guide du Monde Informatique, Le Monde Informatique, Telecoms & Reseaux; **GERMANY'S** Computerwoche, Computerwoche Focus, Computerwoche Extra, Electronic Entertainment, Gamepro, Information Management, Macwelt, Netzwelt, PC Welt, Publish, Publish; **GREECE'S** Publish & Macworld; **HONG KONG'S** Computerworld Hong Kong, PC World Hong Kong; **HUNGARY'S** Computerworld SZT, PC World; **INDIA'S** Computers & Communications; **INDONESIA'S** Info Komputer; **IRELAND'S** ComputerScope; **ISRAEL'S** Beyond Windows, Computerworld Israel, Multimedia, PC World Israel; **ITALY'S** Computerworld Italia, Lotus Magazine, Macworld Italia, Networking Italia, PC Shopping Italy, PC World Italia; **JAPAN'S** Computerworld Today, Information Systems World, Macworld Japan, Nikkei Personal Computing, SunWorld Japan, Windows World; **KENYA'S** East African Computer News; **KOREA'S** Computerworld Korea, Macworld Korea, PC World Korea; **LATIN AMERICA'S** GamePro; **MALAYSIA'S** Computerworld Malaysia, PC World Malaysia; **MEXICO'S** Compu Edicion, Compu Manufactura, Computacion/Punto de Venta, Computerworld Mexico, MacWorld, Mundo Unix, PC World, Windows; **THE NETHERLANDS'** Computer! Totaal, Computable (CW), LAN Magazine, Lotus Magazine, MacWorld; **NEW ZEALAND'S** Computer Buyer, Computerworld New Zealand, Network World, New Zealand PC World; **NIGERIA'S** PC World Africa; **NORWAY'S** Computerworld Norge, Lotusworld Norge, Macworld Norge, Maxi Data, Networld, PC World Ekspress, PC World Nettverk, PC World Norge, PC World's Produktguide, Publish& Multimedia World, Student Data, Unix World, Windowsworld; **PAKISTAN'S** PC World Pakistan; **PANAMA'S** PC World Panama; **PERU'S** Computerworld Peru, PC World; **PEOPLE'S REPUBLIC OF CHINA'S** China Computerworld, China Infoworld, China PC Info Magazine, Computer Fan, PC World China, Electronics International, Electronics Today/Multimedia World, Electronic Product World, China Network World, Software World Magazine, Telecom Product World, **PHILIPPINES'** Computerworld Philippines, PC Digest (PCW); **POLAND'S** Computerworld Poland, Computerworld Special Report, Networld, PC World/Komputer, Sunworld; **PORTUGAL'S** Cerebro/PC World, Correio Informatico/Computerworld, MacIn; **ROMANIA'S** Computerworld, PC World, Telecom Romania; **RUSSIA'S** Computerworld-Moscow, Mir - PK (PCW), Sety (Networks); **SINGAPORE'S** Computerworld Southeast Asia, PC World Singapore; **SLOVENIA'S** Monitor Magazine; **SOUTH AFRICA'S** Computer Mail (CIO),Computing S.A.,Network World S.A., Software World; **SPAIN'S** Advanced Systems, Amiga World, Computerworld Espana, Communicaciones World, Macworld Espana, NeXTWORLD, Super Juegos Magazine (GamePro); PC World Espana, Publish; **SWEDEN'S** Attack, ComputerSweden, Corporate Computing, Macworld, Mikrodatorn, Natverk & Kommunikation, PC World, CAP & Design, DataIngenjoren, Maxi Data,Windows World; **SWITZERLAND'S** Computerworld Schweiz, Macworld Schweiz, PC Tip; **TAIWAN'S** Computerworld Taiwan, PC World Taiwan; **THAILAND'S** Thai Computerworld; **TURKEY'S** Computerworld Monitor, Macworld Turkiye, PC World Turkiye; **UKRAINE'S** Computerworld, Computers+Software Magazine; **UNITED KINGDOM'S** Computing/Computerworld, Connexion/Network World, Lotus Magazine, Macworld, Open Computing/Sunworld; **URAGUAY'S** PC World Uraguay; **UNITED STATES'** Advanced Systems, AmigaWorld, Cable in the Classroom, CD Review, CIO, Computerworld, Computerworld Client/Server Journal, Digital Video, DOS World, Electronic Entertainment Magazine (E2), Federal Computer Week, Game Hits, GamePro, IDG Books, Infoworld, Laser Event, Macworld, Maximize, Multimedia World, Network World, PC Letter, PC World, Publish, SWATPro, Video Event; **VENEZUELA'S** Computerworld Venezuela, PC World; **VIETNAM'S** PC World Vietnam.

Dedication

This one's for VaRene...

Acknowledgments

Many people are responsible for getting a book like this into your hands, so I don't take all the blame. There's not room to acknowledge them all, so I'll simply mention a few who played a major role in the process. First, thanks to all the talented behind-the-scenes folks at IDG Books. I've done several projects with this publisher, and consider them the best in the business. More specifically, thanks to Janna Custer and Megg Bonar in the Acquisitions department. Also thanks to my editors — Erik Dafforn, John Edwards, Michael Simsic, Jeff Waggoner, and Bill Helling, who helped convert my words into even better words. I'm also indebted to Stuart Stuple, who did a thorough job with the technical review (and set me straight on a few things).

The book looks as good as it does because of the fine work done by the Production team at IDG Books. I'm also grateful to Borland International for coming up with such a good product in the first place (I just hope Novell is as easy to get along with as the people at Borland have been). Last but not least, thanks to my good friend VaRene, who provided unfailing support and good times throughout the process.

(The Publisher would like to give special thanks to Patrick J. McGovern, without whom this book would not have been possible.)

Credits

Publisher
David Solomon

Acquisitions Editor
Megg Bonar

Brand Manager
Judith A. Taylor

Editorial Director
Diane Graves Steele

Editorial Managers
Tracy L. Barr
Sandra Blackthorn

Editorial Assistants
Tamara S. Castleman
Stacey Holden Prince
Kevin Spencer

Acquisitions Assistant
Suki Gear

Production Director
Beth Jenkins

Production Coordinator
Valery Bourke

Pre-Press Coordinator
Steve Peake

Project Editor
Erik Dafforn

Editors
John C. Edwards
Diane L. Giangrossi
Michael Simsic
Bill Helling
Jeffrey Waggoner

Technical Reviewer
Stuart Stuple

Production Staff
Tony Augsburger
Paul Belcastro
Linda M. Boyer
Sherry Dickinson Gomoll
Drew R. Moore
Mark Owens
Carla Radzikinas
Dwight Ramsey
Patricia R. Reynolds
Kathie Schnorr
Gina Scott

Proofreader
Jenny Kaufeld

Indexer
Sharon Hilgenberg

Cover Design
Kavish + Kavish

Contents at a Glance

Introduction 1

Part I: First Things First 9
Chapter 1: What This Thing Can (and Can't) Do 11
Chapter 2 Starting, Stopping, and Begging for Help 23
Chapter 3: The Obligatory Tour of the Screen 37
Chapter 4: Jumping Right In (A Hands-On Experience) 51

Part II: Basic Stuff That You Just Can't Ignore 69
Chapter 5: Ways to Fill Up All Those Cells 71
Chapter 6: The Inside Scoop on Menus, Dialog Boxes, and Toolbars 85
Chapter 7: How to Prevent Losing Your Work (and Ruining Your Whole Day) ... 107
Chapter 8: Formulas: Not Just for Babies Anymore 127
Chapter 9: Making Formulas More Functional 147
Chapter 10: Making Changes to Your Work (and Living to Talk about It) 167
Chapter 11: Putting it on Paper 193

Part III: How to Impress the Easily Impressed 211
Chapter 12: Dressing up Your Work 213
Chapter 13: Presto Chango: Turning Numbers into Graphs 233
Chapter 14: Making the Most of Notebooks 253
Chapter 15: Making Quattro Pro for Windows Your Slave 263

Part IV: Faking It 271
Chapter 16: The Lowdown on Lists and Databases 273
Chapter 17: Cool Formulas You Can Steal 291
Chapter 18: Just Enough about Macros to Get By 303
Chapter 19: How Do I 317

Part V: The Part of Tens 329

Chapter 20: Ten Good Habits You Should Acquire 331

Chapter 21: Top Ten (or So) Shortcut Keys 335

Chapter 22: Ten Concepts Every Quattro Pro for Windows User Should Understand 337

Chapter 23: The Ten Commandments of Quattro Pro for Windows 341

Appendix A: If You Gotta Install it Yourself 343

Appendix B: Glossary 347

Index 365

Reader Response Card .... Back of Book

Cartoons at a Glance
By Rich Tennant

page 9

page 35

page 69

page 125

page 211

page 106

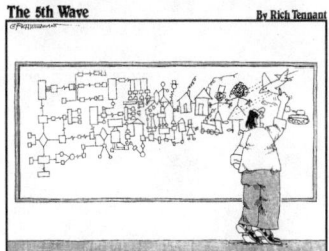
page 271

page 302

page 329

page 340

Table of Contents

Introduction *1*

What This Book Covers 2
Read the Whole Thing? Naah... 2
What to skip, what to read 3
Yes, this book is organized (sort of) 4
Foolish Assumptions About You 5
Conventions — Typographical and Otherwise 6
Of mice and keyboards 6
I think icon, I think icon 7
Now What? 8

Part I: First Things First *9*

Chapter 1: What This Thing Can (And Can't) Do 11
Spreadsheets 101 (This Will Be on the Final Exam!) 11
So what is a spreadsheet? 12
Borland? WordPerfect? Novell? 14
Quattro Schmattro 14
Yes, but does it taste good? 15
Excursions into versions 15
What Can This Puppy Do? 16
Crunch numbers 16
Make killer graphs 17
Manage your lists 18
Manage databases 19
Access other data 20
Automate with macros 20
Activate fun stuff 20
Who knows what else 20
What Can't This Puppy Do? 21
How Spreadsheets Are Put Together (Secret Stuff) 22

Chapter 2: Starting, Stopping, and Begging for Help 23
Starting Quattro Pro for Windows 24
Starting Quattro Pro for Windows from the Windows
Program Manager 24
Starting Quattro Pro for Windows from DOS 25
Switching Out of Quattro Pro for Windows 26

Quattro Pro 6 For Windows For Dummies

Quitting Quattro Pro for Windows 28
  The right way to exit 28
  The wrong way to exit 29
Help! I Need Help! 30
  An example of using Help 32
  Pointers for using Help 33
  Help with Help 34
Using the Built-in Coaches 34

Chapter 3: The Obligatory Tour of the Screen 37

The Screen Tour (It's the Law) 37
More About Notebooks 40
May I See a Menu? 41
Belly Up to the Toolbar 42
Property Band 42
Some Useless Terminology 43
  Rows, columns, cells, and pages 43
  Gimme your address 44
  The active cell 45
Move It Along 45
  Moving around with a mouse 46
  Moving around with the keyboard 46
  When the arrow keys don't work 48
  Really advanced secret stuff 48
  Summary of movement options 49

Chapter 4: Jumping Right In (A Hands-On Experience) 51

What You'll Be Doing 52
First Steps 53
  Putting in the column headings 54
  Making the headings bold 55
  Adjusting the column widths 56
Entering the Data 57
Formatting the Dollar Amounts 57
And Now, a Formula 59
  Inserting new rows 60
  Sticking in the formula 60
  Ready for another formula? 61
Adding a Title 62
Saving This Masterpiece 63
Working with the Notebook 64
Saving It Again 64
Quitting Quattro Pro for Windows 65
Retrieving Your Work 65
Still Afraid? 66
Food for Thought 66
Other Stuff for Overachievers 67

Part II: Basic Stuff That You Just Can't Ignore 69

Chapter 5: Ways to Fill Up All Those Cells 71

What to Do with a Blank Notebook 71
What Goes in a Cell? 72
More About What Goes in a Cell 72
Putting Numbers into Cells 73
Making Numbers Look Right 74
    What is formatting? 74
    How to format numbers 75
Entering Labels 76
Some Weird Stuff about Labels 77
    More useless terminology 78
    What if the words don't fit? 78
Aligning Labels and Numbers 79
When Enter Isn't Good Enough 81
Changing Things You've Done 81
    Overwriting a cell 81
    Editing a cell 82
    Nuking a cell completely 83

Chapter 6: The Inside Scoop on Menus, Dialog Boxes, and Toolbars 85

Quattro Pro for Windows: At Your Command 86
Two Types of Menu Systems 86
    The main menu bar 87
    SpeedMenus 87
Using Menus 88
    With a mouse 88
    With the keyboard 90
More About Menus 90
What the Menus Are Good For 92
    The File menu 92
    The Edit menu 92
    The View menu 93
    The Block menu 93
    The Notebook menu 93
    The Graphics menu 93
    The Tools menu 93
    The Window menu 93
    The Help menu 94
Carrying On a Meaningful Dialog 94
    The anatomy of a dialog box 94
    Dialog box controls 95
    Mousing through dialog boxes 101
    If you prefer the keyboard 101

Toolbars 102
    Why Toolbars? 102
    True facts about Toolbars 102
    So many Toolbars, so little time 103
    Toolbars at your disposal 103
    Using Toolbars 103
The Property Band 104
    Using the Property Band 104
    Property Band pull-down lists 104
In Conclusion 105

Chapter 7: How to Prevent Losing Your Work (and Ruining Your Whole Day) 107

Protecting Your Work 107
Using Files with Quattro Pro for Windows 109
    A new notebook 109
    Saving files 110
A Visit to the File Menu 110
    Files and windows 110
    The file-related File menu commands 112
    Non-file-related File menu commands 117
Doing Things with a File — Step by Step 118
Making Backups 120
    Backing up from Quattro Pro for Windows 121
    Backing up from the Windows File Manager program 122
    Backing up from DOS 124
    Other ways to back up your work 124

Chapter 8: Formulas: Not Just for Babies Anymore 127

Formulas: The Definition 128
Hello, Operator? 130
    Using parentheses 131
How to Enter Formulas 135
Just How Complex Can Formulas Be? 138
Relative and Absolute References 139
    It's all relative 139
    Absolutely absolute 140
    Why use absolute references? 141
    And it gets even uglier 142
Even More about Formulas 143
    Controlling recalculation 143
    Using built-in functions 145
    Other types of formulas 145

Chapter 9: Making Formulas More Functional 147

Getting Functional 147
    OK, what is an @function? 148
    A functional example 148
    Cells, blocks, and cell blocks 149
    Adding pages to cell references 151
Entering @functions 151
    The direct approach 151
    The pointing method 152
    Let's have an argument 152
    Editing @functions 153
    Insert @function here, insert @function here! 154
@function Categories 156
Some Useful Numeric @functions 157
    @MAX 157
    @MIN 158
    @SQRT 158
    @ROUND 158
@functions for Dates and Times 159
    @DATE 159
    @TODAY 160
    @TIME 160
Combined @functions in Formulas 161
    The nesting instinct revisited 162
    Testing conditions 162
Naming Cells and Blocks 163
    An example 164
    Another example 164
    How to name cells and blocks 164

Chapter 10: Making Changes to Your Work (and Living to Talk about It) 167

Types of Changes You Can Make 168
Cutting and Pasting — Scissors and Glue Not Required 169
    How cutting and pasting works 169
    Why cut and paste things? 171
    Cutting and pasting a cell 171
    Cutting and pasting a block 172
    Cutting and pasting formulas 172
    The E-Z way to move things 172
Copying Things Things Things 173
    How copying works 174
    Why copy? 174
    Copying a cell to a cell 174
    Copying a cell to a block 175
    Copying a block to a block 175

   Copying formulas 176
   Drag-and-drop copying 177
  Adjusting Column Widths 178
   Why widen columns? 178
   Adjusting column widths using the menu 179
   The E-Z way to adjust column widths 180
  Changing Row Heights 182
  Erasing Cells and Blocks 183
  Adding New Rows and Columns 184
   Why do it? 184
   Adding new rows 185
   Adding new columns 185
  Getting Rid of Rows and Columns 185
   Why do it? 186
   Eliminating rows 186
   Deleting columns 186
  Transposing Rows and Columns 186
   Why do it? 186
   How to do it 187
  Finding and Replacing — Wherefore Art Thou, Text String? 188
  Sorting Blocks of Cells — Head 'em Up and Move 'em Out 189
   Why do it? 189
   How to do it 189

Chapter 11: Putting It on Paper 193

  The Seedy Side of Printing 193
  Printing 101 194
  Getting a Sneak Preview 196
  Printing 202 197
   Specifying what to print 198
   Printing multiple copies 199
   Page Setup options 199
   Sheet options 205
   Printing charts, drawings, and other neat stuff 206
  Printers Du Jour 207
   Laser printers 207
   Inkjet printers 208
   Dot-matrix printers 208
   Daisywheel printers 208

Part III: How to Impress the Easily Impressed 211

Chapter 12: Dressing Up Your Work 213

What is Stylistic Formatting? 213
When Plain Old Text Won't Cut the Mustard 214
General Principles of Formatting 215
    When to format 215
    Screen vs. printer 216
    General formatting how-to 216
Introducing the Format Toolbar 217
Dealing with Fonts 218
    Types of fonts 219
    Changing fonts 220
Borders, Lines, and Frames 222
    Adding lines or borders 223
Color, Color Everywhere 225
Alignment and Misalignment 226
    Horizontal alignment 226
    Vertical alignment 227
    Word wrap 227
    Centering across cells 228
    Changing orientation 229
And Now, the E-Z Way to Format Tables 229
Some Final Words 230

Chapter 13: Presto Chango: Turning Numbers into Graphs 233

The Graph's Parts 234
Graph Tidbits 235
How to Create a Graph 235
Making a Graph Be Your Eternal Slave 237
    Changing the graph type 238
    Adding titles 239
    Changing the graph series 239
    Swapping rows and columns 241
    Moving and resizing a graph 242
    Graph annihilation techniques 243
    Printing graphs 243
Rearranging Your Graph's Furniture 244
Hungry for More Graph Power? 245
Gallery of Gorgeous Graphs 245
    An annotated line graph 245
    A combination graph 246
    A rotated bar graph 246
    Stacked bars 247

An XY graph 248
A doughnut graph 249
A very fancy graph 249
A stock market graph 249
A surface graph 251
Another XY graph 251

Chapter 14: Making the Most of Notebooks 253

Why Use More Than One Page? 253
Ideas for Using 3-D Notebooks, No Weird Glasses Needed 254
Things You Should Know about 3-D Notebooks
  (Things That Your Mother Never Told You) 255
Fundamental Stuff 256
  Naming pages 256
  Displaying more than one page at a time 256
  Moving pages 257
  Printing multiple pages 258
Navigating in the Third Dimension (without the Help of Captain Picard) ... 258
  Activating other pages 259
  Selecting 3-D ranges 260
Group Mode 260
  Naming a group of pages 261
  Getting into group mode 261
  Using group mode 262
A Final Note 262

Chapter 15: Making Quattro Pro for Windows Your Slave 263

Have It Your Way 263
  Hiding and showing things 264
  Zoom in, zoom out 265
The Paneful Way of Seeing More of Your Notebook 267
Freezing Rows and Columns (Even in the Dead of Summer) 268
Chekking Your Speling 270

Part IV: Faking It 271

Chapter 16: The Lowdown on Lists and Databases 273

Lists and Databases 273
  A sample list 274
  A sample database 274
What You Can Do with a Database 275
Database Basics 276
  The database block 277
  The criteria table 277
  The output block 278

Table of Contents

Creating a Database 278
    Setting up field names 278
    Entering data into a database 279
An Example 281
    The database 281
    The objective 282
    Setting up the criteria table 282
    Setting up the extract block 284
    Performing the query 284
    Changing the criteria 286
    Locating records 286
Using Formulas with Databases 288
Printing Databases 290

Chapter 17: Cool Formulas You Can Steal 291

Read This First 291
Common, Everyday Formulas 292
    Calculating a sum 292
    Computing an average 292
    Calculating a percentage change 293
    Finding the minimum and maximum in a block 293
    Calculating a loan payment 294
Mathematical Formulas 295
    Finding a square root 295
    Finding a cube (or other) root 295
    Checking for even or odd values 295
    Generating a random number 296
    Rounding numbers 296
Label Formulas 297
    "Adding" labels 297
    Working with labels and values 297
Date Formulas 298
    Finding out what day it is 298
    Determining the day of the week 299
    Determining the last day of the month 299
Miscellaneous Formulas 299
    Displaying the notebook name 299
    Looking up a corresponding value 300
    Converting measurements 301

Chapter 18: Just Enough about Macros to Get By 303

What Is a Macro? 303
More about Macros 304
Your First Macro 305
    Creating the macro 305

Quattro Pro 6 For Windows For Dummies

    Running the macro 306
    Modifying the macro 307
    Some macro rules 308
The Macro Recorder 309
Recording and Executing a Macro 309
    Recording it 309
    Naming it 310
    Playing it 310
    Fixing it 311
Getting More Advanced 312
Using Other People's Macros 314
What Next? 315

Chapter 19: How Do I... 317

Editing 317
    Changing the contents of a cell 317
    Selecting a block of cells 318
    Copying a block of cells 318
    Copying between notebooks 318
    Copying a cell or block, but not its formats 319
    Copying only the formats from a cell or block 319
    Moving a block of cells 319
    Deleting a cell or block 319
    Reversing the effects of a command 320
    Inserting a new column 320
    Inserting a new row 320
    Entering dates 320
    Sorting a block 321
    Converting formulas to values 321
    Converting vertical data into horizontal data (and vice versa) 322
    Searching and replacing 322
Formatting 322
Graphing 323
    Making a graph 323
    Changing the graph type 323
    Adding things to a graph 323
    Making changes to elements in a graph 323
    Moving or resizing a graph 324
Printing 324
    Printing the current notebook page 324
    Printing part of a notebook page 324
    Printing all used pages in a notebook 324
    Previewing your work 324
    Adding a page header or a footer 325
    Printing page numbers 325

Files and Notebook Windows 325
    Opening a notebook 325
    Saving a notebook 325
    Activating a particular notebook 325
    Seeing more than one notebook 326
    Moving a window 326
    Resizing a window 326
    Splitting a window 326
Miscellaneous 326
    Switching to another program (temporarily) 327
    Finding a circular reference 327
    Changing the clock display 327
    Saving your notebook automatically 327
    Leaving Quattro Pro for Windows 327

Part V: The Part of Tens 329

Chapter 20: Ten Good Habits You Should Acquire 331

Use the SpeedBar buttons and property band 331
Don't save your worksheet files only to a floppy disk 331
Take advantage of multiple worksheet files 331
Use cell and block names whenever possible 332
Don't forget that you can work with more than one
    program at a time 332
Take advantage of the on-line help in Quattro Pro for Windows 332
Don't be afraid to try new things 332
Don't waste time printing drafts 333
Don't go overboard with fancy formatting 333
Don't be afraid of macros 333

Chapter 21: Top Ten (Or So) Shortcut Keys 335

Chapter 22: Top Ten Concepts Every Quattro Pro for Windows User Should Understand 337

There are lots of versions of Quattro Pro out there 337
Quattro Pro for Windows works well with other Windows
    applications 337
The Quattro Pro for Windows window has other windows 338
There are many different ways to select ranges 338
You have lots and lots of command options 338
You can preselect a range to simplify data entry 338
There are more @functions than you'll ever need 339
The on-line help system is very comprehensive 339
Hard disks crash for no apparent reason 339
The more you use Quattro Pro for Windows, the easier it gets 339

Chapter 23: The Ten Commandments of Quattro Pro for Windows 341
    I   : Thou shalt always maketh backup copies 341
    II : Thou shalt check thy work carefully 341
    III : Remember thy right mouse button 341
    IV : Thou shalt not take the name of Philippe Kahn in vain 341
    V : Honor thy toolbar buttons and shortcut keys 342
    VI : Thou shalt not copyeth the program from others 342
    VII : Save thy file before taking drastic measures 342
    VIII: Thou shalt enable undo and forgeteth not that it exists 342
    IX : Thou shalt consult thy local guru with matters of importance .. 342
    X : Feareth not to experiment 342

Appendix A: If You Gotta Install It Yourself 343
    For Do-It-Yourself Types 343
    Preflight Checkout 343
    Installing Quattro Pro for Windows 344

Appendix B: Glossary 347

Index 365

Reader Response Card .... Back of Book

Introduction

● ●

*G*reetings, computer book consumer...

Let me take a wild guess. You need to learn Quattro Pro for Windows, but you don't want to get bogged down with all the technical details. And I'll bet that you don't know much about computers, and you certainly have no aspirations of becoming a spreadsheet guru. In other words, you're probably a bottom-line kind of person who likes to cut to the quick. And, unlike the stereotypical computer user, you also have a sense of humor. If that's true, you've come to the right place.

Welcome to *Quattro Pro 6 For Windows For Dummies* — the best beginner's guide to one of the best spreadsheet programs available. The title not with-standing, owning this book doesn't make you a dummy; that's a reputation you must earn on your own.

If you already bought this book, thanks — now I can feed my turtle this week. If you borrowed it from someone, please give it back and buy your own copy. If you're standing around in a bookstore trying to make up your mind about it, just buy it and be on your way (the clerk's getting suspicious).

Here's a sneak preview of what you'll find here:

- Down-to-earth information about the most useful parts of Quattro Pro for Windows that will get you up to speed in no time (well, actually it takes *some* time).
- Informative examples that demonstrate things that you may want to do with this software (or things that someone *else* wants you to do with it).
- Very few extraneous details about topics that you don't really care about anyway.
- Lively, entertaining, and easy-to-read text, with subtle humor sprinkled liberally throughout its pages (I just love describing my own writing).
- Lots of things you can say and do to make you seem smarter than you really are.
- Cartoons by Rich Tennant that are guaranteed to be funnier than those Bazooka Joe comics you find wrapped around pieces of bubble gum.

Have no fear; this is not an advanced reference book. So if the office computer geek needs to look up all the gory details on macro command arguments, you won't find *this* book missing from your desk.

What This Book Covers

The astute reader will notice that the title of this book isn't *The Complete Guide to Quattro Pro For Windows For Dummies*. That's because I don't cover everything about this spreadsheet product — but then again you don't want to *know* everything about Quattro Pro for Windows, right?

This book is for people who are just starting out with Quattro Pro for Windows Version 6. But anyone can buy the book — we won't check. This does *not* cover Quattro Pro for DOS — which is a completely different animal that has virtually nothing in common with Quattro Pro for Windows. If you need to learn Quattro Pro for DOS, check out *Quattro Pro For DOS For Dummies* (also by yours truly).

Version 6 of Quattro Pro for Windows began shipping in the summer of 1994. If you have Version 5 of this product, this book will still be useful, since the basic procedures haven't changed much. However, the menus have undergone a serious facelift in the latest version, so some of the commands won't match — and your screen will look different than the picutres in this book. My advice? Just bite the bullet and upgrade to Version 6. Upgrading is cheap, and the latest version is actually quite a bit easier to use than Version 5.

Read the Whole Thing? Naah...

My intention is not that you read this book from cover to cover. Frankly, the plot stinks, the character development leaves much to be desired, and you'll have to do a lot of page turning before you get to the steamy sex scenes.

But if you're foolish enough to read the book straight through, you'll find that the chapters *do* move along in a quasi-logical progression — but they also pretty much stand on their own. After you learn the basics of Quattro Pro for Windows, you can safely put the book aside until you need to move on to the next challenge. When that time comes, follow these simple steps:

1. **Refer to the table of contents for a general topic.**

    If you're in a real hurry, go straight for the index. If your problem is "How do I get rid of these stupid decimal points?," look under Decimal points, not Stupid.

2. **Based on what you discover in the table of contents or index, turn to the page that discusses the topic.**

3. **Read the informative and often jocund text that introduces the topic.**

4. **If that doesn't help, take a look at any examples provided and work your way through them.**
   5. **If you still can't figure it out, panic.**

   Then settle down and try to find someone who knows what they're doing and bribe them.

Unless the task you're trying to do is a fairly sophisticated or unusual one, this book will certainly shed some light on it. Even if an example for a topic doesn't seem to be related to what you're trying to do, you might find that working through it step-by-step provides some insights that let you figure it out on your own. But what I hope to get across more than anything is that you should feel free to play around in Quattro Pro for Windows and experiment with things. That's the best way to learn.

What to skip, what to read

The topics in this book usually start out with some introductory comments, and often include one or more examples and maybe even some step-by-step instructions. You can skim through the introductory text to see whether it's really what you want.

If you're just starting out, I recommend that you read some of the chapters in their entirety — or at least until the subject matter exceeds the level of complexity that you can stomach. For example, if you've never printed anything before, you'll find it helpful to start reading Chapter 11 from the beginning. Doing so gives you enough background so that you'll at least have a vague idea of what you're doing. At the very least, it steers you to the right menu or dialog box so that you can figure it out by yourself.

Some topics have additional information for those overachievers who want to know even more about what they're doing. Reading these sections will only increase the depth of your knowledge of Quattro Pro for Windows — and that's certainly not what this book is all about. So you may want to make a mental note: *See the Technical Stuff icon, skip the section.*

As long as you have your mental notepad out, here's another one for you: *See the Warning icon, read the section.* The Warning icon signals something that might eat your data, cause your computer to go into warp speed nine, wipe out half the population of a small country, or otherwise ruin your whole morning. More about icons later.

Yes, this book is organized (sort of)

Personally, I think that my editors and I are the only ones who really care how this book is organized. I started out with an outline — the part of the term paper you always hated writing, remember? The outline eventually turned into the table of contents, which you can peruse if you're really into organizational issues. But you may prefer the following synopses of the book's major parts.

Part I: First Things First

The four chapters in this section are for people who don't have a clue as to what a spreadsheet — much less Quattro Pro for Windows — is all about. Chapter 1 tells you lots of interesting things so that you can hold your own should you ever find yourself at a cocktail party populated with spreadsheet junkies. Chapter 2 tells you how to start and exit the program, and also discusses how to get to all the help information at your fingertips. Chapter 3 gives you a quick tour of the screen so you'll know what all the weirdness is. If you want some quick and dirty experience, you can wade through Chapter 4. I'll walk you through a real-life Quattro Pro for Windows session, and you can pretend I'm standing over your shoulder helping you. If you make it through this chapter, you can honestly say, *"Yeah, sure. I've used Quattro Pro for Windows."*

Part II: Basic Stuff That You Just Can't Ignore

Like it or not, you can't just jump into Quattro Pro for Windows and expect to start doing meaningful things immediately — you need some basic background information. Part II imparts this knowledge upon you in the form of seven short (usually) chapters. You'll learn about entering data, menus and dialog boxes, saving files, creating formulas, using built-in functions, avoiding parking tickets, printing, and lots of other things that you may or may not be interested in (but you should know about). You don't have to read everything in these chapters; you can always refer to them when the need arises.

Part III: How to Impress the Easily Impressed

The four chapters in this section can be described as "gee whiz" stuff (with a bit of "jeepers" and "golly" stuff thrown in for good measure). You can probably get by for quite a while by pretending these topics don't even exist. But sooner or later, you might need to expand your horizons. In the unlikely event that this actually occurs, you'll learn how to make your work look great (or at least good), how to create and customize graphs, how to make the best of Quattro Pro's cool notebook pages, and how to use all kinds of shortcuts that can save you valuable minutes each day, giving you more time for important things like goofing off.

Part IV: Faking It

Aptly named, this is the section in which I tell you just enough about some of the more advanced topics so that you can get by. If you're so moved, you can learn about databases, steal some nifty formulas that I developed, and even learn how to use and create (horrors!) macros. And the final chapter covers even more topics that might get you out of a jam or two — and will *surely* make you the hit of the next spreadsheet geek festival.

Part V: The Part of Tens

For some reason, most of the books in the ... *For Dummies* series include short chapters with lists of 10 or so things in each. This book is no exception, and you'll find these chapters collected in Part V. You'll get concise lists of habits you should acquire, things you definitely must know, and (holy Moses!) even the Ten Commandments of Quattro Pro for Windows.

The Appendixes

Shortly before going to press, I met with a team of surgeons. Following a thorough examination, they decided against the appendectomy. Consequently, you'll find two (count 'em) appendixes in this book: one covers the details of installing Quattro Pro for Windows; the other is a glossary of weird terms you're likely to encounter in this book or throughout your life's travels.

Foolish Assumptions About You

People who write books usually have a target reader in mind. In the case of this book, my target reader is a conglomerate of dozens of beginning computer users that I've met over the years. The following points more or less describe this typical new user (and may even describe you):

- ✓ You have access to a PC at work, but working on the computer isn't the most interesting part of your job.

- ✓ Your computer has a hard drive, a printer, some version of the DOS operating system, and Microsoft Windows 3.1 or later installed on it. Although a mouse is not required, I do strongly suggest you buy one. Using Windows products without a mouse is like sweeping the kitchen floor with a toothbrush; it can be done, but who wants to do it?

- ✓ You have some experience with computers (probably word processing), and have even gone so far as to copy a few files from the hard drive to a floppy.

- ✔ Someone just installed Quattro Pro for Windows on your computer, and you have to learn how to use the sucker.
- ✔ You've never used a spreadsheet before — and if you did, you didn't really know what you were doing.
- ✔ You need to get some work done and have a low tolerance for computer books that weigh more than you do.

Conventions — Typographical and Otherwise

As you work your way through the book, you may notice that it uses different type styles. This was done for two purposes: to show off the typographic skills of the IDG Production Department, and to make it easy for you — the reader — to distinguish various word meanings.

When I tell you to enter something into a cell, the "something" appears in a distinctive typeface (called *monospace*). If I want you to enter some words into a cell, it would look like this:

```
Expenses disapproved by the IRS
```

This means that you should type exactly what you see. Most the time, you'll also have to press the Enter key to signal the end of what you're typing. If I want you to enter something that's short, I don't waste a whole line of valuable computer book paper; I simply stick it in the text in **bold type**. Here's an example: "Enter **256** into cell A1." In this case, you simply type the three numbers and press the Enter key.

Occasionally, Quattro Pro for Windows displays some messages to you on its screen. When I talk about such messages, I use the monospace typeface, as so: READY.

Sometimes, you'll need to press a *key combination* — which means you hold down one key while you press another. For example, the Ctrl+Z key combination means that you should hold down the Ctrl key while you press Z once.

Of mice and keyboards

You can use Quattro Pro for Windows with or without a mouse — although I strongly recommend a mouse for everyone; they are cheap and fun to use. But if you work in a high crime area and one day discover that someone has stolen

Introduction

your mouse, there's no reason to go home and watch game shows on TV until a new mouse is delivered. You can continue to be as semi-productive as ever using only the keyboard. You can still access commands, make selections, and move the cell pointer all over the place. You just can't use the toolbar icons and do a few other mouse-only things.

To issue a Quattro Pro for Windows command, mouse users simply click the menu and then click a command from the list that drops down. Without a mouse, you have to press Alt to access the menu, use the arrow keys to move to the selection you want, and then press Enter. Some people actually prefer to use the keyboard for commands. They think it's faster.

In this book, when I ask you to select a command, I *don't* waste time by giving directions for both keyboarders and mouseketeers. Rather than say something such as: "If you're using the keyboard, press **Alt+F** and then press **S** to save your file. Mouse users should click File and then click Save," I say, "Save your file by issuing the File⇨Save command." Then you can choose your method of payment. A lot simpler, no?

Chapter 4 is an exception to this rule. Because that chapter might be your first hands-on experience with Quattro Pro for Windows (yes, having a photographer present to document the occasion might be appropriate), I describe how to issue the commands in agonizing detail.

By the way, did you notice that I underlined two letters when I mentioned the File⇨Save command above? These represent the "hot keys" that keyboard users can press to issue the commands. Whenever I mention a command, the hot keys will always be underlined (just as they appear on screen) for the convenience of our mouseless readers. But be careful, because the hot keys aren't always the first letter of the command.

I think icon, I think icon

Somewhere along the line, some market research company must have shown that computer books sell more copies if they have icons stuck inside their margins. Icons are those little pictures that are supposed to draw your attention to various features or help you decide whether something is worth reading. Whether the research is valid remains to be proven, but I'm not taking any chances. So here are the icons you'll see scattered liberally throughout the following pages:

8   Quattro Pro 6 For Windows For Dummies

This icon signals material that no one in their right mind should care about. Read this only if your interested in the nitty-gritty details — for the nerd in all of us.

Don't skip these. They tell you about a shortcut that can save you lots of time and make you a hit at the next computer-geek party.

This icon tells you when you need to store information away in the deep recesses of your brain for later use.

Read these, otherwise you may lose your data, put your eye out, cause a nuclear holocaust, or worse.

This icon alerts you to features found only in Version 6 of Quattro Pro for Windows. If you're still using Version 5 the stuff you read here won't apply to you. See what you're missing by not upgrading?

Now What?

If you've never used a spreadsheet, I strongly suggest that you peruse Chapters 1 through 3 before you do anything else. Chapter 1 tells you what a spreadsheet is and exactly what Quattro Pro for Windows can do. Chapter 2 tells you how to start the program (and how to get out of it when you've had enough). Chapter 3 describes some of the important screen elements so we'll be on the same wavelength.

But it's a free country (at least it was when I wrote this book), so I won't sic the Computer Book Police on you if you opt to thumb through randomly and read whatever strikes your fancy. If you have a particular task in mind — such as, "How do I sort all of these numbers?" — go to the index. Go directly to the index. Do not pass Go, do not collect $200.

Good luck and have fun.

John Walkenbach
LaJolla, CA

Part I
First Things First

The 5th Wave   **By Rich Tennant**

"My gosh Barbara, if you don't think it's worth going a couple of weeks without dinner so we can afford Quattro Pro for Windows, just say so."

In this part...

This part has only four chapters. But if you've never used a spreadsheet before or if you need a refresher course on the subject, you won't want to miss these chapters. In Chapter 1, you get some essential background information about spreadsheets. Chapter 2 tells you how to start Quattro Pro for Windows, put it aside temporarily, and (importantly) how to exit gracefully when you've had enough. Chapter 3 tells you what all of the weird stuff on your screen is for. You get the opportunity to acquire some hands-on experience with Quattro Pro for Windows in Chapter 4. And, if you follow my instructions, you'll have a real, live spreadsheet to hang on your refrigerator door.

Chapter 1
What This Thing Can (And Can't) Do

In This Chapter
- What is a spreadsheet? And, more important, what is Quattro Pro for Windows?
- What is Borland? What is Novell? What is WordPerfect? And why does this spreadsheet have such a strange name?
- What version of Quattro Pro do you have? Does it matter?
- What sort of things can you do with this program?
- What things can't you do?
- How do real people go about using a spreadsheet?

This chapter definitely qualifies as background information. It's sort of like photography. Any idiot can press a button and take snapshots of Aunt Florence, but those who spend some time learning about composition, f-stops, depth of field, shutter speeds, and so on, take much better pictures of Aunt Florence. So bear with me and see what develops.

Here's an incentive for you. After reading this chapter you'll have more background information about spreadsheets and Quattro Pro for Windows than 99.9 percent of the people on this planet (it's true). That, and about two bucks, will get you a cup of cappuccino at your local trendy coffee shop.

Spreadsheets 101 (This Will Be on the Final Exam!)

Until about ten years ago, computers were large monstrosities accessible only to techies in white lab coats. But right now we're in the midst of the PC revolution — which means that even people like you can now use (and even own) computers. Computers are pretty much worthless without software. Sure, they add a high-tech look to just about any decor (and make decent, if bulky, doorstops), but it's the software programs that make a computer compute. One without the other is completely useless. Think of it like this: your VCR is hardware; videotapes are software. Your CD player is hardware; your CDs are software. Your toaster is hardware; a loaf of bread is software. Get the picture?

Hundreds of thousands of software programs are available for your PC. Some of them are good (like Quattro Pro for Windows); some of them are bad (product names omitted to protect the guilty). Software can be divided into several basic categories: word processing software, graphics software, database software, game software, and so on. One of these categories is *spreadsheet software*. Coincidentally enough, Quattro Pro for Windows just happens to fall into this category.

So what is a spreadsheet?

Back in the old days, accountants wore green visors and sleeve garters, and used spreadsheets that consisted of paper with grid lines drawn on it. In today's high-tech world, we now have the electronic equivalent of accountant's spreadsheet paper — although we still don't have a good replacement for those green visors (some things just *never* go out of style).

This electronic version of accountant's paper appears on your computer monitor when you run Quattro Pro for Windows. The electronic version is huge — so big, in fact, that you can see only a tiny portion at one time in a window on your screen. You can use the keyboard or mouse to move around this huge grid so that you can see the other parts of the spreadsheet.

In place of the grid lines, the electronic spreadsheet has rows and columns. The place where each row and column intersects is called a *cell*. You enter numbers and words into the cells. You can print the information in the cells if you want others to see it. It's also very easy to copy cells and move them around. You can save the results of your efforts in a file on your hard disk and work on it later. So far so good, but any decent word processing software can do this sort of thing.

The real fun starts when you learn how to enter formulas into cells. Formulas bring a spreadsheet to life; they perform calculations using the information in other cells. Suppose that you entered your bowling scores for your past 12 games into a column in Quattro Pro for Windows. You can enter into a cell a formula that says, in effect, "Add up all the scores in the first column and then divide by the number of values in the column." This formula displays in its cell the average of the numbers (your 12-game average). Best of all is that formulas recalculate the results if you change the numbers in any of the cells that the formulas use. So if you want to improve your average, just replace that 79 with a 245 and the average cell displays the new result. You may not appreciate this now, but you will when you need to improve your bowling average.

Chapter 1: What This Thing Can (And Can't) Do

Other goodies? Quattro Pro for Windows, like all other electronic spreadsheets, lets you apply slick formatting to the cells. You can use different fonts, make some cells larger, use different colors, draw lines, and so on. You also can create graphs from the numbers in your spreadsheet that look like they came from a professional artist (no lie).

But wait, there's more (he says in a Ginsu knife pitchman's voice). Each Quattro Pro for Windows file you use actually contains 256 of these humongous spreadsheets arranged as if in a notebook, making it easy to keep your work organized and accessible. So roll up your sleeve garters, put on your visor, and be prepared to crunch some numbers!

How big is a spreadsheet?

Imagine, for a minute, that you entered a number into every cell in a Quattro Pro for Windows spreadsheet. We're talking 256 pages, each with 256 columns and 8,192 rows — which works out to 536,870,912 cells. (Filling every cell is actually impossible because your computer doesn't have nearly enough memory to hold all of this information. But bear with me on this, OK?)

If you enter the numbers manually into each cell, the task takes about 34 years (figuring a relatively rapid two seconds per cell, with no coffee breaks or time out for sleep). Hopefully, you save your work often while entering this amount of data because it would be a shame to have to repeat five or six years of data entry as a result of a power failure.

You would hate to lose all this work, so you make a backup of this 5.9GB file. Before you start the backup procedure, however, you make sure that you have about 4,765 blank floppy disks on hand. (I suggest that you use high-density floppies.)

You want a hard copy of the data to give to your boss. Using the default column width and row height, Quattro Pro for Windows can print 55 rows and 8 columns (or 440 cells) on a sheet of 8 1/2-by-11-inch paper. Printing the entire notebook requires 1.22 million pages of paper. If you use cheap photocopier paper, your printout is a stack of pages about 407 feet tall — roughly the height of a 40 story building. If you splurge for thicker paper, your printout is about as tall as the St. Louis Gateway Arch.

Using a standard four-page-per-minute laser printer, printing the entire spreadsheet takes about 212 days (not counting the time you spend changing paper and replacing toner cartridges). If you have a faster laser printer, you can easily print the entire job in less than three months.

If this worksheet has formulas in it, you have to take recalculation time into account. I have no way of estimating how long it would take to recalculate the formulas in such a worksheet, but it would probably be a good time to take that round-the-world cruise after pressing F9.

Borland? WordPerfect? Novell?

As I wrote this paragraph, Quattro Pro for Windows was undergoing a change of ownership. Quattro Pro for Windows originally was developed by a company called Borland International. While Borland was in the middle of upgrading Quattro from Version 5 to Version 6, a company called Novell bought Borland's entire spreadsheet business (which took more than a bit of pocket change). They also bought WordPerfect Corporation (the famous word processor company) at the same time. The prerelease version that I used to write this book said Borland in some places and Novell in others. I assume that the transaction will be complete by the time you read this, and that your copy will not even mention Borland. However, you may have gotten your copy as part of the Perfect Suite — which also includes a copy of WordPerfect. Bottom line? Who cares? Software companies pull the old switcheroo all the time. Quattro Pro for Windows is a good spreadsheet, regardless of the company name on the box.

Quattro Schmattro

Which brings us to the next topic — why does this product have such a weird name?

Many software products have names that describe what they do. WordPerfect makes perfect words, and Harvard Graphics creates graphics for Ivy League professors. Other products have names that were assigned for no apparent reason — for example, QuarkXpress. And some products have misleading names. Xtree, for example, is not a program that lumberjacks use to determine which trees need to be chopped down but a program that helps you manage the files on your disks.

To understand where the name Quattro comes from, you have to know that Quattro was originally developed to compete with Lotus 1-2-3 — which traditionally has been the best-selling spreadsheet software. My guess is that someone in Borland's Software Naming Department was trying to come up with a name for this product and thought, "Let's see now, what comes after 1-2-3?" As fate would have it, this person happened to be listening to "Woolly Bully," the classic tune by Sam the Sham and The Pharaohs. If you're as old as I am, you know the rest of the story.

Actually, *quatro* is the Spanish word for *four*. Since 4 comes after 1, 2, and 3, it's a somewhat apropos name for a product that they hoped would be the successor to 1-2-3. But I have no idea why they spelled it wrong. By the way, wouldn't it be cool if Pro were the Spanish word for five?

Yes, but does it taste good?

There are several spreadsheet programs on the market, so you may be curious about how Quattro Pro for Windows stacks up against the competition. Quattro Pro for Windows is most often compared to Microsoft Excel and Lotus 1-2-3 for Windows — two other leading spreadsheet products than run under Windows. People (like me) who know about such things think that Quattro Pro for Windows is an excellent product (especially Version 6). So you can rest assured that someone made a good purchase decision, and you're using an excellent product.

Excursions into versions

Software companies continually come up with new versions of their products because computer users are a demanding bunch who always gripe that their favorite software doesn't do enough. Software companies also release new versions so that they can correct bugs in the previous version and charge their loyal customers for upgrades at the same time.

The latest version of Quattro Pro for Windows is Version 6. To find out which version you have, try to find the box the program came in and read the version number off the box. If you trashed the box, try to find the original disks and read the version number off of one of the disks. If you lost the original diskettes or acquired the product through illegal means (which I do not condone), you can tell what version you have by selecting the Help⇨About command from the menu. The box that pops up on screen proudly displays the version number.

So that you can get an idea of where this product came from, I've pulled together a quick rundown of the differences between the three versions of Quattro Pro for Windows.

- **Quattro Pro for Windows Version 1:** This version came out in October, 1992. It was pretty good for a first product.

- **Quattro Pro for Windows Version 5:** This upgrade to the original Windows version adds a great deal more analytical power and dozens of ease-of-use features.

- **Quattro Pro for Windows Version 6:** The latest version has rearranged menus, a handy draw layer, easier graphing, and many other features that keep it competitive.

What about Versions 2, 3 and 4? They don't exist. Borland skipped these version numbers so their DOS and Windows spreadsheets would be in synch, version numberwise. Geez. You'd think a company that makes spreadsheets would know how to count!

Part I: First Things First

What Can This Puppy Do?

People use Quattro Pro for Windows for lots of things — for business, educational, scientific, and personal purposes, and who knows what else.

Here's a quick rundown of its primary uses.

Crunch numbers

Spreadsheet programs are made primarily for calculating numbers. If you use Quattro Pro for Windows to create a budget (probably the most common task people use spreadsheets for), you enter your budget category names and values for each month into cells. Then you include some formulas to add up each month's total and the annual total for each category. (And, if necessary, you fiddle around with the numbers until the formulas come up with the results your boss wants to see.) Figure 1-1 shows an example of a budget that's set up in Quattro Pro for Windows. It's all pretty easy after you get the hang of it.

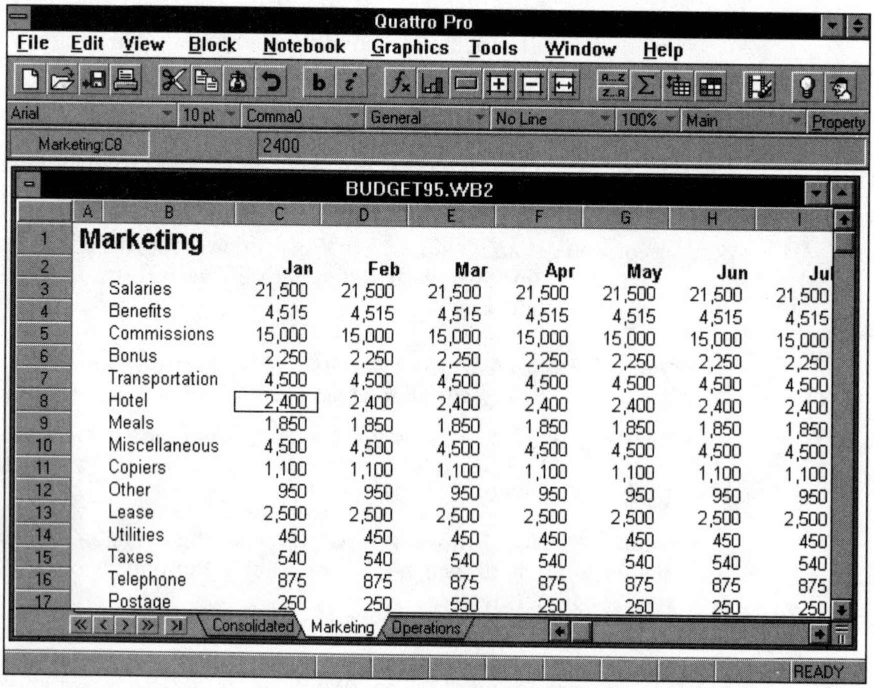

Figure 1-1: Quattro Pro for Windows hard at work crunching numbers.

Chapter 1: What This Thing Can (And Can't) Do

Here are a just a few examples of the types of worksheets you can develop in Quattro Pro:

- **Budgets.** These include simple household budgets, corporate department budgets, budgets for a whole company, or even a budget for an entire country.
- **Financial projections.** Figure out how much money you're going to make or lose this year, using formulas that rely on various assumptions.
- **Sales tracking.** Keep track of who's selling the most (and how much they receive in commissions) and who's falling down on the job (and when they should get their pink slips).
- **Loan amortizations.** How much of that mortgage payment goes to interest (a lot) and how much to principal (not much)? A spreadsheet can tell you information like this for every month of the loan's term.
- **Scientific things.** Quattro Pro for Windows has many specialized built-in functions that only white-coated laboratory inhabitants understand.
- **Statistical stuff.** Again, there are lots of built-in functions for people who think in terms of standard deviations.

These examples just scratch the surface. If you have a problem that involves numbers, chances are Quattro Pro for Windows is a good tool to use — especially if you can't find a Phillips-head screwdriver.

Make killer graphs

Quattro Pro for Windows can take the numbers you put into a spreadsheet and transform them into a magnificent graph in just about any style you can imagine. And here's the best part: You can waste hours of your company's time playing around with the graphs to make them look just right. Even if your numbers aren't worth diddly-squat, you can still impress your boss with the quality of the graph. And that's what life is all about, right?

Figure 1-2 shows a modest example of a Quattro Pro for Windows graph. (I made a vow to avoid using trite phrases such as "a picture is worth a thousand words," so it's up to *you* to figure out how many words a picture is worth.)

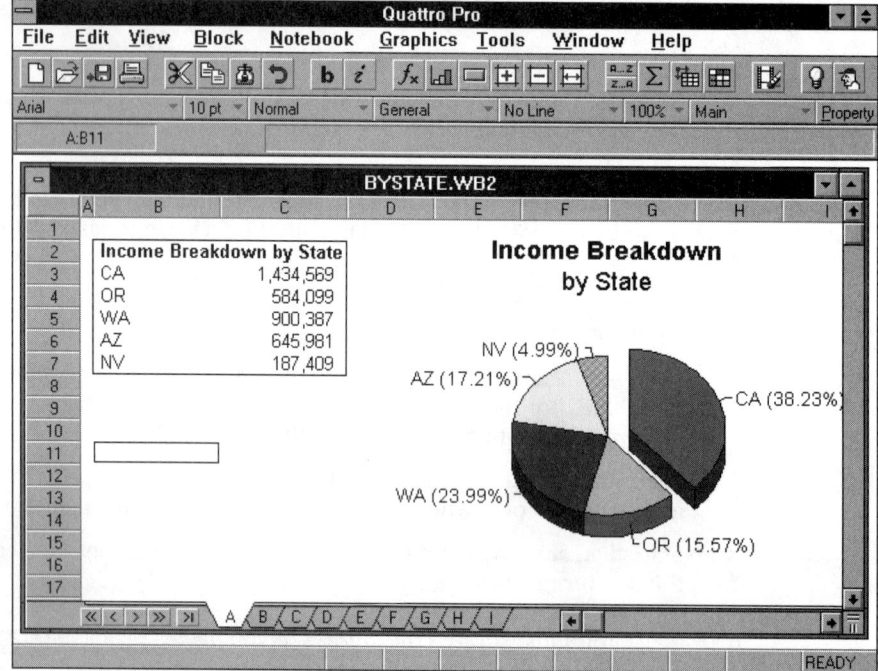

Figure 1-2: Quattro Pro for Windows lets you transform dull numbers into more interesting graphs.

Manage your lists

Quattro Pro for Windows, like all spreadsheet programs, has ready-made rows and columns. Because you can make the columns as wide as you want, your spreadsheet is a natural choice for keeping track of items in lists (it's even better than a mere word processor). The following are a few lists that you may want to store in a Quattro Pro for Windows spreadsheet:

- Things to do today
- Things to avoid doing today
- Questions you need to ask the office computer geek
- Any of David Letterman's Top Ten lists
- A list of the logical flaws in the *Gilligan's Island* plots (use a separate worksheet for each episode; otherwise you'll quickly run out of room)

Lists (such as the preceding) can include only words, or they can include a combination of words and numbers. If you use numbers in your lists, you can even create formulas that perform calculations on the numbers. Here are some ideas for lists that use numbers:

- Bills you need to pay this month
- Bills you can get by without paying this month
- Itemized costs for fixing your wrecked car
- The amount of time the person in the next cubicle spends goofing off each day

Figure 1-3 shows a simple list that uses three columns (the third column has formulas that compute a running total of the values in the second column). You'll learn all about formulas in a later chapter.

Manage databases

If the term *database* conjures up images of dull, obsessively tidy, compulsive people whose socks always match their pocket protector color, you're right on track. Actually, a database is nothing more than an *organized* list. If you have a lot of friends, you may use a database to keep track of them, storing on it their names, addresses, phone numbers, and the amounts of money they owe you.

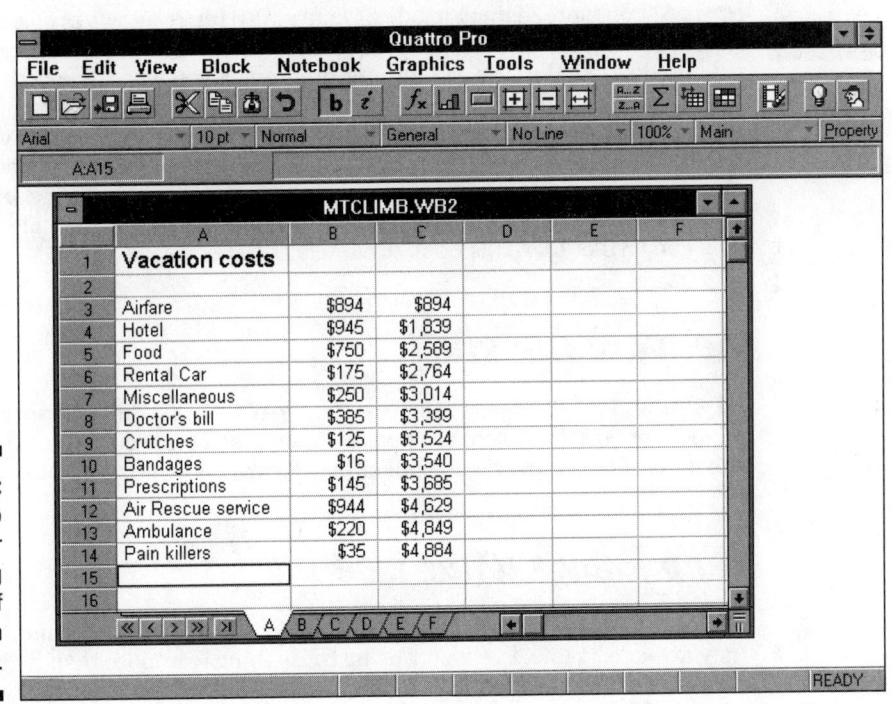

Figure 1-3: Quattro Pro is great for keeping track of things in lists.

	A	B	C
1	Vacation costs		
2			
3	Airfare	$894	$894
4	Hotel	$945	$1,839
5	Food	$750	$2,589
6	Rental Car	$175	$2,764
7	Miscellaneous	$250	$3,014
8	Doctor's bill	$385	$3,399
9	Crutches	$125	$3,524
10	Bandages	$16	$3,540
11	Prescriptions	$145	$3,685
12	Air Rescue service	$944	$4,629
13	Ambulance	$220	$4,849
14	Pain killers	$35	$4,884

Truth is, Quattro Pro for Windows is pretty good at helping you work with databases. You can sort the data, search for something in particular, display items that meet certain criteria, and so on. You learn the ins and outs of databases in Chapter 16.

Access other data

If you have to deal with a humongous database — such as your corporate accounting system that lives on a different computer — you probably won't have enough memory in your computer to be able to load it all into Quattro Pro for Windows. Fortunately (or perhaps unfortunately), you can still access such "external" databases from Quattro Pro for Windows. If you learn how to work with external databases in Quattro Pro for Windows, you may not even have to buy a real database program. This is a fairly advanced topic, but I touch on it lightly in Chapter 19 if you're so inclined.

Automate with macros

For hard-core spreadsheet junkies, Quattro Pro for Windows provides a feature known as macros. A *macro* consists of instructions that tell the spreadsheet what to do — kind of like a computer program. If you want to take the time to learn, you can write macros for Quattro Pro for Windows. Developing macros isn't as difficult as you may think, because you can simply "record" your keystrokes and play them back again (much like a tape-recorded message). You also may need to *execute* a macro that someone else wrote. Those with inquiring minds will learn how to execute macros (and even create simple ones) by going no further than this book (Chapter 18, to be precise).

Activate fun stuff

All work and no play makes Quattro Pro for Windows a dull spreadsheet. In a moment of boredom (actually several moments), I once developed a spreadsheet that lets you play video poker (see Figure 1-4 if you don't believe me).

Who knows what else

The neat thing about spreadsheets (including Quattro Pro for Windows) is that they are so versatile. Even after using these things for more than a decade, people are still showing me new uses for spreadsheets that I had never dreamed of. Once you learn the basics, don't be surprised if you come up with a brand new use for Quattro Pro for Windows. (Let me know if you do, so I can steal your idea and put it in my next book.)

Figure 1-4: The author developed this video poker game using Quattro Pro for Windows. It works like the casino machines — except you don't lose real money.

> Try not to be overwhelmed by the potential of Quattro Pro for Windows. Sure, it's a complex product, and people do some amazing things with it. But the vast majority of users (including you, I would bet) can get by just fine using only a small fraction of its features. As you'll see, you can do quite a bit with this small fraction of features.

What Can't This Puppy Do?

Quattro Pro for Windows is a great program, but it can't do everything — and it's probably not the only software program you'll ever need. For example, it can work with small amounts of text and manipulate labels, but it's certainly no substitute for a real word processing program. It has some great graphing features, but if you're really into creating some cool computer graphics and images, many other products are available that are more versatile. And although you can do some simple project management, better project management packages are available. In other words, learning Quattro Pro for Windows is no reason to close your mind to other types of available software (especially all the cool games).

How Spreadsheets Are Put Together (Secret Stuff)

OK, now you know a bit about the category of software known as spreadsheets, and you even have a pretty good idea of what types of tasks Quattro Pro for Windows is good for. But you still may have some lingering doubts as to how all this magic actually happens. To dispel these doubts, just keep reading and I'll let you in on the secret.

When you have a problem that you can solve with spreadsheet software, here are the general steps you should take:

1. **Turn on your computer.**
2. **Run Microsoft Windows (if it doesn't run automatically when you turn on your machine).**
3. **Start Quattro Pro for Windows (see Chapter 3 for detailed instructions).**

    Quattro Pro for Windows starts up with a blank notebook.

4. **Figure out what you want to do and enter the appropriate values, text, and formulas into the notebook.**

    You learn how to do this in the remaining chapters.

5. **Save the notebook.**

    This action creates a file on your hard disk, lets you retrieve your work later, and also protects you if some clod accidentally trips over your computer's power cord.

6. **Apply formatting to your work — change the type fonts, make the numbers look different, add borders, change the colors, and so on.**
7. **Save it again.**

    Saving frequently is a good idea.

8. **When it looks good, print it.**
9. **Show the printout to your boss.**
10. **When the boss tells you that you're totally off base, figure out where you went wrong and correct it.**
11. **Repeat Steps 4 – 10 until the old geezer is satisfied.**

Chapter 2
Starting, Stopping, and Begging for Help

In This Chapter
- What to do if Quattro Pro for Windows isn't on your computer
- How to start Quattro Pro for Windows (a necessary step if you expect to get anything done)
- How to temporarily leave Quattro Pro for Windows so you can do something else
- How to quit Quattro Pro for Windows (the right way and the wrong way)
- The types of additional help included with Quattro Pro for Windows — at no extra charge

Before you can use Quattro Pro for Windows — or just about any software for that matter — you must install it on your computer. When you install software, you're simply copying files from floppy disks to your hard disk in such a way that everything will work when you execute the program. Back in the prehistoric days, you could run software directly from floppy disks. But those days are pretty much over, and virtually every program must now be installed on your hard disk.

If Quattro Pro for Windows isn't already installed, refer to Appendix A for assistance. Better yet, bribe your office computer genius to do it for you (with a new pocket protector, perhaps?).

After Quattro Pro for Windows is installed, you can run the program, do all sorts of interesting spreadsheety things with it, and then exit the program when you're finished. Exiting a program simply means stopping it from running. While a program is running, however, you can put it aside temporarily and do other things (such as run other programs, jump to another program that's already running, delete files, and so on). You learn about all this stuff right here in Chapter 2.

Starting Quattro Pro for Windows

In order to benefit from having Quattro Pro for Windows, you need to run the program — otherwise, it just eats up space on your hard disk and you've wasted your company's money (or, even worse, *your* money). There are a number of ways to start Quattro Pro for Windows, most of which I explain in the next few paragraphs.

Starting Quattro Pro for Windows from the Windows Program Manager

Using the Program Manager is the best way — and by far the most common way — to start Quattro Pro for Windows. When Quattro Pro for Windows is installed, the installation program puts several icons in one of the Program Manager program groups. (It may even create a whole new program group.) Depending on how your system is set up, this icon may always be visible, as it is in Figure 2-1. But, in some cases, the program group may be "minimized," or the Quattro Pro for Windows icon may be in a program group with a different name.

Figure 2-1: In the program group called Quattro Pro, double-click the Quattro Pro for Windows icon to start the program.

If you can't find the Quattro Pro for Windows icon, try double-clicking some of the program group icons at the bottom of the Program Manager windows. (If there's one called Quattro Pro, that would be a good place to start.) When you double-click a program group icon, it opens up to display the program icons in the program.

If you received Quattro Pro for Windows as part of the "Office" version (a collection of software that weighs about 800 pounds), the Quattro Pro for Windows icon is most likely located in a program group called Perfect Office, or something similar.

After you locate the Quattro Pro for Windows icon, just double-click this icon and Quattro Pro for Windows starts up. Most likely you'll be greeted with a dialog box that says, "Welcome to Quattro Pro." If this dialog box doesn't appear, it means that someone turned it off (which can get rather annoying). If the dialog box *does* appear, you see two buttons: one labeled Quattro Pro and the other labeled Coaches. Unless you want to go through some rather tedious on-screen lessons, click the Quattro Pro button.

Starting Quattro Pro for Windows from DOS

When you turn on your computer, if the blank screen shows only the DOS prompt, then you have to do the following two things to get Quattro Pro for Windows running:

1. **Start Windows**
2. **Start Quattro Pro for Windows**

To start Windows from the DOS prompt, just type **WIN** (upper- or lowercase) and press Enter. You are greeted with the Program Manager, which shows a bunch of icons. The preceding section explains how to locate the Quattro Pro for Windows icon in the Program Manager. After you find the icon, just double-click it to load the program.

Or, if you like, you can start up Windows and Quattro Pro for Windows in one fell swoop by typing **WIN QPW** at the DOS prompt.

If the WIN QPW command doesn't work properly, then the directory that holds the Quattro Pro for Windows files isn't in your DOS path. If you know what you're doing, you can edit the PATH line in your AUTOEXEC.BAT file (located in your C:\ root directory) to include the Quattro Pro for Windows directory. You can use any text editor, including Notepad, a program that comes with Windows.

If Quattro Pro for Windows is the only program that you ever use (what a boring life *you* must have), you can set things up so that Quattro Pro for Windows starts whenever you turn on your computer (also known by the odd term *booting* your system). You do this by editing your AUTOEXEC.BAT file. Insert an additional line at the end of this file by typing **WIN QPW**. If your AUTOEXEC.BAT file already has a line that simply says WIN, just edit this line so that it says WIN QPW.

If you don't know what you're doing, be on the safe side and get your computer guru to help you out. (Try bribing this person with Doritos!) Editing AUTOEXEC.BAT can be tricky — and even dangerous.

Switching Out of Quattro Pro for Windows

When you start Quattro Pro for Windows, the Windows program itself is still running in the background. In fact, any other Windows programs that you may have started prior to Quattro Pro for Windows also continues to run. One of the real benefits of using Windows is that you can run more than one software program at a time and switch among the programs whenever you like. You can even display multiple programs on the screen at one time, as demonstrated in Figure 2-2.

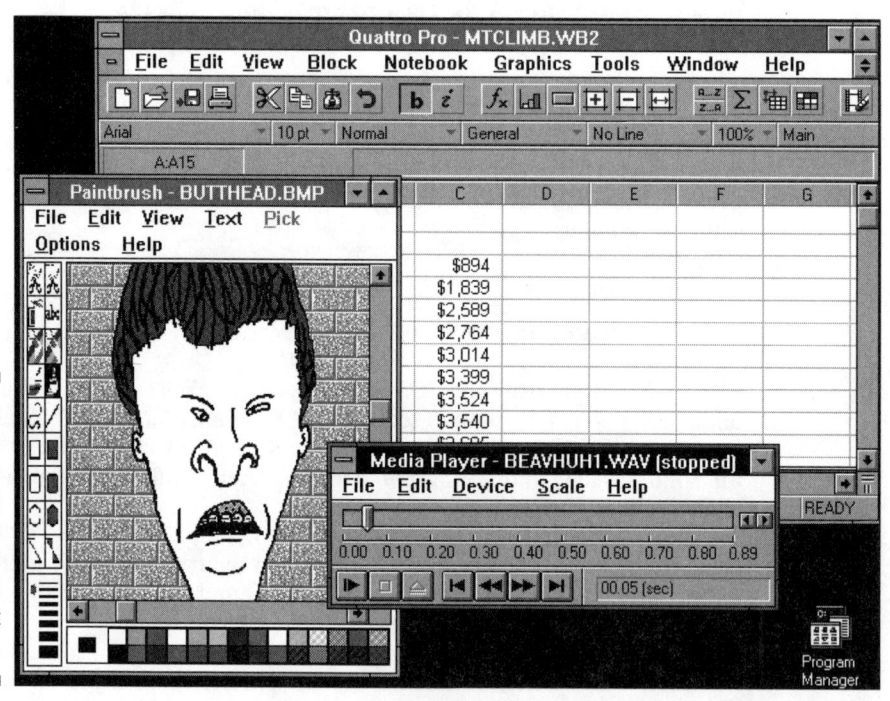

Figure 2-2: One of the benefits to using Windows is that you can run several programs at once.

Why would you want to run more than one program at a time? Most busy people tend to work on more than one project at the same time. For example, you may be plugging away in your word processor (working on your resume) when your boss barges in and asks to see the latest sales figures. When you are working in Windows, you don't have to exit your word processing program to deal with this rude interruption. You can leave the word processor running, jump over to Program Manager, and fire up Quattro Pro for Windows to check the sales results (although you may want to minimize the window your word processing document is in if you're working on your resume).

Chapter 2: Starting, Stopping, and Begging For Help   27

Or suppose that you've been working all day on a spreadsheet that will revolutionize the way your company tracks employee potty breaks. You're burned out and need a break. Take a few minutes to jump into Program Manager and execute one of your favorite games (try Tetris, if you have it). In Windows, you can leave Quattro Pro for Windows running so that you can return to it after you finish playing your game.

> **TIP**
>
> Get into the habit of saving the file that you're working on before you jump to another program. You never know when another misbehaved program may cause everything to crash and die — including the latest (unsaved) version of your Potty Break Tracker spreadsheet.

Use the following steps to activate other programs while you're in Quattro Pro for Windows:

1. **Press Ctrl+Esc to bring up the Windows Task List, which shows a list of all programs currently running, as illustrated in Figure 2-3.**

2. **If the program you want is on the list, select the program.**

   Click the Switch To button to activate the new program.

   If the program you want isn't running, it isn't listed.

3. **To run the program, select Program Manager from the list and then click Switch To.**

   In Program Manager, locate the icon for the program you want and double-click it.

4. **To return to Quattro Pro for Windows, press Ctrl+Esc again, select Quattro Pro for Windows, and click Switch To.**

Figure 2-3:
When you press Ctrl+Esc, the Windows Task List appears, letting you jump to other programs that are running.

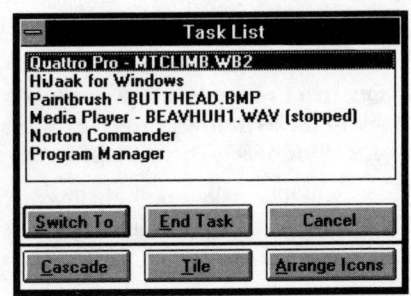

Part I: First Things First

> **TIP:** To save yourself a step when switching out of Quattro Pro for Windows, just double-click the program name in the Task List and avoid the Switch To button altogether. You also can use Alt+Tab to cycle through all the active programs, including Program Manager. When you see the program you want, take your fingers off of the Alt+Tab keys and the program will be activated.

You won't learn all the ins and outs of Windows here, but picking up on some tips just may give your overall productivity a healthy kick in the pants.

> **REMEMBER:** While Quattro Pro for Windows is running, you can use other programs without exiting your spreadsheet. Use Ctrl+Esc to bring up the Windows Task List and then choose the program you want. If the program isn't running, switch to Program Manager and start the program you want.

Quitting Quattro Pro for Windows

Once you get Quattro Pro for Windows started, you'll be staring at a blank notebook. You'll find out what you can do with this blank notebook later on — in fact, that just happens to be the subject matter for the remainder of this book. But you need to know one more thing now: how to quit Quattro Pro for Windows. There are two ways to do this: the right way and the wrong way.

The right way to exit

To exit Quattro Pro for Windows, use the menu and perform the following steps:

1. **Click the File menu.**

   Figure 2-4 shows the pull-down menu that appears. Then click Exit to get out of Quattro Pro for Windows. When you follow this procedure, you're actually executing the File⇨Exit command. You learn all about issuing commands later in the book.

2. **If you've saved your work, Quattro Pro for Windows unloads from memory, and you are be back in the Windows Program Manager (assuming that Quattro Pro for Windows is the only program running.)**

   If you haven't saved your work, you'll be asked politely if you want to do so. Unless the stuff you've been working on is totally bogus or simply for practice, you probably want to save it. I discuss all the ins and outs of dealing with files in Chapter 7.

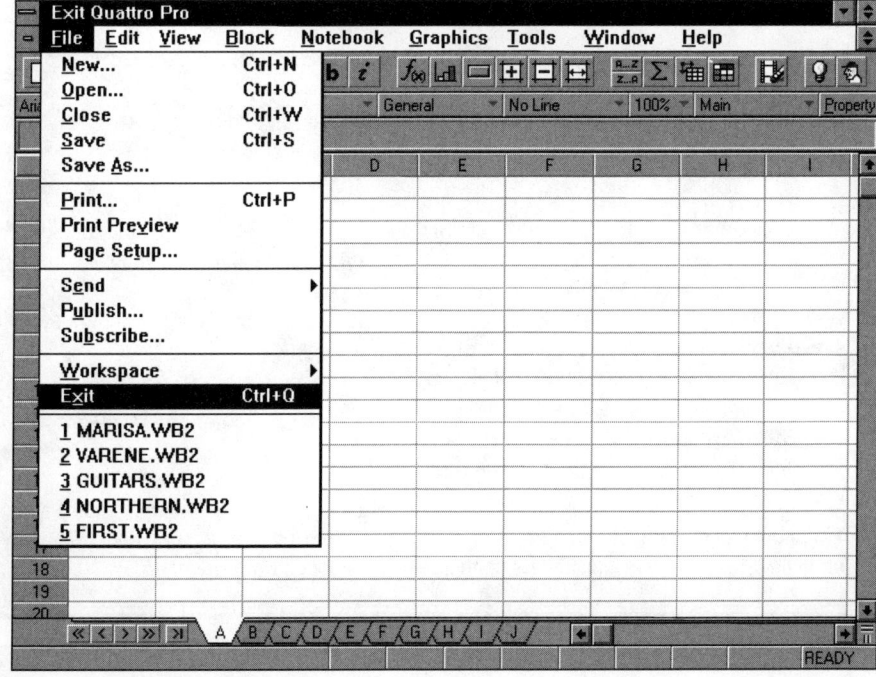

Figure 2-4: Choose the E_x_it command on the F_ile menu to quit Quattro Pro for Windows.

For a shortcut that saves you two to four seconds (depending on how fast you can type), get into the habit of using Alt+F4 to exit Quattro Pro for Windows. In fact, the Alt+F4 shortcut works in just about all Windows programs. If you learn the shortcut now, you'll have a head start on subsequent programs you may want to learn.

The wrong way to exit

One of the worst ways to exit any program is to simply turn off the computer. Even if you saved your file first, you should *never* use the power switch method to exit Quattro Pro for Windows. Why? Both Windows and Quattro Pro for Windows use lots of other files that you don't even know about. If any of these files is not closed properly, you can potentially mess up your hard disk and scramble some information. Or you may end up with dozens of temporary files that just take up space on your hard drive and do you no good.

So exit gracefully, as they say, by using the File➪Exit command. Then you can turn off your computer and do what you normally do after you turn off your computer — such as head for the local pub, practice your couch-potato act in front of the TV, get some Zs, and so on.

To power off or not: the ongoing debate

Over the past several years, I've read lots of articles debating the question of whether to turn off the computer at night or to leave it running all the time. (It seems computer people will argue about anything.) Those who vote for leaving the system on claim that the act of powering up can strain the system components. To avoid this strain, leave the computer on at all times. (Most believers in this camp do recommend that you turn off the monitor when it's not in use.) If leaving an electronic unit on all the time sounds strange to you, think about alarm clocks.

Those who align themselves on the side of powering down after they've finished using the computer believe that they save money by reducing power consumption. These people don't buy the claim that switching components on and off causes any damage. (Some even say that the money you save on your electric bill can be used to replace any components damaged by on/off switching.)

So who do you believe? Beats me. I hardly ever turn my computer off — unless I'll be gone for a few days. Leaving my computer on lets me get to work faster by avoiding the two-minute boot-up delay the next morning. I guess the jury is still out on this one, so you can do what you want.

Help! I Need Help!

By using this book, you've already demonstrated that you're not afraid to seek out help in learning computer programs. Congratulations. But you also know that this book doesn't tell you everything there is to know about Quattro Pro for Windows. Fortunately, there's a quick and easy way to get some help with this program. I'm talking about the on-line help system that's always at your beck and call.

The easiest way to get help is to press the F1 function key (located either along the top of your keyboard, on the left side of the keyboard, or both). Often, this key displays help information that deals with what you're doing at the time. If you're not doing anything when you press F1 (or if Quattro Pro for Windows can't figure out what you're doing), you receive the Help Contents screen (shown in Figure 2-5).

You can navigate through these help screens by clicking the underlined words. For example, if you click the word *Essentials* in the Help Contents screen, you get another screen, shown in Figure 2-6. Just keep clicking away until you find what you're looking for.

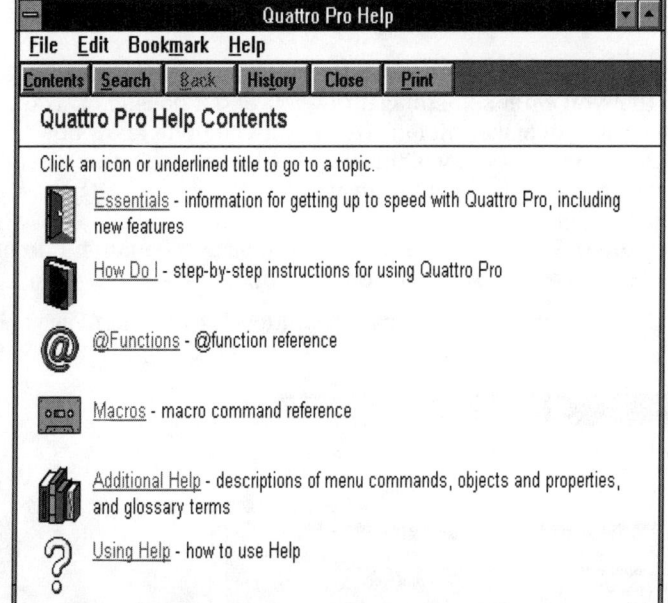

Chapter 2: Starting, Stopping, and Begging For Help 31

Figure 2-5:
The on-line help system actually has more information than the manuals that come with Quattro Pro for Windows.

Quattro Pro Help Contents

Click an icon or underlined title to go to a topic.

Essentials - information for getting up to speed with Quattro Pro, including new features

How Do I - step-by-step instructions for using Quattro Pro

@Functions - @function reference

Macros - macro command reference

Additional Help - descriptions of menu commands, objects and properties, and glossary terms

Using Help - how to use Help

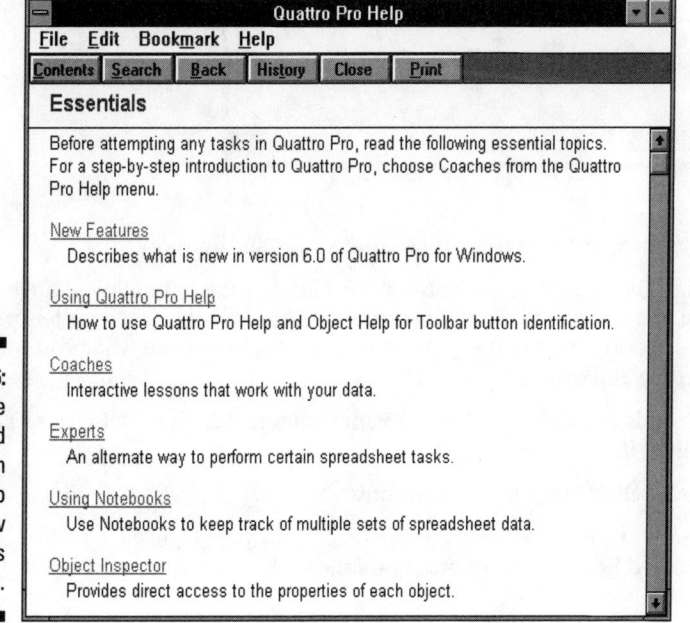

Figure 2-6:
Clicking the underlined phrases in the Help window provides more help.

Essentials

Before attempting any tasks in Quattro Pro, read the following essential topics. For a step-by-step introduction to Quattro Pro, choose Coaches from the Quattro Pro Help menu.

New Features
  Describes what is new in version 6.0 of Quattro Pro for Windows.

Using Quattro Pro Help
  How to use Quattro Pro Help and Object Help for Toolbar button identification.

Coaches
  Interactive lessons that work with your data.

Experts
  An alternate way to perform certain spreadsheet tasks.

Using Notebooks
  Use Notebooks to keep track of multiple sets of spreadsheet data.

Object Inspector
  Provides direct access to the properties of each object.

An example of using Help

One of the best ways to use Help is to take advantage of its searching capability. Suppose that you enter something into a cell, and it doesn't fit. You've heard a rumor that you can make columns wider, but you don't know how to do it (and somebody swiped your copy of this very book from your desk). Here's how you can use the on-line help to get the answer:

1. **Click the Help menu and then click the Search command (in other words, use the Help⇨Search command).**

   Quattro Pro for Windows displays a window like the one shown in Figure 2-7.

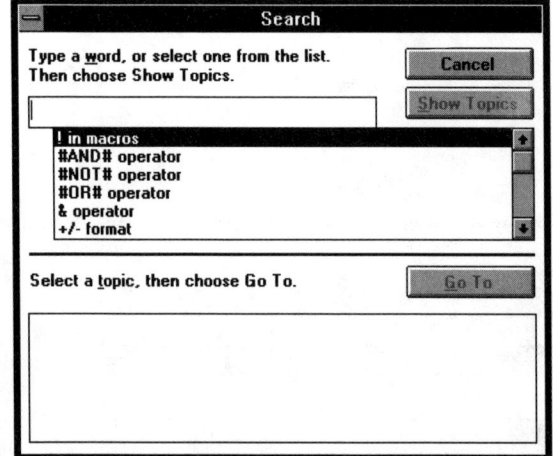

Figure 2-7: This window is where you enter a phrase that describes what you want help on.

2. **Type a word that describes what you want help on.**

   For this example, type **column**. Notice that the list below changes, based on what you type. For example, after you type the first four letters of the word **column**, you'll see some phrases that look like what you want. Stop typing and examine the list.

3. **The phrase Column Width Property looks like it may help, so click it to select it.**

4. **Next, click the Show Topics button.**

   You'll see a list of topics in the box below (see Figure 2-8). The topic labeled Resizing Rows and Columns looks promising, so click it.

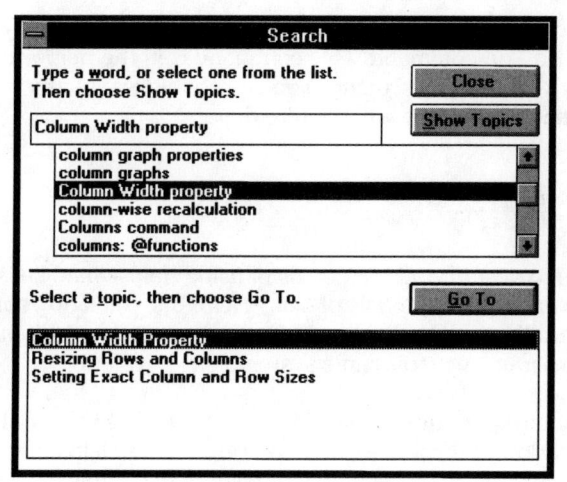

Figure 2-8: Choose a topic from the list and click Go To. Then read all about it.

5. **Click the Go To button to display help for the selected topic.**

   A window that lists several ways to change the width of a column appears.

6. **Click any of the underlined phrases to receive detailed instructions.**

Pointers for using Help

Most people find the Help system easy to use, once they get used to it. Fortunately, nearly all Windows systems use this same technique for providing on-line help. The key thing to remember is don't be afraid to click underlined words. Often, they'll lead you exactly to what you want. Here are some more things to remember about Help:

- If you click something that leads you to something else that's completely off base, just click the Back button to go back to where you were. In fact, you can keep clicking Back to back up even farther.

- If the Help window is too big and obscures your work you can change its size just by clicking and dragging a border

- You also can move the Help window. Just click its title bar (the thick thingy at the top that says Quattro Pro Help) and drag the window to where you want it to be.

- You'll find that when you click back in your spreadsheet, the Help window seems to disappear. Actually, it's still there — it's just in the background. Press Alt+Tab to get it back.

✔ If you want to keep the Help window displayed while you work, choose the Help Always on Top command. This command is in the Help window, not in Quattro Pro for Windows' menu. You'll probably want to move it or resize it so that you can see what you're doing.

Help with Help

I don't have space to describe all the details of using Help — and I'm sure that you don't want to *know* all the details of using Help. But you'll do yourself a favor by getting familiar with the on-line Help system, because just about all other Windows programs use this same system.

If you ever have some spare time on your hands, call up the Quattro Pro for Windows' Help window and choose the Help⇨How to Use Help command (yes, there's even help on how to use Help). If you need help on how to use the How To Use Help command, you're in trouble! Note that the Help⇨How to Use Help command is in the Help window, not in the Quattro Pro for Windows menu.

Using the Built-in Coaches

Besides all of the Help screens at your disposal, Quattro Pro for Windows gives you something known as Coaches. Coaches walk you through the steps required to perform command tasks — but they don't pat you on the butt after you hit a home run.

To access the Coaches, click the Coaches button on the toolbar. (It's the icon that shows the guy with the baseball cap.) You are greeted with a screen that gives you complete instructions on how to proceed.

Clicking the Coaches button may give you a message stating that the Coaches are not installed. If so, you'll have to rerun the Install program and request that the Coaches be installed. But, on the other hand, you may want to pass on it. Many people find them tedious to use and prefer other methods — like books.

Chapter 2: Starting, Stopping, and Begging For Help

The 5th Wave By Rich Tennant

"Yeah, my people are still getting headaches - DANG these VGA screens!"

Chapter 3
The Obligatory Tour of the Screen

In This Chapter
▶ What you need to know about all those weird things that show up on your screen when you run Quattro Pro for Windows
▶ What a notebook is, and how notebooks relate to files
▶ Some rudimentary information about menus and Toolbars
▶ Lots of marginally useful terminology that you can read once and then forget
▶ How to move around in a notebook

*Y*ou already know that this book is designed to cut to the chase and protect you from the gory details that prevent you from becoming adequately proficient in Quattro Pro for Windows. Unfortunately, there are some things that you just can't overlook. Bear with me as I tell you about them.

The Screen Tour (It's the Law)

Federal Statute CB324.21.190 states that every computer book published in the U.S. must include a tour of the screen within its first 50 pages. I developed Figure 3-1 to satisfy this legal requirement. After you start Quattro Pro for Windows, the screen shows a blank notebook just waiting to be used, abused, or misused.

Your screen may look a bit different, depending on what type of display driver you have installed for Windows. The screen in Figure 3-1 is in standard VGA mode, which shows 640 x 480 pixels (think of a pixel as a screen dot). You may have a display driver installed that has a higher resolution. The other two common display resolutions are 800 x 600 and 1024 x 768. If you have a choice, you're usually better off going with a higher resolution, because you can see more stuff on the screen. But make sure that your monitor can display high resolutions and that the text is not too small for you to read.

Part I: First Things First

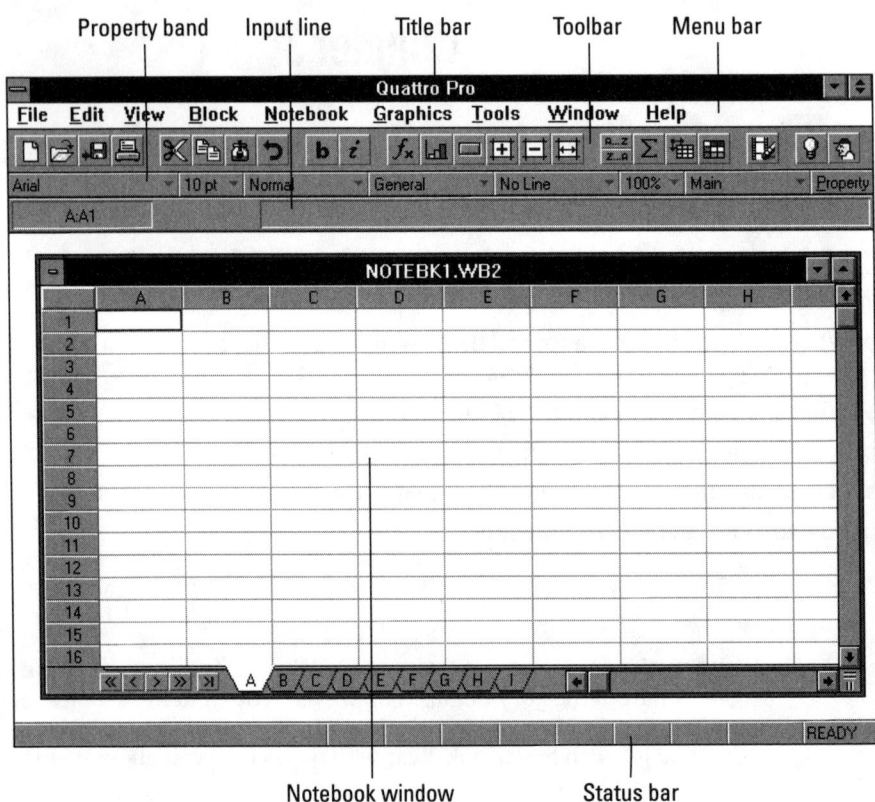

Figure 3-1: The opening screen from Quattro Pro for Windows.

Like the human body, a spreadsheet consists of various parts, some of which definitely are more interesting than others. Table 3-1 lists the parts that you eventually need to know. Don't be too concerned if you don't understand the terminology. It'll almost become crystal clear as you go through this chapter.

A notebook window has its own parts. Figure 3-2 shows a typical Quattro Pro for Windows notebook with its parts labeled. The parts are described in Table 3-2.

Chapter 3: The Obligatory Tour of the Screen   39

Table 3-1   The More Popular Quattro Pro for Windows Body Parts

Screen Part	What It Does
Title bar	Displays the name of the program you're running — if it's not Quattro Pro for Windows, you're reading the wrong book. The title bar also displays a handy description of the toolbar buttons and menu command descriptions.
Menu bar	Displays the commands that you can choose to get Quattro Pro for Windows to work for you.
Toolbar	Contains little buttons with pictures that, when clicked, perform shortcuts. There are several toolbars to choose from.
Property band	Contains pull-down menus for quickly setting things such as fonts, text size, and so on.
Input line	Where you enter and edit data in cells (even though you also can enter and edit data directly in cells).
Notebook window	Designed to hold your work in its many cells. Each notebook has its own window, and you can have many notebook windows open at once.
Status bar	Tells you Quattro Pro for Windows' current "state," whether NumLock is on, and other (usually worthless) details.

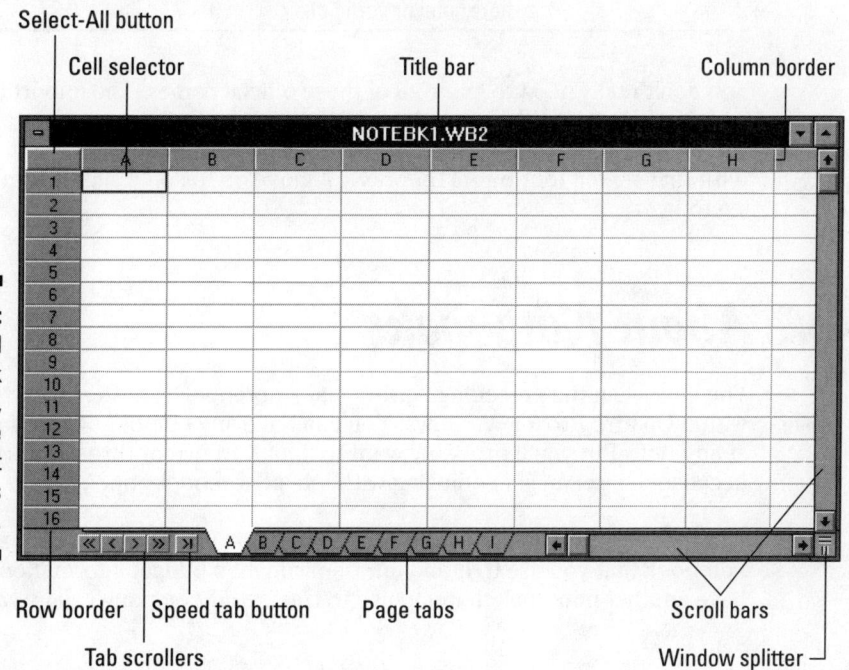

Figure 3-2: A typical notebook window, with the important parts pointed out.

Select-All button
Cell selector
Title bar
Column border
Row border
Speed tab button
Page tabs
Scroll bars
Tab scrollers
Window splitter

Table 3-2: Body Parts of a Notebook Window

Notebook Part	What It Does
Title bar	Tells you the name of the notebook.
Select-All button	Selects all cells on the active notebook page.
Column border	Identifies columns (columns are named by letters).
Row border	Identifies rows (rows are named by numbers).
Cell selector	Identifies the active cell.
Scroll bars	Click on the vertical scroll bar to move up and down in a notebook page. Click on the horizontal scroll bar to move sideways in a page.
Page tabs	Provides quick access to the additional pages in your notebook. Normally you label them with letters, but you can give them meaningful names, too.
Tab scrollers	If the page tab you want isn't displayed, you can click on these buttons to show other page tabs.
Speed tab button	Instantly moves you to a special page known as the Objects page. If you're already in the Objects page, the Speed tab button takes you back to the notebook page you were working in prior to going to the Objects page.
Window splitter	Lets you divide the notebook window into two panes (either horizontal or vertical).

You don't really need to know all of these official names. The important thing is that you know what the parts do.

With that screen tour out of the way, I'll move on to some slightly more interesting topics.

More About Notebooks

You can see in the preceding figures that a notebook is basically a window within Quattro Pro for Windows. You can have any number of notebooks open at any time. But you'll probably want to limit it to two or three at the most, because things can get confusing with lots of notebooks open.

A notebook corresponds to a particular project. For example, you may have a notebook that you use to hold your department's budget information. You may have another notebook that you use to track your company's daily sales. And you may have yet another notebook that holds the entries in the office football pool. A single notebook is certainly large enough to hold all of these projects, but you'll do yourself a favor by keeping your notebooks organized by project and not putting unrelated stuff into the same notebook.

A notebook corresponds to a file saved on your hard disk. Every notebook is stored in its own file. Even if you use all 256 pages in a notebook, that notebook still resides in one file.

May I See a Menu?

The row of words at the top of the screen (officially called the Menu bar) is vitally important. In fact, you won't get very far with Quattro Pro for Windows unless you use the Menu bar. The Menu bar is the primary way that you give commands to this program.

You use the menus by clicking a word, called a *menu item,* which causes a list of menu commands to drop down. Figure 3-3 shows what happens when you click Block. You then can click on one of the commands from the drop-down list.

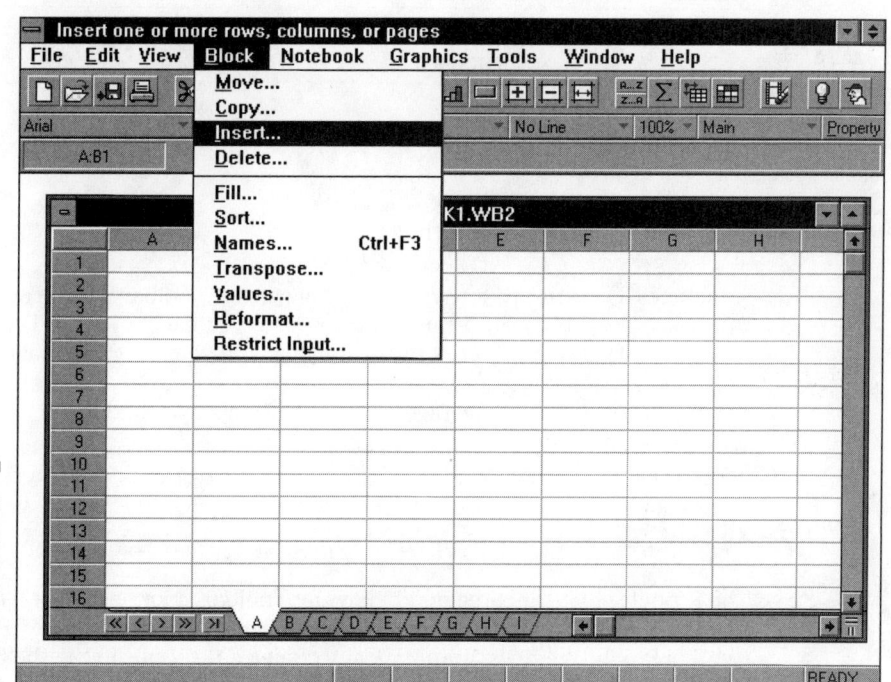

Figure 3-3: Clicking Block displays a set of menu commands.

Part I: First Things First

You learn more about menus in Chapter 6. At this point, I just want to make sure that you know they're there. So there.

Belly Up to the Toolbar

Besides using the menus, Quattro Pro for Windows provides a boatload of picture buttons that you can use to issue commands. A collection of such buttons is called a Toolbar. Normally, Quattro Pro for Windows displays its Main Toolbar, shown in Figure 3-4. However, you can replace it with any of four other prebuilt Toolbars — or even create your own if you're really ambitious.

Figure 3-4: The Main Toolbar has lots of shortcuts on it. Hold the mouse pointer over a button, and a little box pops up that tells you what the button does.

Sometimes, Quattro Pro for Windows changes the Toolbar for you automatically (nice guy, huh?). For example, when you create a graph, the Toolbar changes and gives you access to new buttons relevant to graph-making.

Toolbars receive more coverage in Chapter 6, so stay tuned.

Property Band

The Property band, located just below the Toolbar, contains several different items that make it easy for you to perform certain actions. Like the Toolbar, Quattro Pro for Windows automatically changes the items in the the Property band pull-down menu depending on what you happen to be doing at the time.

Some Useless Terminology

What do you call the thing that you're working on in Quattro Pro for Windows? The official name is a *notebook,* but lazy types often call it just a *sheet.* Some people call it a *spreadsheet,* and others simply call it a *file.* Still others refer to it as a *document.* Many prefer the more colorful term, &%#@!. I call it several things throughout this book (but never &%#@!). All of this terminology gets even more confusing when you consider that every Quattro Pro for Windows notebook actually has 256 pages in it. The bottom line? Don't worry about terminology. Don't forget: the goal is to get your work done so that you can move on to more important things.

Rows, columns, cells, and pages

A notebook page is made up of a bunch of cells. (I'll define the technical term *bunch* later.) Each cell is at the intersection of a row and a column. Rows are numbered 1, 2, 3, and so on up to 8,192. Columns are numbered A, B, C, and so on.

A notebook page contains 256 columns, but because the English alphabet stops at the letter Z, a team of experts was formed to determine how to label spreadsheet columns after you run out of letters. The experts arrived at an ingenious solution: use two letters. After column Z comes column AA, which is followed by AB, AC, and so on. After AZ comes BA, BB, BC, etc. If you follow this train of thought to its logical conclusion, you discover that column 256 is IV.

Every notebook has 256 pages, all of which are exactly the same size. Just click on one of page tabs at the bottom of the screen to activate a different page (see Figure 3-5).

Figure 3-5: The page tabs let you activate any of 256 pages in a notebook.

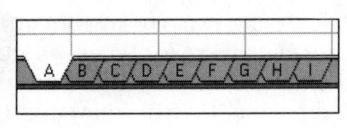

Every Quattro Pro for Windows notebook has one additional page beyond page IV. This page is called the Objects page and is used to store graphs and other things. You don't have to be concerned with this until Chapter 13 (and even then you can ignore it if you want).

Part I: First Things First

So how may cells are in a notebook? If your math is rusty, I'll fire up Quattro Pro for Windows and do the calculation for you: 8,192 rows x 256 columns x 256 pages comes to 536, 870, 912 cells. If you need more cells than this, you're reading the wrong book.

[Technical Stuff icon] You may be curious about why Quattro Pro for Windows uses such odd numbers. Why not 250 columns instead of 256? Why not an even 10,000 rows instead of 8,192? Why not 200 pages? Good questions. Using these strange numbers is a by-product of the binary system rearing its ugly head. Computers rely heavily on the binary system (you know, the number system that consists of only 0s and 1s). Two hundred fifty-six is 2 to the 8th power, and can be represented using exactly eight binary digits; 8,192 is 2 to the 13th power, and can be represented with 13 binary digits. Using these nice binary numbers actually optimizes the way things are stored within Quattro Pro for Windows.

Gimme your address

With a half billion cells in a notebook, the normal person may have trouble keeping track of them. Actually, because each cell has its own address (but not its own ZIP code), it's not all that difficult to keep track of the cells.

The address of a cell is made up of three things: its page letter (optional), its column letter and its row number. The page letter has a colon after it, but the column letter and row number are stuck together with no space in between. For example, the upper left cell is known as cell A:A1. The last cell, way down at the bottom of the fifth page and in the last column, has an address of E:IV8192.

[Remember icon] If you're working with only one page of a notebook (which is a fairly common thing to do), you don't have to be concerned with page letters. In fact, cell addresses don't even use the page letter when you have only a single page. I discuss working with multiple notebook pages in Chapter 14.

Cell addresses, by the way, are used in formulas, which I'll cover in Chapter 9. As you may already have noticed, cell addresses can quickly turn into a bowl of alphabet soup. To combat this problem, Quattro Pro for Windows lets you give meaningful names to the pages in a notebook. For example, you can name the first page *Income* and the second page *Expenses*. Then, if you want to refer to the upper-left cell on the second page, you can use a reference such as Expenses:A1. Much simpler, eh?

To change a page letter into a more meaningful name, just double-click on the page tab, type in the new name, and press Enter.

Chapter 3: The Obligatory Tour of the Screen 45

> **TIP**
> Often you can omit the page letter part of a cell address. If you don't include the page letter, Quattro Pro for Windows simply uses the current page. For example, if you're working on the second page, you can refer to the upper-left cell on that page as A1 rather than B:A1. But if you're on the second page and need to refer to the upper left cell on the *first* page, then you have to use the full A:A1 reference (which makes sense if you think about it).

The active cell

Take a look at the notebook in Figure 3-6. Notice that one of the cells has a darker outline than the others. This cell, called the *active cell,* is where the cell selector is. In this case, the active cell is cell A:C4. The box in the left part of the input line also tells you which cell is the active cell. When you move the cell selector around, the active cell changes. Isn't technology grand?

Move It Along

So how do you move the cell pointer? It's easy — with a mouse or your keyboard.

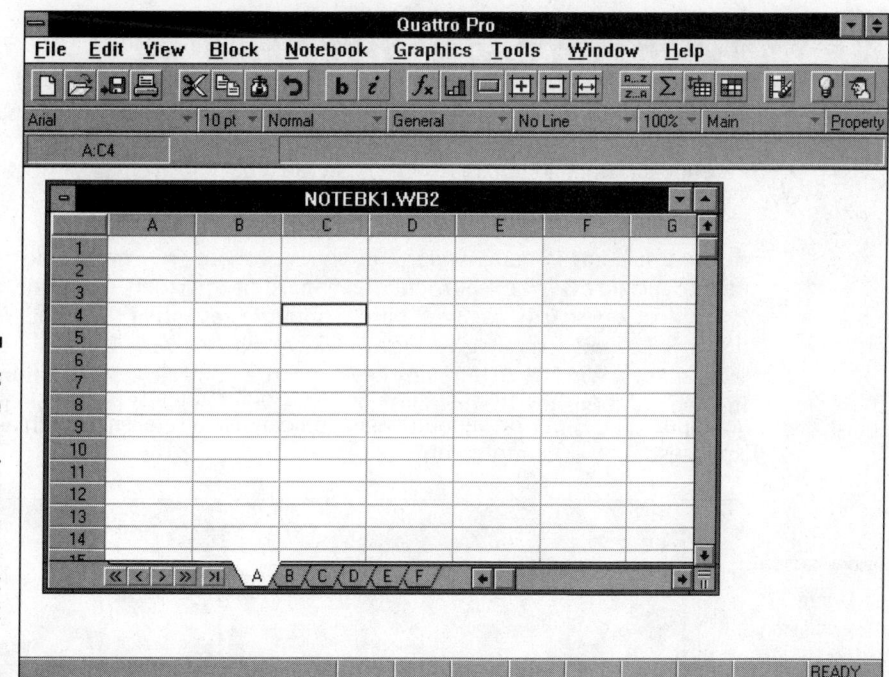

Figure 3-6: The active cell has a darker outline, and its address appears in the left part of the input line.

Moving around with a mouse

When you move your mouse around, notice how the little mouse arrow (otherwise known as the mouse pointer) moves on the screen. When the pointer is over one of the cells, click the left mouse button. The outline around the cell becomes thicker, and this cell magically transforms into the active cell.

Mouse freaks also can use the scroll bars to move to other cells. There are two scroll bars, the vertical one and the horizontal one. To move down one full screen in a notebook page, click toward the bottom of the vertical scroll bar. To move up a screen, click toward the top of the vertical scroll bar. To move one screen to the right, click the right side of the horizontal scroll bar. To move one screen to the left, click the left side of the horizontal scroll bar. You also can drag the little button that appears on the scroll bar to scroll the page either up or across. This scroll bar stuff is easier to do than it is to describe, so play around with clicking and dragging the scroll bars until you get the hang of it.

Using the scroll bars doesn't change the active cell — it just scrolls the page. To change the active cell, you have to click a cell after you use the scroll bars.

You can activate another page in the notebook by clicking on the appropriate tab at the top of the screen. If the tab for the page you want isn't visible, use the little VCR-like buttons to the left of the page tabs to scroll the tab display.

Moving around with the keyboard

Because you have to remove your hand from the keyboard to use your mouse, you may find that using the keyboard is more efficient for moving around a notebook. (I do, and I'm an expert.) Use the cursor movement keys, the keys with the arrows on them.

Keyboards come in many styles, but yours probably resembles the one depicted in Figure 3-7. This particular keyboard has two sets of cursor movement keys. Most keyboards have a separate numeric keypad at the right. This numeric keypad actually gives you *two* keypads: one with numerals and one with arrows. When the NumLock key is on, the numeric keypad's numerals are in effect. And (surprise, surprise) when the NumLock key is off, the numeric keypad's arrows are in effect.

Figure 3-7:
A common keyboard layout.

Chapter 3: The Obligatory Tour of the Screen   47

> ## Taming the wild rodent
>
> If you've never used a mouse before, don't be alarmed if you find it all very awkward at first. I've found that a four-year-old can master a mouse faster than most adults (feel bad now?). One way to get in some practice with a mouse is to run the Windows Solitaire game (which should be located in your Games program group). A few hands of this mildly addicting game will make you more comfortable with the mouse — and probably less interested in Quattro Pro for Windows.
>
> You need to know some basic mouse techniques and terminology, that apply to all the other Windows programs you'll ever use. The following list of terms covers just about everything you need to know about using the mouse:
>
> - **Click:** Move the mouse pointer over an object, press the left button, and release it right away.
> - **Right-click:** Move the mouse pointer over an object, press the right button, and release it right away.
> - **Double-click:** Move the mouse pointer over an object and press the left button twice in quick succession.
> - **Drag:** Move the mouse pointer over an object, press the left button (but don't release it), and then move the mouse (drag it). You can select cells like this, and even move things by dragging them and then releasing the mouse button.
>
> If you run out of room to move the mouse on your desk top or mouse pad, just pick up the mouse and reposition it somewhere else. Picking up the mouse doesn't move the mouse pointer, but it does give you more room to move around. Some people have trouble with double-clicking an object after they pick up the mouse. Just remember that you need to keep the mouse pointer in the same location for both of the clicks in a double-click.

The keys with the arrows move the cell pointer one cell at a time in the direction of the arrow. When you hold down one of these keys, the cell pointer zips along until you let go. A better way to move the cell pointer long distances is to use the keys labeled PgUp and PgDn. These keys move the cell pointer up or down one full screen. To move one screen to the right, use Ctrl+right-arrow key. And, to move quickly to the left, use Ctrl+left-arrow key. Pressing Ctrl+PgDn moves you to the next page in the notebook, while pressing Ctrl+PgUp moves you to the preceding page — unless you're already in the first page (then it does nothing but exercise your fingers).

Moving by one screen gives you different results, depending on how large the notebook window is. For example, if you make the notebook window very small (say, five rows high), PgDn only moves you down five rows. If the notebook window is large and shows 20 rows, PgDn moves you down 20 rows.

At some point in your spreadsheeting life, you may find yourself lost deep in the bowels of a notebook and desperate to get back home (back to cell A:A1). To take the express route, just press Ctrl+Home and you'll find yourself safe and sound back in cell A1 of the first page. To quickly jump to cell A1 of the *current* page, just press Home.

When the arrow keys don't work

If the arrow keys spit out numbers after you press them, just press the key labeled NumLock. Most keyboards have a little light that tells you the status of the NumLock key (either on or off). If your NumLock light is on, the numeric keypad produces numbers. If the NumLock light is off, the numeric keypad produces cursor movements. It's as easy as that.

Really advanced secret stuff

If, for some unknown reason, you need to move the cell pointer to an off-the-wall cell address such as R:FE459, you can bang away on the cursor control keys all day and still not find your way there. Or you can use a shortcut: Press the F5 key on your keyboard (found either in a row along the top or in a separate section along the left side). Quattro Pro for Windows displays a dialog box called Go to (see Figure 3-8). Simply type **R:FE459** (or whatever obscure cell address you want to get to) and select OK. Voila! You're there.

Figure 3-8: Press F5 and you get this handy Go to dialog box that can instantly send you to any of the 536,870,912 cells in a notebook.

Summary of movement options

When you're starting out with Quattro Pro for Windows, you may have trouble remembering all the specific navigational options. Fortunately for you, I've put together a handy summary of keyboard movements in Table 3-3. Eventually you'll discover the keyboard movements that you enjoy using, or you may decide to use them all, depending on what you're doing.

Table 3-3	Navigational Options	
Movement	*Keyboard*	*Mouse*
One cell up	Up-arrow key	Click the cell
One cell down	Down-arrow key	Click the cell
One cell left	Left-arrow key	Click the cell
One cell right	Right-arrow key	Click the cell
One screen down	PgDn	Click bottom of vertical scroll bar
One screen up	PgUp	Click top of vertical scroll bar
One screen left	Ctrl+left-arrow key	Click left side of horizontal scroll bar
One screen right	Ctrl+right-arrow key	Click right side of horizontal scroll bar
Next page	Ctrl+PgDn	Click page tab
Preceding page	Ctrl+PgUp	Click page tab
Move a long distance	F5, then enter address	Drag scroll-bar button

Chapter 4
Jumping Right In (A Hands-On Experience)

In This Chapter
▶ Overcoming your fears about working with a computer
▶ Receiving a once-in-a-lifetime opportunity to get some hands-on experience with Quattro Pro for Windows (and you don't even have to know anything)
▶ Creating a marginally useful notebook
▶ Learning about Quattro Pro for Windows' toolbars — useful little clickable pictures that can save you time and energy
▶ Getting some practical experience with dialog boxes

*I*t's no secret that many people (maybe even you) are deathly afraid of computers. At the mere mention of a computer-related term, their hands sweat, their hearts race, their glasses fog up, and they exhibit other strange physiological phenomena. I've found that fear of computers seems to be related to age: the older you are, the more fear you're likely to have. I know a four-year-old who has absolutely no fear of jumping into a new program and clicking away to see what happens. I also know an 81-year-old who never fails to ask me whether it's all right to click the Help menu.

The best way to overcome your fear of computers is to do things on a computer and to realize that you can't really cause too much damage. (Well, you *can* cause some damage to a computer, but I'll tell you how to minimize this possibility.) This chapter is designed to help you conquer your computer phobia by demonstrating that you (yes, even *you*) can do something reasonably productive with a computer — and that your computer will still be operable after you're finished.

Even if you're fearless when it comes to computers, taking the time to work your way through this chapter may teach you a thing or three. At the very least, you will get your feet wet with Quattro Pro for Windows, and you can decide whether it's really something you want to learn. (Let's hope so; otherwise, you've wasted 20 bucks on this book.)

What You'll Be Doing

By the time you reach the end of this chapter, you will have created a Quattro Pro for Windows notebook that can help you catalog your music collection. If you don't have a music collection, you still can use this chapter. (Just pretend that you have a music collection.)

If this were a *typical* computer book, the example in this chapter would probably be a notebook that calculates monthly payments on a mortgage, keeps track of your business expenses, or some other equally boring exercise. My example, though certainly not the most exciting spreadsheet you'll encounter, is slightly more interesting than the run-of-the-mill financial examples.

How to avoid causing damage

Avoid the following pitfalls if you're afraid that you'll screw things up while working on your computer. You may want to photocopy this page and nail it to your computer monitor (just kidding!). If you don't understand all the points, don't worry. You'll learn about this stuff later in this book.

- Don't delete any files unless you know *exactly* what they do. The fact is, deleting one critical file can keep your computer from starting. If you have a doubt about a file, don't delete it (or ask someone who has a degree in Computerfilology).

- Don't turn off your computer until you exit all your programs properly. Exit Quattro Pro for Windows by selecting the File⇨Exit command (or Alt+F4). Also, don't kick the plug out, don't knock your PC off of the desk, and don't drop the computer from tall buildings or airplanes.

- If you plan to make major changes to a file that already works, start by saving the notebook under a different name by using the File⇨Save As command. That way, the original notebook remains intact, and all your changes (for better or for worse) go to another notebook. If your changes mess things up, you can open the notebook that originally worked and pretend that nothing happened.

- Make a floppy disk backup copy of every important file. The worst damage that can occur to your files may not even be your fault. Hard disks tend to crash on their own for no apparent reason (I think it has something to do with astrological signs). A crashed hard disk usually means that everything stored on it has entered the big bit bucket in the sky — never to return.

- Keep your floppy disk backups in a safe place — *not* next to your computer. If your office burns down during the night, your backups suffer the same fate as your computer — they're fried.

- Be very careful when formatting floppy disks (formatting a disk is necessary the first time you use it). First, make sure that the disk you format doesn't have anything good on it. Second, make sure that you're actually formatting a *floppy* disk, not your hard disk. When in doubt, call your computer guru over for help. Or you can just buy pre-formatted disks.

Chapter 4: Jumping Right In (A Hands-On Experience)

More specifically, the notebook you develop does the following:

- Lets you keep track of CDs, cassettes, and even LPs and 8-track tapes (remember them?)
- Stores the artist, title, format, and total time of the recording in four columns
- Tells you the total number of recordings in the notebook
- Calculates and displays the total amount of money you spent on the collection

First Steps

I'm assuming that your system is all set up to run Quattro Pro for Windows and that you know how to start it. If my assumption is not valid, check out Appendix A (which covers installation details) and Chapter 2 (which explains how to start Quattro Pro for Windows).

For this exercise, you start out with a blank notebook, the way Quattro Pro for Windows normally starts up. Usually, it's a good idea to spend a few seconds thinking about what you want to do before you enter data into a notebook. Because you're just starting out, this time I'll do the thinking for you.

You're going to set up a notebook that will hold information about the recordings in a music collection. Each recording occupies one row of the notebook. For each recording, you'll keep track of the following four things:

- The recording artist's name
- The title of the recording
- The recording medium (CD, cassette — and even LP and 8-track tape if you're living in a time warp)
- The amount you paid for the item

You'll use four notebook columns to record the information. OK, that's enough time to think about the spreadsheet — now it's time to do it.

REMEMBER If you've never used a spreadsheet before, many of the things in this chapter will seem foreign to you. Don't worry if you don't understand everything that's going on. The point of this chapter is to give you an opportunity to do something, not to explain every detail. There'll be plenty of time for the details later.

Putting in the column headings

Throughout this chapter I refer to cell addresses. As you may already know from reading Chapter 3, a *cell address* consists of three parts: a page letter, a column letter, and a row number. Because you're only going to work with one page in the notebook, you don't need to bother with the page part of the cell address. So, for example, A1 is a cell address that refers to the upper-left cell of the notebook (column A, row 1).

Start by entering labels for the four column headings that correspond to the information in each column. To enter column headings, carefully follow these steps:

1. **Make sure that the cell pointer is in cell A1.**

    The input line tells you which cell the cell pointer is in. Use the arrow keys or the mouse to move the cell pointer to cell A1 or press Home to take the express route there.

2. **Type Artist and then press the right-arrow key to move the cell pointer to cell B1.**

    You don't have to press Enter after you type the word — the right-arrow key serves double-duty.

3. **Type Title into cell B1 and press the right-arrow key to get to cell C1.**

4. **Type Format into cell C1 and press the right-arrow key to get to cell D1.**

5. **Type Cost in cell D1 and press Home to return to cell A1.**

You've now entered the column headings, and your screen should look like Figure 4-1.

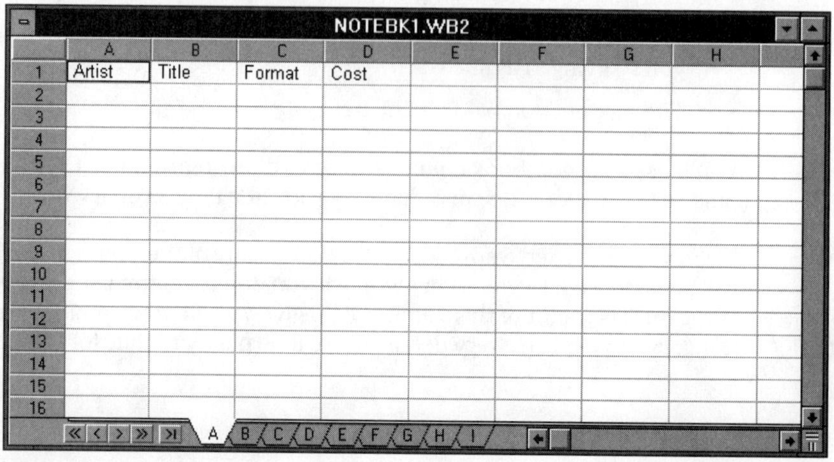

Figure 4-1:
Your notebook, after entering labels into the top row to serve as column headings.

Chapter 4: Jumping Right In (A Hands-On Experience) **55**

Making the headings bold

Next, you're going to boldface the headings. This step isn't essential, but it will make the notebook look a bit nicer. Follow these steps to boldface the headings:

1. **Make sure that the cell pointer is in cell A1 (the cell with the first column heading).**

   Use the arrow keys, the mouse, or press Home.

2. **Click the mouse and drag it so that it highlights all the other cells that have labels (cells A1 through D1).**

   You've just selected a range of cells.

3. **Examine the row of little icons in the toolbar at the top of the screen and find the one that looks like Figure 4-2. Click on it.**

   You've just used a Toolbar button to make the selected cells appear in bold type. There are other ways to do this, but the Toolbar technique is the fastest.

Your notebook now should look like Figure 4-3.

Figure 4-2: This Toolbar button makes the contents of the selected cells bold.

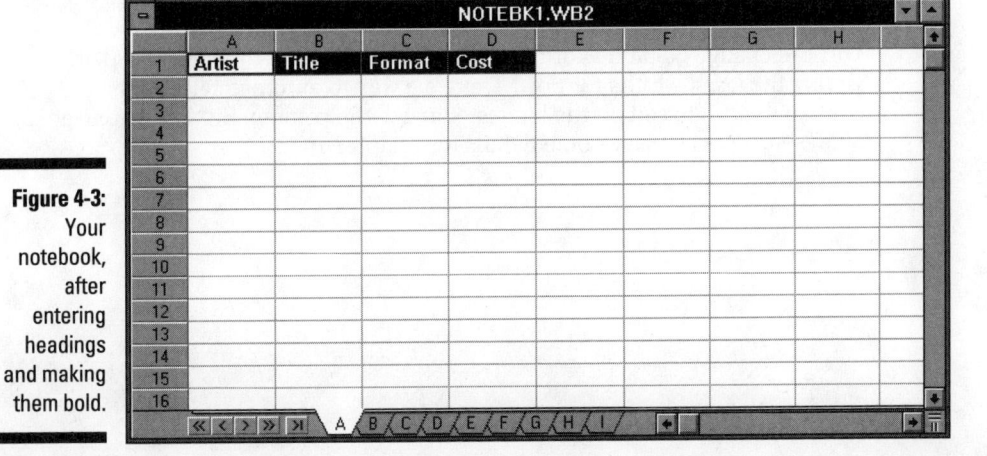

Figure 4-3: Your notebook, after entering headings and making them bold.

Adjusting the column widths

Unless your music collection consists exclusively of one-word titles by artists with a single name, the columns won't be wide enough to display everything properly. You can increase the widths of the columns by following these steps:

1. **Move the mouse pointer to the right border of column A.**

   The mouse pointer changes shape and looks like two arrows pointing in opposite directions, as in Figure 4-4.

2. **While the mouse pointer sports this new shape, click and drag the column border to the right.**

   As you do so, watch the column width expand before your very eyes. Keep dragging until the column is about three times its original size.

3. **Repeat Steps 1 and 2 for column B.**

4. **Repeat Steps 1 and 2 for column D, except this time drag the border to the *left* to make the column a bit narrower.**

   Column C is OK as it is.

Figure 4-4: When you drag the mouse over a column border, the mouse pointer changes shape.

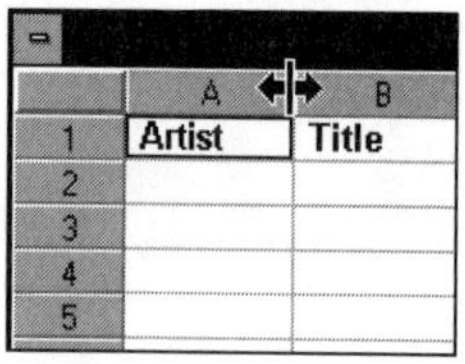

You can change column widths at any time, so don't be too concerned about getting the exact widths for now. There's a way to automatically adjust a column's width based on the longest entry in the column. But I'm getting ahead of myself. I need to save some details for Chapter 10.

Entering the Data

Now you're ready to put some entries into the notebook. Remember, each recording goes into a separate row, and you'll use four columns in each row. Just follow these steps:

1. **Move the cell pointer to cell A2 (using the arrow keys or the mouse) and enter the name of a recording artist.**

   If you can't think of one, type **Eric Clapton**. Press the right-arrow key to move to the next cell.

2. **In cell B2, enter the title of the recording.**

   If you lack imagination, type **Unplugged**. Use the right-arrow key to move to the cell next door.

3. **Enter the format of the recording in cell C2.**

   If you're using my example, type **CD**. Press the right-arrow key again to go to cell D2.

4. **Enter the cost of the item.**

   The CD in the example I'm using cost $13.99, so type **13.99** (don't put in a dollar sign because Quattro Pro will just ignore it).

5. **Press Enter to end this entry.**

After you finish with this row, use the down-arrow key to move the cell pointer to the next row (row 3) and then press the left-arrow key until you're in cell A3. Repeat the preceding procedure until you've entered your entire CD, cassette, and record collection. (Not really. You can stop after four or five entries, or whenever it gets boring.)

Your notebook should look something like Figure 4-5. If it looks *exactly* like this figure, you either have excellent taste in music, or you have no imagination and simply copied my example.

Formatting the Dollar Amounts

You may have noticed that if you enter a dollar amount such as $13.99 with a dollar sign tacked on, Quattro Pro for Windows ignores the dollar sign (I told you it would) and simply displays the number. Does this mean that you can't use dollar signs in your spreadsheet? Of course not. Why would I include this section if you couldn't?

Figure 4-5: Your notebook, after entering some recordings.

	A	B	C	D
1	Artist	Title	Format	Cost
2	Eric Clapton	Unplugged	CD	13.99
3	Steel Pulse	Smash Hits	Casette	7.99
4	Beausoleil	La Danse de la Vie	CD	15.99
5	John Mayall	Wake Up Call	CD	13.99
6	Enya	Watermark	CD	15.99
7	Traveling Wilburys	Volume 3	Casette	8.99
8	Tangerine Dream	Canyon Dreams	CD	13.99
9	Loreena McKennitt	The Mask and the Mirror	CD	14.99
10	Rabih About-Khalil	Al-Jadida	CD	15.99
11	Willie Nelson	Red-Headed Stranger	LP	8.95
12	Art Pepper	Laurie's Choice	CD	6.99
13	David Bromberg Band	Midnight on the Water	LP	8.95
14	Philippe Kahn	Paradiso	CD	0
15	Philippe Kahn	Pacific High	CD	0
16	Bob Dylan	Blonde on Blonde	LP	11.95

In these steps, you'll apply formatting techniques to column D. More specifically, you'll set it up so that values entered into this column will *automatically* include a dollar sign (you don't even have to enter it). You're going to change the style property of the cells in column D. Here's how to do it:

1. **Select the entire column D.**

   Move the mouse pointer to the D in the column headers (the mouse pointer changes to a downward-pointing arrow). Click the left mouse button to select the entire column.

2. **Click on the Style pull-down list in the Property band and select Currency from the list.**

   The Property band is located just below the Toolbar (see Figure 4-6). Usually, the Style pull-down list reads "Normal" (since cells have a Normal style by default).

   After you change the style to Currency, all of the values in the selected column take on a slightly different look — they have dollar signs. Also, if any of your dollar amounts didn't have decimal places (for example, if you entered **14** with no decimal point), they do now. Using the Currency style, all numbers have a dollar sign and two decimal places.

> **TIP** If some of the cells in Column D display asterisks after you apply the Currency style, you'll need to make the column width wider. Asterisks signal that the column isn't wide enough to display the values. If you don't remember how to change the width of a column, go back and reread the section "Adjusting the column widths."

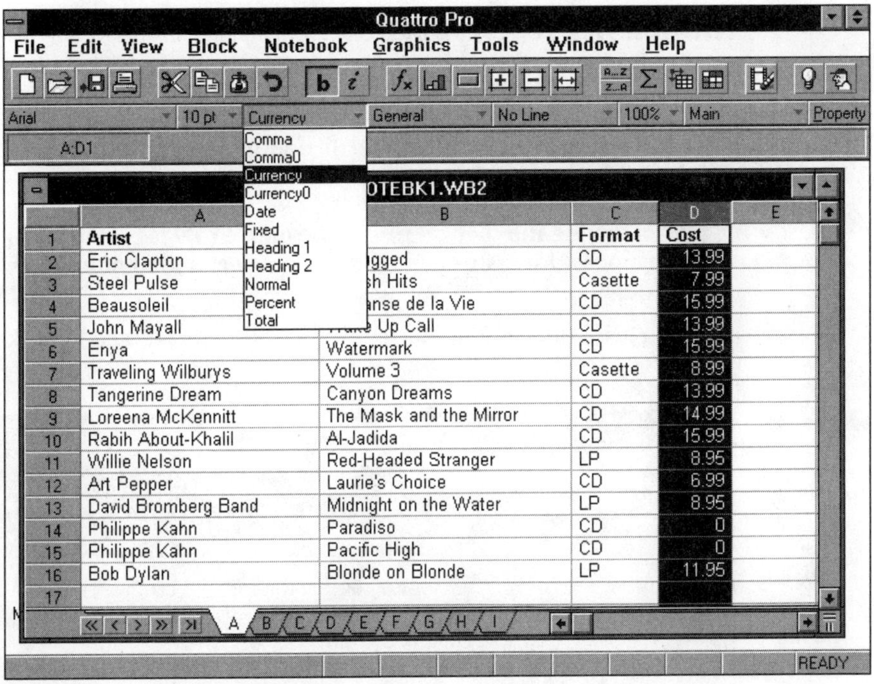

Figure 4-6: The Style pull-down list makes it easy to change the look of your cells. In this case, you're applying the Currency style to column D.

And Now, a Formula

If you have only a few sample lines of data, you can tell at a glance how many recordings are in the list. But what if you have several hundred? Or several thousand? You would have to move down to the end of the list, make a note of what row number the last entry is in, and then mentally subtract one from the number of the last entry to account for the row containing the column headings. But why do all these mental gymnastics when you can use a formula to do the counting? This is the age of computers, no?

A *formula* is something that you put into a cell that uses information in other cells to display a result (usually a calculation of some kind). The formula you'll work with uses one of the built-in functions provided by Quattro Pro for Windows to count the number of nonblank cells in a range of cells. This product has many built-in functions, as you discover in Chapter 9.

A good place to put a formula is at the top of the notebook. But because the top rows are occupied, you need to move the rows down by inserting new rows to make room for the formula.

Inserting new rows

In this part of the exercise, you insert four new blank rows at the top of the notebook. After you add the new rows, everything else gets pushed down (but you don't lose anything you've already done). To insert new rows at the top of the notebook, do the following:

1. **Click on the number on row 1 (the entire row is highlighted) and drag the mouse down three more rows to select a total of four rows (rows 1 through 4).**

   You just selected four entire rows. Your screen should look like Figure 4-7.

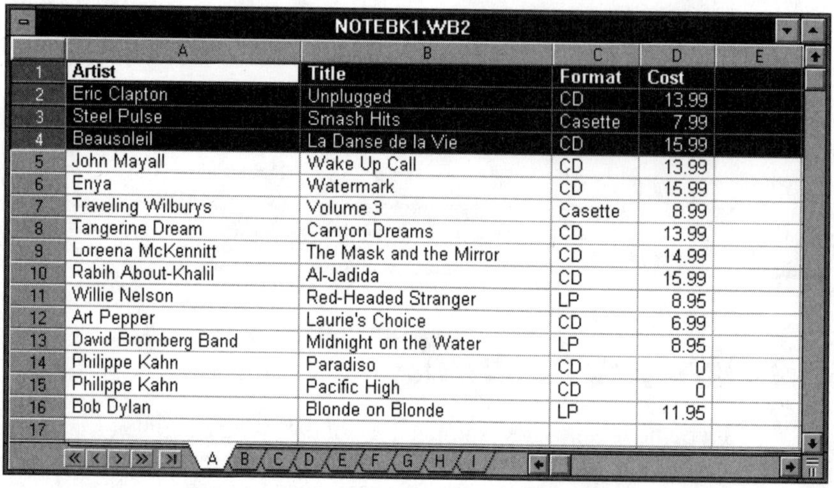

Figure 4-7: The first step in inserting rows is to select the rows where the insertion will take place by clicking and dragging on the row number.

	A	B	C	D
1	Artist	Title	Format	Cost
2	Eric Clapton	Unplugged	CD	13.99
3	Steel Pulse	Smash Hits	Casette	7.99
4	Beausoleil	La Danse de la Vie	CD	15.99
5	John Mayall	Wake Up Call	CD	13.99
6	Enya	Watermark	CD	15.99
7	Traveling Wilburys	Volume 3	Casette	8.99
8	Tangerine Dream	Canyon Dreams	CD	13.99
9	Loreena McKennitt	The Mask and the Mirror	CD	14.99
10	Rabih About-Khalil	Al-Jadida	CD	15.99
11	Willie Nelson	Red-Headed Stranger	LP	8.95
12	Art Pepper	Laurie's Choice	CD	6.99
13	David Bromberg Band	Midnight on the Water	LP	8.95
14	Philippe Kahn	Paradiso	CD	0
15	Philippe Kahn	Pacific High	CD	0
16	Bob Dylan	Blonde on Blonde	LP	11.95
17				

2. **Click on the Insert button on the Toolbar. This button has a small blue plus sign on it.**

   Quattro Pro for Windows goes to work and inserts four new rows for you in a jiff (pushing everything else downward). Your screen now should look like Figure 4-8.

Sticking in the formula

Now that you have some extra room at the top of the notebook, you can put in a formula to count the number of occupied cells. The formula can go in any unused cell, but cell B2 is a good place to put it. To enter the formula, take the following steps:

Chapter 4: Jumping Right In (A Hands-On Experience)   61

Figure 4-8: Your notebook, after inserting four new rows at the top.

	A	B	C	D
5	Artist	Title	Format	Cost
6	Eric Clapton	Unplugged	CD	13.99
7	Steel Pulse	Smash Hits	Casette	7.99
8	Beausoleil	La Danse de la Vie	CD	15.99
9	John Mayall	Wake Up Call	CD	13.99
10	Enya	Watermark	CD	15.99
11	Traveling Wilburys	Volume 3	Casette	8.99
12	Tangerine Dream	Canyon Dreams	CD	13.99
13	Loreena McKennitt	The Mask and the Mirror	CD	14.99
14	Rabih About-Khalil	Al-Jadida	CD	15.99
15	Willie Nelson	Red-Headed Stranger	LP	8.95
16	Art Pepper	Laurie's Choice	CD	6.99
17	David Bromberg Band	Midnight on the Water	LP	8.95

1. **Move the cell pointer to cell B2.**
2. **Type the formula @COUNT(A:A)-1 into cell B2 and press Enter.**

   After you press Enter, you don't see the formula in the cell; instead, you see the formula's result, which tells you how many recordings you've entered. When the cell pointer is on the cell, however, you can see the formula in the edit line at the top of the screen.

   This formula uses a special function (@COUNT) that counts the number of nonblank entries in a range; the range is in parentheses. In this case, the range is the entire column A of page A. The first A refers to the page and the second A refers to the column. The formula subtracts one from this count to account for the column heading.

3. **Move to cell C2 and type Recordings, a label that reminds you of what the number in cell B2 refers to.**

Add another record or two and watch as the count is updated automatically. Are you in love with spreadsheets yet?

Ready for another formula?

Now you can add another formula that calculates the total amount of money spent on this collection. Follow these steps carefully:

1. **Move the cell pointer to cell B3.**
2. **Type the formula @SUM(A:D) and press Enter.**

   The @SUM function adds all of the values in a range. Here, the range consists of the entire column D. The A refers to the page that you're on.

3. **With the cell selector still in cell B3, open the Style pull-down list and assign the Currency style to this cell.**

   The values in the column are now displayed with a dollar sign.

4. **Move to cell C3 and type** Total cost **to remind you of what the number in cell B3 is.**

To see whether the formula works, add another record or two and watch as the total cost is updated to include the new amounts. Now your notebook should look something like Figure 4-9. The actual numbers in cells B2 and B3 depend, of course, on how many recordings you entered and how much you spent on them. Your mileage may vary.

Figure 4-9: Your notebook, after entering the formula to count the recordings and compute the total cost.

	A	B	C	D
1				
2		15	Recordings	
3		158.75	Total cost	
4				
5	Artist	Title	Format	Cost
6	Eric Clapton	Unplugged	CD	13.99
7	Steel Pulse	Smash Hits	Casette	7.99
8	Beausoleil	La Danse de la Vie	CD	15.99
9	John Mayall	Wake Up Call	CD	13.99
10	Enya	Watermark	CD	15.99
11	Traveling Wilburys	Volume 3	Casette	8.99
12	Tangerine Dream	Canyon Dreams	CD	13.99
13	Loreena McKennitt	The Mask and the Mirror	CD	14.99
14	Rabih About-Khalil	Al-Jadida	CD	15.99
15	Willie Nelson	Red-Headed Stranger	LP	8.95
16	Art Pepper	Laurie's Choice	CD	6.99
17	David Bromberg Band	Midnight on the Water	LP	8.95

Adding a Title

Now you can add one last finishing touch — a title for your spreadsheet, at the top — and you can make it a bit fancy, just for fun. To add a title to your spreadsheet, use this procedure:

1. **Move the cell pointer to cell A1.**

   The Home key gets you there in a jiff.

2. **Type** List of Recordings **and press Enter.**

3. **Use the Size pull-down menu on the Property band and select a larger typeface for this cell.**

Something like 18-point type should do the trick.

4. **Click on the Bold button on the Toolbar to make the text bold.**

5. **Just for fun, click on the Italic button on the Toolbar to make the text italic.**

Your notebook now looks something like Figure 4-10.

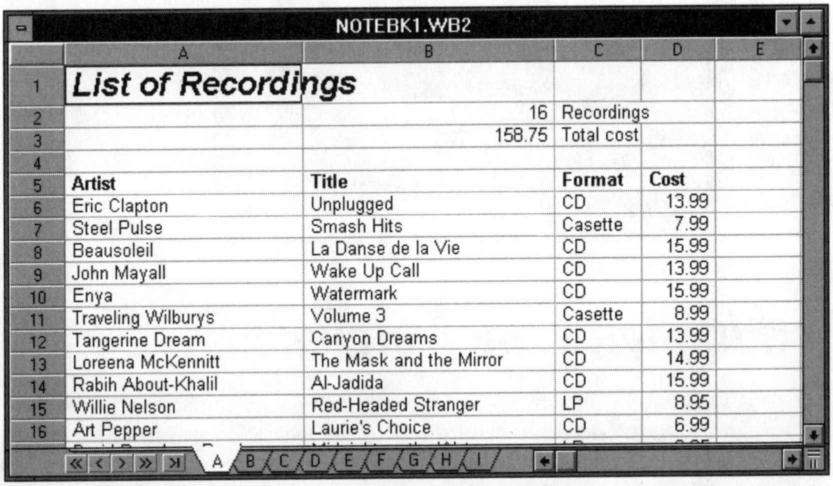

Figure 4-10: The notebook, after modifying some of the properties of cell A1.

	A	B	C	D	E
1	*List of Recordings*				
2		16	Recordings		
3		158.75	Total cost		
4					
5	Artist	Title	Format	Cost	
6	Eric Clapton	Unplugged	CD	13.99	
7	Steel Pulse	Smash Hits	Casette	7.99	
8	Beausoleil	La Danse de la Vie	CD	15.99	
9	John Mayall	Wake Up Call	CD	13.99	
10	Enya	Watermark	CD	15.99	
11	Traveling Wilburys	Volume 3	Casette	8.99	
12	Tangerine Dream	Canyon Dreams	CD	13.99	
13	Loreena McKennitt	The Mask and the Mirror	CD	14.99	
14	Rabih About-Khalil	Al-Jadida	CD	15.99	
15	Willie Nelson	Red-Headed Stranger	LP	8.95	
16	Art Pepper	Laurie's Choice	CD	6.99	

Saving This Masterpiece

Nothing you've done so far has been saved in your computer's memory. Your hard disk has been completely idle. If you (or some clod) should accidentally kick your PC's plug out of the wall socket, all this fine work would go down the proverbial tube. To prevent such a disaster, you need to save your notebook with the following steps:

1. **Click on the Save Notebook button on the Toolbar. It's third from the left and has a picture of a disk on it.**

   Because you haven't given your notebook a filename yet, Quattro Pro for Windows pops up the dialog box shown in Figure 4-11 that asks you to enter a name for the file. This dialog box also shows you a list of other notebook files that may be in this directory.

2. **Type MUSIC (the name you'll use for this file) and press Enter.**

   Quattro Pro for Windows saves your work as MUSIC.WB1. This filename now shows up on the title bar of the notebook window to remind you of what you're working on.

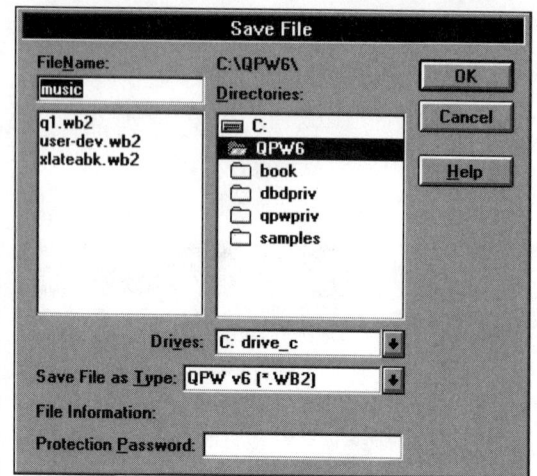

Figure 4-11: Name your notebook file in this dialog box.

Working with the Notebook

This notebook is in pretty good shape. Now you can use the techniques you've learned to add more recordings to the list. The formulas at the top will always tell you exactly how many recordings you've entered and the total amount of cash you've spent.

For practice, add some more recordings.

Saving It Again

If you made any changes to the notebook since you saved it, you need to save it again to keep from losing this additional work. Click on the Save Notebook button to save your file. Because the notebook already has a name, Quattro Pro for Windows doesn't waste your time asking you for the name again — it simply saves the file using its existing name. This process all happens so quickly that you may not even notice anything. However, if you watch your hard disk drive light, you see that it flashes on for a split second while the file is being saved. That flash tells you that Quattro Pro has saved your file again.

Chapter 4: Jumping Right In (A Hands-On Experience) **65**

A personal anecdote

At one point in my college days, I had four roommates who also happened to be music lovers and computer buffs. Between the five of us, we had approximately 3,000 LPs. (This was long before CDs were available.) One of these guys was taking a computer class and needed a project.

Believe it or not, we actually keypunched all the titles, artists, and other information from these recordings onto IBM cards and created a data file on the campus mainframe. Using FORTRAN (an ancient computer language), we wrote a program to summarize and print the data. Then, when we were all sitting around in various states of consciousness and couldn't decide what to listen to, someone would call out a random number. We had a mutual agreement that we would play the record that corresponded to the number on the printout. Because our musical tastes were all pretty good, this usually resulted in an agreeable outcome, and we often heard an album that we would never think of playing otherwise. Occasionally, however, the scheme backfired, and we had to endure 45 minutes of the Carpenters or some other equally obnoxious group.

The point of this story is that we all learned a great deal about programming because the project involved a topic that we were *interested* in. The same goes for learning Quattro Pro for Windows or any other software for that matter. If you try to learn software by using stupid examples, you probably won't get too far. The best way to learn is by working on projects that are important to you.

Quitting Quattro Pro for Windows

Now that you've set up this notebook and saved it, you can call it quits. Press Alt+F4 (a shortcut way to exit Quattro Pro for Windows). If you've made any changes since the last time you saved the file, Quattro Pro for Windows prompts you and gives you a chance to save your file before you exit. Otherwise, the program ends and you're back at the Windows Program Manager screen.

Retrieving Your Work

The next time you start Quattro Pro for Windows, you can work on this notebook again by retrieving it from your disk. This process is also known as "opening a file." To open an existing notebook file, follow these steps:

1. **Click on the Open Notebook button on the Toolbar. (It's second from the left and has a picture of a file folder with a blue arrow.)**

   The Open File dialog box appears, which looks remarkably like the one you use when you save a file (see Figure 4-12).

Figure 4-12: Use this dialog box to tell Quattro Pro for Windows what file you want to retrieve.

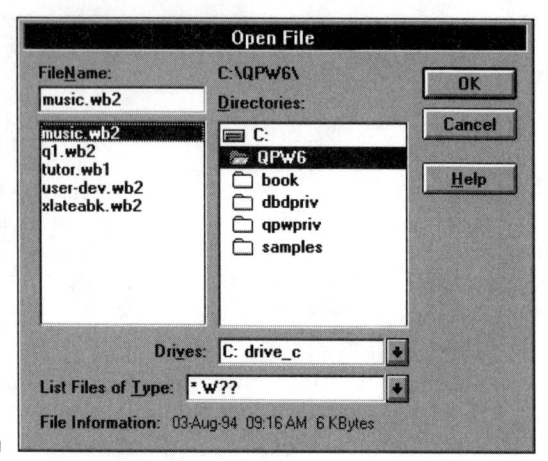

2. **Type in the filename of the file you want to open and choose OK. Or you can avoid typing and simply select the filename from the list of files shown.**

    The file opens and looks just as it did the last time you saved it.

    An even faster way to open a notebook file is to click File. The File menu drops down, and the bottom of the menu displays a list of the last four notebook files you worked on. Just click the filename you want and it will open. This works only if the file you need is one of the last four that you worked on.

Still Afraid?

If you followed along with these exercises and had no problems, congratulations. If you found yourself getting lost and even more confused, don't despair. Try it again, starting with another blank notebook. Take your time and follow the instructions carefully. I guarantee that you'll eventually get the program to work right. Your last vestiges of fear will begin to vanish as your confidence increases. If they don't, try some Valium.

Food for Thought

You may not know it, but during the course of this exercise you've actually created a database. For the uninitiated, a database is simply a collection of data arranged in an organized manner. As you learn in Chapter 16, Quattro Pro for

Windows is a good tool for working with databases. Chapter 16 teaches you how to sort the information and generate reports to summarize the information and display only selected data (such as a list of only the CDs in your collection).

If you think about it, you probably can come up with several other ideas for databases that would be useful for you. Believe it or not, you already have enough knowledge about Quattro Pro for Windows to create them. And you're only on the fourth chapter!

Other Stuff for Overachievers

Normal users can consider this chapter over and done with, and they can move on to other topics. But those who always turn in their science projects early will probably want to read more.

The notebook you developed in this chapter is only a start. Imaginative users can do even more to it. Here's a list of some potential additions you can make to the spreadsheet:

- A formula to calculate the average cost of the items in your collection (hint: use the @AVG function).
- Another column for the year the album was recorded.
- Another column for your evaluation of the recording: excellent, good, poor, pure garbage, and so on. If you use numerical ratings, eventually you will be able to sort the data according to this column and instantly see your recordings sorted from best to worst. Sorting is covered in Chapter 10.

You also can change the formatting. Changing the formatting simply means making the contents of the cell look different. Feel free to select some cells by dragging the mouse over them and then experimenting with the Toolbar buttons. Have some fun and be as outrageous as you want.

> **TIP**
> To find out what a Toolbar button does, just move the mouse pointer over it (but don't click). A little yellow box pops up and gives you the button's name. To learn even more, hold down Ctrl and right-click the button. A larger box, known officially as Object Help, appears. If you *still* want to learn more, click the Help button in the box. The on-line help system will tell you everything you ever wanted to know. And more — lots more.

Part II
Basic Stuff That You Just Can't Ignore

The 5th Wave — By Rich Tennant

"I SAAIID WHAT COMPANY DO YOU REPRESENT?"

In this part...

The information in these chapters is best described as fundamental. In other words, you won't get too far with Quattro Pro for Windows unless you know how to do these basic operations. Or, to put it another way, if you're just starting out with Quattro Pro for Windows, this is *not* the section to skip.

Chapter 5
Ways to Fill Up All Those Cells

In This Chapter
▶ Learning not to panic when faced with a blank notebook
▶ Putting numbers and words into cells
▶ Changing the contents of cells
▶ Removing the information in a cell

Part I of this book covers quite a bit of ground: you have at least some idea what Quattro Pro for Windows is all about. You know what the screen parts are, and you even know how to move the cell pointer to any cell in the notebook. A lot of good that does on an empty notebook, right? Your boss wants *information* in the cells of your notebook. In this chapter you learn all the gory details on how to put information into those cells.

If you took the time to walk through the example in Chapter 4, some of this material may be old hat to you. But don't skip anything in this chapter — you learn *why* you did what you did in Chapter 4.

What to Do with a Blank Notebook

If you're really observant, you may have noticed the little word in the bottom right corner of your screen (in the status line) that reads READY. This is the *mode indicator*. When you start it up, Quattro Pro for Windows is in READY mode, which means that the program is ready for you to perform a task, such as move to another cell (which you already know how to do) or put information into a cell (which you're about to learn).

What Goes in a Cell?

A notebook cell can hold the following four types of information:

- **A number** (also known as a value). You won't have to stray any farther than this chapter to learn how to enter numbers.
- **A label** (which you may recognize as normal words). You also learn how to enter labels in this chapter.
- **A formula** (which does miraculous things using the contents of other cells). You learn about formulas in Chapter 8.
- **Nothing** (zip, nada, zilch, blankissimo, nil). Cells can be completely empty, void of all content (like some of the chapters in this book).

A cell can hold only one of these four items at a time. But because a cell holding a formula displays the answer to the formula and not the formula itself, a cell holding a formula *looks* as if it's holding either a number or a label.

TIP

The preceding list of cell contents applies only to notebook *cells.* As you learn later, a notebook also can hold graphs, pictures, and drawings. But these items aren't *in* cells; they kind of *float* on top of cells and can be moved around and resized independently of the cells.

More About What Goes in a Cell

Why is there a distinction between numbers and labels? When do you need numbers, and when do you need labels? What good are formulas? And does the refrigerator light really go out when you close the door?

You use numbers when you work with a subject that uses quantities or values. If you make a notebook to keep track of your gambling losses, for example, you may enter a number for the amount you lose on each bet. A nice fact about numbers is that you can refer to them in your formulas. For example, you can enter a formula that adds up a bunch of numbers and displays the total in a separate cell (but for your gambling loss notebook, you may not *want* to know the total damage).

You use labels, on the other hand, to describe what the numbers in cells represent and to add titles to your work. In your gambling loss notebook, you can put the following labels next to your numbers: Reno blackjack table, Santa Anita Racetrack, and so on. You also can use words just to make a simple list without getting any numbers involved.

Leave cells blank (or empty) when you don't have anything to put in them or when you want to have some space between cells that have information in them. By default, all cells are blank.

Figure 5-1 shows a notebook with numbers, labels, formulas, and blank cells. Notice that you can't see the formulas, just the results of the formulas. Actually, if a formula is in the active cell, the formula appears in the edit line at the top of the screen.

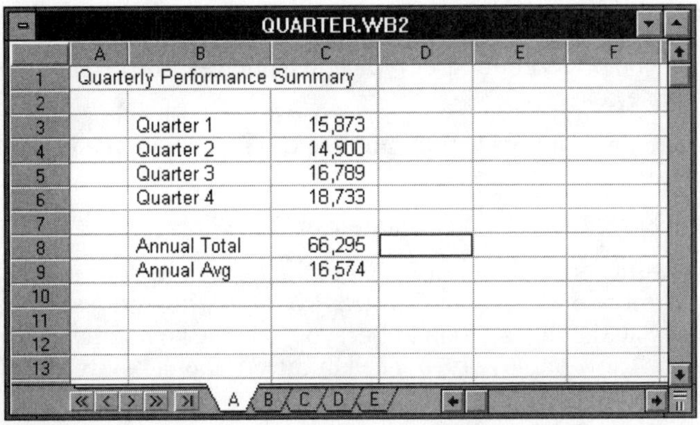

Figure 5-1: A notebook, showing examples of numbers, labels, formula results, and (yes) even blank cells.

	A	B	C
1	Quarterly Performance Summary		
2			
3		Quarter 1	15,873
4		Quarter 2	14,900
5		Quarter 3	16,789
6		Quarter 4	18,733
7			
8		Annual Total	66,295
9		Annual Avg	16,574

Putting Numbers into Cells

Throughout the course of recent history, spreadsheets have acquired a reputation for being good to use with numbers. Therefore, it's only fitting that you get your feet wet by learning how to enter a number into a cell.

Before you put anything into a cell, make sure that you're in READY mode. If not, press Esc once or twice to get into this mode.

When you're ready to enter a number (and Quattro Pro for Windows is READY too), you have the following two choices for entering the numbers into the cells:

- You can use the number keys along the top of your keyboard (not the keys with Fs on them, but the keys with punctuation characters above the numbers).
- If your NumLock light is on, you can use the keys on the numeric keypad to input numbers.

Ready? Try entering some data into your spreadsheet by following these steps:

1. **Move to a cell — use cell B3 just for grins.**
2. **Type 236, or a number of your choice (but don't press Enter).**

    Notice that you're now in VALUE mode. After you type the first number, Quattro Pro for Windows reads your mind and realizes that you are entering a number (or value) into a cell.

3. **Press Enter to make the number stick in the cell.**

    Take a peek at the mode indicator — you're back in READY mode.

    When you press Enter after typing in a number, the cell pointer stays on the same cell.

4. **Use the down-arrow key to move to the cell below (cell B4) and type another number, such as 314.**
5. **Press Enter to record the number in the cell.**

    Repeat this procedure until you get the hang of it. Your numbers can have any number of digits (but Quattro Pro for Windows doesn't necessarily display all the digits). Remember, you can use any of the techniques you already know to move to any cell in the notebook before entering a number into it.

You may not realize it, but you've come a long way. You now have enough knowledge to fill the entire notebook with numbers. (But don't try it; it gets boring really fast.)

Making Numbers Look Right

After you start entering numbers into cells, you may not be happy with how the numbers look. If you have a really long number, Quattro Pro for Windows displays it using scientific notation. You may want other numbers to show up with commas in them. Or you may want all numbers to be displayed with two digits to the right of the decimal point. Accountants usually like to see dollar signs tacked on to their numbers. And what if you work with percentages? The answer, my friend, is formatting.

What is formatting?

Figure 5-2 shows some numbers. The numbers in the first column are plain old numbers, and the numbers in the second column are formatted. Which numbers do you like better?

Figure 5-2: The difference between plain and formatted numbers.

	A	B	C
1	Plain Numbers	Formatted Numbers	Numeric Format Used
2	123.45	$123.45	Currency (two decimal places)
3	7873623	7,873,623	Comma (no decimal places)
4	0.128	12.80%	Percent (two decimal places)
5	6.1289231E+14	6.13E+14	Scientific (two decimal places)
6	1234.54	1234.54000	Fixed (five decimal places)
7	34777	19-Mar-95	Date
8	34777.78	06:43 PM	Time

Formatting only affects how the numbers look; formatting does *not* change the actual number. In Figure 5-2, the cells in each row hold exactly the same number. The only difference in the numbers is the way the numbers look — one column is formatted and the other is not.

How to format numbers

You can format numbers by following these steps:

1. **Move the cell pointer to the cell that has the number you want to format.**

    You also can select a range of cells.

2. **Click the right mouse button.**

    Quattro Pro for Windows displays its shortcut menu.

3. **Choose Block Properties from the shortcut menu.**

    Quattro Pro for Windows displays the dialog box in Figure 5-3, which is also known as an *Object Inspector* dialog box. It lists ten categories along the left side. You are interested in the first category, Numeric Format. It's already selected. The middle of the dialog box lists a bunch of names for numeric formats.

4. **Click these format names until you find a format that looks appropriate.**

    Watch the sample box at the bottom-right corner of the dialog box to see what your number looks like for the format you select. For most numeric formats, you can also indicate how many decimal places to use by clicking the appropriate arrow. (You can have between 0 and 15 decimal places displayed.)

Part II: Basic Stuff That You Just Can't Ignore

Figure 5-3: From the Object Inspector dialog box, you can select the numeric format you want.

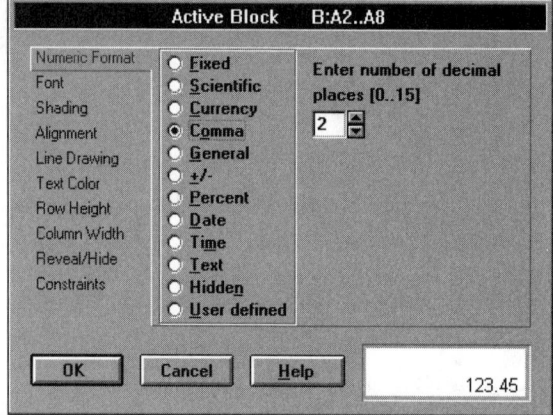

5. **Select OK to close the dialog box, and the number's appearance changes.**

   After you format a number, you're not stuck with it. You can keep applying different numeric formats until you have the one you want.

   > **TIP:** You can even format empty cells. Then, if you ever decide to put a number in the cell, the number appears in the format that you gave it when the cell was empty. Even better, you can preformat entire rows or columns. If you have been through the exercises in Chapter 4, you've already formatted empty cells.

   > **TIP:** Right clicking and using the Object Inspector dialog box is only one way to apply numeric formatting to the selected cell or cells. In some cases, you can simply apply a predefined style to the selection by clicking the Style pull-down list in the Property Band. By default, cells have the Normal style. Figure 5-4 shows the choices you receive when you click the Style pull-down list. As you can see, the Style pull-down list doesn't offer nearly as many formatting choices as the Object Inspector dialog box. Experiment with this list to discover what the various styles do to your numbers.

Entering Labels

Spreadsheets are boring enough as they are, but just think how much worse they would be if they held only numbers. As you already know, Quattro Pro for Windows can cope with words (known as labels) as well as with numbers. The steps for entering a label into a cell are similar to the steps for entering a number. To enter a label into a cell, do the following:

Chapter 5: Ways to Fill Up All Those Cells   **77**

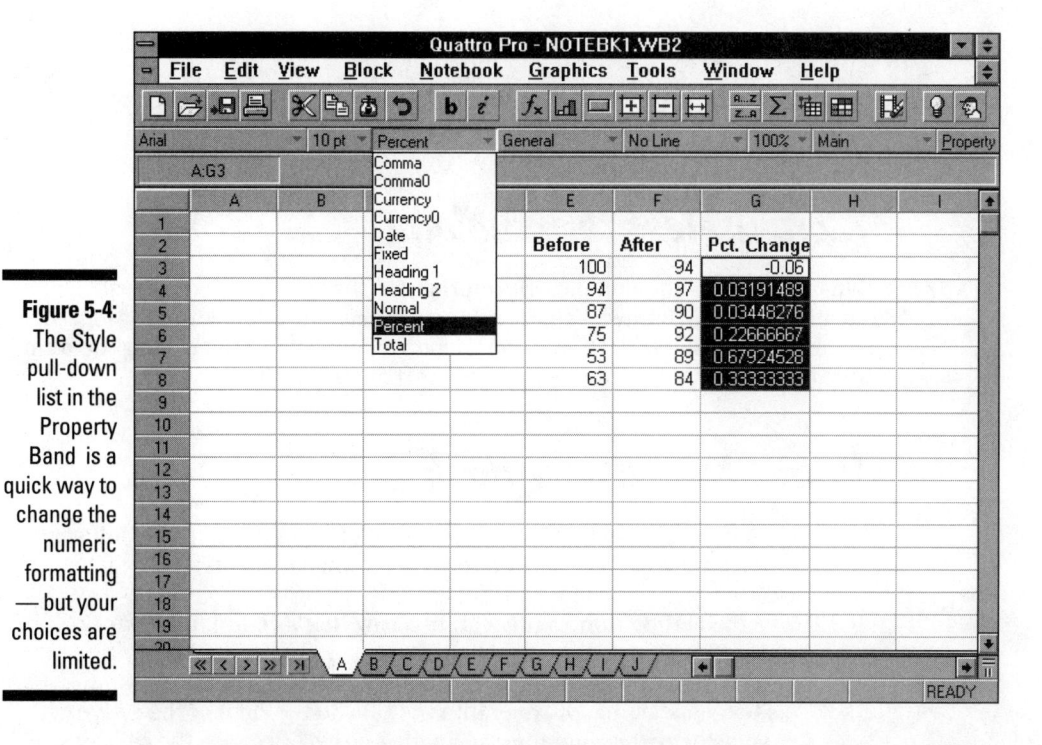

Figure 5-4: The Style pull-down list in the Property Band is a quick way to change the numeric formatting — but your choices are limited.

1. **Move to the cell you want and type a word or letters.**

    Quattro Pro for Windows reads your mind and changes the mode indicator to LABEL.

2. **Press Enter.**

    A label can consist of more than one word, so you can use the spacebar as you normally would.

Some Weird Stuff about Labels

Here's something to keep in mind. Sometimes, you might have a label that starts with a quotation mark ("). For example, enter something like **"Hello"** into a cell (and type the two quotation marks). You'll find that Quattro Pro for Windows leaves off the first quotation mark. What's going on?

Well, what you're seeing is a hold out from the old days of spreadsheets. Back in prehistoric times, people had to use special *label prefixes* to specify the alignment of labels in a cell. A quotation mark is one of those special label prefixes that signaled right alignment. The others are apostrophe (') for left alignment, and caret (^) for center alignment. So, to avoid surprises, don't start your labels with any of the three label prefixes. If you must, just start your label with a space and you won't have any trouble.

More useless terminology

What do you call the nonnumeric information that you enter into a cell? The Quattro Pro for Windows manual refers to nonnumeric cell entries as *labels*. Some people call it *text*. Others call it *words*. You may catch me using the term *string*. The bottom line? It doesn't matter what you call it.

What if the words don't fit?

What if you have a really long label that doesn't fit into the cell? The following procedure shows what happens on the screen when you enter a long label:

1. **Move the cell pointer to any cell in a row that's completely empty.**
2. **Type the following:** Bills I Need to Pay This Month

   This text appears to spill over into the cells to the right of the active cell. Actually, the text is contained all in the one cell. Because the cells next door are empty, Quattro Pro for Windows simply borrows their space to display the spillover from the active cell.
3. **In cell B3, type a number, such as** 198.
4. **Move the cell pointer one column to the left (to cell A3) and type** Car Payment Amount **into this cell.**

   Because cell B3 is occupied, Quattro Pro for Windows can't borrow its space to display the spillover from cell A3. Therefore the program appears to shorten its display for this cell. Don't worry, all the text is still in there — it just doesn't show up on the screen.

When you start with a new notebook, the columns are wide enough to display about 10-12 characters (more or less, depending on the size of the font you use). The solution to the "failure to spill over problem" is to make the entire column A wider. To do so, move the mouse to the right border of the column label. The mouse pointer changes shape and looks like two arrows pointing in opposite directions. While the mouse pointer has this new shape, click and drag the column border to the right. As you do so, the column width expands before your very eyes. Keep dragging this border until the column is as wide as you want it to be.

Chapter 5: Ways to Fill Up All Those Cells   79

> **REMEMBER:** You don't have to adjust the column width to accommodate a long label unless the cell to its immediate right has something in it. If this cell is empty, the text just spills over and borrows its space.

Aligning Labels and Numbers

Normally, when you enter a label into a cell, Quattro Pro for Windows aligns it to the left in the cell (a liberal move). When you enter a number, the program aligns it to the right in the cell (a more conservative approach). You're not stuck with this political alignment, however. You easily can change how numbers and labels are aligned within cells. Figure 5-5 illustrates several alignment choices you can make with labels and numbers.

Figure 5-5: Different types of alignment for labels and numbers.

	A	B	C	D
1	Missouri			Left aligned (default)
2		Montana		Right aligned
3		Washington		Centered
4		The State of California		Centered across three columns (A-C)
5	The Beautiful State of Oregon			Left aligned with wrap-text
6	At the bottom			Bottom vertical alignment (default)
7	Centered			Center vertical alignment
8	At the top			Top vertical alignment
9	D o w n			Vertical orientation

The easiest way to change the alignment is to use the Align pull-down list — which is designed expressly for this purpose (see Figure 5-6). Start by selecting the cell or cells you want to align. Then open the Align pull-down list and make your selection. As you can see, only the most common alignment options are available here. For other types of alignment you need to use the Object Inspector dialog box.

> **TECHNICAL STUFF:** After you enter a label, Quattro Pro for Windows adds a new character, which you can see only when you're in EDIT mode, to the beginning of the text. This initial character, called a *label prefix,* which is a single quotation mark ('),

Part II: Basic Stuff That You Just Can't Ignore

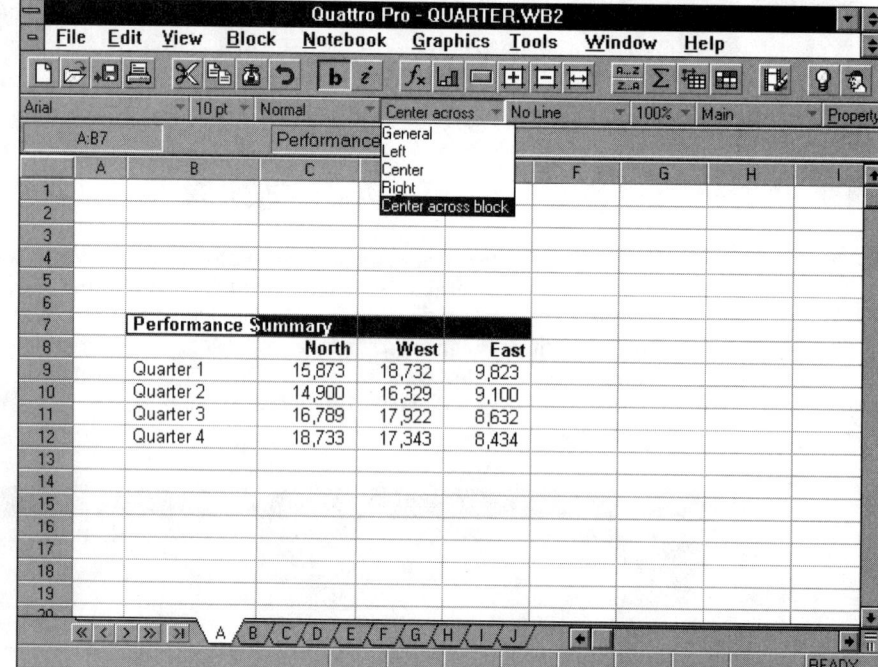

Figure 5-6: The Align pull-down list on the Property Band is a quick way to make changes to the alignment of labels or numbers.

automatically aligns the contents of the cell to the left (the default setting). Actually, you can put your own label prefix at the beginning of a label to change how it's aligned. Table 5-1 is a list of the label prefixes that you can use. (By the way, you definitely can forget the term *label prefix* as soon as you finish this chapter.)

Table 5-1	Label Prefixes and What They Do	
Label Prefix	**English Translation**	**How the Label Is Displayed**
'	Single quote	Left-aligned in the cell
"	Double quote	Right-aligned in the cell
^	Caret	Centered in the cell

When Enter Isn't Good Enough

TIP

Up until now, you've probably been using Enter to signal the end of your numbers and labels. Actually, you also can use any of the arrow keys. Using the arrow keys has a dual effect: the label or numbers stick in the cell, and the cell pointer moves in the direction of the arrow key. Over the past 10 years, this technique has saved me a cumulative total of 3 minutes and 18 seconds.

Changing Things You've Done

The time will come when you realize that you have entered something incorrectly into a cell. (Although this has never happened to me personally, I have heard stories about people making such mistakes.)

Suppose that you have typed the following label into a cell: **An Analisys of 1994 Investments.** Your boss, a former elementary school spelling bee near runner-up, points out the misspelled word. To soothe his ruffled feathers, you have the following two choices (three, if you include taking spelling lessons from your boss):

- Move the cell pointer back to the offensive cell and reenter the entire label.
- Edit the cell.

TIP

For all of you major-league bad spellers out there, Quattro Pro for Windows has a built-in spelling checker that you can invoke with the <u>T</u>ools⇨Spell Check command. (For more on the spelling checker, refer to Chapter 11.) But don't rely on this stuff too much. Like all computerized spelling checkers, it can't tell you whether a properly spelled word is used incorrectly in a sentence. For example, the spelling checker doesn't warn you if you enter **United Snakes of America** into a cell, because *snakes* is a legitimate word.

Overwriting a cell

To replace the information that is already contained in a cell, do the following:

1. **Move the cell selector to the cell that contains the information you want replaced.**
2. **Type in the new information.**
3. **Press Enter.**

    The old stuff is replaced by the new stuff. You can replace a number with a number, a label with a number, a number with a label, and so on.

Editing a cell

If you need to make only a minor change to a cell, you can save a few seconds by *editing* the cell rather than reentering the information. Use the following steps to edit a cell:

1. **Move the cell selector to the cell you want to edit.**
2. **Press F2 (located either along the top of your keyboard or along its left side).**

   Notice that the mode indicator reads EDIT, a sure sign that you are, in fact, editing a cell.

3. **Type new characters, delete unwanted characters, or replace existing characters to make the cell correct by using the editing keys (described in the next section).**

   The flashing vertical bar thingamajig that indicates where you are in the cell you're editing is known by the provocative term *insertion point.* (After you finish this chapter, you can safely forget the official name for this item.)

4. **Press Enter when everything is the way it's supposed to be.**

The editing keys

Knowing the functions of a few keys in EDIT mode can speed up the editing process. If you're interested, check out Table 5-2. If not, prepare to waste lots of time reentering data.

Table 5-2	Handy Keys to Use While Editing Cells
Key	*What It Does*
Backspace	Erases the character to the left of the insertion point
Left-arrow key	Moves the insertion point by one character to the left (and doesn't erase anything)
Right-arrow key	Moves the insertion point by one character to the right (and doesn't erase anything)
Delete	Erases the character to the right of the insertion point
Esc	Leaves the cell just as it was before you started this escapade (for the times you screw up royally and want to start over)

Use these keys to move around within the contents of a cell, to erase unwanted characters, and to insert new characters. When the edit line looks right, just press Enter (or any of the arrow keys). Pretty painless, eh?

Insert or overwrite?

When you edit a cell, inserting new characters causes the current contents to shift to the right. But you can change this process by pressing Insert when you edit. The characters that you type then *overwrite* (or replace) those that are in the way. When you are in the overwrite mode, Quattro Pro for Windows displays OVR in the status line.

Why would you ever want to be in overwrite mode? Because overwrite prevents you from having to erase a character and then type a new one, it is a minor time saver. In overwrite mode, you can add a good character and get rid of a bad one with a single keystroke. When you press Enter to end the editing, you're returned to the normal Insert mode. Over the course of a lifetime of heavy spreadsheet use, overwriting may save you about 11 seconds.

Nuking a cell completely

You know how to change the contents of a cell, but what if you want to wipe the contents of a cell completely off the face of the earth? Easy! Move the cell pointer to the undesired cell, press Delete, and kiss it good-bye. Any formatting that you applied to the cell remains there — only the cell's contents go away.

Another way to remove the contents of a cell is to use the Edit⇨Clear command. This method is a bit more destructive because it also wipes out the cell's formatting. In other words, if you want to return a cell to its normal, unformatted state, use Edit⇨Clear. Otherwise, just use Delete.

> **WARNING!** Never erase a cell by pressing the spacebar. Although this technique appears to get rid of the cell contents, it actually inserts an invisible space character into the cell. This invisible character can cause serious problems for some formulas, and it can be difficult to diagnose. Take my word for it — pressing the spacebar to erase a cell is a no-no.

Chapter 6
The Inside Scoop on Menus, Dialog Boxes, and Toolbars

In This Chapter
▶ Learning useful information about the Quattro Pro for Windows menu system
▶ Giving commands to make Quattro Pro for Windows do what you want
▶ Exploring the functions of some of the more useful menu items
▶ Learning about dialog boxes, and how to use them efficiently
▶ Making the most of those weird little pictures at the top of your screen
▶ Finding out what a Toolbar button does
▶ Becoming familiar with the Property Band

*I*f you graduated from Chapter 5, you now have enough knowledge to enter information into any of more than half a billion cells in a notebook. That's pretty useful stuff, but you ain't seen nothing yet. The real power of Quattro Pro for Windows is apparent when you start issuing commands.

Unless you aspire to be a Quattro Pro for Windows instructor (or a spreadsheet book author), there's no reason to learn all the program's commands. But it is a good idea to know where to go to find an unfamiliar command, so a general understanding of the menu system is definitely in your best interest.

In this chapter you encounter Toolbars, which contain clickable buttons that you often can use as quick alternatives to the menus. Quattro Pro for Windows — like most other Windows programs — displays dialog boxes when you issue certain commands. You learn how to use dialog boxes to provide Quattro Pro for Windows more specific instructions about what you want to do. You also discover the wonderful world of the Property Band — weird name, but useful nonetheless. In short, this chapter explains everything you need to know about menus, dialog boxes, Toolbars, and the Property Band.

After you learn how to use the menus and dialog boxes in Quattro Pro for Windows, you can apply most of this hard-earned knowledge to other Windows programs that you want to learn — all Windows programs work in much the same way.

Quattro Pro for Windows: At Your Command

You can give orders to Quattro Pro for Windows by using any of the following methods:

- The menu system
- Dialog boxes that are displayed by some commands
- The seemingly endless supply of Toolbar buttons
- The Property Band
- Shortcut-key combinations
- The function keys
- Inserting formulas into cells
- Running macros

In this chapter, we focus on the biggies: menus, dialog boxes, Toolbars, and the Property Band. Working with formulas is the topic of Chapter 9, and I briefly cover macros in Chapter 18.

Two Types of Menu Systems

Quattro Pro for Windows has two menu systems:

- The *main menu bar,* which is always visible and appears at the top of the screen, just below the title bar
- *SpeedMenus,* which are hidden but spring to life when you right-click the mouse after selecting something

The main menu bar

When you're running Quattro Pro for Windows, the main menu bar is always available at the top of the screen. The main menu bar consists of a series of menu items. To refresh your memory, take a look at Figure 6-1.

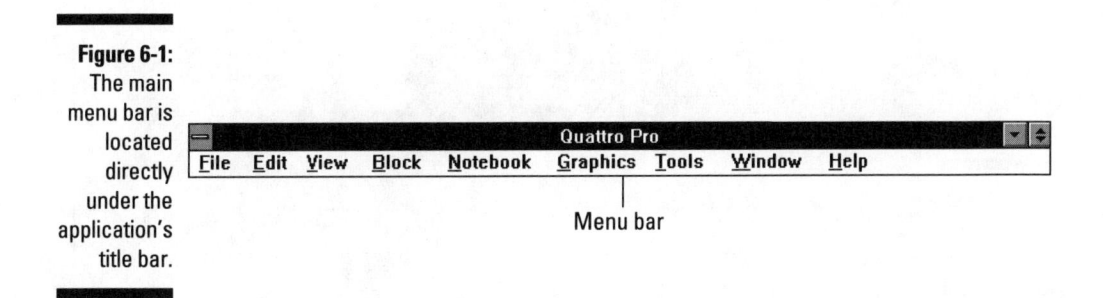

Figure 6-1: The main menu bar is located directly under the application's title bar.

[Quattro Pro menu bar showing: File Edit View Block Notebook Graphics Tools Window Help — labeled "Menu bar"]

As you may know by now, after you select an item, such as File, Edit, and so on, the menu drops down a list of commands. You can select a menu item by clicking it, or by pressing Alt plus the *hot key* (the underlined letter in the menu item) for the menu command.

SpeedMenus

The second type of menu is a shortcut menu called a *SpeedMenu*. This menu isn't visible until you press the right mouse button after you've selected an item (such as a cell, a range, or a chart). A SpeedMenu pops up wherever the mouse pointer is, making it very convenient to select a command from the list. The actual commands on the SpeedMenu vary, depending on what you click. The SpeedMenus include the most common commands that you can perform with the selection you have made. It's almost as if Quattro Pro for Windows can read your mind. But it can't — at least the current version can't.

Figure 6-2 shows the SpeedMenu that appears when you right-click after selecting a range of cells.

The only way to access a SpeedMenu is by right-clicking the mouse button. If you're running Quattro Pro for Windows on a mouseless system, you'll be forced to lead a life without SpeedMenus. Sad, but true.

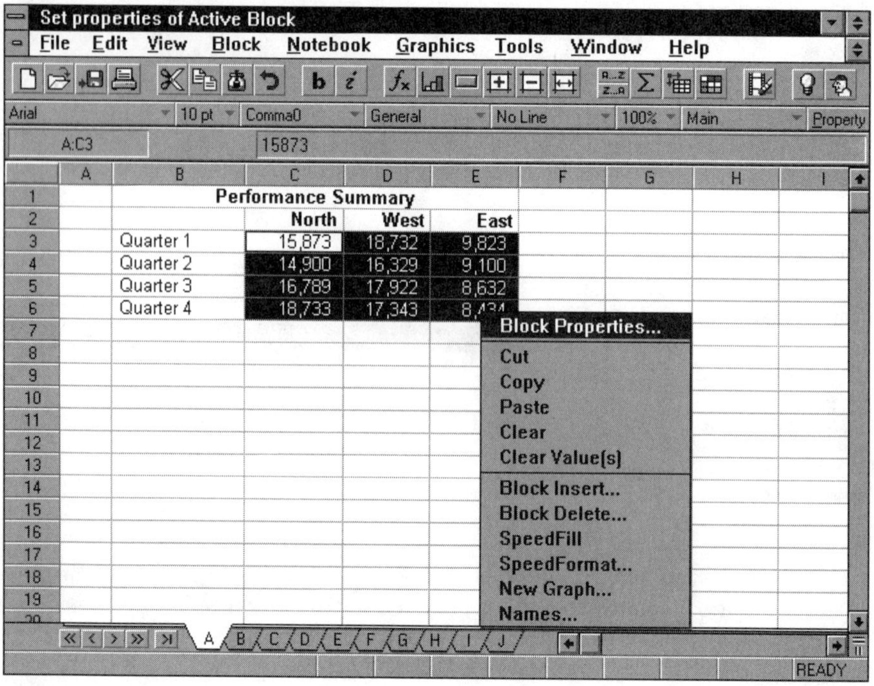

Figure 6-2: A context-sensitive SpeedMenu appears when you right-click after making a selection.

Using Menus

This section tells you how to access menus using either a mouse or the keyboard.

With a mouse

To access a menu with your mouse, simply click the name of the menu on the menu bar. The menu drops down to display its list of commands. Then click the command you need. For example, when you click the File menu, the list of commands includes New, Open, Close, and so on.

After you select an object (such as a cell, a block of cells, or a chart), you can access the SpeedMenu by right-clicking the mouse button to display a list of relevant commands. Not all commands show up on the SpeedMenu, however. If the command you want isn't there, you have to use the normal menu system (or a Toolbar button, if one exists).

Another type of menu

As you work with Windows programs, you encounter yet another menu, the Control menu. Every Windows program (including Quattro Pro for Windows) has a Control menu that is used to control various applications of the program. You access the Control menu by clicking the control button in the upper-left corner of an application's title bar. It's the square button that has a short horizontal line through it.

The Control menu, as shown in the accompanying figure, lets you do things such as minimize the window (to make it an icon), maximize the window (to make it fill the screen), close the application, or switch to another application that's already running.

And to confuse things even more, the windows within an application usually have their own Control menus. Because every Quattro Pro for Windows notebook is actually a separate window, each notebook (window) has its own Control menu.

If you want to know more about this stuff (or more about the wonderful world of Microsoft Windows), I suggest getting a copy of *Windows For Dummies*.

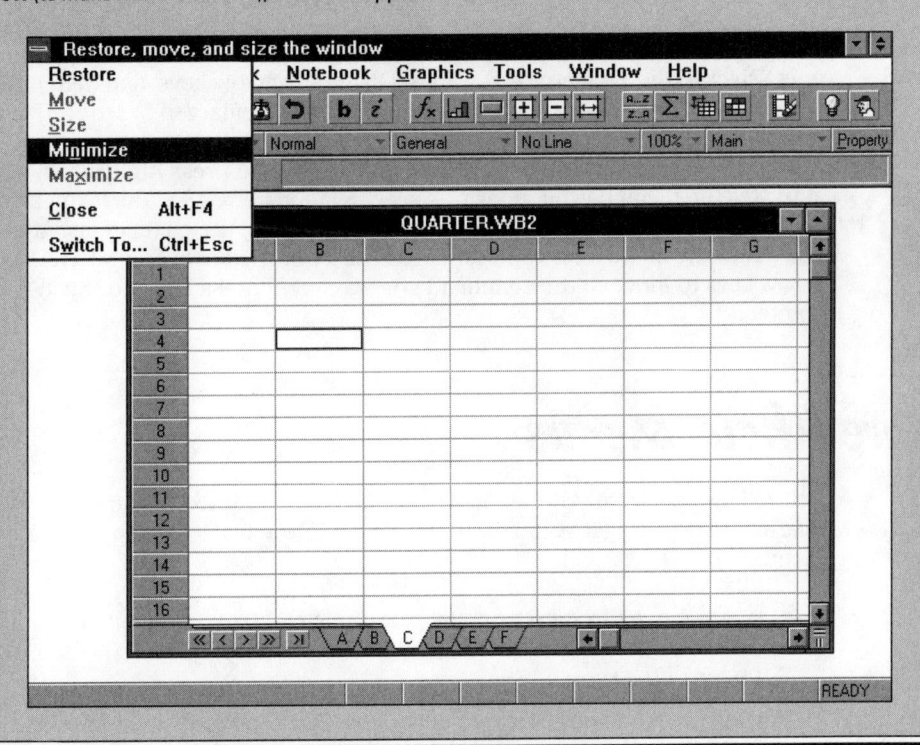

With the keyboard

If you prefer, you also can access the main menu bar by using the keyboard (but SpeedMenus require a mouse). The easiest way to select a menu item is to use a key combination that combines Alt with the underlined letter in the menu item (the hot key).

For example, to access the View menu from the keyboard, press Alt+V. The View menu drops down, just as if you clicked View with the mouse. Then you simply press another letter that corresponds to the underlined letter of the command that you want (no need to keep holding down the Alt key, but it doesn't hurt). As you explore the menus, you notice that the hot key isn't always the *first* letter in the command.

Suppose that you want to change the zoom factor of your notebook. The zoom factor determines the magnification of what you see on the screen. You use the View⇨Zoom command for this task. First press Alt+V, and then press Z. Notice that both V and Z are underlined in the menu — these are the hot keys. After you issue this command, a dialog box pops up to get more information from you. Select the zoom factor you want by using the arrow keys, and then press Enter. The image on your screen will be miraculously enlarged or reduced in size.

> **TIP**
>
> Another way to access a menu with the keyboard is to press Alt by itself, which activates the menu bar but does not select a menu item. After the menu bar is activated, you can use the arrow keys to move among the menu items. After you get to the menu item you want, press Enter or the down-arrow key. Use the arrow keys to move to the command you want, and press Enter to execute the command.

More About Menus

Before I discuss what you can do with menus, you need to know the following characteristics. To get your bearings, refer to Figure 6-3, which shows the Edit menu.

- As you move through the menu selections and their commands, Quattro Pro for Windows displays a brief description of the items in the title bar at the top of the screen.

- If you press F1 while working in a menu, Quattro Pro for Windows displays on-line help that tells you about the menu item or the command.

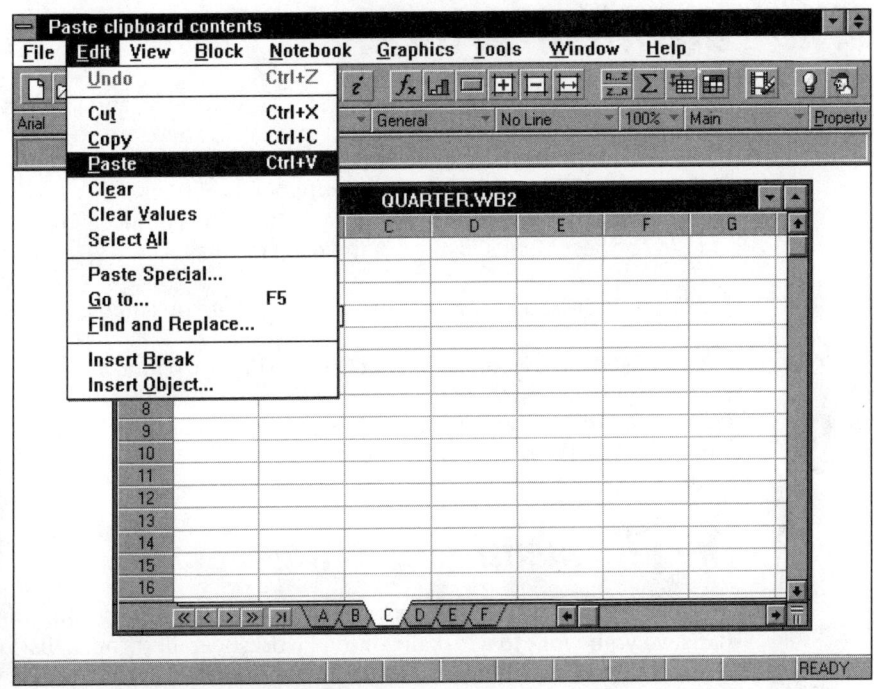

Figure 6-3:
A typical menu, pulled down to show its commands.

- When a command on a menu isn't appropriate for what you're doing, Quattro Pro for Windows *dims* the command (lightens the color). You still can see the command, but you cannot select it.
- Menu commands that are followed by three dots (an *ellipsis*) display a dialog box after you select the command.
- Menu commands that have a shortcut key display the shortcut key combination on the pull-down menu. For example, the Cut command on the Edit menu displays Ctrl+X on the right side of the menu; therefore, pressing Ctrl+X accomplishes the same thing as selecting the Edit⇨Cut command.
- Some commands are followed by a small right-pointing arrow. These commands, after being selected, display yet another list of commands. This secondary command list is known as a *cascading menu.* But you can call it a *whatchamadoojie,* and it still has the same effect. See the Tools menu for several examples of this type of menu.
- The horizontal lines in the pull-down menus simply divide the commands into logical groups; these lines have no great significance.

Now that you have a decent background in the Quattro Pro for Windows menus, let's see just what you can do with them.

What the Menus Are Good For

The Quattro Pro for Windows menu system is extensive, and it offers many commands for your dining and dancing pleasure. There are so many commands that you may feel overwhelmed at times. (I do, and I've used this program for years!) The good news is that you'll probably need to use only a few of these menu commands and can safely ignore the rest. You often can use Toolbar buttons or SpeedMenus instead of the main menus.

Here's a quick and dirty general overview of what you'll find under each menu.

If you've used a previous version of Quattro Pro for Windows, you'll notice that the menus in Version 6 are completely different. While this may take some getting used to, the new menu arrangement is actually much better and less confusing than the previous versions.

The File menu

The File menu deals with (you guessed it) files. Here you find the commands that save your work to a disk file or load worksheet files from a disk. Odd as it may seem, the File menu also has the commands to print and preview your work.

Putting the print commands under the File menu is not a quirk of Quattro Pro for Windows. For some reason, this arrangement is standard practice for virtually all Windows programs. So when it comes time to put your work on paper, don't waste time looking for a print menu — head straight for the File menu. Think of the printing function as printing a file, not a notebook.

The Edit menu

If you want to rearrange cells in your notebook, chances are you'll find the commands you want in the Edit menu. The Edit menu has what you need to copy cells and blocks of cells (using Copy and Paste), move cells and blocks of cells (using Cut and Paste), and perform lots of other functions.

You can even search for text in your notebook and automatically replace the text with something else. The Edit menu also houses the all-important Undo command (which can reverse the effects of almost anything you do in Quattro Pro for Windows).

The View menu

The View menu controls some aspects of what you see in Quattro Pro for Windows. You probably won't have too much use for this menu — except for maybe the Zoom command.

The Block menu

When you're working with a block of cells, this menu is quite useful. You can use commands here to insert and delete rows and columns, sort cells, and do a few other things.

The Notebook menu

This menu handles things that are done at the "notebook level." For example, you can move a notebook page to a different location in the notebook, copy a notebook page to a separate file, and even insert an entire file into your notebook.

The Graphics menu

Care to guess what purpose this menu serves? You got it. This menu deals with graphs and slide shows. (Yes, you can use Quattro Pro to deliver a slide show — on your monitor, that is.)

The Tools menu

If TV's Tim (the Toolman) Taylor used Quattro Pro for Windows, he'd probably spend most of his time with this menu. The Tools menu has plenty of commands on it, including such special tools as numeric stuff, database commands, spelling checker, and macros.

The Window menu

You won't have much use for the Window menu commands unless you work with more than one notebook file at a time. These commands let you arrange the windows neatly on-screen, jump to a different notebook, or even open a new window for your notebook so you can see two different pages at once.

The Help menu

Everyone needs a little help now and then when working with a computer program, and the Help menu is the place to go when you find yourself in that predicament. The Help commands let you access the very comprehensive on-line help system. You also can find out which version of the program you're using (Help⇨About Quattro Pro), and you can even start an interactive tutorial lesson to help you learn more about specific topics.

> **TIP**
>
> Pressing F1 also gives you on-line help. Most of the time, the help that appears is relevant to what you're currently doing (known in the trade as *context-sensitive help*). Try it; you'll like it.

Carrying On a Meaningful Dialog

Menu commands tell Quattro Pro for Windows what you want to do. But dialog boxes go a step further and let you tell the program exactly what you want to do. All menu commands that end with an ellipsis lead to a dialog box. A dialog box is, essentially, a convenient way for you to make your wishes known to the program.

To understand how a dialog box works, picture yourself in your favorite restaurant: After you arrive, you look at the menu and give your order to the waiter. The waiter looks down at you and asks you to choose between soup or salad, baked potatoes or french fries, and coffee or tea. Using a dialog box is like responding to the waiter's questions. In other words, you use a dialog box to clarify your order to Quattro Pro for Windows. And a benefit of using the dialog box is that you don't have to leave a tip for Quattro Pro for Windows.

Because dialog boxes appear in almost every Windows application, you need to understand these animals as best as you can. The dialog boxes you encounter in Quattro Pro for Windows all have a similar look and feel. After you learn a few dialog box techniques, you'll feel fairly comfortable with just about any dialog box that the program throws your way.

The anatomy of a dialog box

Figure 6-4 shows a typical dialog box — this box happens to be the dialog box that appears when you choose the Block⇨Insert command.

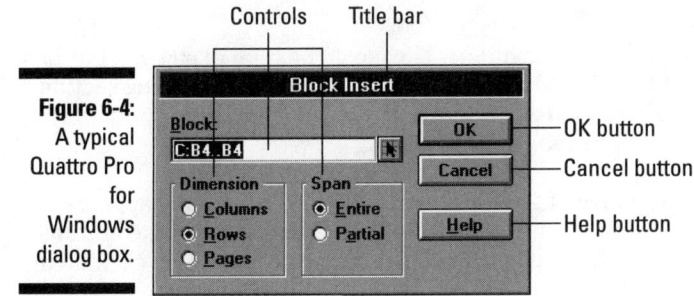

Chapter 6: The Inside Scoop on Menus, Dialog Boxes, and Toolbars

Figure 6-4: A typical Quattro Pro for Windows dialog box.

[Dialog box illustration showing Controls, Title bar, OK button, Cancel button, and Help button labels pointing to a "Block Insert" dialog with Block field "C:B4..B4", Dimension (Columns, Rows, Pages), and Span (Entire, Partial) options]

All dialog boxes in Quattro Pro for Windows have the following characteristics in common:

- **Title bar.** The title bar simply tells you the name of the dialog box (which is usually the command that you select to get there).

- **OK button.** Click this button when you have made all your choices. This action dismisses the dialog box, and Quattro Pro for Windows processes your command. Pressing Enter is the same thing as clicking the OK button.

- **Cancel button.** Click this button if you decide you really didn't want to work with this dialog box after all. Even if you've made changes in the dialog box, clicking the Cancel button eliminates all the changes, just as if you had never opened the dialog box in the first place. Pressing Esc is the same as clicking the Cancel button.

- **Help button.** Click this button if you're not sure what to do. Quattro Pro for Windows' on-line help fires up and displays a help topic for the particular dialog box you're using. Pressing F1 is the same as clicking the Help button.

- **Controls.** Every dialog box has at least one control — usually more. You use dialog box controls to make your choices. I discuss dialog box controls in the next section.

TIP: Occasionally, a dialog box pops up and covers up what you want to see. You can move the dialog box by clicking and dragging its title bar.

Dialog box controls

Items that you manipulate in a dialog box are called *controls*. People who design dialog boxes are called control freaks.

A common type of control is a button (such as OK or Cancel). I discuss several other types of dialog box controls in this section. Learning to use these controls efficiently makes your life much easier, so pay attention. If this book had sound effects, bells would be ringing loudly.

Buttons

Dialog box buttons have many functions. The most common dialog box buttons are the OK, Cancel, and Help buttons, which I discuss in the preceding section. If the text in the dialog box button is followed by an ellipsis (three dots), clicking this button leads to another dialog box.

Figure 6-5 shows an example of some buttons in the dialog box that appears when you select the Block⇨Names command. Notice that three of the buttons (Generate, Labels, and Output) display another dialog box after you click them.

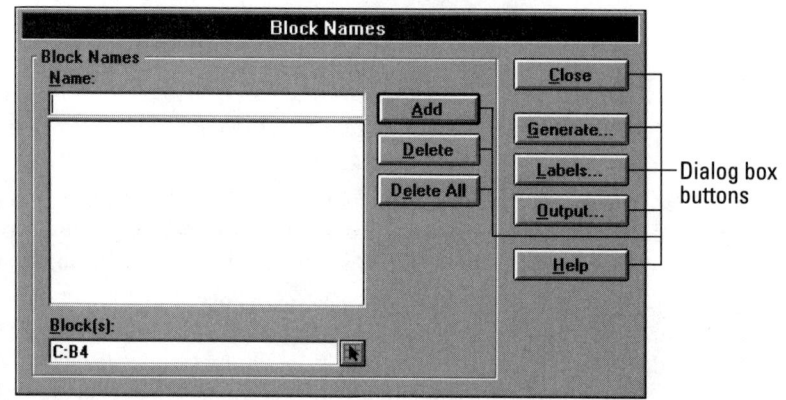

Figure 6-5: An example of some dialog box buttons.

Option buttons

Option buttons are sometimes called *radio buttons,* because — like an old-fashioned car radio — when you click a radio button, the previously selected button pops out or is no longer selected. Option buttons always come in groups from which you choose one (and only one) option from a list of options.

Figure 6-6 shows an example of some option buttons in a dialog box that appears when you choose the View⇨Zoom command. In this case, the dialog box has two sets of option buttons.

Check boxes

A check box is either checked or not checked, which means that an option is either selected or not selected — as simple as that (or not). Unlike option buttons, clicking a check box does not affect any other check boxes. You can select more than one check box at a time.

Figure 6-7 shows an example of some check boxes in a dialog box. This dialog box appears when you select the View⇨Display command. Notice how all the

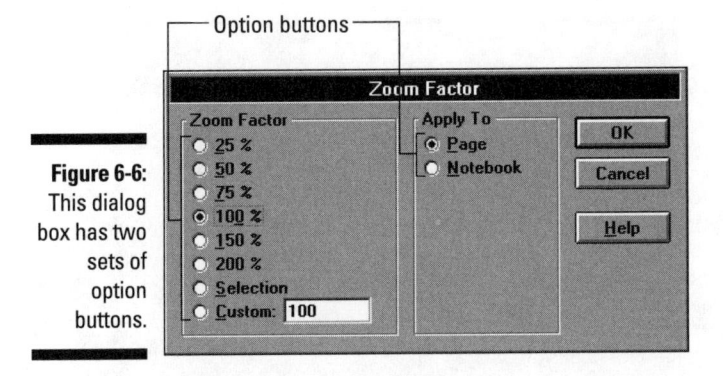

Chapter 6: The Inside Scoop on Menus, Dialog Boxes, and Toolbars *97*

Figure 6-6: This dialog box has two sets of option buttons.

Figure 6-7: An example of selected check boxes.

check boxes are selected, indicating that all of these options are in effect. By the way, the right side of the dialog box shows two sets of option buttons (which you already know about, right?).

List boxes

A *list box* is just what its name suggests, a box with a list of items in it. You can choose only one of the items in each list box. If the list box contains a vertical *scroll bar,* the list contains more options than you can see at one time. To see the additional options, click the scroll bar.

Figure 6-8 shows an example of a list box within a dialog box that appears when you choose the File⇨Page Setup command. In this case, the list box shows a list of paper sizes to choose from.

Object Inspector: the mother of all dialog boxes

When is a dialog box not a dialog box? When it's a bunch of dialog boxes all rolled into one. Quattro Pro for Windows has a special dialog box — Object Inspectors — that you may encounter frequently throughout your spreadsheeting journeys. These things are very powerful, so you'll do well to get to know them.

The only way to get to an Object Inspector dialog box is to select an object (cell, block, graph, and so on) and then right-click to get the SpeedMenu. The first choice is always xxxxxx Properties. If you select a cell or block, the first SpeedMenu choice is Block Properties. If you select a graph, it reads Graph Properties. And so on.

The following figure shows the Object Inspector dialog box for a cell or block. Notice the ten words on the left (Numeric format, Font, Shading, and so on). When you click one of these, the dialog box changes completely, giving you a whole new set of choices relevant to what you clicked. In the following figure, I clicked Font — so the dialog box shows all of the settings appropriate for messing around with fonts.

These Object Inspector dialog boxes are worth getting to know. Think of them as your one-stop shopping place for changing just about anything related to the current selection.

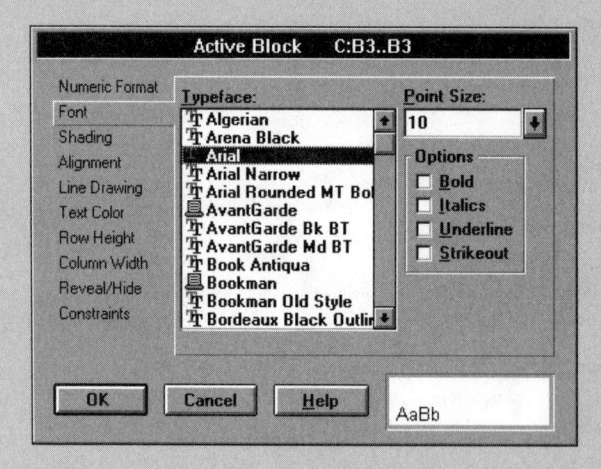

Block selection boxes

Many of the dialog boxes used by Quattro Pro for Windows have *block selection boxes*. When you select a block of cells before you issue a command, that range appears in the block selection box. You can then change the block in the dialog box by clicking the block and then pointing to the range in your notebook. If you need to make only a minor change, you also can manually edit the block specification.

Figure 6-9 shows an example of a dialog box with two block selection boxes. This dialog box appears when you choose the Block⇨Move command.

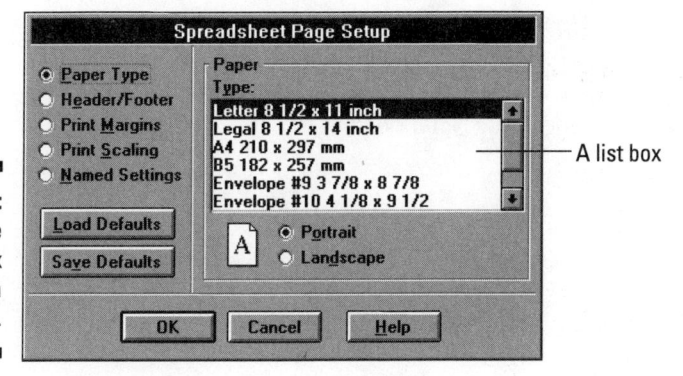

Chapter 6: The Inside Scoop on Menus, Dialog Boxes, and Toolbars 99

Figure 6-8: An example of a list box within a dialog box.

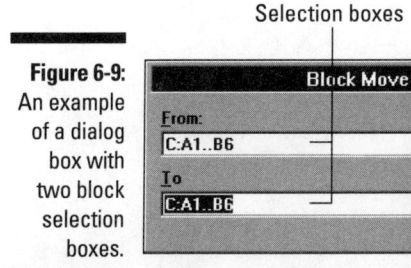

Figure 6-9: An example of a dialog box with two block selection boxes.

Spinner controls

A spinner control lets you change a number in a dialog box by clicking one of the two arrows to increase or decrease the value of the number. Figure 6-10 shows several examples of spinner controls in the dialog box that appears when you choose the File⇨Print command.

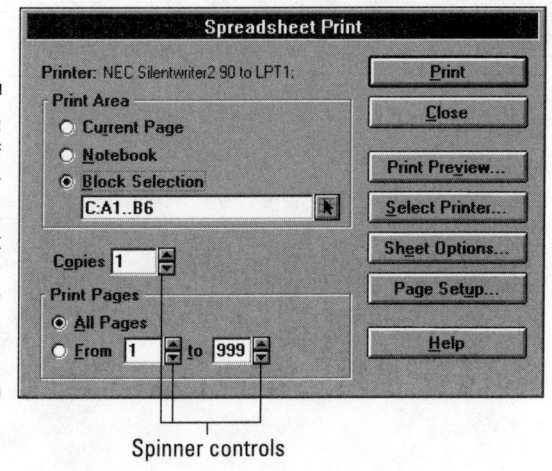

Figure 6-10: Examples of spinner controls, which let you select a number by clicking an arrow.

Part II: Basic Stuff That You Just Can't Ignore

Text box

A *text box* is simply a white box into which you enter some text. Figure 6-11 shows an example of some text boxes within a dialog box. You see this dialog box when you choose the Notebook⇨Define Group command.

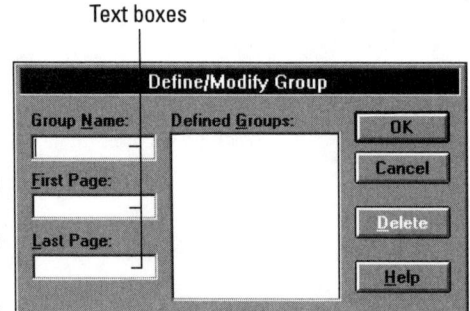

Figure 6-11: Examples of text boxes.

Sample box

The items in a *sample box* show you examples of what you get as you make changes to other controls. You cannot choose or select any items in a sample box — you can only look at them. Figure 6-12 shows an example of a sample box within a dialog box. This is the Object Inspector dialog box for a cell or block (Alignment section).

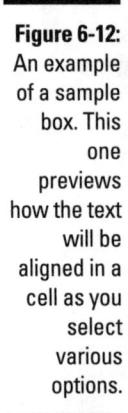

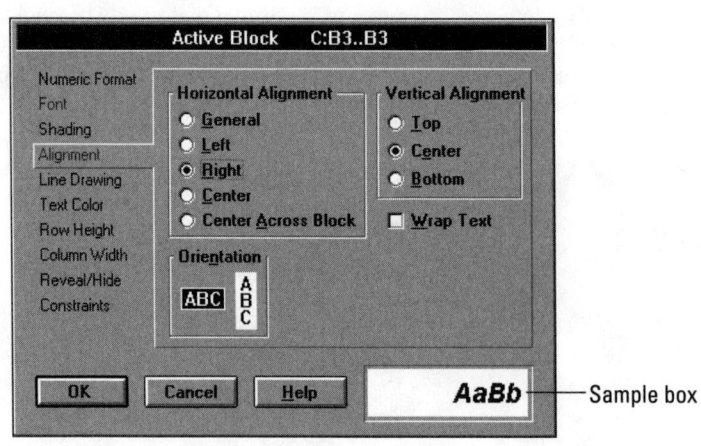

Figure 6-12: An example of a sample box. This one previews how the text will be aligned in a cell as you select various options.

Mousing through dialog boxes

Dialog boxes were invented with mouse users in mind, so it's not surprising that most people prefer to use the mouse for most of their dialog box action.

Generally, you click the control that you want in order to activate it. After you have activated the control, you can make your selection. The exact technique varies with the specific control, but the controls work pretty much as you expect them to work. In other words, the process is very intuitive. To check or uncheck a check box, click it. To select an option in an option button, click it. To select an option from a drop-down list box, click the arrow and make your choice from the list by clicking. My best advice to you is to start clicking away and see what happens. You'll get the hang of it in no time. But save any work you have started before you go clicking away, just in case your mouse goes rabid!

If you prefer the keyboard

Although most people like to use the mouse in a dialog box, other people find that the keyboard is actually faster because they don't have to move their hands from the keyboard. The truth is, after you get the hang of it, using the keyboard to work with dialog boxes can be more efficient than using the mouse. But this is largely a matter of personal preference, so feel free to mouse your way through everything if that's what you like.

Table 6-1 lists some useful keys and key combinations that are active when you work with a dialog box from the keyboard.

Table 6-1	Keyboard Combinations to Use with Dialog Boxes
Key Combination	**What It Does**
Alt+hot key	Selects the control of the hot key (underlined letter) that you press
Tab	Moves forward and activates the next control
Shift+Tab	Moves backward and activates the preceding control
Spacebar	Checks or unchecks an option button or check box
Arrow keys	Moves within a group of controls (such as option buttons)
Enter	Completes the command and closes the dialog box (just like clicking OK)
Esc	Closes the dialog box without completing the command (just like clicking Cancel)
F1	Provides help for the dialog box
Ctrl+PgUp	Changes to the preceding category in an Object Inspector dialog box
Ctrl+PgDn	Changes to the next category in an Object Inspector dialog box

Part II: Basic Stuff That You Just Can't Ignore

> **REMEMBER:** I've tried to get across to you in this chapter that understanding how to use menus and dialog boxes is pretty important in learning how to use Quattro Pro for Windows. You spend lots of time using menus and commands — especially dialog boxes. So the sooner you master these features, the better off you'll be. 'Nuff said.

Toolbars

New Quattro Pro for Windows users usually wonder about those cryptic little pictures at the top of their screen. What do they mean? Are they some form of computer hieroglyphics? Secret messages from Elvis? As you may or may not have figured out by now, these pictures are called Toolbar buttons. They can save you a great deal of time and trouble if you learn what they're all about and how to take advantage of them.

> **TIP:** In previous versions of Quattro Pro for Windows, Toolbars were called SpeedBars. I'm not sure why they changed the name, but you may still see a few references to SpeedBars lurking around. When you see the word "SpeedBar," just mentally substitute "Toolbar" and you won't get confused.

Why Toolbars?

Somewhere along the line, someone figured out that software users tend to use some commands more often than others. Because clicking a button is usually faster than accessing the menu and dealing with a dialog box, software companies put together collections of buttons to serve as shortcuts for the more commonly used commands.

Today, most Windows programs include a collection of such buttons, and these puppies are worth getting to know.

True facts about Toolbars

Before getting down to the nitty gritty, take a minute to digest the following appetizers:

- Remember, you have to use your mouse to access the Toolbar buttons.
- You can choose from several different Toolbars, each with different buttons.
- If you don't like the clutter, you can get rid of the Toolbars.
- You can create custom Toolbars consisting of the buttons that you like the most.

So many Toolbars, so little time

When you start Quattro Pro for Windows, you see the Toolbar known affectionately as Main. Figure 6-13 shows the Main Toolbar.

Figure 6-13: The Main Toolbar. Even more Toolbars lurk behind the scenes, just waiting to be useful.

Toolbars at your disposal

Table 6-2 provides a description of the Toolbars that you can use. Don't be too overwhelmed; most people are perfectly satisfied using only the Main Toolbar.

Table 6-2	Toolbars Available in Quattro Pro for Windows
Toolbar	**What It Does**
Main	Filled with common, everyday tools
Format	Contains lots of buttons that deal with formatting cells
Block	Handy for manipulating cells and blocks of cells
Draw	Lets you add and manipulate drawings on your notebook
Modeling	Contains tools for Data modeling desktop (you probably won't be needing this one)

Using Toolbars

You can change which Toolbar is displayed by using the Toolbars pull-down list on the Property Band (which is explained in the next section).

To find out what a particular Toolbar button does, just move your mouse pointer over the button and pause for about one second. A little box pops up

Part II: Basic Stuff That You Just Can't Ignore

and provides the name of the button. A description of the button also appears in Quattro Pro for Windows' title bar. To learn even more, hold down Ctrl and right-click on a button.

I'm not going to describe each Toolbar button. You can explore these buttons on your own. However, throughout the rest of the book I'll be referring to them when appropriate.

The Property Band

The Property Band is the thing that lives just below the Toolbar (see Figure 6-14). The Property Band, new to Version 6, is very handy. It'll definitely save you some time, and you'll find that you often can avoid using the menus and dialog boxes by using the Property Band.

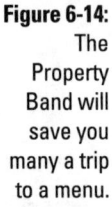

Figure 6-14: The Property Band will save you many a trip to a menu.

| Arial | 10 pt | Normal | General | No Line | 100% | Main | Property |

Using the Property Band

To use the Property Band, just click one of the pull-downs (these are described later) and make your selection. You can't use the Property Band from the keyboard.

Property Band pull-down lists

Table 6-3 describes what each of the eight pull-down lists in the Property Band can do for you.

Table 6-3	The Property Band Pull-Down Lists
Pull-Down List	*What it Does*
Font	Lets you change the font for the selected cell or block of cells
Font Size	Lets you change the size of the type for the selected cell or block of cells
Style	Lets you apply any of the predefined styles to the selected cell or block of cells
Align	Lets you change the alignment of the selected cell or block of cells
Underline	Lets you set the type of underlining for the selected cell or block of cells
Zoom Factor	Lets you choose the zoom factor for the current page
Toolbars	Lets you choose a toolbar to display
Property	Displays an Object Inspector dialog box for a particular object

In Conclusion

If you're more confused than ever after reading through this chapter, I understand. There are many ways to issue commands to Quattro Pro for Windows. But as you work with this program, you'll discover that you need only a very small number of these commands. Most of the time you can use the Toolbars or Property Band for what you want to do. If you can't find what you want there, try right-clicking and using the SpeedMenu. It'll all eventually make sense. Trust me.

106 Part II: Basic Stuff That You Just Can't Ignore

The 5th Wave — By Rich Tennant

"IT WAS CLASHING WITH THE SOUTHWESTERN MOTIF."

Chapter 7
How to Prevent Losing Your Work (and Ruining Your Whole Day)

In This Chapter
- Why computer users lose their work — and how you can prevent such a tragedy
- Why you should learn about files, disks, saving notebooks, and related topics
- Why you should save frequently and make backup copies of important files
- How to save Quattro Pro for Windows files so that other programs can use them

If you work with computers, sooner or later you will lose some work and be mighty upset. There's no denying it, because it happens to everybody. When you've exhausted your supply of obscenities, you simply have to repeat things you've already done.

You can do several things to minimize the heartbreak of data loss. But, if you like to live on the edge and don't mind wasting time redoing hours of work that disappeared, feel free to skip this chapter.

This chapter tells you a great deal about working with files — things that I think are very important for every computer user to understand. If you want to cut to the chase and simply learn how to do common file operations with Quattro Pro for Windows, skip ahead to "Doing Things with a File — Step By Step," later in this chapter.

Protecting Your Work

Use these three guidelines to avoid losing data when using Quattro Pro for Windows (or any computer program, for that matter):

✔ **Save your work to a disk frequently.** I've seen too many people spend the whole day working on a notebook without saving it until they're done with it. Most of the time, this practice doesn't get you into trouble. But computers do crash occasionally, and power failures also can occur. Both of these events cause you to lose everything that hasn't been saved, and you have to restart your system. It can ruin your whole day.

Saving a file takes a few seconds, but re-creating eight hours of lost work takes about eight hours. So, to avoid headache, panic, confusion, fatigue, and general hysteria, save your work often!

Is it disk or is it Memorex?

One thing I've noticed over the years is that new computer users often get confused about memory and disks. This isn't surprising, because both of these objects are places where you can store data. Here's the difference:

✔ **Memory:** This is the part of your computer that stores things you are currently working on. It also goes by the name of *random-access memory* (RAM). Computer memory is very fleeting — a flick of the power switch and it's wiped out immediately.

Computers vary in the amount of memory that is installed in them. Nowadays, most computers have at least 4 megabytes (MB) of RAM, and systems with 8 to 16MB are common. When you're working in a program with a great deal of data, you may get an Out of memory error. This means that your system doesn't have enough memory to handle what you want to do. It does *not* mean that your disk is full (that's a completely different problem and has nothing to do with memory).

An out-of-memory error often has nothing to do with memory. It just means that the system resources used by Windows have been exhausted. You can regain these resources by closing Windows and then restarting it. Usually, the memory problem you had will disappear.

✔ **Disks:** A disk stores information more permanently. Information stored on a disk is in files. If you turn off the power to your PC, the files that you've stored on the disk remain there. Disks come in a variety of sizes that correspond to how much information they can hold. Your computer has at least one built-in *hard disk* (that holds many files); you also can use removable *floppy disks* (that hold less information and may or may not actually be floppy).

If you have many programs and data files stored on your hard disk, you may get a Disk full message. This means that your disk can hold no more information. (This message has nothing to do with the amount of memory in your computer.) To free up some space, you must erase files that you no longer need on that disk. You can do this directly from DOS or use the Windows File Manager program.

Chapter 7: How to Prevent Losing Your Work (and Ruining Your Whole Day) 109

- **Use your software's automatic backup feature, if it has one.** Fortunately, Quattro Pro for Windows has such a feature. To activate this feature, right-click on the Quattro Pro for Windows title bar, and choose File Options from the Object Inspector dialog box. Set a time interval and click on the Activate option. For example, if you set the time interval to 10, your file will be backed up every ten minutes. If your system crashes, you will be prompted to recover any open files the next time you start Quattro Pro for Windows. This can be a real lifesaver.

- **Make a backup copy of all your important files.** Most people who back up their work religiously do so because they've been burned in the past (and you can count me among these folks). Hard disks aren't perfect — one bad byte, if it's a critical byte, can make the entire disk unreadable. If a file has any value to you at all, you should make a copy of it on a floppy disk and keep the disk in a safe place. And don't leave the backup disk next to your computer — if the building burns down during the night, a melted floppy disk doesn't do you much good.

If you don't understand the preceding paragraphs, the remainder of this chapter provides enough information so that you will. And, by the way, much of the information in this chapter applies to other programs as well.

Using Files with Quattro Pro for Windows

When you start Quattro Pro for Windows, the program is loaded from your hard disk into your computer's memory. The program stays on the hard disk and loads a *copy* of itself into memory. Actually, the complete program isn't loaded into memory — only the most important parts are. The program leaves enough memory available so that there's room for you to work on your notebooks. As you use Quattro Pro for Windows, other parts of the program are automatically loaded as required. The program loads these parts from the hard disk in the background, and you don't notice the activity unless you keep an eye on your hard disk light.

A new notebook

When you start working on a new notebook, you're simply storing information in your computer's memory. Therefore, if you turn off your PC without saving the notebook, your work is gone to the big PC graveyard in the sky. To keep your work from being just an unpleasant memory, you need to save the notebook that's in memory to a file on your hard disk.

Saving files

The first time you save a notebook (also called a file) to disk, you have to tell Quattro Pro for Windows what filename to use for the notebook. After that, it uses that same filename every time you save the file, unless you specify a different filename (using the File⇨Save As command). Every time you save the file, it replaces the file on the disk with the updated information from memory. It's a good idea to save your work at least every 15 minutes. Otherwise, an unexpected power outage or an ungainly coworker who kicks the plug out of the wall can destroy everything you did since the last time you saved.

You need to remember some simple rules about filenames. First, they can be no longer than eight characters, with no spaces. Second, they must start with either a letter or a number. And finally, you can't use the following characters in a filename: period (.), quotation mark ("), slash (/), backslash (\), brackets ([ ]), colon (:), semicolon (;), vertical bar (|), equal sign (=), or comma (,). After you name a file, Quattro Pro for Windows attaches WB1 as the file's extension.

A Visit to the File Menu

When you're working in Quattro Pro for Windows, everything you do with your files is controlled through the File menu item (somewhat intuitive, eh?). As with all menu items, when you select File from the menu (by choosing File or pressing Alt+F), Quattro Pro for Windows drops down a list that shows more commands, as seen in Figure 7-1. All these options can be somewhat intimidating at first, but they all seem straightforward after you get used to them.

Files and windows

Quattro Pro for Windows has a *multiple document interface*. In plain language, this means that you can work with more than one notebook file at a time; you don't have to close one project to work on another one. If you tend to juggle many things at once (which is fairly common where I've worked), you'll enjoy this capability.

Every notebook file that's open appears in its own window within the Quattro Pro for Windows window (got that?). You can move the windows, resize them, compare their data, and do many other things. Only one window can be active at a time; the others just lurk in the background waiting for their turn to be useful. Figure 7-2 shows several notebook files, each in a separate window, arranged nicely on the screen. This way you can see what's in them and jump around among them.

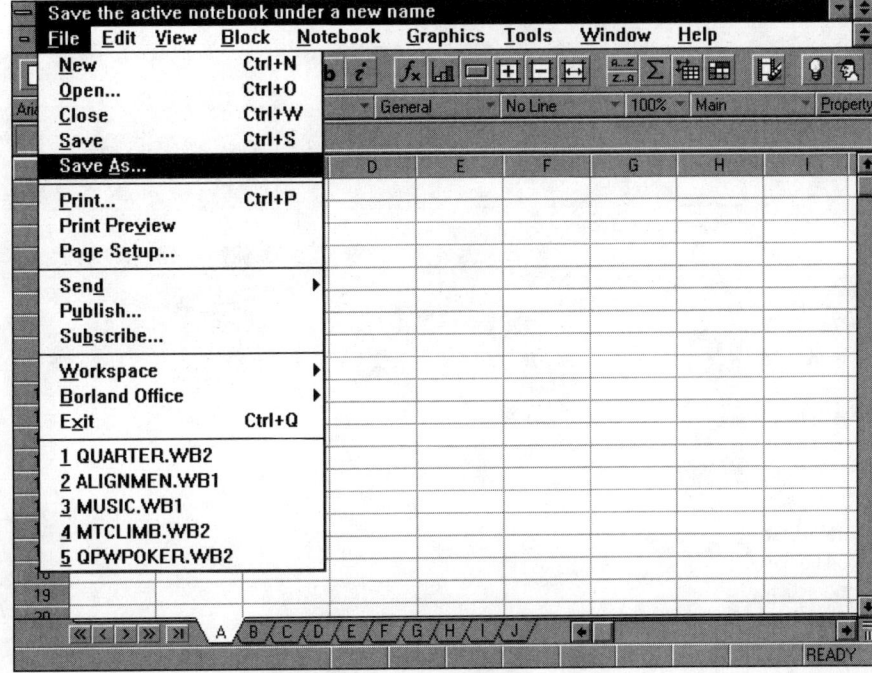

Chapter 7: How to Prevent Losing Your Work (and Ruining Your Whole Day) 111

Figure 7-1:
The File menu commands become very familiar to you as you gain more experience with Quattro Pro for Windows.

But there's one more thing to remember: Every notebook file has 256 pages in it. These pages are stacked one behind another, and all of the pages in a notebook are in one window. Use the page tabs to move to different pages within a notebook.

Windows that hold notebook files can be *maximized* to fill the entire Quattro Pro for Windows workspace, or they can be *minimized*, reduced down to a tiny icon. If a notebook window is not maximized or minimized, you can move it around and resize it within the Quattro Pro for Windows workspace. Only one window at a time can be the *active window*. The active window is the one your cursor is currently in; it is on top of the stack of windows and its title bar is a different color than the others'.

To activate a different window, do one of the following things:

- If the window that you want to reach is showing, just click on it with your mouse, and it will miraculously appear at the top of the stack.
- Keep pressing Alt+F6 to cycle through all of the notebook windows until the one you want appears.
- Select the Window command. This command in turn drops down a list of commands, and at the bottom of the list you will see a list of all the windows you have open. Select the window you want to activate, and you're off and running.

Part II: Basic Stuff That You Just Can't Ignore

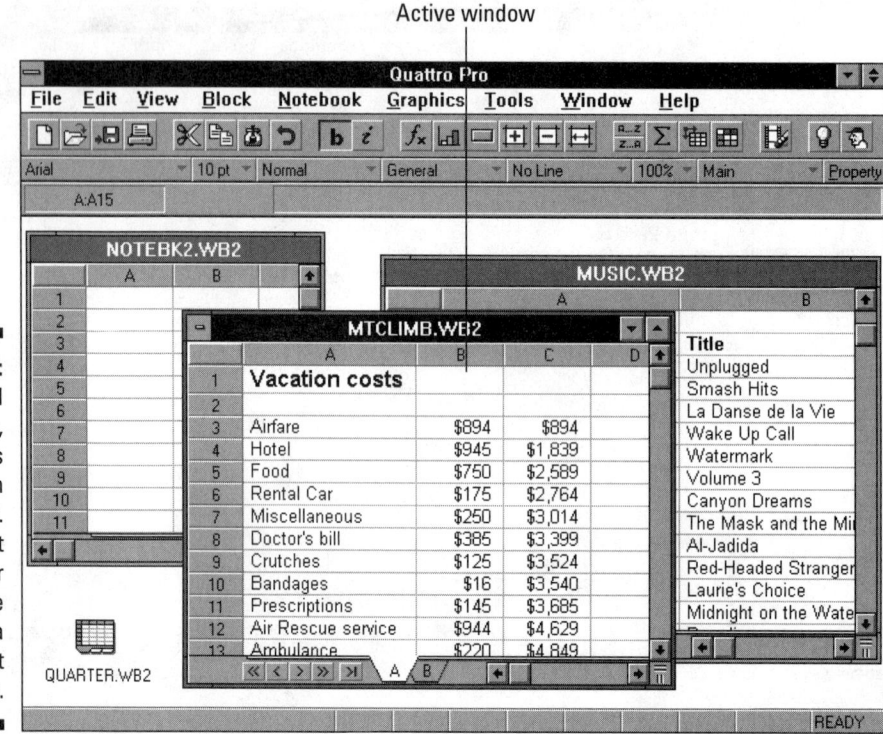

Figure 7-2: Several notebooks, each in its own window. Notice that the title bar of the active window is a different color.

> To minimize a notebook window (that is, to iconize it), click on the down arrow in the upper right corner of the notebook window's title bar. Double-click on the icon to restore it to its previous size. To maximize a window, click on the up arrow. If a window is maximized, you can restore it to its former size by clicking on the button with two arrows (one up, one down) that's directly below the Quattro Pro for Windows title bar.

If you have several notebook windows open, the screen can become a bit cluttered, and some windows may even be hidden behind others. Quattro Pro for Windows provides two commands to clean things up. The Window⇨Cascade command arranges all the windows in a tidy stack so you can see their title bars (see Figure 7-3). The Window⇨Tile command sizes and moves the windows so that each one is showing, with no overlaps (much like floor tiles — and you wondered where they got the names of these commands, didn't you?).

The file-related File menu commands

OK, here comes the meaty stuff — a summary of the important File commands and their functions.

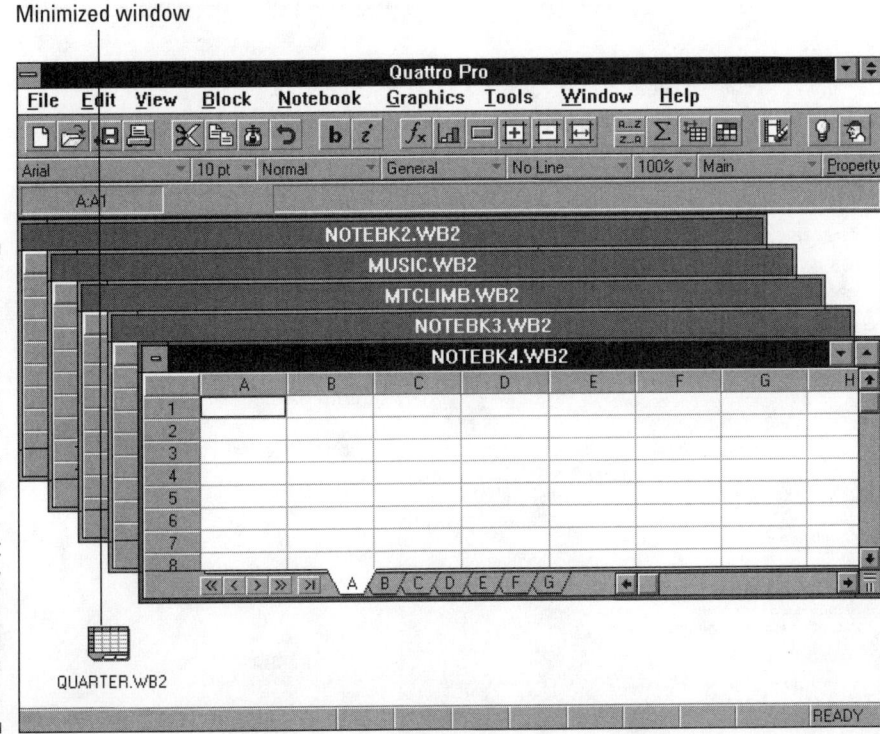

Chapter 7: How to Prevent Losing Your Work (and Ruining Your Whole Day) *113*

Figure 7-3: These windows were arranged with the Window⇨Cascade command. Notice that one window has been minimized and appears as an icon.

File⇨New

When Quattro Pro for Windows starts up, you will have a blank notebook called NOTEBK1.WB2. You can use this notebook to start a new project.

Version 6 has a brand-new feature called QuickTemplates @md pre-built notebooks that make it easy to perform some common tasks. When you choose File@->New, you may be greeted with a dialog box that lets you choose one of the QuickTemplates. See the sidebar "About those QuickTemplates" for more details.

About those QuickTemplates

Most of the notebooks that you create with Quattro Pro for Windows will be unique to your own needs. For example, you may need a notebook to keep track of your company's sales leads and how they are followed up. But some other notebooks are more general in nature. The new QuickTemplate feature in Quattro Pro 6 for Windows is designed to make your life easier. These QuickTemplates are pre-built notebooks for 17 common tasks. You can often use a QuickTemplate rather than create a new notebook from scratch.

(continues)

Part II: Basic Stuff That You Just Can't Ignore

> *(continued)*
>
> When you choose File@->New, you get the dialog box shown in the figure. If you want a plain notebook, just click on the Plain Notebook Option and click OK. To open a QuickTemplate, click the From QuickTemplate option and scroll through the QuickTemplates in the list box. Choose the one you want and click OK. You get a new, formatted "fill-in-the-blanks" notebook.
>
> The QuickTemplates provided with Quattro Pro for Windows are
>
> Accounts Payable Register
>
> Accounts Receivable Register
>
> Auto Expenses
>
> Checkbook Reconciliation
>
> College Savings Plan
>
> Household Inventory
>
> Meeting Room Schedule
>
> Mortgage Calculator
>
> Personal Net Worth
>
> Product Invoice
>
> Purchase Requisition
>
> Purchase Order (Landscape)
>
> Purchase Order (Portrait)
>
> Sales Order Form
>
> Sales Quotation
>
> Service Invoice
>
> Travel Expense Report
>
> Quick Template Builder
>
> For example, you may have a kid who's going to be ready for college in ten years. You can use the College Savings Plan notebook to figure out how much you need to save each month to meet the anticipated costs (it's a lot). You could set up your own notebook to do the calculations, but why reinvent the wheel?
>
> If you find yourself with a few spare minutes, you may want to check out the QuickTemplates. One of them just may be useful to you. Or not.

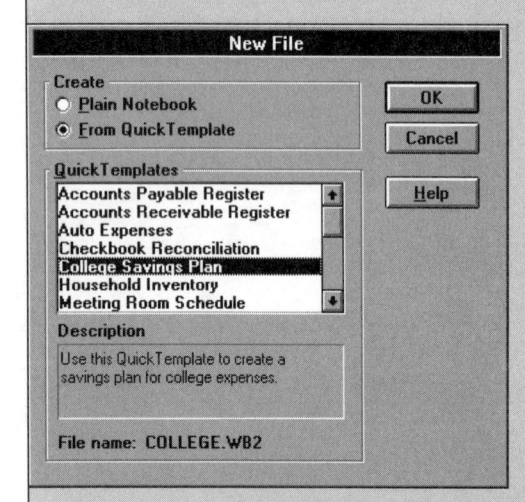

If you need to start another new project, use the File⇨New command. This command creates a new blank notebook on your screen but doesn't save it to disk. If you're already working on a notebook, this command starts a new notebook (and doesn't close the other one). Every new notebook begins life with a generic name such as NOTEBK2.WB2. Create another one and it'll be named NOTEBK3.WB2.

Chapter 7: How to Prevent Losing Your Work (and Ruining Your Whole Day) 115

TIP
When you start a new project and create a new notebook, it's a good idea to save it immediately (even though it's empty). Saving it forces you to give it a name — hopefully something more meaningful than NOTEBK1.WB2. Do this with the File⇨Save command (see "File⇨Save," later in this chapter).

TIP
The New Notebook button on the Toolbar is equivalent to the File⇨New command.

File⇨Open

Use this command when you want to open a notebook that already exists on your hard disk. If you have one or more notebooks open, this command brings yet another one on-screen (and doesn't close any of the others). When you issue this command, you'll see the Open File dialog box, which is shown in Figure 7-4.

Figure 7-4: Selecting the File⇨Open command opens this dialog box. You then specify which notebook file you want.

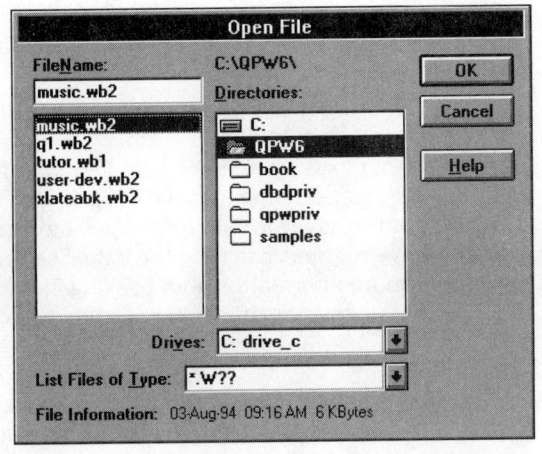

Usually, the file you want will be displayed in the list box on the left. Just scroll through the list until you find it. You may have to select a different directory or drive. When you change the drive or directory, you'll see a new list of files. When you find your file, double-click on it or highlight it with the arrow keys and press Enter.

TIP
If the file you want to open is one of the last five files you've worked with, it will appear at the bottom of the command list that drops down when you select the File menu. You can simply select the file from the list — saving yourself several valuable seconds (and over the years those seconds add up to many many many minutes).

TIP
You can save a few more nanoseconds merely by clicking the Open Notebook button on the toolbar. Like the File⇨Open command, this brings up the Open File dialog box.

File⇨Save

This command saves your notebook to a file on-disk. If you've already saved the file before, Quattro Pro uses the same name. If it's a new notebook with a generic NOTEBKx.WB2 filename, Quattro Pro for Windows prompts you to name the file. Just type a valid filename — the program supplies the WB2 extension that identifies it as a Quattro Pro for Windows notebook file. If you want to rename an existing file with a different name, use File⇨Save As (see the following section).

> **REMEMBER:** Filenames can be no longer than eight characters (with no spaces). Also, a few characters are verboten [\ (backslash), + (plus sign), : (colon), and a few others]. If you try to use one of these characters, Quattro Pro for Windows returns an error message that is itself erroneous. It tells you that the directory does not exist. Actually, the error message should say that the file name is invalid. See? Even software writers make mistakes.

> **TIP:** You also can select the Save Notebook button on the Toolbar to save your notebook.

File⇨Save As

Use this command when you want to save your existing notebook with a different name, or save it to a different directory or disk. This is also the command you use when you want to save a Quattro Pro for Windows file in a different file format so that other programs can read the data. See the sidebar "Working with foreign files" for more information about saving files in different file formats. Figure 7-5 shows the dialog box that appears when you choose the File⇨Save As command.

> **REMEMBER:** When you save a file for the first time using the File⇨Save command, Quattro Pro for Windows is smart enough to know that you really meant to use the File⇨Save As command. Consequently, you see the dialog box you normally get when you select the File⇨Save As command.

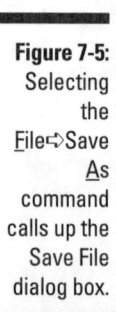

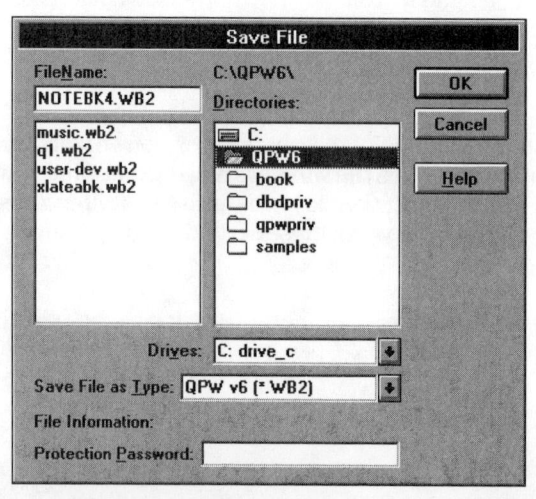

Figure 7-5: Selecting the File⇨Save As command calls up the Save File dialog box.

Working with foreign files

If you have a VHS video cassette player, you probably know that you can't play old Beta video cassettes in your machine. Besides being different sizes, the tapes are in different formats, too. Even if you took the tape out of a Beta cartridge and spooled it onto a VHS cartridge, your VHS machine can't understand it.

Similarly, if you save a file from Quattro Pro for Windows, you normally can't use that file in your word processor because the two programs use different file formats. By the same token, if you tried to load a Quattro Pro for Windows notebook file into dBASE, dBASE can't recognize the information — again, different file formats.

Actually, there is a way to save Quattro Pro for Windows files so that the information can be used in most other programs. The trick is to save the file in a *foreign* file format — one that the other program can understand.

Quattro Pro for Windows can open and save files in the following formats:

- Notebooks produced by earlier versions of Quattro Pro
- Files produced by Microsoft's Excel spreadsheet (but not Excel 5.0 files)
- Files produced by Lotus 1-2-3
- dBASE database files
- Paradox database files

When you use the File⇔Open command, choose the drop-down list labeled List Files of Type, and select the file type that you want. This selection displays only those types of files that are in the file list. To save a notebook in one of these formats, use the File⇔Save As command. You also have to specify the appropriate file extension.

File⇔Close

This command removes the current notebook from memory. If the notebook that you're trying to close hasn't been saved since you made any changes, Quattro Pro for Windows asks you whether you want to save it; it asks you this by displaying a dialog box like the one in Figure 7-6. To save it before closing it, select the Yes button. To abandon your changes and close it anyway, choose No. Select Cancel if you get cold feet and decide not to close the file after all.

File⇔Workspace

You already know that you can have several notebooks open at once. Let's say you're diligently working on, say, five notebooks — switching back and forth, having a grand old time. You have the windows arranged just the way you like them. Then the whistle blows: time to go home. It would be nice if you could save the position of all of these windows so you could resume where you left off. Well, you'll be glad to know that such a feature is indeed available.

Figure 7-6:
If you try to close a file that includes unsaved information, Quattro Pro for Windows warns you with this message.

The File⇨Workspace⇨Save command will save the current notebook window configuration. After it does, you can use the File⇨Workspace⇨Restore command to restore Quattro Pro for Windows to the same place you were when you left. Cool, eh?

TIP

The File⇨Workspace command is one of those cascading menus. When you select Workspace, the menu expands to show two more choices: Save and Restore.

WARNING!

Saving your workspace does not actually save the notebook files. You have to remember to save these files on your own.

TECHNICAL STUFF

When you save a workspace, it is saved in a file with a WSB extension. You can save any number of workspaces and then retrieve the one you want.

File⇨Exit

Use this command when you are finished using Quattro Pro for Windows. If you have any unsaved work, Quattro Pro for Windows lets you know about it and gives you the opportunity to save it to disk before quitting.

TIP

Alt+F4 is the standard Windows shortcut for File⇨Exit — it also works with Quattro Pro for Windows. You also can use Ctrl+Q to quit — but this shortcut is unique to Quattro Pro for Windows and doesn't work in other programs.

Non-file-related File menu commands

The File menu also has several other commands that really don't have anything to do with files on your disk. You use these other commands to print or view your notebook. Because these commands are irrelevant to the current topic, I put off discussing them until Chapter 11.

Doing Things with a File — Step by Step

Now it's time to put all your file knowledge to work. You'll create a new notebook file, put some information into it, save it, close it, and then open it again. These are the tasks you will perform every time you work with Quattro Pro for Windows.

Start by running Quattro Pro for Windows. As always, it will start up and give you an empty notebook window called NOTEBK1.WB2.

In this exercise, just ignore the NOTEBK1.WB2 window. Run the exercise as follows:

1. **Select the File⇨New command.**

   Quattro Pro for Windows creates a new (empty) notebook file called NOTEBK2.WB2. This file exists only in memory and is not saved on disk.

   If the QuickTemplate option is set, you get a dialog box labeled File New that lets you choose a QuickTemplate (see the sidebar earlier in this chapter). Just select the Plain Notebook option and click OK. This will give you a fresh notebook to work with.

2. **Enter some information in the notebook.**

   It doesn't matter what; just put in some numbers or labels. Your screen should look something like Figure 7-7.

3. **Save this notebook by selecting the File⇨Save command.**

   Because this notebook doesn't have a name (NOTEBK2.WB2 is not considered a real name), Quattro Pro will ask you to supply one in the Save File dialog box.

4. **Type MYFILE in the dialog box (refer to Figure 7-8), and click on the OK button.**

   Quattro Pro for Windows creates a new file on your hard disk called MYFILE.WB2.

5. **Close the file you're working on by selecting the File⇨Close command.**

   The file will be unloaded from memory. But that's OK, because it was saved to disk. If you hadn't saved the file before closing it, Quattro Pro for Windows would have politely asked you if you wanted to do so (it does all it can to save you).

6. **Now you'll open the file again to work on it some more. Choose File⇨Open. Figure 7-9 shows the Open File dialog box that appears.**

Part II: Basic Stuff That You Just Can't Ignore

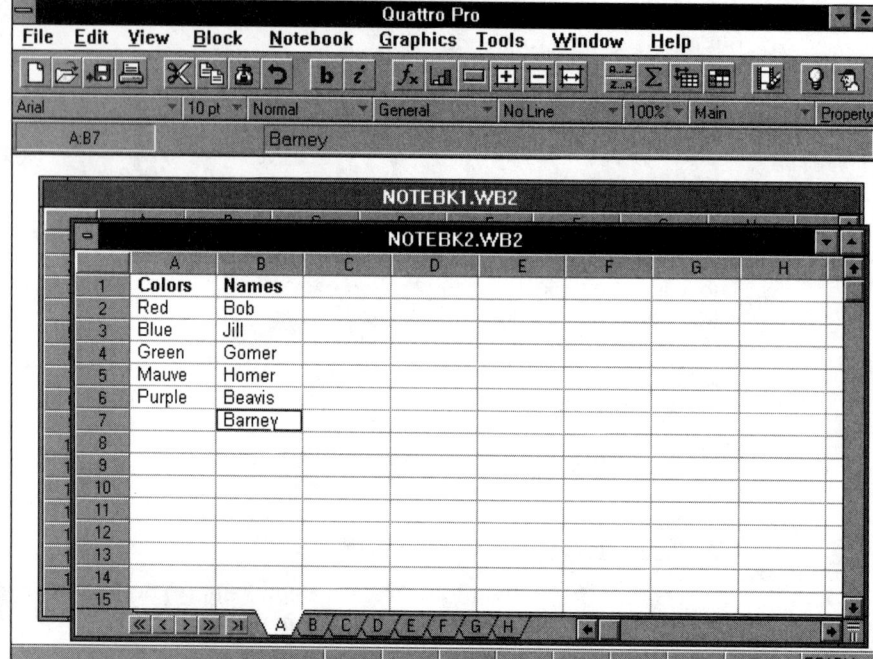

Figure 7-7: Your new notebook file after putting some information into it.

Figure 7-8: The Save File dialog box is where you give your notebook a filename.

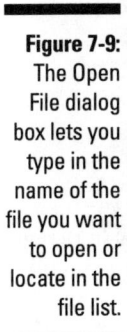

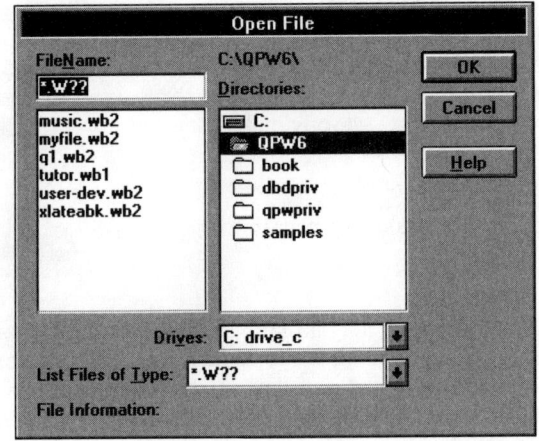

Chapter 7: How to Prevent Losing Your Work (and Ruining Your Whole Day) **121**

Figure 7-9:
The Open File dialog box lets you type in the name of the file you want to open or locate in the file list.

7. **In the Open File dialog box, enter** MYFILE **into the FileName box and press Enter (or choose OK).**

    If you can't remember the filename, you can look for it in the file list. You may have to use the scrollbar to display more filenames. When you find MYFILE.WB2, click on it to select it, and then choose OK (or just double-click on it and bypass the OK button).

    Quattro Pro for Windows will open the notebook file, which will look just as it did when you last saved it.

TIP

The preceding steps are actually the long way to do things. Quattro Pro for Windows has Toolbar buttons to open and save a file — letting you avoid the menu altogether for these actions.

Making Backups

If there's one thing that almost all beginning computer users have trouble with, it's managing files on their hard drive and floppy disks. Most people don't take the time to learn the cryptic DOS commands normally used to copy files, rename files, move files, and do other things. I don't blame you if you are one of these people — those commands are very confusing, and much better ways exist. Don't let the computer nerds tell you otherwise.

Although this book isn't really the place for you to learn the ins and outs of managing your files, I do want to tell you how to make a backup copy of a file — in fact, I'll show you several different ways. That way, if you ever lose an important file, you can't blame me!

Making a backup of a file simply means placing a copy of the file in another location — usually on a floppy disk. Some people make their backups to another hard drive on their system, to a network file server, or to magnetic tape. To keep things simple, I'm going to show you three ways to get a Quattro Pro for Windows notebook file on a floppy disk. They are

- Using Quattro Pro for Windows
- Using the Windows File Manager program
- Using DOS

You (or the office computer nerd) may already have some procedures in place to make a complete backup copy of all the files on your hard disk. For example, you may own software that's designed specifically to back up all the files on your hard drive to a tape storage unit. I encourage you to make such backups regularly. But you need to realize that you still need to make separate backups of important files that you work on. (What if someone breaks into your office and steals your PC?) The procedures in this section tell you how to save your own files.

Backing up from Quattro Pro for Windows

You can search the Quattro Pro for Windows menus all day and never find the File⇨Backup command — there's no such animal. However, you still can save your notebook to a floppy disk. (If you haven't fallen asleep yet, you probably already have a pretty good idea of where this section is heading.) The key is to use the File⇨Save As command, and then specify saving your files to drive A. Say you're ready to head for home after a long afternoon working on your department's budget. After juggling all that electronic money, you're tired and don't feel like thinking any more, but you know you have to save your data. Here's the easy way to save a copy of your file to a floppy disk:

1. **Save your notebook to your hard drive as you normally do.**
2. **Insert a formatted floppy disk into drive A.**
3. **Issue the File⇨Save As command.**

   In the Save File dialog box, click on the arrow in the list box labeled Drives. Select A: from the list and choose OK. Quattro Pro for Windows saves your current notebook to the floppy disk in drive A.

4. **You now can use File⇨Exit to get out of Quattro Pro for Windows.**

   You should rejoice, because you have *two* copies of your file: the one on your hard disk and the one you just saved to the floppy disk.

5. **For good measure, put that diskette into your pocket and take it home with you.**

Chapter 7: How to Prevent Losing Your Work (and Ruining Your Whole Day) *123*

> **TIP**
>
> If you prefer, you can use drive B rather than drive A in all these procedures. It doesn't matter, as long as your diskette is in drive B rather than drive A.

When you come back to work the next day, use File⇨Open to open the file on your hard drive. If you make any changes to the file, repeat the floppy disk backup procedure after saving the file to your hard disk. Because the file already exists on your backup floppy, Quattro Pro for Windows makes you verify that you want to overwrite this file with your newer version.

Backing up from the Windows File Manager program

Microsoft Windows includes a program called *File Manager* that every Windows user should become familiar with. Figure 7-10 shows what File Manager looks like. Unless your hard drive is an exact clone of mine, your File Manager window will look somewhat different.

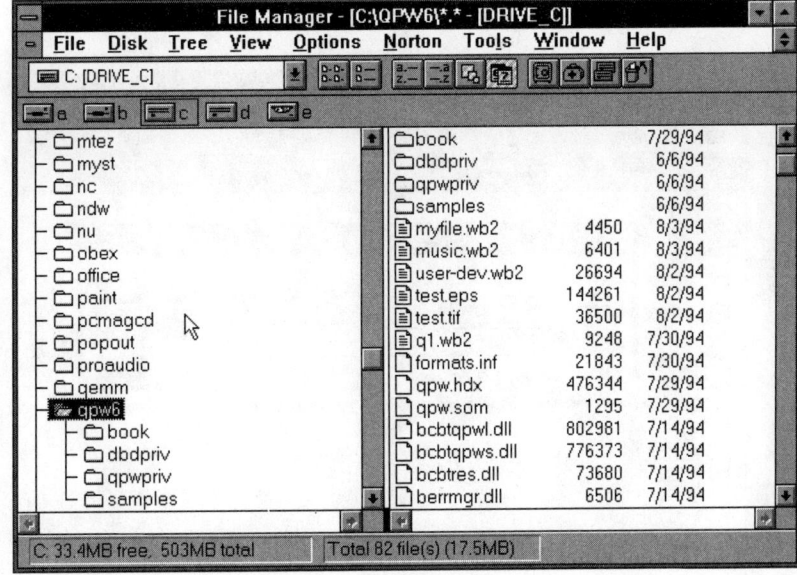

Figure 7-10: A File Manager is included with Microsoft Windows at no extra charge (what a bargain!).

This isn't the place to teach you all about using File Manager (*Windows For Dummies* explains this program pretty well). But I do want to give you step-by-step instructions for copying a file using File Manager:

1. Save your notebook as usual using the File⇨Save command (or use the Save Notebook Toolbar button). If you haven't named the file yet, Quattro Pro for Windows asks for a name.

2. Press Ctrl+Esc to bring up the Windows Task List. If File Manager is listed in the task list, double-click on it. If File Manager is not listed, select Program Manager to get to the Program Manager screen. Then locate the File Manager icon in the Main program group (it looks like a file cabinet with two drawers) and double-click on it.

3. When File Manager starts, its window usually is split into two vertical panes. Directories appear on the left, and the files in the selected directory appear on the right.

4. In the pane on the left, locate the directory on your hard drive in which you save your notebook files, and click on that directory's name. The pane on the right then displays the files in that directory.

5. In the pane on the right, click on the file that you were just working on to select it.

6. Issue the File⇨Copy command (or press F8). File Manager displays the dialog box shown in Figure 7-11.

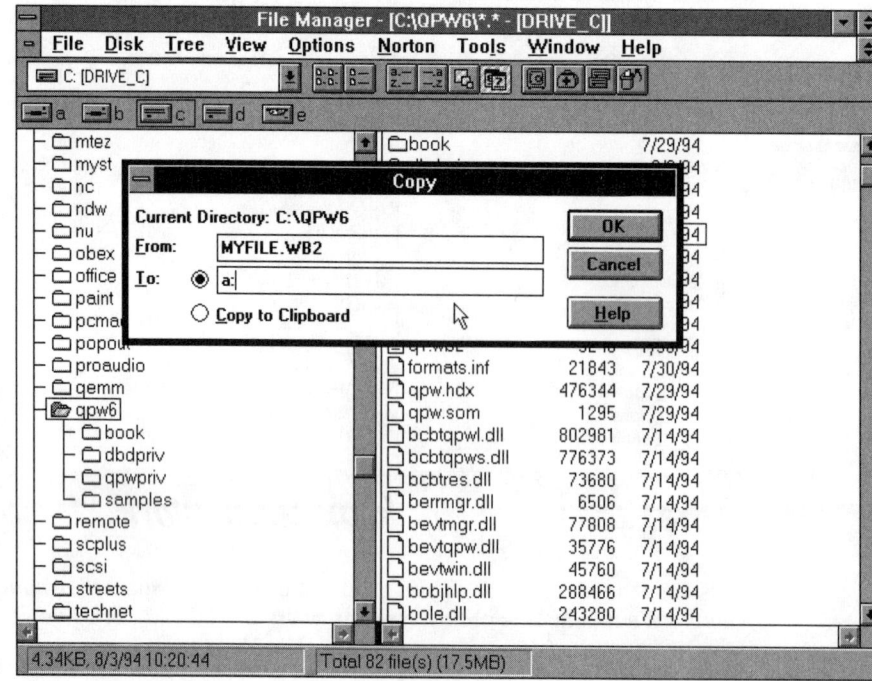

Figure 7-11: Here's where you tell File Manager where to copy your file.

Chapter 7: How to Prevent Losing Your Work (and Ruining Your Whole Day)

REMEMBER

7. In the To: text box, enter a: and choose OK. File Manager makes a copy of the file and puts it on the disk in drive A.

8. You can copy more files to the floppy disk using the same procedures. When you're finished copying, choose File⇨Exit to close File Manager.

9. If you're not back in Quattro Pro for Windows, press Ctrl+Esc and choose Quattro Pro from the task list.

10. Remove the floppy disk and put it in a safe place.

11. With your file safely backed up, you now can exit Quattro Pro for Windows, leave work, and get some elbow exercise at Joe's Place.

Backing up from DOS

Another way to make a backup copy of a notebook is to use the DOS COPY command. You can access DOS from Windows (using the MS-DOS icon), or you can exit Windows to return to DOS. In either case, you start this procedure at the DOS prompt (which is usually C:>):

1. **Insert a formatted diskette into drive A.**

2. **At the DOS prompt, type** CD C:\xxxx, **where xxxx is the name of the directory that you store your notebook files in.**

   For example, if you keep your notebooks in the QPRO directory, type **CD C:\QPRO**. After you have correctly entered the command, press the Enter key.

3. **Next, type**

   ```
   COPY filename.wb2 a:
   ```

   where **filename.wb2** **is the name of your file. When you press Enter, DOS copies the notebook file to the floppy disk. (You'll see your floppy disk light come on if you have one.)**

4. **Remove the floppy disk, and store it in a safe place (that weird neighbor's bomb shelter, for example).**

Other ways to back up your work

Your computer may have other file-management programs on it, such as Norton Desktop, PC Tools, XTree, or Norton Commander. These programs can copy, organize, move, and rename files very easily. Consult the documentation that came with these programs (or buy a ...*For Dummies* book!) to learn how to use them.

Part II: Basic Stuff That You Just Can't Ignore

> **REMEMBER**
>
> I just wrote several pages telling you stuff that you won't fully appreciate until that fateful day comes when you realize that your only copy of an important file has bit the dust. Take some precautions — now — and practice safe spreadsheeting.

The 5th Wave   By Rich Tennant

"I ALWAYS BACK UP EVERYTHING."

Chapter 8
Formulas: Not Just for Babies Anymore

• •

In This Chapter
▶ Why spreadsheets are so popular and appealing
▶ What formulas are and why you need them
▶ How to enter a formula into a worksheet
▶ How to use the mathematical operators you thought you were finished with in high school (but maybe now you'll understand them)
▶ What goes on when you enter a formula into a cell, with exclusive, behind-the-scenes photos
▶ A necessary discussion of absolute and relative cell references

• •

OK, here's what you've been waiting for: the chapter that makes it all worthwhile. This is the chapter that finally makes your notebooks come to life, the chapter that gives you the skills necessary to actually do something useful, the chapter that teaches you about formulas.

If you're following this book in chapter number order, you now know just enough about moving around through a worksheet to be dangerous. You can enter numbers and labels into cells with the best of them, and you even know about menus, dialog boxes, Toolbars, and the importance of saving your work. Now you're ready for the next logical step to earn your degree in Quattro Pro for Windows.

Formulas: The Definition

A notebook without formulas is like the fake food you see displayed in the window of a Chinese restaurant — it looks pretty good on the surface, but it doesn't do a whole lot for you. In fact, without formulas, you may as well be using a word processing program. Therefore, it's in your best interest to get turned on to formulas as soon as possible. Hey, now's a good time!

After you enter a number or a label into a cell, Quattro Pro for Windows displays that number or label in the cell. A formula, like a number or a label, is something that you enter into a cell. But the difference is that a formula does some type of calculation and displays the *answer* in the cell. However, you can still see the formula in the contents box of the input line when you move the cell pointer to a cell that has a formula in it. Therefore, a cell that has a formula in it may display different things, depending on the current values of the cells it uses.

Simple formulas use only numbers and no cell addresses. For example, try entering the following formula into a cell (any cell will do):

```
+100+45
```

You'll find that Quattro Pro for Windows displays the answer, which is 145. (Figure 8-1 proves that I'm not lying.) Cell B2 has this simple formula in it, but the cell itself shows the result of the calculation that the formula performs. The actual formula appears in the contents box of the input line.

However, formulas are most interesting when you use cell addresses rather than actual values. Allow me to demonstrate. Take a look at Figure 8-2, which shows a worksheet with labels in column A and numbers in column B. But cell B5 contains a formula. What you're seeing displayed in the worksheet is the formula's *answer* (or its result). Because the active cell happens to be cell B5, the contents of this cell (the *formula*) appear in the contents box of the input line. Here it is again:

```
+B1+B2+B3+B4
```

What this formula is saying, in plain English, is this: *Hey, Quattro Pro for Windows, take the number in cell B1 and add it to the number in B2. Then add the number in B3 to the total. And while you're at it, add the number in B4 to that total. Now, display the final answer in my cell. Thanks, dude.*

You may think that entering **+B1+B2+B3+B4** is a rather lengthy way to get the sum of these numbers. But you'll have to admit that it's sure easier than typing out the instructions in English.

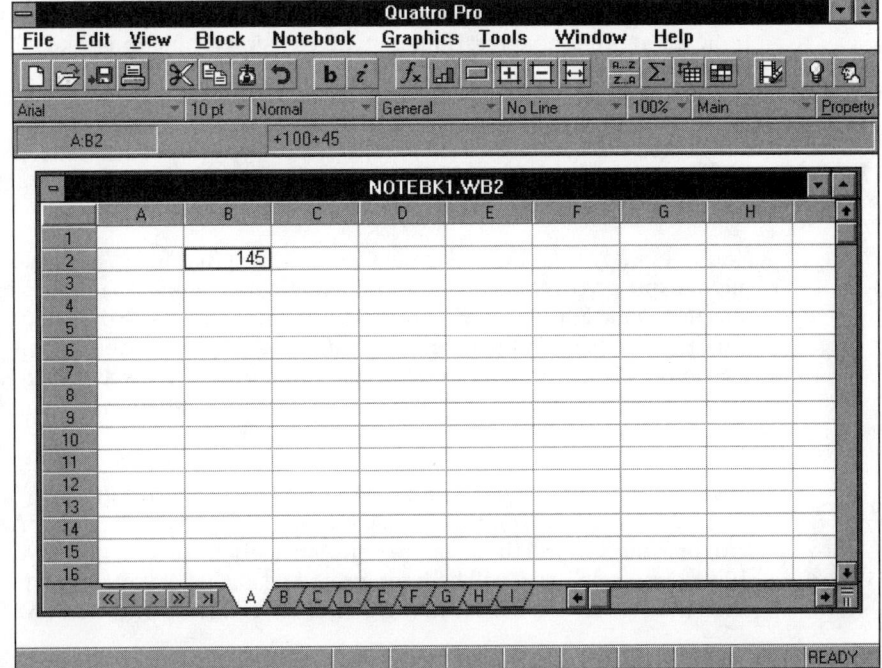

Chapter 8: Formulas: Not Just For Babies Anymore *129*

Figure 8-1: A formula displays its results in the cell. To see the actual formula, look at the input line.

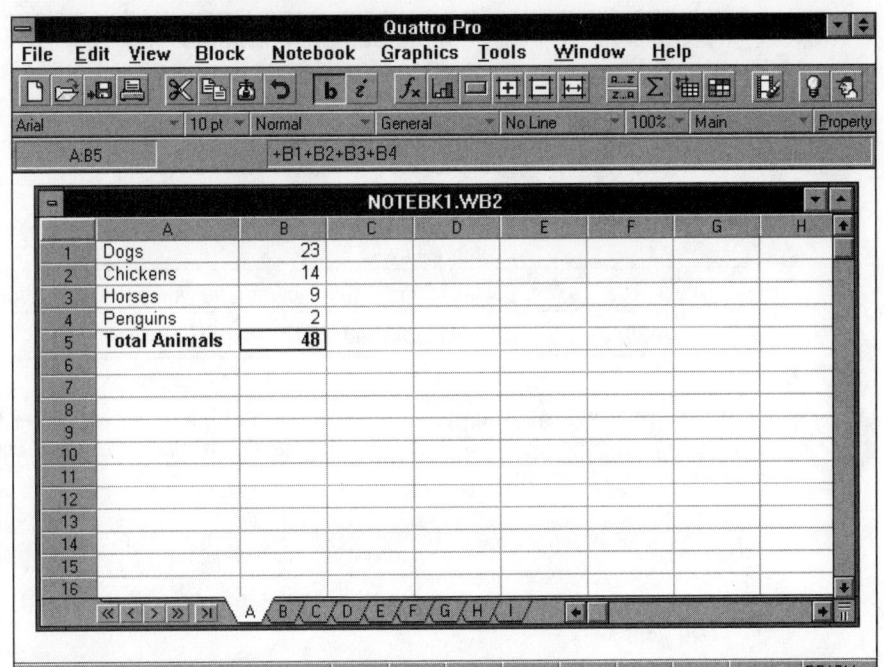

Figure 8-2: A bunch of numbers? No way, Jose. Cell B5 has a formula in it.

Actually, there's a much easier way to get the sum of several cells, but that's a topic for another chapter. Hint: It involves using @ functions, and a Toolbar button is available.

Hello, Operator?

You've already seen how a formula can use the plus sign to add values. As you might expect, you can use other mathematical *operators* to perform even more amazing feats. For example, you can subtract values using the minus sign and multiply values using an asterisk (not an X, as you might think). And you can't overlook the ever-popular division operation that uses a slash. Finally, those with a penchant for large numbers might be interested in the exponential operator (^), which raises a number to a power.

Always start your formulas with a plus sign (+) so Quattro Pro for Windows won't get confused. Think about it. If a formula starts with a cell address, Quattro Pro for Windows will think you're entering a label. For example, if you enter **A1+A2** into a cell, this will be intereprated as a label. If you want a formula that adds the contents of cell A1 to the contents of cell A2, enter **+A1+A2** in a cell.

Table 8-1 shows some examples of formulas using these operators.

Table 8-1	Some Sample Formulas that Use Various Operators
Formula	*What It Does*
+A1*23.5	Multiplies the value in cell A1 by 23.5
+A1-A3	Subtracts the value in A3 from the value in A1
+A4/A3	Divides A4 by A3
+A3^3	Raises A3 to the third power (equivalent to +A3*A3*A3)
+(A1+A2)/A3	Adds A1 to A2 and then divides the answer by A3

The cell references in the preceding table don't include a page letter because they are contained in a single notebook page. Formulas, of course, can use page letters in formulas, such as this:

```
+B:A1*C:A1
```

This particular formula multiplies the upper left cell on page B by the upper left cell on page C.

Using parentheses

The observant reader may have noticed that the last entry in Table 8-1 introduced something new — parentheses. You can use parentheses to tell Quattro Pro for Windows in what order you want the calculations to occur. Why is this necessary? Here's how that example would look without any parentheses:

```
+A1+A2/A3
```

In this form, the example is ambiguous. Do you want to add A1 to A2 and divide the result by A3? Or do you want to divide A2 by A3 and then add A1 to it? Does it matter? Yep. Read on to find out why.

A formula with two answers

Just for the sake of argument, assume that you have three cells in column A, each with a value. The values are

```
A1:    4
A2:    10
A3:    2
```

Take another look at this now-familiar formula: +A1+A2/A3.

If you forget about cell addresses and use the real numbers, the formula would look like this:

```
+4+10/2
```

Add 4 to 10 and you get 14. Divide 14 by 2 and you get 7. That's the answer, right? Well, you also can look at it like this: Divide 10 by 2 and get 5. Add the 4 to this 5 and you get 9. Hmmm. It turns out that this formula can produce an answer of either 7 or 9, depending on the order in which the operations are done. Computers, like some people, can't handle ambiguity well. Therefore, you need to be very specific at times. If you don't believe me, look at Figure 8-3 (figures don't lie).

> **REMEMBER:** The result of a formula may depend on the order in which the arithmetic operations are performed. You can control this by using parentheses.

How Quattro Pro for Windows copes with ambiguity

So what happens if you leave out the parentheses? Does Quattro Pro for Windows go into an endless loop trying to resolve the ambiguity? Will smoke start coming out of your floppy disk drive? Not quite. The program has some rules built into it that determine how it handles ambiguities such as these. These rules are called *orders of precedence* (a term that you can safely forget after you understand the concept).

Figure 8-3: Visual proof that a formula can produce different results by changing the order of the calculations.

```
         A     B    C           D    E
  1      4
  2     10
  3      2
  4
  5      9    <---  +A1+A2/A3
  6      7    <---  (A1+A2)/A3
  7
  ...
```

For example, multiplication has higher precedence than addition; therefore +2+3*4 produces an answer of 14, not 20. In other words, when it doesn't find any parentheses to guide it, Quattro Pro for Windows first does the multiplication (3*4) and then performs the addition.

Table 8-2 lists some of the world's most popular mathematical operators and numbers that indicate their precedence levels. Operations with lower precedence numbers are performed first, and those with equal precedence are performed from left to right.

Table 8-2   Some of the More Commonly Used Mathematical Operators and Their Precedence

Operator	Description	Precedence
^	Exponentiation	1
*	Multiplication	2
/	Division	2
+	Addition	3
-	Subtraction	3

REMEMBER: If a formula doesn't have any overriding parentheses, Quattro Pro for Windows always performs the exponentiation (^) operator. Then it performs multiplication and division. And, finally, it performs subtraction and addition.

The nesting instinct

Frankly, I've been using spreadsheets for more than a decade, and I confess that I never can remember how this precedence business works (and I just don't trust it, for some reason). Therefore, I tend to use more parentheses than are necessary — which isn't bad, because multiple parentheses make it very clear how the formula is calculated.

Examine the following formula:

```
(((A1+B1)*2)-((C1+D1)*2))/4
```

Notice that the number of left parentheses is exactly equal to the number of right parentheses. If this were not true, Quattro Pro for Windows would not accept the formula when you press Enter. Matching parentheses is not all that difficult, because Quattro Pro for Windows color codes the parentheses as you enter them into a formula. Keep your eye on the cell when you enter a formula with parentheses and you'll notice that parentheses show up in different colors. A red parenthesis is an unmatched parenthesis. Green parentheses are matched.

When Quattro Pro for Windows evaluates a formula like the one above, it starts in the middle and works its way out. Whatever is enclosed by the most deeply nested parentheses gets first attention, and the result of that calculation is used to evaluate the remaining parts of the formula.

Here's how Quattro Pro for Windows might tackle the preceding formula. It starts at the most deeply nested level. Actually, two sets of parentheses exist at the deepest level: (A1+B1) and (C1+D1). Quattro Pro finds these two answers and then evaluates the next level. Again, two sets of parentheses exist at the next level. In this case, Quattro Pro uses the answers from the preceding level and multiplies them by 2.

At the next level up, it takes these two answers and subtracts the second one from the first. And, at the top level, it takes the preceding answer and divides it by four. This final calculation gives the answer that shows up in the cell.

All this figuring, of course, happens in the blink of an eye (actually, a bit faster than that). The point I'm trying to make is that using more parentheses than you really need can actually help you make sense of cryptic formulas such as the preceding one.

The thing about formulas

Here's the thing about formulas: They always look more complicated than they really are. That's because most people are used to seeing things that have some inherent meaning in them. A cell address such as F13, however, is meaningless. Face it: Things would be much less intimidating if you could write a formula such as this:

```
(current-previous)/previous
```

rather than this:

```
(C12-B12)/B12
```

Fact is, you *can* write formulas that use meaningful names. As you discover later in this book, you can give a name to a cell, to a block of cells, and even to a complete notebook page.

> **TIP:** Sometimes it's useful to include a note to yourself (or to others) that explains what's going on in a formula. That clever trickery you came up with last March may totally baffle you by July. You can add a note to a formula by placing a semicolon at the end of the formula and then typing in some descriptive text. Quattro Pro for Windows ignores everything appearing after the semicolon when calculating the formula. Your description then appears in the input line when the cell pointer is on the cell, as shown in Figure 8-4. This is an *annotated* formula.

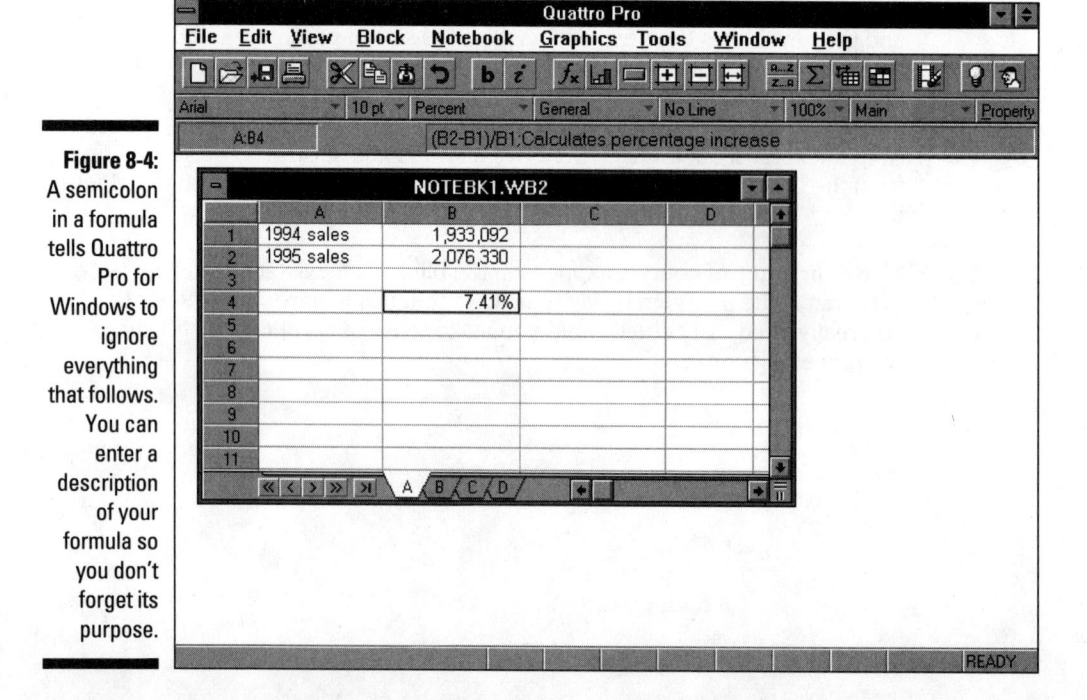

Figure 8-4: A semicolon in a formula tells Quattro Pro for Windows to ignore everything that follows. You can enter a description of your formula so you don't forget its purpose.

Chapter 8: Formulas: Not Just For Babies Anymore

How to Enter Formulas

One way to enter a formula is to type it into a cell, beginning the formula with a plus sign. You can enter any of the formulas you've seen so far just by typing them exactly as they appear. This includes all the cell addresses, worksheet letters (if they're necessary), mathematical operators, parentheses, actual values, and whatever else is required.

But the best way to enter a formula is to *point* to the cells and let Quattro Pro for Windows help you build the formula. When you're entering a formula, Quattro Pro for Windows offers a slick alternative to typing the actual cell references. The typing method can be tedious (not to mention error-prone). This alternative method is called *pointing*. The best way to understand this is to follow along with an example.

In this example, you build a formula that adds three cells and displays the results in another cell. And you do it without typing a single cell address. Figure 8-5 shows what my screen looked like when I was trying this.

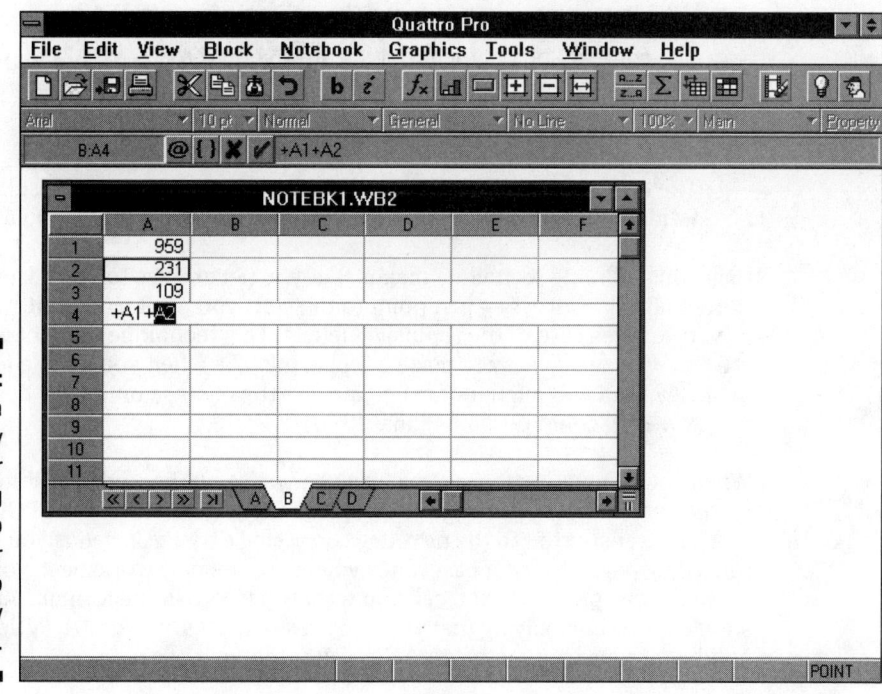

Figure 8-5: Building a formula by pointing or letting Quattro Pro for Windows do the dirty work.

Follow these steps to learn how to use the pointing method:

1. **Enter some numbers into cells A1, A2, and A3.**

   Any numbers will do.

2. **Move the cell pointer to cell A4.**

3. **Enter + (the operator that means add) to tell Quattro Pro for Windows that a formula is on the way.**

4. **Use the up-arrow key to move the cell pointer to cell A1.**

   Notice that the mode indicator at the bottom of the screen now reads POINT. Also notice that the formula is being created in the cell before your very eyes — and it's also being created in the input line at the same time.

5. **Enter + again.**

   The cell pointer jumps back to cell A4, where the formula is being built.

6. **Use the up-arrow key to move the cell pointer to cell A2.**

7. **Press + again.**

8. **Use the up-arrow key to move the cell pointer to cell A3.**

   The contents box in the input line now should read +A1+A2+A3 (which is just what you want).

9. **Press Enter to place the formula into cell A4.**

   The formula is evaluated, and the cell shows the formula's result, not the formula (but the input line continues to show the actual formula).

Using this pointing technique means that you never have to be concerned with the actual cell address — just point to the cells you want, and Quattro Pro for Windows takes care of the repulsive details. This technique also cuts down on errors. After all, it's easy to make a typing mistake when you enter a formula manually (and you might not even discover the mistake until your boss asks you how 12+9 could possibly equal 197).

> **TIP:** When you're pointing to create a formula, you're not limited to pointing to cells on the current notebook page. If you press Ctrl+PgDn while in the POINT mode, you'll be transported to the next page. Pressing Ctrl+PgUp sends you to the preceding page. In either case, after you get to the new worksheet, you can move the cell pointer to the cell you want to refer to in the formula. And it should go without saying that you can press Ctrl+PgDn and Ctrl+PgUp any number of times until you get to the right notebook page.

If your formula returns ERR

It's not unusual to enter a formula into a cell and be greeted with ERR instead of a more friendly result. In a nutshell, ERR means that you made a boo-boo. This notation appears for a number of reasons:

- You made a mistake by typing a cell reference that doesn't exist (such as +ZA1). A formula with this nonexistent cell reference would return ERR.

- You're trying to do something impossible, such as calculate the square root of a negative number or divide by zero (operations that aren't allowed on this planet).

You'll learn later that cells and ranges can be given meaningful names, and Quattro Pro for Windows lets you use such a name in a formula even if it doesn't exist. Formulas with nonexistent cell or range names always return ERR.

- Your formula is trying to use a cell that is returning ERR. If the formula uses a cell that is returning ERR, the formula also returns ERR. This is known as the *ripple effect,* because a single ERR can ripple through an entire worksheet.

Usually, if you examine the formula that's returning ERR, you can figure out the problem — look for unusual cell references or undefined range names. You then can edit the cell to correct the problem, and the formula will return a better result.

Behind the scenes

You may be curious about what goes on behind the scenes when you enter a formula into a cell. If you've ever wondered what a computer thinks about, you'll find out here.

When you start entering a formula into a cell, Quattro Pro for Windows goes through the following thought process:

1. **OK, this person is entering a formula.** It's not just a number or a label, so she must know *something* about Quattro Pro for Windows.

2. **Is she using the POINT mode?** If so, I'll need to show her the cell addresses as she points to them and place them in the formula (sheesh, I have to do *all* the work).

3. **She just pressed Enter.** That means she's finished with the formula.

4. **Before I display the result, I'll just check this formula to make sure that it follows all my rules.** If it doesn't, I'll beep and make her feel foolish.

5. **Looks OK to me.** Now I'll calculate the results using the values in the cells she specified.

6. **Now I'll finish up by displaying the answer in the cell.**

Your computer continues to think as you do your work. Every time you put a value into a cell or create a new formula, it checks every single formula on the worksheet to see whether it needs to be recalculated based on your new input. But this all happens so quickly that you usually don't even realize it.

Just How Complex Can Formulas Be?

Like personalities, formulas can be simple or complex. All the formulas you've seen so far in this chapter fall into the Simple category. Yes, even the formula that demonstrated nesting parentheses is pretty elementary in the whole scheme of things.

TECHNICAL STUFF

Here's an example of an actual formula that I once developed in a moment of boredom (actually, it took me quite a few moments):

```
@IF(B$25<>$A27,(((@COUNT(@@(B$25))*@SUMPRODUCT(@@(B$25),@@($A27)))-
    (@SUM(@@(B$25))*@SUM(@@($A27))))/
    (@SQRT((@COUNT(@@(B$25))*@SUMPRODUCT(@@(B$25),@@(B$25)))-
    @SUM(@@(B$25))^2)*@SQRT((@COUNT(@@(B$25))*@SUMPRODUCT(@@($A27),
    @@($A27)))-(@SUM(@@($A27))^2))),"      —")
```

This formula is used to calculate correlation coefficients using indirect referencing. Believe it or not, some people actually have a use for this sort of thing. But the most amazing thing is that this monster actually works — although I no longer understand exactly *how* it works. By the way, Quattro Pro for Windows now has a built-in function that can simplify this formula significantly. This means I can replace this monster with something as simple as @CORREL(@@(B$25),@@($A27)).

The point of presenting this formula is not to impress you with my formula-building prowess (although you *should* be impressed), but to demonstrate that you really don't have to worry about creating formulas that Quattro Pro for Windows can't handle.

External cell references

A cell reference can be even more complex than what's described in this chapter. In addition to a page letter, a column letter, and a row number, a reference also can include a filename. Here's an example of a simple formula that uses cells stored in two different worksheets (BUDGET93.WB1 and BUDGET92.WB1):

+[BUDGET93]A:A1-[BUDGET92]A:A1

To refer to a cell in another notebook, precede the normal cell reference with a filename enclosed in square brackets (you can omit the file extension).

You can get Quattro Pro for Windows to create this reference automatically by pointing to a cell in the other notebook as you're building a formula.

There's a good chance that you won't be using this feature much, if at all. But if you ever run across a formula with all those strange brackets in it, you'll know that the formula is using cells from a different notebook. This phenomenon is called an *external cell reference*.

By the way, when you enter or edit very lengthy formulas such as the preceding one, the formula wraps around in the cell and in the input line so that you can see the entire thing. In general, you should avoid lengthy formulas and use several different formulas instead.

Relative and Absolute References

There's one additional topic that I just can't put off any longer: relative vs. absolute references. This can be rather confusing, but it's important stuff. So bear with me, OK?

It's all relative

When you put a formula into a cell, you can copy that formula to other cells. In fact, copying formulas is one of the most common things that spreadsheet users do. You'll learn all about copying in Chapter 10. But, for now, just understand that you can enter a formula once and then copy it so that the same formula works on another cell. For example, if you have six columns of numbers, you can put a formula below the first column to add the preceding numbers. Then you can copy that formula to the five cells to the right to add the other columns. Copying a formula to five cells is a lot easier than entering it five more times.

Until now, all the cell references you've used in formulas have been *relative*. If you copy a formula that has relative references, the copies of the formula change. Here's an example. Assume the following formula is in cell A3:

```
+A1+A2
```

If you copy this formula to the cell next door (B3), the formula in cell B3 would read:

```
+B1+B2
```

In other words, copying the formula changed the cells in a *relative* manner. No matter where you copy the formula, it always computes the sum of the two cells directly above it. This is a good thing and, most of the time, exactly what you want to happen. This concept is demonstrated in Figure 8-6.

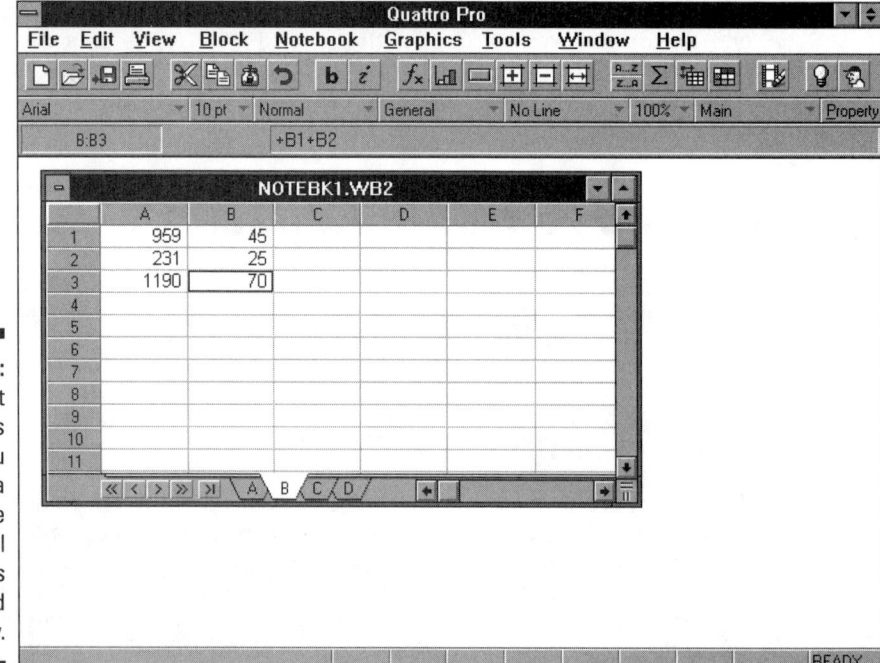

Figure 8-6: This is what happens when you copy a formula. The cell addresses are changed automatically.

By default, all cell references are relative.

Absolutely absolute

What if you wanted the copy of the formula to return exactly the same result as the cell it was copied from? In this case, you need to specify *absolute* cell references. Here's a formula with absolute cell references:

```
+$B$1+$C$1
```

I told you that this can get complicated. Using a dollar sign before the column part and the row part of a cell reference tells Quattro Pro for Windows that the cell reference is absolute — that it always refers to those specific cells, even if you copy the formula.

Why use absolute references?

The best way to understand why to use absolute references is to go through an example. Figure 8-7 shows a worksheet designed to calculate the sales tax on several purchase prices. The sales tax rate is in cell B1. Column A has labels, column B has amounts, and column C has formulas that calculate the sales tax on the amount in column B.

The formula in cell C4 is

```
+B4*$B$1
```

The first cell reference (B4) is a normal relative cell reference, but the second part of the formula ($B$1) is an absolute reference. When we copy this formula down the column, the first part of the formula will change to reflect the price in the cell to the left of it, but the copied formula will *always* refer to cell B1 — which is just what we want. For example, the formula, when copied to cell C5 reads:

```
+B5*$B$1
```

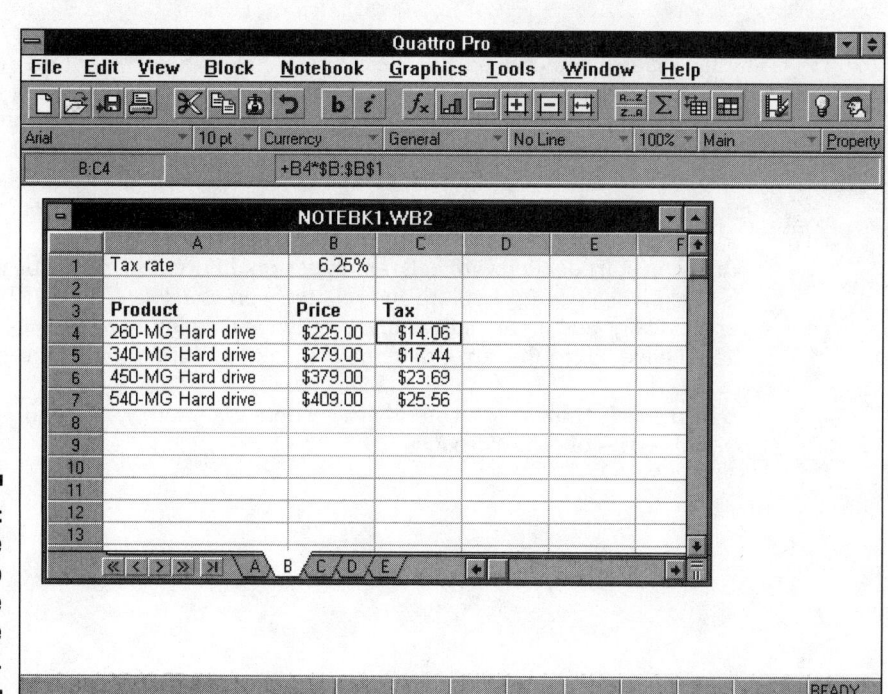

Figure 8-7: An example of when to use absolute references.

If we used a relative reference (B1) rather than the absolute reference ($B$1), the copied formula would be

```
+B5*B2
```

This formula would return the wrong answer, because the sales tax rate is not in cell B2. If this point doesn't make sense, read it again until it does. Believe me, this is important stuff.

If you're really eating this stuff up, you can find more about copying formulas in Chapter 10.

And it gets even uglier

If you think that you understand the difference between relative and absolute cell references, let me throw some more things at you.

Cell references also can be mixed. That is, one part can be relative and the other can be absolute. Here's an example of a mixed-cell reference:

```
+A$1
```

In this case, the column part of the cell reference is relative, but the row part is absolute because it's preceded by a dollar sign. What happens when you copy a formula that includes a mixed-cell reference like this? Copying a formula with this particular mixed reference always results in a reference to row 1, because that part of the formula is absolute. The column part changes in a relative manner.

When you start dealing with cell references on different worksheets, you can also get involved with absolute and relative worksheet references. This works very logically, and if you understand relative and absolute references, you should have no trouble extending the concept to include sheet letters.

To help clarify things (or to muddy the waters completely), Table 8-3 shows all possible types of cell references.

Table 8-3	Types of Cell References
Example Reference	*Type of Reference*
A:A1	All relative
A:$A1	Sheet and row relative, column absolute
A:A$1	Sheet and column relative, row absolute
A:$A$1	Sheet relative, row and column absolute
$A:A1	Sheet absolute, row and column relative
$A:$A1	Sheet and column absolute, row relative
$A:A$1	Sheet and row absolute, column relative
$A:$A$1	All absolute

Even More about Formulas

I'll wrap up this chapter with a few additional random thoughts. This section can be considered lagniappe.

Controlling recalculation

As you know, a formula displays a different result if you change the values in any of the cells that the formula uses. Normally, Quattro Pro for Windows performs this recalculation automatically. Whenever you change anything in a worksheet, Quattro Pro scans all the formulas and checks to see whether any of them needs to be updated to show a new answer.

Some people, however, create very large worksheets that have hundreds or even thousands of formulas. In such a case, Quattro Pro for Windows continues to scan each formula every time you make a change in the worksheet, and Quattro Pro then makes the appropriate recalculations. But because it takes a while — even for a computer — to scan thousands of formulas, you'll notice that you often have to wait for Quattro Pro for Windows to do its scanning. The net result is that your computer slows down, and it may even take some time for what you type to show up on the screen (a delayed reaction).

Part II: Basic Stuff That You Just Can't Ignore

To speed up such a delay, tell Quattro Pro for Windows that *you* want to control when it does its recalculation. In other words, you want to turn off automatic recalculation and set it to manual recalculation. Here's how:

1. **In READY mode, choose the Property pull-down in the Property Band, and select Active Notebook.**
2. **In the dialog box that appears, select Recalc Settings — which changes the right part of the dialog box to resemble Figure 8-8.**
3. **Select the Manual option button, and then choose OK.**

To switch back to automatic recalculation, use the same steps, but select the Automatic or Background option button.

If you choose to use manual recalculation, it's up to you to remember to recalculate. You do this by pressing F9.

By the way, Quattro Pro for Windows reminds you when a recalculation is needed by displaying CALC in the status bar at the bottom of the screen. If the CALC indicator is showing, you know that you can't always trust that what's displayed on the screen (or on paper) is accurate. After you press F9, the worksheet is recalculated and the CALC indicator disappears.

If things start slowing down because you have many formulas, switch to Manual recalculation.

Figure 8-8: Here's where you tell Quattro Pro for Windows that you want to control when the notebook is calculated.

Using built-in functions

Formulas take on even more muscle when you use some of Quattro Pro for Windows' built-in @functions (pronounced "at functions"). The reason for the unusual name is that they all begin with an *at sign:* @. For example, @functions can calculate the sum of a range of cells (@SUM), compute the average (@AVG), do square roots (@SQRT), and many other more or less useful things.

I cover some of the more common @functions in the next chapter, so don't go away.

Other types of formulas

This chapter has focused exclusively on arithmetic formulas — formulas that deal with numbers and values. Two other types of formulas exist that you may run across:

- **Text formulas:** These formulas work with labels (that is, words) that you put into cells. You can do some clever things with text formulas. For example, you can create a formula such as this:

  ```
  +"Hello"&" there"
  ```

  This formula uses the ampersand (&) operator to join two strings of text — sort of like adding them together. This formula, when evaluated by Quattro Pro for Windows, displays **Hello there** in the cell.

- **Logical formulas:** These formulas return either True or False. Most people really don't have much need for logical formulas, so this book pretends that they don't exist.

If you want to learn more about formulas and see some fairly useful ones, check out Chapter 17 of this very book.

Chapter 9
Making Formulas More Functional

In This Chapter
▶ Solutions for simple formulas that just can't cut the mustard
▶ An overview of @functions — what, why, when, and how
▶ Pointing skills that deal with blocks of cells
▶ @functions that just may come in handy some day
▶ An introduction to the delightful (and useful) concept of named blocks

Formulas are great — as I tried to convince you in Chapter 8. But, as the saying goes, you ain't seen nothin' yet. This chapter tells you how to coax even more power from formulas by using some of the built-in functions that Quattro Pro for Windows provides for your analytical pleasure.

Getting Functional

Sooner or later — probably later — you'll discover that your formulas need something more than the capability to refer to cell addresses and to use numbers, awesome as that is. There's gotta be more, right? You betcha.

The developers of Quattro Pro for Windows, realizing that number crunchers like yourself may actually want to do something useful with their spreadsheets, included more than 300 @functions (374 to be exact) to help you out.

> ### So what's with the at sign (@)?
>
> The at sign (@) is weird — I admit it. But the built-in functions in Quattro Pro for Windows are called @functions (pronounced *at functions*). The at sign is used to distinguish its functions from other information that you may type into a cell.
>
> The reason for the name is mainly historical (and slightly hysterical). You see, the original version of Quattro Pro, developed a long time ago, was modeled after Lotus 1-2-3. For some reason, the developers of 1-2-3 used @ to distinguish functions from other information. Because the designers of Quattro Pro wanted their product to be compatible with 1-2-3, they also went with the @ sign. Don't worry; it doesn't take long to get used to this weirdness. And besides, the at sign makes it very easy to spot an @function stuck in a long formula.
>
> The vast majority of the @functions aren't covered in this chapter, because they are beyond the scope of this book. Some are for very specialized purposes. Others, frequently called *@dysfunctions,* are just plain worthless.

OK, what is an @function?

Think of an @function as a shortcut for telling Quattro Pro for Windows to do something (usually using information in other cells). For example, there's an @function called @AVG, which computes the average of the numbers in a block of cells. This function saves you the trouble of adding up the numbers in the block and then dividing by the number of elements in the list. Another example is the @PMT function, which produces the monthly payment on a loan. (You only need to supply the loan amount, the interest rate, and the length of the loan.)

Using the @functions is like having your own personal calculator built into your personal computer. The calculating capabilities of the @functions stretch well beyond yours or mine. As a matter of fact, many @functions enable you to perform some feat that simply can't be done in any other way. @SQRT, for example, returns the square root of a number. Try to do that without using an @function!

A functional example

I start with an example so that you can see how to use @functions. Study the notebook in Figure 9-1. This notebook contains a block of numbers for which you need a total. Your knowledge level so far produces the following formula:

```
+B1+B2+B3+B4+B5+B6+B7+B8+B9+B10+B11+B12+B13+B14+B15
```

Chapter 9: Making Formulas More Functional

This formula certainly gets the job done, but a much easier and quicker way to create a formula is by using — you guessed it — an @ function. In this case, the @SUM function does the trick just fine. Instead of typing the preceding unwieldy formula, simply type the following @ function into any cell (cell B16 is a good place for it):

```
@SUM(B1..B15)
```

This formula consists of a single @function. The stuff in the parentheses is called the @function's *arguments* (more about arguments later). In this case, there is just one argument, and it is a block of cells.

TIP

You already may have discovered the Toolbar button in Figure 9-2 that automatically adds up cells; this is called the SpeedSum button. If you click the SpeedSum button when the cell selector is in a blank cell, Quattro Pro for Windows analyzes the surrounding cells in your notebook and inserts an @SUM function. In other words, it does the dirty work for you.

Cells, blocks, and cell blocks

A cell is a cell, but a group of contiguous (consecutive) cells is a *block*. A cell block is a living unit in a prison and has absolutely nothing to do with this discussion.

Figure 9-1:
An @function enables you to determine the sum of these numbers.

	A	B
1	Date	Num Sold
2	August 3, 1994	93
3	August 4, 1994	221
4	August 5, 1994	243
5	August 6, 1994	290
6	August 7, 1994	183
7	August 8, 1994	277
8	August 9, 1994	289
9	August 10, 1994	304
10	August 11, 1994	189
11	August 12, 1994	200
12	August 13, 1994	205
13	August 14, 1994	211
14	August 15, 1994	304
15	August 16, 1994	198
16	Month-toDate	

Figure 9-2:
The SpeedSum button creates a formula automatically by using the @SUM function.

An example of a block is the cells A1 through A10 in a notebook. You can specify a block of cells in a formula by using the following format:

```
FirstCell..LastCell
```

FirstCell and *LastCell* represent normal cell addresses. A *block reference* is simply two cell addresses separated by two periods (for example, A1..A12). The reason for using two periods goes back to the way the original Lotus 1-2-3 was designed. (Quattro Pro was modeled after 1-2-3, you know.) It's just another strange practice that you'll have to live with.

I'll let you in on a big secret: You can use only *one* period in a block reference. Quattro Pro for Windows automatically adds the other one. Knowing this could save you countless milliseconds over the course of your life.

The following examples of block references give you an idea of how to interpret them:

A1..A12   12 cells, beginning in cell A1 and extending down to and including cell A12

A1..Z1   26 cells, beginning in cell A1 and extending across to and including cell Z1

A1..B12   24 cells, beginning in cell A1, going down to cell A12, back up to include cell B1, and then going down to cell B12
(In other words, this block consists of 2 columns and 12 rows.)

Chapter 9: Making Formulas More Functional

Quattro Pro for Windows also deals with a group of cells that is not contiguous. A group of noncontiguous cells is called a noncontiguous block (great name, eh?). You can refer to a noncontiguous block by using a comma to separate the blocks or cell references that make up the noncontiguous block. For example, here's an @function that refers to cell A1 and the block C1..G1:

```
@SUM(A1,C1..G1)
```

This formula will add the value in cells A1, C1, D1, E1, F1, G1. In other words it skips over cell B1 in the first row.

Adding pages to cell references

If the reference in your @function happens to extend across multiple pages (or if you're referring to cells on a different page), you have to tack on a page reference so that Quattro Pro for Windows knows which pages to use. You simply precede the block reference with a page letter and a colon (or two page letters separated by two dots), as illustrated in the following examples:

A:A1..A12	A block of 12 cells, all on page A, starting in cell A1 and going to cell A12 (In this case, use the page letters only if the @function is on a page other than page A.)
A..C:A1..A12	A three-dimensional block of 36 cells, beginning in cell A1 of page A and extending to cell A12 on page C

Entering @functions

As you may recall from Chapter 8, you can build a formula either by typing it into a cell or by pointing to the cells that you want to include in the formula. Use the same two processes for entering @functions into your cells.

The direct approach

Entering an @function into a cell involves, well, entering an @function into a cell. In other words, if you want to add the numbers in the block A1..C12 and have the answer appear in cell A13, type the following into cell A13:

```
@SUM(A1..C12)
```

Part II: Basic Stuff That You Just Can't Ignore

> **TIP:** You can type the @function in uppercase, lowercase, or mixed-case characters. The case doesn't matter at all, because Quattro Pro for Windows always converts the letters to uppercase, anyway.

The pointing method

Sometimes it may be faster to point out the cell or block (called an argument) rather than to type it. To point out a block, using the example in the preceding section, do the following:

1. **Move the cell pointer to cell A13.**
2. **Type @SUM(**
3. **Use the arrow keys to move to cell A1, the first cell in the block.**

   Notice that the edit line displays the cell.
4. **Press Shift and hold it down.**

   Holding down the Shift key makes the first cell "stick" so that you can point to the last cell in the block (this procedure is also known as *anchoring* the cell).
5. **Use the arrow keys to move to the last cell in the block, cell C12.**

   You'll notice that the block you are pointing to is highlighted. Also notice that @SUM(A1..C12 is now displayed in the input line and in cell A13.
6. **Type a closing parenthesis and press Enter.**

> **QUATTRO PRO 6:** Actually, the closing parenthesis is optional — if you prefer, you can just press Enter. If you do omit the closing parenthesis, Quattro Pro for Windows automatically puts it in for you — just another example of how this program is trying to be your friend.

> **TIP:** Rather than go through all the preceding steps with your keyboard, you can simply click and drag the mouse over the block after you have typed **@SUM(** in cell A13. As you do so, Quattro Pro for Windows displays the selected block in the edit line. After you're finished, type the closing parenthesis in cell C12 (or just press Enter and let Quattro Pro for Windows do the work). If you're using a mouse, you can also click on the little check-mark in the input line as a substitute for pressing Enter.

Let's have an argument

The information that an @function uses to perform its calculations is called its *argument*. Arguments are always enclosed in parentheses, directly following the @function name. You should remember the following information about @function arguments:

- Some @functions need more than one argument. In these cases, the arguments are separated with a comma.
- Some @functions need a single cell for an argument, and others need a block reference.
- Some formulas need numbers for arguments, and others need text (or labels).
- You can usually use a normal number or text in place of a cell reference.
- You also can use a block name as an argument for a block reference, or a cell name as an argument for a cell reference.

The following examples illustrate how the different arguments work in the @SUM function:

@SUM(A1..A12)	Adds the numbers in the block A1..A12
@SUM(A1)	Displays the number in cell A1 (not a very useful formula, but it is valid)
@SUM(A1,A2,A3,A4)	Adds the numbers in cells A1, A2, A3, and A4. You can do this calculation more efficiently by using @SUM(A1..A4)
@SUM(1,2,3,4)	Adds the numbers 1, 2, 3, and 4 and displays the result (which is 10)
@SUM(A1..A12)/2	Adds the numbers in the block A1..A12 and then divides the result by 2
@SUM(A..C:A1..A12)	Adds the numbers in the three-dimensional block, starting in cell A1 on page A and extending through cell A12 on page C (the third page)

Editing @functions

It should come as no surprise that you can edit formulas that contain @functions. You tell Quattro Pro for Windows that you want to begin editing the contents of a cell by using any of these signals:

- Pressing F2
- Clicking the input line with your mouse
- Double-clicking the cell

Part II: Basic Stuff That You Just Can't Ignore

When you use any of these signals, the formula is displayed in the cell (and in the input line). Then you can use the normal editing keys (arrow keys, Backspace, Delete) to change the formula. After you get the formula right, press Enter (or click on the checkmark in the input line).

Insert @function here, insert @function here!

With 374 to choose from, how can you possibly remember the names and correct spelling of all the @functions? Well, chances are you'll only be using a small percentage of them — but you can get a complete list when the need arises.

When you're entering a formula and need an @function, you can just click on the @ button on the input line. If the @function is at the start of your formula, this button won't be visible, so you must press F2 first, or just double-click on the cell. Either of these methods will display the @ button.

Clicking on the @ button displays the dialog box shown in Figure 9-3.

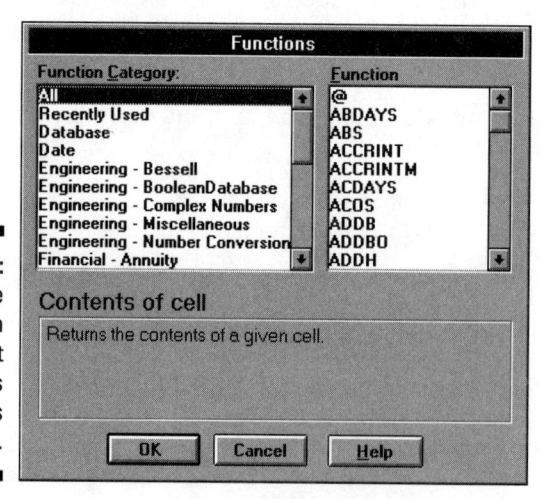

Figure 9-3: Clicking the @ button in the input line gives you this dialog box.

The @function dialog box lists all of the @function categories. So start by double-clicking on a category to narrow your search. Let's say you're helping your boss's son with his trigonometry homework (it never hurts to know the boss's kids). He needs to calculate the tangent of a number that happens to be in cell A1 of your notebook. You think Quattro Pro for Windows might be able to help, so you go through the following steps.

Chapter 9: Making Formulas More Functional   155

1. **Move the cell selector to cell B1**

   This cell will hold the answer.

2. **Double-click the cell.**

   This step opens the input line and displays the little buttons.

3. **Click on the @ button to get the dialog box that lists all of the @function categories.**

4. **Scroll through the list of categories.**

   Since there's not a category called Trigonometric, click the Numeric category (it seems like a logical place for it). The dialog box changes and now lists all of the @functions in the Numeric category (see Figure 9-4).

5. **Scroll through this list and eventually you'll see TAN.**

   TAN sounds like it might be what you're looking for (however, it might be an @function that calculates the amount of time it takes to get a suntan).

6. **Just to make sure, glance down at the bottom of the dialog box for a discription.**

   Sure enough. That's the one. You can also click on the Help button to get a help window that will tell you everything you need to know about the @TAN function. For example, you'll discover that the @TAN function requires its argument to be in *radians,* not *degrees.* You need to know this; otherwise you will get the wrong result.

7. **Click OK in the dialog box.**

   Quattro Pro for Windows inserts @TAN(for you).

8. **Use the mouse and click on cell A1.**

   That cell reference will be inserted as the argument for @TAN.

9. **Click on the checkmark button on the input line.**

   This step provides the closing parenthesis and enters the formula. The formula in cell B1 now returns the tangent of the number in cell A1 (which is assumed to be in radians, not degrees).

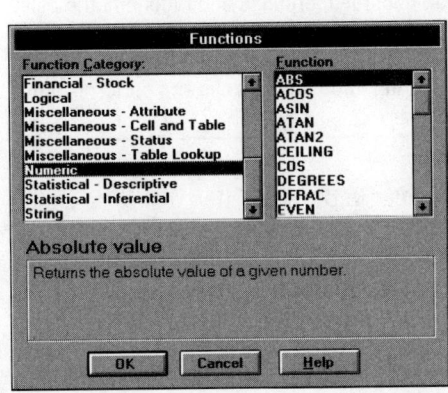

Figure 9-4: A list of all @functions in the Numeric category.

Part II: Basic Stuff That You Just Can't Ignore

If the value in cell A1 is in degrees, you can use two @functions in your formula: one to convert degrees to radians and another to calculate the tangent. The formula you need in order to accomplish these two functions is

```
@TAN(@RADIANS(A1))
```

This is an example of a *nested* @function (more about this later). Quattro Pro for Windows first converts the value in cell A1 to radians using the @RADIAN function, and then Quattro Pro uses the result of this conversion to calculate the tangent.

@function Categories

Quattro Pro for Windows divides its laundry list of @functions into eight main categories, many of which also have subcategories. These categories and subcategories make it easier to narrow your search when you need an @function but don't know its name. The @function categories are shown in Table 9-1.

Table 9-1   @ Function Categories

Category	What It Does
Database	Performs queries and calculations in database tables
Date	Calculates values that deal with dates and times
Engineering	Performs engineering calculations and other advanced mathematical operations
Financial	Deals with investments, annuities, securities, depreciation, cash flows, and loans
Logical	Calculates the results of logical or conditional formulas
Miscellaneous	Provides cell information, lookups, and so on
Numeric	Performs mathematical operations and trigonometric calculations
Statistical	Performs statistical calculations
String	Provides information about text in cells and performs other operations on text

The categories in this table appear in the @function dialog box, many with subcategories. In addition, there's a category called All that lists all @functions in alphabetical order. Another category shows a list of the functions you used most recently — handy for repeat offenders.

The on-line help feature has a great deal of information on every @function. Use it to determine which @function is best for the job at hand.

Some Useful Numeric @functions

So far, you know about the @SUM function, and I also mentioned the ever-popular @AVG function (which works just like @SUM, except that it returns the average of the cells in its argument). Because you're probably yearning for more, I won't keep you in suspense any longer. Keep reading for details on some more useful @functions.

@MAX

Suppose that you've started a notebook with the monthly sales figures for the people in your organization. The notebook may look something like Figure 9-5. You want to give an award to the top salesperson of the month. You can scan the numbers and try to figure out which number is highest — or you can use the @MAX function. Just type the following formula into the cell where you want to display the maximum sales figure:

```
@MAX(B2..B19)
```

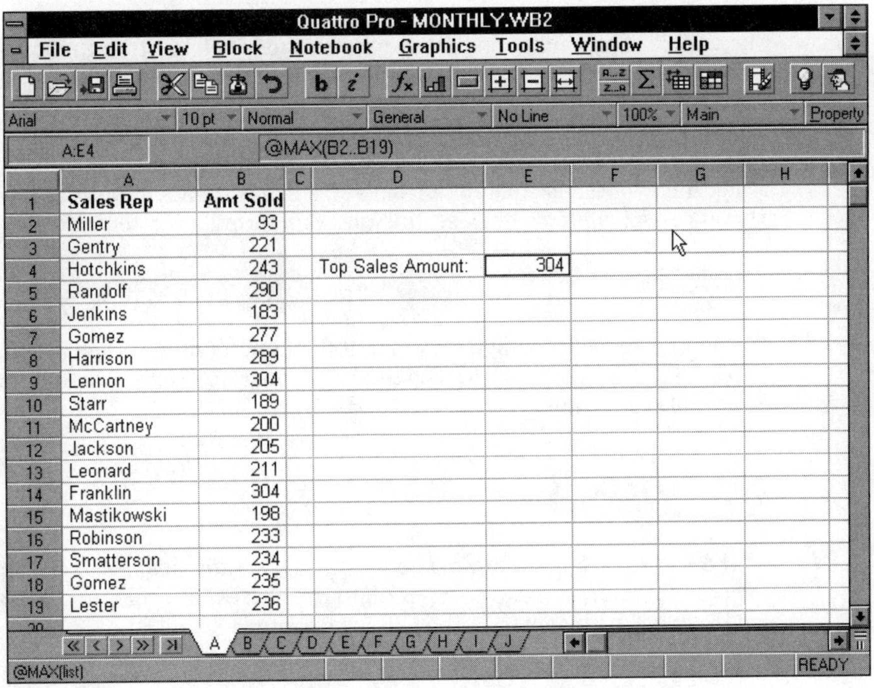

Figure 9-5: The @MAX function tells you the highest sales figure.

@MIN

If you need to locate the lowest sales volume in the list — to determine which underachiever gets your monthly private motivational talk — you can use the following @MIN function, which works like @MAX but displays the lowest sales figure:

    @MIN(B2..B19)

@SQRT

The @SQRT function is a shortened version of the term *square root*. The square root of a number is the number that, when multiplied by itself, gives you the original number. For example, 4 is the square root of 16 because 4 x 4 = 16.

You can calculate the square root of the value in cell A1 by entering the following formula in any cell:

    @SQRT(A1)

If cell A1 contained the value 225, the formula would return 15. @SQRT is an example of an @function that requires a single cell for its argument — which is perfectly logical, because it doesn't make sense to calculate the square root of an entire block of cells.

Here's another example that involves trigonometry (more specifically, calculating the hypotenuse of a right triangle). If cell A1 contain the triangle's height and cell A2 contains its base, the following formula will return the hypotenuse:

    @SQRT(A1^2+A2^2)

You may recall from high school that the hypotenuse is equal to the square root of the height squared plus the base squared. That's exactly what this formula calculates.

@ROUND

The @ROUND function rounds off its argument and displays the result. If cell A1 contains 12.67, you can round it off to the nearest integer and display the result (13) in cell B1 by entering the following formula in cell B1:

    @ROUND(A1,0)

Chapter 9: Making Formulas More Functional

Does this formula look different than you expected? To produce the correct results in your notebook, this function needs two arguments. The first argument tells the program what cell you want to round off; the second argument tells Quattro Pro for Windows how many decimal places to round the number to. In this case, the second argument is 0, which tells the program to round off the number in cell A1 to no decimal places.

To round off the number to the first decimal place, 12.7, change the formula to look like this:

```
@ROUND(A1,1)
```

REMEMBER: Manipulating the value in a cell by using an @function affects the actual value of the cell. For example, after you change the value of 12.67 to 12 with the @ROUND function, the value of the cell becomes 12, and you lose the decimal value. Using @functions to manipulate the value in a cell is very different than using numeric formatting, which only changes the way the number looks.

@functions for Dates and Times

WARNING! The @functions that deal with dates and times get their information from your computer's internal clock. Make sure that your computer's clock is set properly, or these functions return the wrong dates and times. Procedures for setting computer clocks vary, so check your hardware manual.

If you want to enter dates into your notebook, make sure that you read the next sidebar. After you understand how Quattro Pro for Windows works with dates, you can do some interesting things with the date functions.

@DATE

You can either enter a date into a cell with the formats you learned in the sidebar or you can use the @DATE function. The @DATE function has three parts to its argument: a year, a month, and a day. To enter December 25, 1994 into a cell, use the following formula:

```
@DATE(94,12,25)
```

The program displays the number 34693, its special date number for the date that you entered. To make the date number appear as a date, select Date from the Style drop-down on the Property band (or right-click the cell and use the Object Inspector dialog box).

> ## How about a date?
>
> Adventurous types may have discovered that Quattro Pro for Windows doesn't always know what to do after you enter a date into a cell. Try entering the date *12-25-94* into cell A1. It looks pretty good, but try using that date in a formula. For example enter +A1+1 into cell A2. This formula should return 12-26-94, right? Well, it actually returns 1. Quattro Pro for Windows misinterpreted your date as a label.
>
> Now try putting *12/25/94* into cell A1. Now Quattro Pro for Windows recognizes it is a date and the formula in cell A2 returns 34694 — which is its serial number for December 26, 1994. To make cell B1 look like a real date, you need to change the numeric format of the cell to one of the date formats. Select Date from the Style drop-down on the Property band (or right-click the cell and use the Object Inspector dialog box).
>
> Because Quattro Pro for Windows doesn't recognize all date formats, you must enter dates by using one of the formats the program recognizes, such as 7/31/91 or 31-Jul-91. If you leave off the year (as in 31-Jul), Quattro Pro for Windows assumes the current year.
>
> Quattro Pro for Windows stores dates in a special number system in which each number corresponds to a day. The date number system starts with January 1, 1600 (-109,571) and goes up to December 31, 3199 (474,816) — more than half a million days, or 1,601 years — enough for even the most aggressive budget projection. Day 0 happens to be December 30, 1899.

@TODAY

This function doesn't need an argument. It simply returns the date number that corresponds to the current date stored in the computer's clock. For example, if you entered @TODAY into a cell on October 6, 1994, the function would return 34613 — the date number that corresponds to that date. If you save the notebook and load it again the next day, the function then would return 34614. In other words, @TODAY always returns the current date.

@TIME

Like the @DATE function, the @TIME function also has three parts to its argument: an hour, a minute, and a second. To enter 5:30 p.m. into a cell, use the following formula:

```
@TIME(17,30,0)
```

Why the number 17? Remember that in 24-hour time, 5:00 p.m. is 5 hours past 12:00 noon, so that you add 12 + 5 to get 17 hours. The formula represents 17 hours, 30 minutes, and 0 seconds into the day, or 5:30 p.m. If you enter this @TIME function into a cell, Quattro Pro for Windows displays .7291666667. To see this number as readable time, right-click on the cell and use the Object Inspector dialog box to select an appropriate numeric format.

> ### You got the time?
>
> Quattro Pro for Windows not only deals with dates, but also handles time by extending the date number concept to include decimal values. As you already know, the date number 34963 corresponds to December 25, 1994. By adding a decimal point to the number, you also can work with times during that day. For example, 34963.5 corresponds to 12:00 noon (halfway through Christmas Day, 1994); 34963.1 corresponds to 2:24 a.m. (one-tenth of the way through the day).
>
> Because there are 86,400 seconds in a day, one second works out to be .000011574074074 in this serial number format. One minute, on the other hand, equates to .0006944444. And one hour is .041666667. Therefore, to express 1:00 a.m. on December 25, 1994, you enter 34963.041666667 into a cell. If all these numbers have your head reeling, don't fret. Using the @TIME function makes it all relatively painless.

Combined @functions in Formulas

So far, the example formulas I've shown have consisted only of single @functions. You can, however, combine @functions in formulas. Take a look at the following formula, for example:

```
@SUM(A1..A10)+@SUM(C1..C10)
```

Here, the formula is simply taking the sum of the numbers in block A1..A10 and adding the result to the sum of the numbers in block C1..C10. Another way of looking at the formula is that it's taking the sum of block A1..C10 but skipping block B1..B10. Therefore, the following formula produces the same result:

```
@SUM(A1..C10)-@SUM(B1..B10)
```

You also can work with dates and times in a formula. Suppose that you want to know the number of days between January 1, 1990, and July 16, 1994. Use the following formula to get the desired results:

```
@DATE(94,7,16)-@DATE(90,1,1)
```

In this case, it may be better to put the date formulas into separate cells (such as A1 and A2) and then use a simpler formula (such as +A2-A1) to do the subtraction. By putting the date formulas into separate cells, you easily can change the dates without having to deal with a more complex formula. In other words, you are making the spreadsheet more general, a good idea to keep in mind.

The nesting instinct revisited

The fact is, you can create some very complex formulas by using @functions. You even can use @functions as arguments for other @functions, a concept known as *nested @functions* (a topic that's for the birds).

Figure 9-6, for example, has values in column A, formulas in column B, and a nested @function in cell D13. The formula in cell B3 is @ROUND(A3,0), which rounds the value in cell A3 to zero decimal places. Rows 3 – 9 in column B each have similar formulas that round the values in their corresponding column A cells. The formula for the nested @ function in cell D12 is as follows:

```
@ROUND(@SUM(A3..A9),0)
```

How can you interpret this complex formula? Quattro Pro for Windows tackles the formula as follows: First, the program evaluates the @SUM function and stores the answer in its memory. Then it uses this answer as the first argument for the @ROUND function and combines the answer with the second argument for the @ROUND function (which is 0). The program then displays the final answer in cell D12.

> **TIP**
>
> Rounding off the sum of the values does not produce the same result as summing the rounded-off values. If you don't believe this, examine Figure 9-6 again and take a look at the formulas in cell D10 and cell D11.

Testing conditions

One of the more useful @functions is the @IF function. This essentially allows your formulas to make decisions based on values in your notebook. The @IF function requires the following three arguments:

- A condition to test
- What to display if the condition is true
- What to display if the condition is false

The following example is designed to test whether the number in cell A1 is positive or negative:

```
@IF(A1>0,"Positive","Negative or zero")
```

Notice that the three arguments are separated by commas. The first argument is the condition, which in this case is asking whether the number in cell A1 is greater than zero. If the number is greater than zero, the formula displays the word `Positive`; if the number is zero or less than zero, the formula displays the words `Negative or zero`.

Chapter 9: Making Formulas More Functional   163

	A	B	C	D	E	F
1						
2	Value	Rounded				
3	12.4	12.0				
4	14.5	15.0				
5	18.7	19.0				
6	22.3	22.0				
7	11.2	11.0				
8	13.1	13.0				
9	13.4	13.0				
10			Sum of values	105.6	<---	@SUM(A3..A9)
11			Sum of rounded values	105.0	<---	@SUM(B3..B9)
12			Rounded sum	106.0	<---	@ROUND(@SUM(A3..A9),0)

Figure 9-6: The formula in cell D12 contains a nested @function.

Suppose that you want to know whether the number in a cell is positive, negative, or zero (three responses — an added twist to the same concept). Now you need to use a nested @IF function to produce the desired results. Before you read the explanation, try to figure out the following formula on your own to see how it works:

```
@IF(A1>0,"Positive",@IF(A1<0,"Negative","Zero"))
```

Quattro Pro for Windows first tests to see whether the number in cell A1 is greater than zero. If it is, the program responds with the word Positive and is done with the formula. But if the contents of cell A1 are not greater than zero, the program goes to the third part of the first @IF argument and discovers another @IF function there, which it proceeds to evaluate. This second (nested) @IF function checks to see whether the value of cell A1 is less than zero. If it is, the program responds with the word Negative. If it is not, the program responds with the final choice of Zero.

If you understand how the nested @IF function works, congratulations! You're well on your way to being a more-than-adequate Quattro Pro for Windows user.

Naming Cells and Blocks

Naming cells and blocks may not be absolutely necessary for your well-being, but you may find that it makes your spreadsheeting life easier. You can give a meaningful name to any cell or block (you'll learn how to do this later). After doing so, you can use that name wherever you normally use a cell or block reference.

An example

Suppose that you name cell F2 *num_employees,* because the value in this cell is the total number of employees. Using meaningful names is a good idea, but it's not a requirement. (Quattro Pro for Windows doesn't mind if you name the cell *kh82z1x7y,* but that name certainly doesn't help you to understand your spreadsheet any better.) Cell M12, named *total_salary,* has — you guessed it — the total salary of your employees. Now assume that you want to determine the average salary of your employees. After you choose a cell in the notebook, you can enter the following formula in the cell by using the name of the cell:

```
+total_salary/num_employees
```

You also can write the formula +M12/F2 to make the same calculations. However, the formula with names is much easier to read; anyone who looks at the formula has a pretty good idea of what it does.

Another example

You also can give a name to an entire block. For example, if block G1..G12 is named *expenses,* you then can write the following formula that adds the expenses of the entire block, using the name of the block alone:

```
@SUM(expenses)
```

The formula @SUM(G1..G12) also requests the sum of the block but does not indicate what the formula is adding. Not only does using the name of the block simplify your formula, but it also makes the formula clear to anyone who sees it.

How to name cells and blocks

Naming a cell or block is easy. Just follow these steps:

1. **Move the cell pointer to the cell you want to name.**

   For this example, move the cell pointer to cell C9 to name a single cell.

2. **Select the Block⇨Names command.**

   Quattro Pro for Windows pops up the dialog box.

3. **Type interest in the Name box and choose the Add button.**

   Quattro Pro adds the name to the list of names in the notebook.

4. **Select the Close button to exit the dialog box.**

Chapter 9: Making Formulas More Functional

You also can get to the Block Names dialog box by right-clicking on a cell or selected block and then choosing Names from the shortcut menu. Yet another way is to press Ctrl+F3.

To name a block of cells, you can either begin by selecting the entire block you want to name, or you can select the block from the dialog box after you issue the Block➪Names command.

Keep the following information in mind as you go about naming cells and blocks:

- Names can be up to 64 characters long and must begin with a letter. Don't use any characters that are math operators (such as plus or minus). Also, avoid creating names that look like cell addresses. For example, Quattro Pro might confuse a block named *ab1* with cell AB1. You can use spaces in your names, but it's not a good idea.
- If you already have one or more names in your notebook, Quattro Pro for Windows displays a list of these names in the Block Names dialog box. By choosing a name from this list, you can see the cell or block it refers to in the Block box.
- You can press F5 to jump to a named cell or block.

Chapter 10

Making Changes to Your Work (and Living to Talk about It)

In This Chapter
▶ Cutting and pasting (that is, moving) cells and blocks of cells
▶ Copying cells and blocks of cells (or, how to make many from one)
▶ Changing column widths to avoid the asterisk problem
▶ Making rows taller
▶ Inserting and deleting rows and columns
▶ Turning horizontal data into vertical data — and vice versa
▶ Using Find and Replace to make many changes with little effort
▶ Sorting a block of data — and all kinds of options you have

If you're like most people, you'll spend a large part of your spreadsheeting time changing things that you've already done. This activity is perfectly normal, and it's not a sign of an indecisive personality disorder. (I don't think so, anyway. On second thought, it might be. Well, then again, I'm not sure.) Anyway, you'll soon discover that when you start making changes to a notebook, it's far too easy to take something that used to work and somehow mess it up so it doesn't work anymore.

Therefore, it's in your best interest to understand what goes on behind the scenes when you set out to change something in your notebook. This advice especially applies to copying, cutting, and pasting cells and blocks — particularly when they contain formulas. That's why this chapter has more than its share of Warning icons.

Types of Changes You Can Make

So what do I mean by making changes to a notebook? Here are some examples:

- ✔ You spent five minutes creating a killer formula that does magic with a column of numbers. You have 20 more columns that need the same formula applied to them. What to do? Copy the formula so it works for the other blocks of cells.

- ✔ You have a nice table of numbers, but you fell asleep on the keyboard and put the table about 50 rows below where it should be. So you need to move it up to a more reasonable location in the notebook. This task is known as cutting and pasting.

- ✔ You're just about ready to turn in your department budget when you realize that you forgot to enter a budget item (Pet Neutering) that should go right between the categories Outboard Motor Repair and Quilting Supplies. You need to insert a new row to make room for it.

- ✔ Your boss informs you that you can no longer budget for office mud baths. Eventually, regardless of the resentment you feel, you must zap the entire Mud Bath row in your budget notebook.

- ✔ You have a great notebook, but the numbers are all crammed together and hard to read. You want to widen some of the columns.

- ✔ You have several labels entered in a column — and you realize that you should have put them in a row. You need to transpose these labels, and you don't feel like typing them all again.

- ✔ Marketing just informed you that they changed the name of one of your company's products from Sugar Munchies to Health Munchies. Your notebook has dozens of labels with this product name in it, and you need to change every occurrence of *Sugar* to *Health*. You can do it manually — or let Quattro Pro for Windows do it for you with its Edit⇨Find and Replace command.

- ✔ You just spent two hours entering all of your sales figures in alphabetical order by sales rep name. Then your boss informs you that these names must be in descending order by sales amount. Unless you like to redo your work, you need to sort this block of cells.

The preceding list describes just some of the changes that people make to their notebooks. The rest of this chapter tells you how to make these types of changes — without destroying what you've already done and causing more work for yourself.

> **TIP:** When you start making changes to a notebook, remember that you can reverse the effects of most things that you do by selecting Edit⇨Undo (or Ctrl+Z) immediately after you make the change. But you have to issue this command before you do *anything* else. Therefore, it's good to get into the habit of examining what you did before you move on to something else. It's also good to have a backup copy of your notebook saved to a floppy disk (or saved under a different name).

Cutting and Pasting — Scissors and Glue Not Required

When you enter something into a cell, it's not stuck there for life. You can cut it and paste it anywhere else on the notebook — or even paste it to a different notebook. In other words, if you want to move something from one place to another, you cut it and then paste it.

How cutting and pasting works

If you're going to use Windows, you have to understand the concept of *cutting and pasting.* You cut something out of your notebook, and then you paste it somewhere else. This cutting and pasting involves the infamous Windows Clipboard. (See the sidebar "More about the Windows Clipboard" for additional information on this Clipboard business). When you tell Quattro Pro for Windows to cut, it takes whatever is selected at the time (a cell or a block), removes it from the notebook, and puts a copy of it on the Clipboard. Then, when you tell Quattro Pro for Windows to paste, it takes what's in the Clipboard and pastes it to your current selection (usually a different cell or a block). Once you understand this concept, you should have no problems with moving things.

> **WARNING!** When you paste a cell or block and the area that you're pasting to already contains something, Quattro Pro for Windows overwrites the cells with the pasted information — without warning. So if you have some important material in your notebook, be careful when moving things around.

Part II: Basic Stuff That You Just Can't Ignore

> ### More about the Windows Clipboard
>
> As this chapter so eloquently describes, copying and moving within Quattro Pro for Windows uses something called the Windows Clipboard. Basically, this Clipboard is an area of your computer's memory that's sort of a temporary holding spot. So when you cut or copy a cell or a block, Quattro Pro for Windows puts the information on the Clipboard. When you paste something to a cell or block, Quattro Pro for Windows takes whatever happens to be on the Clipboard and pastes it wherever you want it.
>
> The Clipboard can hold only one thing at a time. So if you copy a cell or block to the Clipboard, it replaces what's already there (if anything). The Clipboard is pretty versatile, and it can hold all sorts of information — the contents of a single cell, a block of cells, an entire graph, or part of a graph.
>
> The neat thing about the Clipboard, though, is that all Windows programs have access to it. This means that you can copy a block of cells from Quattro Pro for Windows and then paste it into your Windows word processing program. The Clipboard works as the intermediary. Learning how the Clipboard works is useful in all the Windows applications you run.
>
> Microsoft Windows includes a program that simply displays what's currently on the Clipboard. This program is called Clipboard Viewer, and you can probably find it in the Windows Program Manager program group called Main. It's not necessary to run this program in order to use the Clipboard to cut, copy, and paste, but you may find it interesting. When you run this program, it simply displays whatever happens to be on the Clipboard. Just for fun, you might want to run the Clipboard program alongside of Quattro Pro for Windows. Then, when you copy something, you can see it show up immediately on the Clipboard.

TIP When you're dealing with the Windows Clipboard, you can save yourself a great deal of time by getting into the habit of using shortcut keys or Toolbar buttons instead of menus. The shortcut keys and Toolbar buttons for cutting, pasting, and copying are shown in Table 10-1.

Table 10-1   Shortcut Keys and Toolbar Buttons

Menu Command	Shortcut Key	Toolbar Button
Edit⇨Cut	Ctrl+X	✂
Edit⇨Paste	Ctrl+V	📋
Edit⇨Copy	Ctrl+C	📑

Chapter 10: Making Changes to Your Work (and Living to Talk about It)

> **TIP:** Throughout this chapter, I talk about the Edit⇨Cut, Edit⇨Paste, and Edit⇨Copy commands. A faster way to access these commands is by right-clicking after you make a selection. This brings up a shortcut menu, which lets you choose Cut, Paste, or Copy.

Why cut and paste things?

Let's say you entered a list of numbers into a notebook column and then discovered that you forgot to leave space for a heading. You *could* insert a new row and place the heading in the new row. But if you have other information in the first row, inserting a new row would also shift *that* information down (which you may not want to do). Therefore, the easiest solution is to move the list of numbers down one row — cut it and then paste it. Another reason to move things around in a notebook is simply to organize it better. We all change our minds occasionally, right?

Cutting and pasting a cell

Here's how to move the contents of a cell from one place to another. We'll assume that we're moving the number in cell A1 to its new home in cell B1. In other words, you're cutting the information from A1 and then pasting it into B1.

1. **Start by moving the cell selector to the cell that you want to move (cell A1, in this case).**

2. **Select the Edit⇨Cut command (or press Ctrl+X).**

   Quattro Pro for Windows removes the contents of the cell and places them on the Windows Clipboard.

3. **Next, move to the new location — which is cell B1 in this example.**

4. **Select Edit⇨Paste (or press Ctrl+V).**

   Quattro Pro for Windows puts the contents of the Clipboard in the selected cell.

It should be clear that using cut and paste on a single cell is no great time-saver — unless the cell contains a long label or a formula. If you just have a value or a short label, it may be faster to delete it and retype it somewhere else. On the other hand, if you're a poor typist, using the Clipboard keeps you from making a typing mistake when retyping the entry.

Cutting and pasting a block

The real value of cutting and pasting becomes apparent when you start dealing with blocks of cells. Moving a block of cells is very similar to moving one cell. Start by selecting the entire block you want to move, and select the Edit➪Cut command (or press Ctrl+X) to remove the block and put in on the Clipboard. Next, move the cell pointer to the new location (you need to select only the upper left cell in the new block — not the entire block). Select Edit➪Paste (or press Ctrl+V), and Quattro Pro for Windows will retrieve the information from the Clipboard and put it in the new location you specified.

You can relocate dozens, hundreds, or even thousands of cells using cut and paste.

Cutting and pasting formulas

You can move cells that contain formulas just like you move other cells. So if you cut and paste a cell that has a formula such as +A1+A2, the formula continues to refer to those same cells no matter where you move it, which is almost always what you want to happen.

Moving cells that contain formulas does not change the cell references in the formulas.

The E-Z way to move things

Now that you know how to use the Clipboard to cut and paste information, you might be interested in learning another, easier way to move cells or blocks — a way that uses a mouse. This method's really easy. Simply select the cell or block that you want to move, drag it to where you want to put it, and then drop it in place.

The only thing you have to remember is that the mouse pointer has to look like a hand before you can drag a cell or block. To get the mouse pointer to turn into a hand, just move it to the selection, click, and wait about a half-second. When it turns into a hand, you can then drag your selection to its new location (you're actually dragging an outline of the cell or block.). When you release the mouse button, the cell or block will appear in its new location, and you're done. Figure 10-1 is an action shot showing a block of cells being moved.

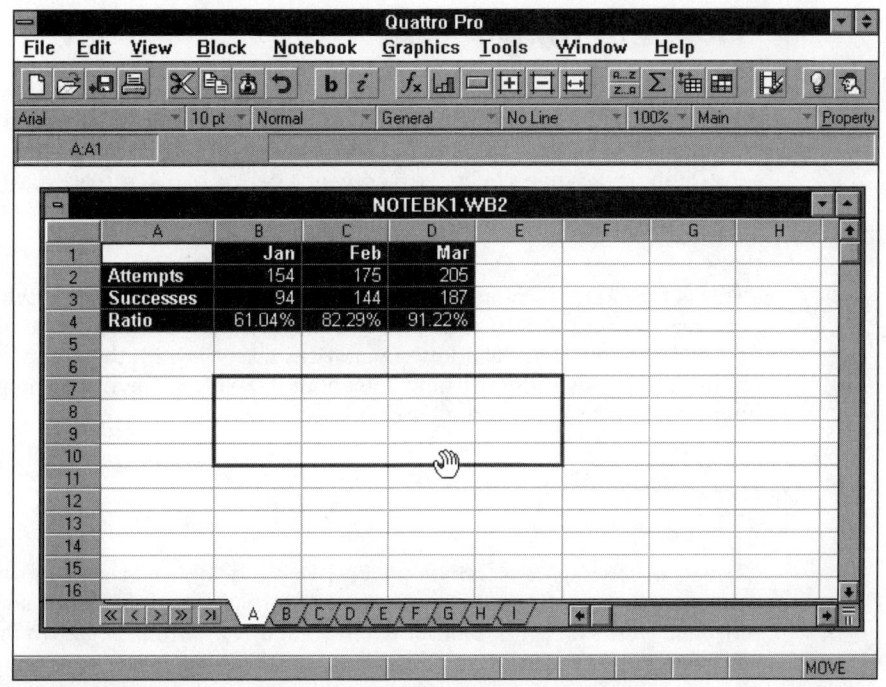

Chapter 10: Making Changes to Your Work (and Living to Talk about It) *173*

Figure 10-1: An easy way to move a cell or block is to drag it — but dragging works only when the mouse pointer looks like a hand.

TIP

If drag-and-drop moving isn't working, it's probably because this feature is disabled. To enable drag-and-drop, select the Tools⇨User Setup command, and make sure the Drag-and-drop cells option is checked.

Copying Things Things Things

One of the most common spreadsheet operations is copying. Here are your three options when it comes to copying:

- Copy a single cell to another cell
- Copy a single cell to a block of cells
- Copy a block of cells to another area

How copying works

As you might expect, copying is rather similar to moving — and both operations use the Clipboard. The difference, however, is that Quattro Pro for Windows leaves the copied cell or block contents intact when it puts them on the Clipboard. When you make a copy of a cell or block, the original cell or block remains the same — you're simply making a replica of it and placing it somewhere else.

WARNING! This is the same warning I gave earlier about cutting and pasting. When you copy something and the area that you're copying to already contains something, Quattro Pro for Windows overwrites the cells with the new copied information — without warning you about it. So if you have some important material in your notebook, be careful when copying.

Why copy?

The most obvious reason to copy a cell or a block of cells is so you won't have to type it in again. Copying is also useful for duplicating a formula so that the formula works on other blocks. When you copy a formula, Quattro Pro for Windows does some interesting things, as I'll explain in the next section.

Copying a cell to a cell

Here's how to copy the contents of cell A1 to B1:

1. **Move the cell selector to A1.**
2. **Issue the Edit⇨Copy command.**

   Quattro Pro for Windows makes a copy of the cell contents and stores it on the Windows Clipboard. The contents of cell A1 remain intact.

3. **Next, move the cell pointer to cell B1, and select the Edit⇨Paste command.**

   Quattro Pro for Windows will retrieve the contents of the Clipboard and insert them into cell B1. Mission accomplished.

Cell B1 will now contain the same information as cell A1.

Copying a cell to a block

Copying a single cell to a block of cells works exactly the same as copying to a single cell. You start by selecting the cell you want to copy, and then issue the Edit⇔Copy command (or press Ctrl+C). The only difference is that you will select a *block* of cells before you issue the Edit⇔Paste command (or press Ctrl+V). After you do so, the single cell you originally copied to the Clipboard will be duplicated in every cell of the block you selected.

Figure 10-2 shows what happens when you copy a single cell to a block of cells.

Copying a block to a block

Copying a block of cells to another block is very similar to the other copy operations I described. Select the block to be copied, and issue the Edit⇔Copy command. Then move the cell pointer to the new location and select Edit⇔Paste. You need to select only the upper left cell before you do the Edit⇔Paste command (you don't have to select the entire block).

Figure 10-3 shows a block of cells that has been copied to another block.

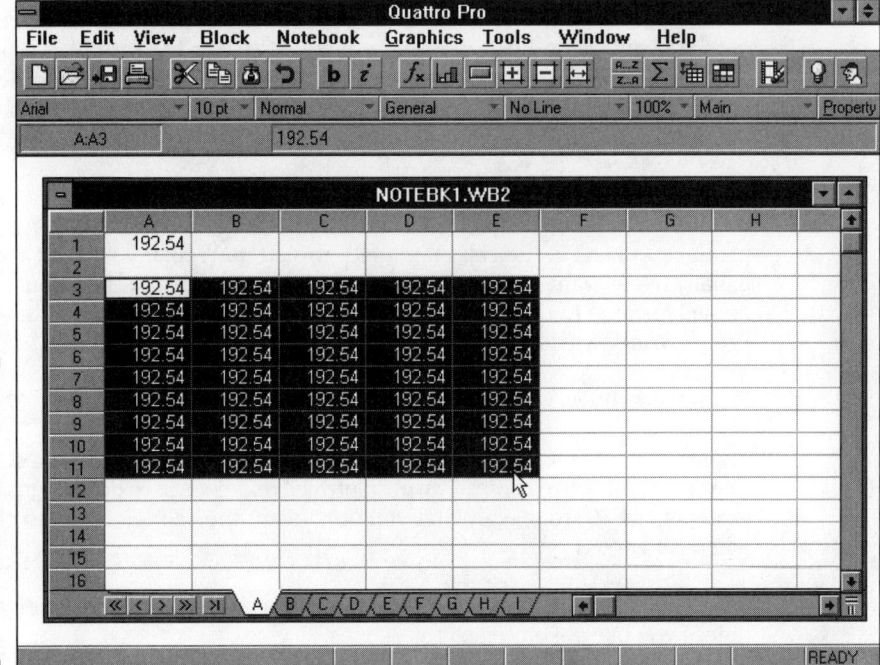

Figure 10-2: Copying a single cell to a block puts the contents of the cell into every cell of the block.

Figure 10-3: Copying an entire block duplicates that block somewhere else.

	A	B	C	D
1	Northern Region			
2		Jan	Feb	Mar
3	Widgets	144	154	165
4	Sprockets	98	76	65
5	Total	242	230	230
6				
7	Southern Region			
8		Jan	Feb	Mar
9	Widgets	144	154	165
10	Sprockets	98	76	65
11	Total	242	230	230

Copying formulas

Copying formulas works exactly like copying anything else. In other words, you can copy a single formula to another cell, copy a single formula to a block of cells, or copy a block of formulas to another block of cells.

When you copy a formula, something special happens: all of the cell references in the formula get adjusted. Assume that cell A3 has the formula +A1+A2. When you copy this formula to cell B3, the formula will read +B1+B2. In other words, the cell references get changed to refer to the same relative cells in their new position.

This might seem contrary to your expectation. If you make a copy of a formula, the copy should be exact, right? Copying a cell that contains +A1+A2 should produce +A1+A2 in the cell that it gets copied to. Well, if you think about it, you usually never want to make an exact copy of a formula. Rather, you want the copied formula to refer to a different set of cells. And that's just what Quattro Pro for Windows does — automatically.

Figure 10-4 shows what happens when you copy a formula.

An exception to this rule is an absolute cell reference, which I discussed in Chapter 8. As you may recall, an absolute cell reference uses dollar signs (for example, +$C$9) to specify that you don't want the cell reference to change when it's copied.

When you copy a formula, the cell references are adjusted automatically — unless you use absolute cell references.

Chapter 10: Making Changes to Your Work (and Living to Talk about It) **177**

Figure 10-4:
When you copy a formula, Quattro Pro for Windows automatically adjusts the cell's references so that the copied formula works as it should in its new home.

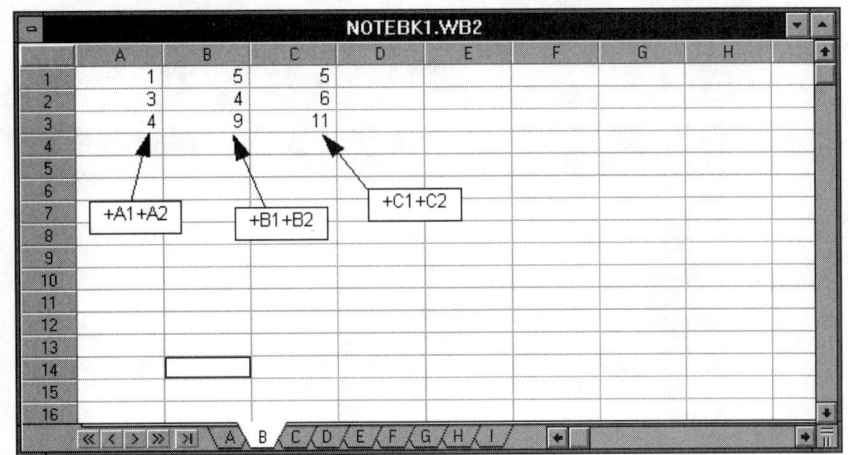

Drag-and-drop copying

If you read the previous section that covered moving cells or blocks by copying and pasting, you know that you can also move things using drag-and-drop. Quattro Pro for Windows extends this procedure and lets you *copy* cells or blocks using drag-and-drop with your mouse.

This procedure has a minor limitation, however. You can copy a single cell to another location, or copy a block of cells to another location — but you *cannot* copy a single cell to a block. You have to use the normal copy-and-paste procedure to do that.

To copy using drag-and-drop, start by selecting the cell or block to be copied. Then, press Ctrl while you click in the selection. In about a half-second the mouse pointer will turn into a hand with a plus sign on it (as in Figure 10-5). Drag the selection to where you want to copy it and release the mouse button. Quattro Pro for Windows will place a copy of your original selection in the new location.

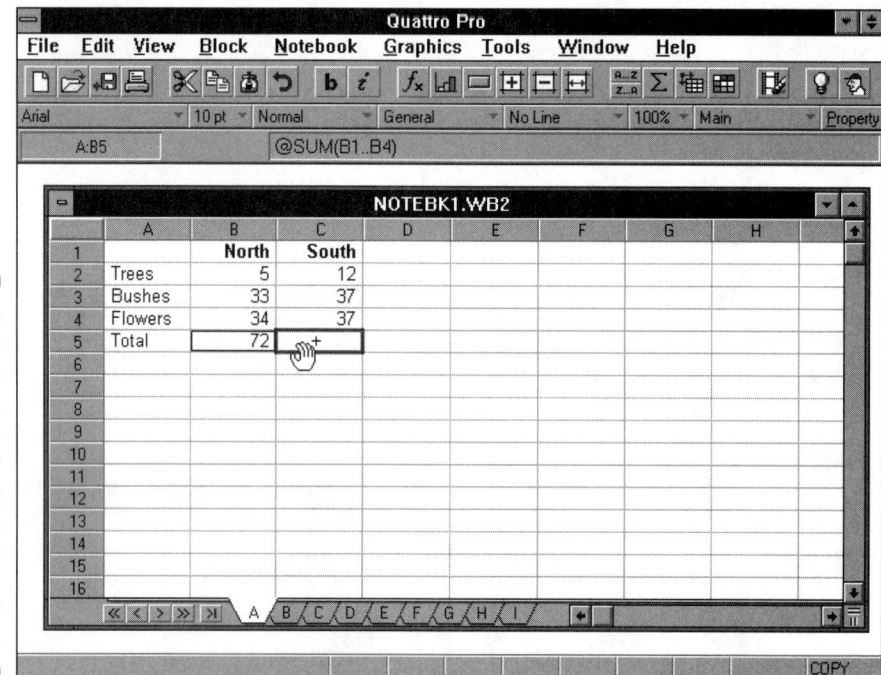

Figure 10-5: If you hold down Ctrl when you click, the hand pointer has a plus sign on it. This lets you copy the selection by dragging it.

Adjusting Column Widths

When you start a new notebook, all the 256 columns in every page are the same width: nine characters. You can make any or all of these columns wider or narrower to accommodate the information you put in them. It should be obvious that when you change a column width, the entire column changes. In other words, you can't adjust the width of individual cells.

> **TIP**
>
> The preceding paragraph stated that a standard column is nine characters wide. Actually, this is a rather arbitrary number, because the number of characters that will display in a nine-character cell depends on the actual characters used, the type size, the font, and whether they're bold. In other words, it's best to adjust column widths based on what you see on-screen, not the number of characters in the cells.

Why widen columns?

I can think of three reasons to adjust column widths:

- To make long numbers display properly. Numbers that are too wide to fit in a column show up as a series of asterisks, like this: *********.

Chapter 10: Making Changes to Your Work (and Living to Talk about It) *179*

- ✔ To make the notebook look better by spacing things out or moving them closer together.
- ✔ To make long labels display properly. Labels that are too wide have a truncated display if the cell adjacent to the right is occupied.

Figure 10-6 shows a notebook that has several different column widths to accommodate various entries.

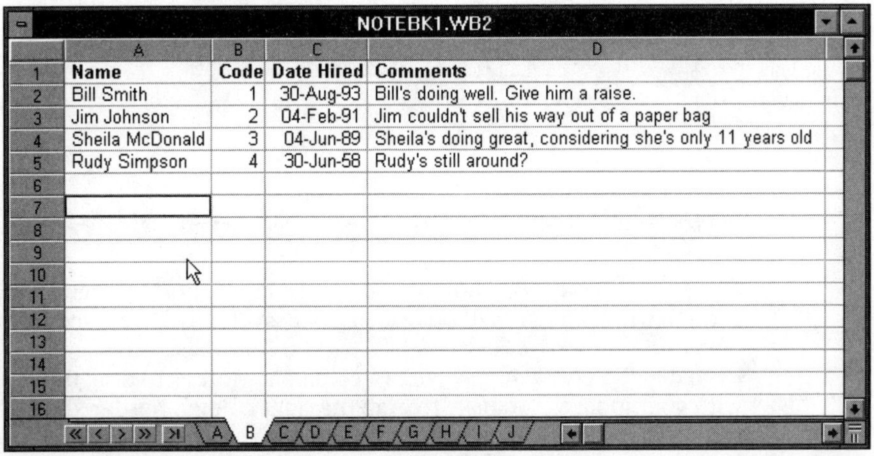

Figure 10-6:
You can adjust the widths of columns to handle practically anything you can put in a cell.

Adjusting column widths using the menu

Here's how to change the width of one or more columns:

   1. **Select any cell in the column or columns you want to adjust.**

      To select nonadjacent columns, hold down Ctrl while you click on cells.

   2. **Right-click to get the shortcut menu.**
   3. **Choose the Block Properties menu option.**
   4. **Select Column Width.**

      The Active Block dialog box will look like Figure 10-7.

   5. **Change the setting to the desired number of characters.**

      If you choose the Auto Width option, each column in the selection will be made just wide enough to handle the widest entry in the column. Choose the Reset Width option to return the columns to their standard width.

   6. **Choose OK to close the dialog box.**

The columns will be adjusted per your specifications.

Figure 10-7: This part of the Active Block dialog box lets you adjust column widths.

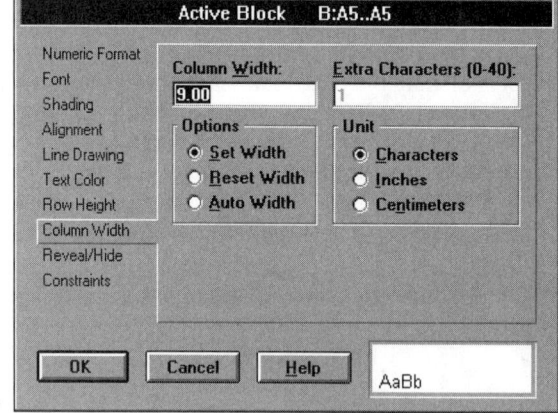

The E-Z way to adjust column widths

The preceding section showed you how to use a shortcut menu to change column widths. That method was pretty easy, but there are even easier ways.

Probably the best way to change a column's width is to drag the column border with your mouse. You have to grab the right column border, directly to the right of the column's letter. When you move the mouse pointer to the column border, the mouse pointer will change shape to let you know that you can drag. Drag the border to the right to make the column wider or to the left to make it narrower. Figure 10-8 shows what dragging a column border looks like.

Global column widths

By default, every column in a Quattro Pro for Windows notebook is nine characters wide. If you ever find yourself wanting narrower or wider columns on an entire notebook page, you don't have to go through the normal steps to set the column widths — just change the default. Right-click the page tab and select Default Width from the Active Page dialog box. Then enter the column width you want.

Changing the global column width for a notebook page will *not* change the widths of any columns that you already changed. For example, if you make column A 24 characters wide and then change the global column width to 15, column A's width will stay at 24 characters, and all the other columns widths will change.

Chapter 10: Making Changes to Your Work (and Living to Talk about It) 181

Figure 10-8: Dragging a column border is the easiest way to change a column's width.

To change the widths of several columns by dragging, first select the complete columns that you want to change by clicking and dragging across the column letters. Then drag the border of any of the selected columns to change the widths of all of them.

If you want to make a column just wide enough to fit the widest entry in the column, just select the Fit button on the Toolbar. (Figure 10-9 shows what this button looks like.) This procedure will work on all the columns that you have selected.

Figure 10-9: This Toolbar button will make the selected column or columns wide enough to handle the widest cell entry.

Changing Row Heights

It should come as no surprise that you can also change the height of rows. Most of the time, you'll be satisfied with the fact that Quattro Pro for Windows handles this task automatically. For example, if you make a cell's font larger, the row height will increase automatically to handle the bigger font. But you can also increase the row heights yourself to adjust spacing between rows.

TIP

If you want to double-space your work, increasing row heights is a a better approach than skipping rows.

Figure 10-10 shows a notebook with several different row heights.

Figure 10-10: You can adjust the height of individual rows to space things vertically.

Here's how to change the height of one or more rows:

1. **Select any cell in the row or rows you want to adjust.**

   To select nonadjacent rows, hold down Ctrl while you click on cells.

2. **Right-click to get the shortcut menu.**
3. **Choose the Block Properties menu option.**
4. **Select Row Height.**

   The Active Block dialog box will look like Figure 10-11.

Figure 10-11:
This part of the Active Block dialog box lets you adjust row heights.

5. **Change the setting to the desired height.**

   You can select the measurement unit by choosing the appropriate option button — points, inches, or centimeters.

6. **Choose OK to close the dialog box.**

   The row heights will be adjusted per your specifications.

TIP

An easier way to change row heights is to drag the row border with your mouse — just like you do when adjusting a column width. Click the bottom border and drag it down to make the row taller, or drag it up to make it shorter.

Erasing Cells and Blocks

Getting rid of the contents of a cell — or a whole block of cells — is easy. This procedure is known as erasing, deleting, wiping out, nuking, killing, annihilating, zapping, and all sorts of other terms that aren't suitable for all family members. Regardless of what you call it, after you do it, the information is gone for good (unless you immediately use the Edit⇨Undo command to get it back).

The alert reader will recall that the Edit⇨Cut command will get rid of the contents of cells and blocks. Another way to erase a cell or a block is to use the Edit⇨Clear command. Start by selecting the offending cell or block, and then issue the command. Or, to save some time, simply press Del and avoid the menu altogether.

Why two commands to do the same thing? The difference is that Edit⇨Clear (or Del) doesn't put the erased information on the Clipboard. So, if you have something on the Clipboard that you want to remain there (so you can paste it later), you can use Edit⇨Clear to erase cells without affecting the Clipboard.

Adding New Rows and Columns

You can insert new rows and columns into your notebook. Actually, the number of rows and columns always remains the same (8192 rows and 256 columns). Inserting a new row simply scoots everything down, and the last row in the notebook disappears.

REMEMBER

Inserting a new column scoots everything to the right, and the last column in the notebook disappears. If the last column has something in it, you can't insert a new column. The same goes for rows. If the last row in your notebook is not empty, you can't insert a new row.

Why do it?

It's not uncommon to discover that you need to insert something between two other cells. You might have a list of products and prices, and discover that you left one out. One approach is to move part of the block down one row to make room for the new entry (cut and paste, remember?). A faster method is to insert a new row, which pushes everything down and makes room for your forgotten material.

If you insert a new row or column, you must be careful that you don't damage other areas of your notebook.

By the way, if you performed the hands-on exercise in Chapter 4, you already have experience inserting new rows.

WARNING!

A word of caution

It may sound like a pretty dumb warning, but you must remember that deleting a row or column does just that — it deletes an entire row or column. Many users tend to focus on just one part of their spreadsheet and forget that there are other parts out of view. They go about inserting and deleting rows and columns, and are then surprised to discover that another area of their notebook is all messed up. So let that be a warning. Actually, if your notebook has many separate parts, you may be better off using separate pages for the various parts. That way, things you do on one page won't affect the other pages in the file. See Chapter 14 for more details on using all those pages in a notebook.

Adding new rows

Here's how to add a new row to your notebook:

1. **Select the complete row that's just below the row that you want to insert.**

    To select a row, click the row number.

2. **Right-click to get the shortcut menu.**

3. **Choose the Block Insert command.**

Quattro Pro for Windows will push all the rows down and give you a new blank row.

TIP

After selecting the row, you can also simply click the Insert button on the Toolbar to insert a new row.

If you want to add more than one row, simply start by selecting more than one row. For example, to add 5 rows below row 10, select rows 10 through 15 before you issue the Block Insert command. In other words, the row or rows that you select before issuing the command to insert rows will be blank rows after you execute the command.

Adding new columns

Adding one or more columns works just like adding rows. The only difference is that you start by selecting one or more columns. Then right-click to get the shortcut menu, and choose the Block Insert command. Quattro Pro for Windows will give you the new columns. The Insert button on the Toolbar also works.

Getting Rid of Rows and Columns

Since you can add rows and columns, you ought to be able to take them away, right? Quattro Pro for Windows lets you remove as many rows and columns as you like. However, the total number of rows and columns always remains the same. If you remove a row, for example, all of the other rows move up one slot, and Quattro Pro for Windows inserts another row at the bottom. The comparable event happens when you remove a column.

Part II: Basic Stuff That You Just Can't Ignore

> **WARNING!** Be careful when removing rows and columns. If they contains cells that are used in any of your formulas, the formulas will be corrupted in a major way — in other words, they will no longer return the correct answer.

Why do it?

If you discover that the information in a row or column is not needed, you can get rid of it quickly by deleting the entire row or column. This is a much faster alternative to deleting the block and then moving everything else around to fill the gap.

Eliminating rows

To get rid of a row, select the entire row, right-click to get the shortcut menu, and then choose the Block Delete command. To delete more than one row, simply extend the row selection before you issue the command.

> **TIP** After selecting the row, you can also simply click the Delete button on the Toolbar to nuke the row.

Deleting columns

Getting rid of entire columns works the same way as deleting rows — except that you start out by selecting the column or columns that you want to zap. Then right-click and choose Block Delete to do the deed. The Delete button on the Toolbar is another option.

Transposing Rows and Columns

Transposing a block means changing its orientation. If you have numbers in a single column, you can transpose them so they appear in a single row — and vice versa.

Why do it?

You transpose rows and columns if you discover that information in the notebook is in the wrong orientation: vertical when it should be horizontal, or horizontal when it should be vertical. Figure 10-12 shows a block of cells before and after being reoriented.

Chapter 10: Making Changes to Your Work (and Living to Talk about It)   *187*

Figure 10-12: Transposing a block changes its orientation.

How to do it

You start by selecting the block to be transposed, and then choose the Block⇨Transpose command. Quattro Pro for Windows displays the dialog box shown in Figure 10-13.

Figure 10-13: The Transpose dialog box.

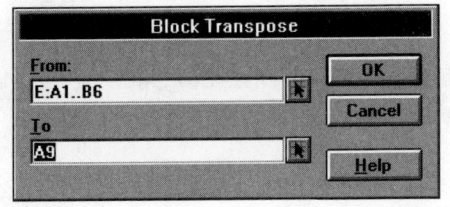

The From box will display the block you selected. In the To box, you need to specify the upper left cell of the block that you want to transpose it to. Then choose OK to close the dialog box. Quattro Pro for Windows will copy the original block to the new area — but transposed.

WARNING!

If the area you specify to hold the transposed data already contains information, Quattro Pro for Windows — in its typical presumptuous fashion — will overwrite that information without telling you about it. So be careful out there.

Finding and Replacing — Wherefore Art Thou, Text String?

Every word processor I've ever seen has a pretty sophisticated find-and-replace feature. You can instruct your software to find a particular text pattern (or *string*) and replace it with something else. You can do this task automatically or have the program stop and ask you each time it finds the string. Quattro Pro for Windows isn't a word processor, but it also has this feature — which is great for making large-scale changes to a notebook.

Fortunately, using this powerful tool is very straightforward. Start by selecting the Edit⇨Find/Replace command. You'll get the dialog box shown in Figure 10-14.

Enter the text or value that you're looking for in the Find box. Enter the text or value that you want to replace it with in the Replace box. If you want to limit your search to a specific block, you can specify the block in the Block(s) box. Normally, you'll want to make sure the Value option is selected.

Choose Find Next, and Quattro Pro for Windows goes to work looking for the string. If the string is found, you'll be asked if you want to replace it — or you can specify that you want to replace automatically all occurrences of the string.

Be careful if you select the Formula option, since this can wipe out formulas and replace them with values — which is usually not what you want.

Figure 10-14: The Find/Replace dialog box.

Sorting Blocks of Cells — Head 'em Up and Move 'em Out

When you rearrange a block of cells so that the order of the rows gets changed, this activity is called *sorting*, which is a very common operation among spreadsheet users.

Why do it?

There are many reasons why you would want to sort a block of data. You may have entered data haphazardly and need to print it out in some order. Or, you may want to sort your data to make it easier to find a particular entry. Or, you may want to see how a group of numbers looks in terms of rank orders. Finally, you may want to change the order before making a graph from the numbers.

> **WARNING!** I've found that sorting mistakes are one of the primary causes of serious spreadsheet problems. Be on the safe side and save your notebook before you sort any data. That way, if you mess up (and Edit⇨Undo can't come to the rescue), you can always go back to the old file and start again.

How to do it

To demonstrate how to sort a block of data, I'll run through an example. Figure 10-15 shows a block of unsorted data. The goal of this exercise is to sort the block alphabetically by state (in ascending order).

What to watch out for when sorting

One of the most common mistakes people make with spreadsheets is to sort them incorrectly. They do this because they don't select the entire intended block as the sort block. For example, suppose you have a block that consists of three columns: Name, Age, and Salary. If you want to sort the block in alphabetical order using Name as the sort key, it's critically important that you select *all three columns* when you specify the sort block. If you only select the column with the names, only the names will be sorted. This means that everyone will have a different age and salary. In other words, the data has serious problems, all the effort you put into entering this information will be wasted, you'll lose your job, the house will go on the auction block, and your dog will hate you.

Part II: Basic Stuff That You Just Can't Ignore

```
                REGIONS.WB2
         A            B      C        D       E    F
  1  California      984   West     Jan
  2  New York        665   East     Feb
  3  New Jersey      589   East     Feb
  4  Illinois        543   Midwest  Feb
  5  Massachusetts   498   East     Mar
  6  Washington      443   West     Jan
  7  Oklahoma        378   Midwest  Apr
  8  Missouri        322   Midwest  Jan
  9  Oregon          143   West     Jan
 10  Rhode Island    143   East     Mar
 11  Nebraska        128   Midwest  Apr
 12  Kansas          124   Midwest  Feb
 13  Nevada           76   West     Apr
 14  Montana          32   West     Mar
 15  Wyoming           5   West     Apr
 16
```

Figure 10-15: Unsorted data.

1. **Select the entire block to be sorted.**

   In this case, it's A1..D15.

2. **Select the Block⇨Sort command.**

   Quattro Pro for Windows displays the Sort dialog box, shown in Figure 10-16.

```
                    Block Sort
  Block: [D:A1..D15]        [Reset]      [ OK ]
  ┌─ Sort Keys ─────────────┐ ┌─ Data ──────────┐
  │        Column  Ascending│ │ ⦿ Numbers First │  [Cancel]
  │  1st  [      ]    [x]   │ │ ○ Labels First  │
  │  2nd  [      ]    [x]   │ └─────────────────┘  [ Help ]
  │  3rd  [      ]    [x]   │ ┌─ Labels ────────┐
  │  4th  [      ]    [x]   │ │ ⦿ Character Code│
  │  5th  [      ]    [x]   │ │ ○ Dictionary    │
  └─────────────────────────┘ └─────────────────┘
```

Figure 10-16: The Sort dialog box.

3. **Specify which column to sort on (the sort key). Choose the box labeled 1st.**

   Because states are in column A, you can select *any cell* in the block A1..A15. This indication tells Quattro Pro for Windows to use that column for the first sort key.

4. **Because we want the states sorted in ascending order, make sure the Ascending box is checked for this column (it's checked by default).**

5. **Select OK to do the sorting.**

Chapter 10: Making Changes to Your Work (and Living to Talk about It) *191*

Quattro Pro for Windows goes to work, and your data will now be sorted per your instructions (see Figure 10-17).

TIP

When you do a sort, Quattro Pro for Windows remembers the settings you give it. The next time you issue the Block⇨Sort command, it will attempt to use exactly the same block and sort keys that you specified earlier. To make Quattro Pro for Windows forget your previous sort specs, select the Reset button in the Sort dialog box. Then you can enter your new sort specs.

TECHNICAL STUFF

Normally, Quattro Pro for Windows considers letters to be "greater than" numbers when it sorts. In other words, if the entries in your sort key column contain both numbers and labels, it will put the numbers before the labels. If you want to change this rule in order to sort labels before numbers, just click first the Labels box.

	A	B	C	D
1	California	984	West	Jan
2	Illinois	543	Midwest	Feb
3	Kansas	124	Midwest	Feb
4	Massachusetts	498	East	Mar
5	Missouri	322	Midwest	Jan
6	Montana	32	West	Mar
7	Nebraska	128	Midwest	Apr
8	Nevada	76	West	Apr
9	New Jersey	589	East	Feb
10	New York	665	East	Feb
11	Oklahoma	378	Midwest	Apr
12	Oregon	143	West	Jan
13	Rhode Isand	143	East	Mar
14	Washington	443	West	Jan
15	Wyoming	5	West	Apr

Figure 10-17: The sorted data.

Chapter 11
Putting It on Paper

In This Chapter
▶ Why printing can be a pain in the drain
▶ How to print what you've done
▶ How to get more control over printing in notebooks
▶ What a crash course on printer types can do for you: the pros and cons of each

Most of the time, you'll want to get a hard copy of the results of your spreadsheeting efforts. You basically have two choices: use a Polaroid camera to photograph your computer monitor, or send the notebook to your printer. Most people choose the latter option because Polaroid prints are too small and are difficult to staple together into reports.

The Seedy Side of Printing

Both beginning and advanced users agree that dealing with printers can be one of the most frustrating parts of working with computers. But it's worth it when you finally have something you can hold in your hand to show for the long hours you spent sweating over your keyboard.

Here are a few observations about printers (maybe you recognize some of them):

- Your printer is never good enough for what you want it to do. And of course, the day after you buy a new printer, the manufacturer comes out with a better model that's several hundred dollars cheaper than what you have just plunked down.
- The paper always jams at the most inopportune times.

Never start printing a 30-page job and then go to lunch. Printers know when you leave the office and purposefully pick that time to jam.

- Printers have minds of their own. When you want to print in Helvetica typeface, sometimes the document comes out in Courier for no apparent reason. (It must have something to do with the phase of the moon.)
- The ribbon dries up, the ink cartridge clogs up, or the toner cartridge bites the dust just as your boss is yelling, "I need that report NOW, you dolt!"
- Nobody really knows what all those little buttons and lights are for. And the 700-page printer manual is printed in Japanese.

That Polaroid print option is looking better and better, isn't it?

Printing 101

To print a document in a perfect world, you would simply issue your software's Print command, and everything would instantly appear on paper just as you would expect it to. Although the world is far from perfect, printing from Quattro Pro for Windows comes fairly close to perfection (except for the *instantly* part).

If you want to print the entire notebook page that you're working on, here's how to do it:

1. **Select the Print button in the Main Toolbar (see Figure 11-1).**

    This displays the Spreadsheet Print dialog box, as seen in Figure 11-2.

2. **Press Return (or choose the Print button in the dialog box).**

Figure 11-1: The Print button on the Main Toolbar is the express route to getting your work on paper.

Figure 11-2: The Spreadsheet Print dialog box is the first step to getting stuff on paper.

That's all there is to it. The active notebook page will be sent to the printer (using the current printer settings). In most cases, the current settings work just fine. But using computers can't be this simple, right? As you may expect, *tons* of options are available so you can change the way your work gets printed and do *tons* of other nifty things. That's why the rest of this chapter exists.

By the way, clicking the Print button on the Toolbar is just a shortcut for the File⇨Print command. You'll get the Spreadsheet Print dialog box regardless of which method you use.

Windows makes printing easy

Before the dawn of Microsoft Windows, every software program that you bought had to be configured for your particular printer. If you used eight different software products, for example, you had to go through the tedious printer configuration routine eight times.

The Windows programs (including Quattro Pro for Windows) have changed this process because they aren't concerned with the mechanics of printing. All the printing is done by Windows, not by the individual programs.

In other words, you have to configure Windows only for your printer. You don't have to go into every Windows program and set it up to work with your new printer. If you're new to computing, you probably don't appreciate how nice this shortcut is. But we old-timers think that it's the cat's pajamas.

Getting a Sneak Preview

Before we get bogged down with all of the print options available to you, you should know about print preview. As you know, printing is not instant. In fact, it's often downright s-l-o-w. You can waste a great deal of time waiting for something to print — only to find that it came out all wrong. Fortunately, Quattro Pro for Windows offers a handy print preview feature that lets you take a peek at your printed page right on your computer screen.

To preview your printout, just select the Print Preview button in the Spreadsheet Print dialog box. Your screen will transform to a full-screen view of the first page of your printout. See Figure 11-3.

Observant users will notice that the mouse pointer looks like a magnifying glass. If you click the left mouse button, the preview will be magnified. Press it several more times, and it gets larger and larger. Pressing the right mouse button reduces the enlarged image.

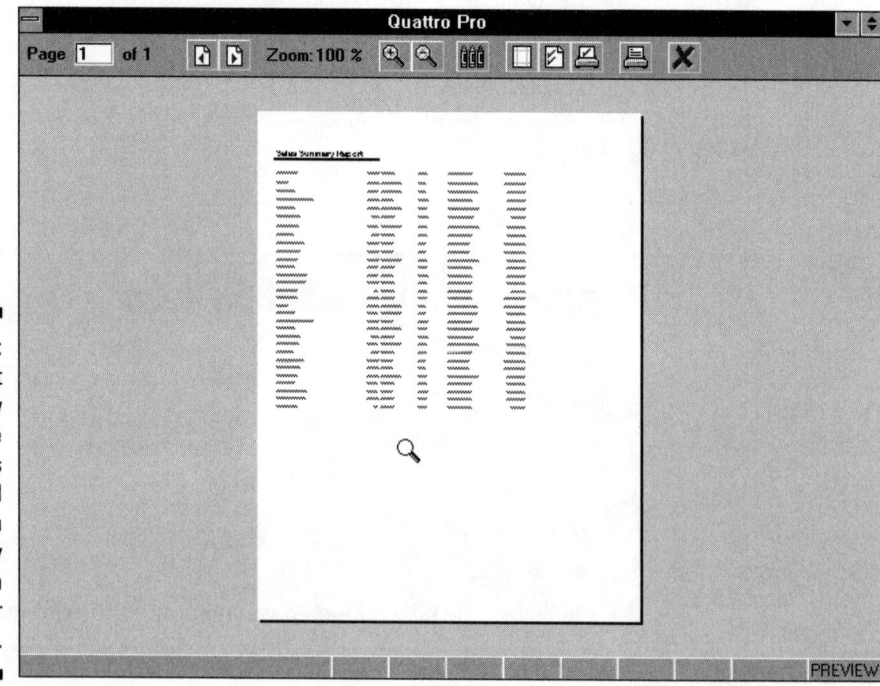

Figure 11-3: Print Preview mode displays your printed results in the privacy of your own computer screen.

There are also several buttons at the top of the preview screen. Table 11-1 summarizes what these buttons can do for you.

Table 11-1   Buttons in Print Preview Mode

Button	What It Does
Previous Page	Displays the previous page (if there is one)
Next Page	Displays the next page (if there is one)
Zoom In	Increases the display magnification
Zoom Out	Reduces the display magnification
Color	Toggles between color and black and white
Margin	Displays margins on the preview page (you can change the margins by dragging)
Setup	Goes to the Spreadsheet Page Setup dialog box (explained later)
Options	Goes to the Spreadsheet Print Options dialog box (explained later)
Print	Prints it (click this if everything looks OK)
Exit Preview	Cancels preview mode and returns you to your notebook

TIP: It's a good idea to get into the habit of previewing your work before you print it. You'll save time, energy, and trees.

Printing 202

As you already learned, the Print Toolbar button brings up the Spreadsheet Print dialog box. This dialog box is the jumping-off place for changing the print settings and options (and also for getting an on-screen preview).

Usually, the default print settings will work fine, but there may be times when you want to make some changes in how your work is printed. The following list contains examples of the printing adjustments you can make in the wonderful world of Quattro Pro for Windows:

- The block of cells to be printed (when you don't want to print everything)
- The number of copies to print
- The pages to print
- Print orientation (tall or wide)
- Paper size

- The margins on the paper
- Headers or footers that appear on every printed page (including page numbers and date/time)
- The cell grid lines (printed or not)
- The row and column borders (printed or not)
- Certain notebook rows or columns that print on each page
- Print compressed, so that it fits on one page

The rest of this chapter tells you how to change some of the more common print options.

Specifying what to print

Figure 11-4 shows the Spreadsheet Print dialog box again. Notice that in this box you can specify what gets printed.

Figure 11-4: The Spreadsheet Print dialog box lets you specify some of your print options.

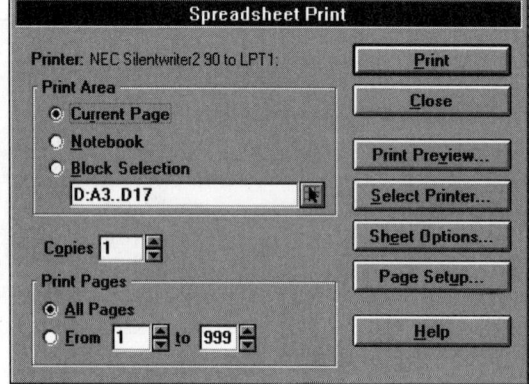

You have the following choices:

Current Page: Prints only the current page. This setting is the default option.

Notebook: Prints all the pages in the notebook — actually it only prints the pages that have something on them. Quattro Pro for Windows is smart enough not to spit out 255 blank pages.

Selection: Prints only the block of cells that you specify.

TIP: If you select the block you want to print before you choose the Print button on the Toolbar, the selected block appears in the Selection range box. Then you simply click on Print, and you're off to the races. As you probably know, you can also select a block of cells directly from the dialog box by clicking in the box and then dragging the mouse over the cells you want to print. Or you can just type in the block address.

Now take a look at the bottom part of the Spreadsheet Print dialog box. If the information you are printing uses more than one sheet of paper, you can also specify a range of pages to print using the From and to spinners. Printing more than one page is only relevant, of course, if your notebook is large enough to use more than one page when it is printed. Imagine that you have a large notebook that normally uses ten sheets of paper when you print it. You print the notebook and notice a mistake on page 8. Rather than reprint the whole job, you can just print that one page by specifying 8 in the From box and 8 in the to box.

TIP: If you want to print all the pages in your job, just select the All pages option (the default).

Here, *pages* refers to printed sheets of paper — not the pages in your notebook.

Printing multiple copies

If you want to print more than one copy, specify the number of copies using the Copies spinner. You can enter a number up to 256 (gee whiz, only 256!). Actually, if you need more than a dozen or so copies, you may want to check out the wonderful world of photocopiers.

Page Setup options

You can gain access to another set of options by choosing the Page Setup button in the Spreadsheet Print dialog box. Selecting this button brings up the Spreadsheet Page Setup dialog box.

This dialog box has more options than you may think. When you choose one of the option buttons on the left, the right part of the dialog box changes. I'll discuss each of these options separately.

REMEMBER: Everything you do in the Spreadsheet Page Setup dialog box is saved with the notebook. So the next time you load the notebook, all these settings are still with the notebook, and choosing the Print button on the Toolbar prints the notebook with the same settings.

Adjusting paper size and orientation

Selecting the Paper type option in the Spreadsheet Page Setup dialog box gives you the options shown in Figure 11-5.

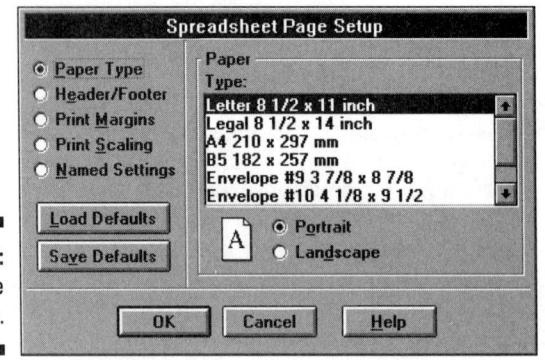

Figure 11-5: Paper type options.

Most of the time, you'll probably use normal-size paper, which is 8 1/2 x 11 inches, for printing. However, if you need to print something that's very tall or wide, you may opt for legal-size paper (8 1/2 x 14 inches). Or you may have some oddball-size paper that you want to use for one reason or another. Quattro Pro for Windows lets you specify different paper sizes, assuming that your printer is capable of handling these different sizes. To specify the paper size, just choose the size from the Paper Type list.

You normally print a page in *portrait* orientation, where the printed page is taller than it is wide. Printing sideways on the page is called *landscape* printing. Use this option when the material you're printing is wide. These terms may seem strange to you — and I have no idea where they come from either — but everybody uses them.

You change the orientation of your paper by choosing either the Portrait or Landscape option button (I'll bet you *never* could have figured that one out!).

Adding headers and footers

Selecting the Header/Footer option changes the dialog box so it looks like Figure 11-6.

Some of you may be curious: What's a header? Furthermore, what's a footer? *Headers* appear at the top of every page, and *footers* appear at the bottom of every page. If you have trouble keeping this straight, think of an upright human body. The head is at the top, and the foot is at the bottom.

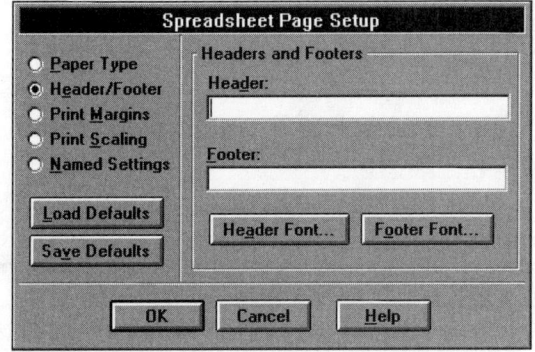

Figure 11-6: Header/Footer options.

Why use headers or footers? Well, some people like to identify what the printout is about. For example, your third quarter report about tardiness can have a header that reads *3rd Quarter Tardiness Report*. You can put whatever you want into the headers or footers, including page numbers, the date, and other goodies.

Quattro Pro for Windows is an incredibly easy program to use. However, I personally think the designers need to work on the header and footer specifications. Inserting special information into a header or footer is — well, not very obvious.

If you want to do anything fancy with a header or footer, you'll need to learn some secret codes. Table 11-2 lists these codes for you.

Table 11-2   Header and Footer Codes

Code	What It Does
I (vertical bar)	Determines the position of the text: left-aligned, right-aligned, or centered
#d	Prints the current date in a format like this: 19-Jun
#D	Prints the current date in a format like this: 06/19/94
#ds	Prints the current date in a format like this: 06/19
#Ds	Prints the current date in a format like this: 19-Jun-94
#t	Prints the current time in a format like this: 11:29:39
#T	Prints the current time in a format like this: 11:29
#ts	Prints the current time in a format like this: 11:29:39 AM
#Ts	Prints the current time in a format like this: 11:29 AM

(continued)

Table 11-2 (continued)

Code	What It Does
#p	Prints the current page number
#p+n	Prints the current page number plus the number *n*
#P	Prints the number of pages in the document
#P+n	Prints the number of pages plus the number *n*
#f	Prints the name of the notebook with no path
#F	Prints the name of the notebook including the path
#n	Prints the remainder of the header or footer on a second line

Think of the vertical bar character as a tab. One vertical bar centers the text; two vertical bars right-align the text.

TIP: If you're having trouble locating the vertical bar character on your keyboard, hold down Shift and press the backslash key (\). On some keyboards, the vertical bar character appears broken in the middle.

If you're confused about these codes, maybe a few examples will clear things up. If you enter the following codes for a header:

```
#Ds|Budget Report|Page p
```

the header will appear at the top of each page as:

```
19-Jun-94           Budget Report           Page 1
```

Here's another example. If you enter the following codes for a footer:

```
|Page p of #P
```

the footer will appear at the bottom of each page as:

```
Page 1 of 6
```

In this case, I used the vertical bar character to center the text.

The best way to learn this material is to enter some codes and see what you get — and use the print preview mode rather than normal printing.

Chapter 11: Putting It on Paper *203*

> **TIP:** For lengthy reports, it's a good idea to add page numbers to the header or footer of your printout. Then if someone opens the door on a windy day and the report blows all over the office, you won't have as much trouble putting the report back together.

> **TIP:** You also can use an @function that updates the date or time in a cell. Go to any cell and type **@NOW;** then format the cell so that it appears as a date, a time, or both. Whenever the notebook gets recalculated, the cell's date or time is updated.

Adjusting margins

The margins on a page refer to the white space along the edges. As you may suspect, Quattro Pro for Windows lets you change the margins to whatever you like. For example, if your company has a policy that all reports must have 1-inch margins on all sides, you can easily set these margins. Or you may want to make the margins even narrower so that everything fits on one page.

Choosing the Print Margins option in the Spreadsheet Page Setup dialog box changes the dialog box to look like Figure 11-7.

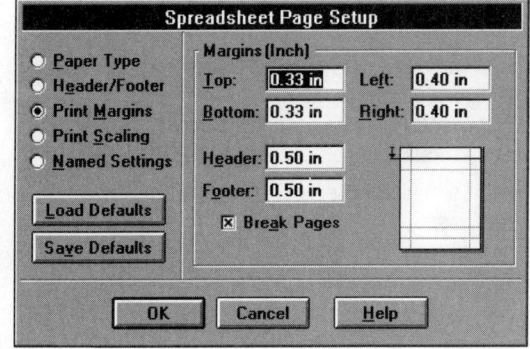

Figure 11-7: Print Margins options.

The Page Setup dialog box lets you change any or all of the six margins on the page. *Six* margins? How can you have six margins if a page has only four sides? Quattro Pro for Windows also lets you specify header and footer margins. A header or footer margin is the distance between the header or footer and the text that's printed.

Scaling your printout

Quattro Pro has some pretty spiffy options that shrink a print selection so that printed data is smaller and more data fits on a printed page. Or you can have the program automatically expand a print selection so that the printed data is larger and less data fits on a printed page.

To adjust the scaling of your printout, choose the Print Scaling option in the Spreadsheet Page Setup dialog box. The dialog box will change and look like Figure 11-8.

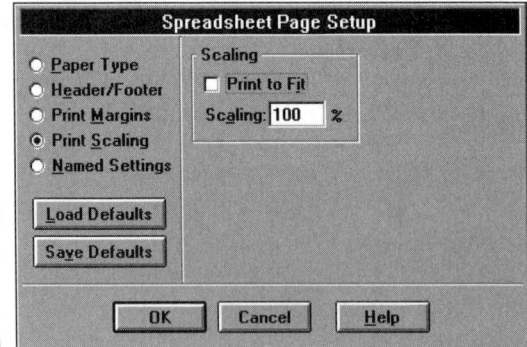

Figure 11-8: Print Scaling options.

You can adjust the size of the printed data with the Scaling box. A setting of 100% means that the printout will be normal size. A value less than 100% makes it smaller, and a value greater than 100% makes it larger. You can enter any value between 1% (extremely tiny) and 1000% (humongous).

Another option here is Print to Fit. If this box is checked, the output will be scaled automatically to fit on a single page. This option is handy for situations in which your printout doesn't quite fit on a single page (it may have one row or one column printed all by itself on the second page).

Naming your print settings

The final option in the Spreadsheet Page Setup dialog box is Named Settings (see Figure 11-9). This option lets you save all your print settings in a file so you can apply them to another notebook — quickly.

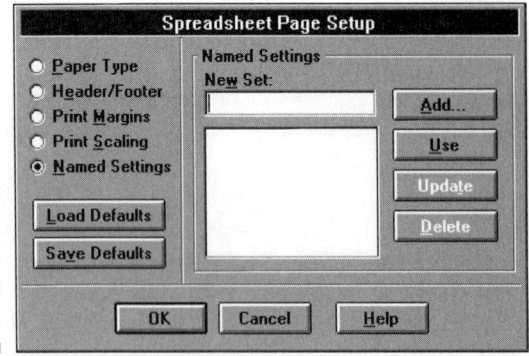

Figure 11-9: Named Settings options.

Say you just spent ten minutes changing several print options. You adjusted the margins, figured out how to get the header to look right, and got the paper size and orientation set up as you like them. Then you realize that you have several other notebooks that will need these same settings. This is a case where you want to give a name to these settings and save them for use later.

Just enter a name (any name will do) in the New Set box, and click on Add to add the set to the list. Then when you want to apply these settings to another notebook, select the name and select Use.

Sheet options

The Spreadsheet Print dialog box (the one that comes up when you choose the Print button on the Toolbar) has another button labeled Sheet Options — which offers still *more* settings. Select this button and you'll get the Spreadsheet Print Options dialog box shown in Figure 11-10.

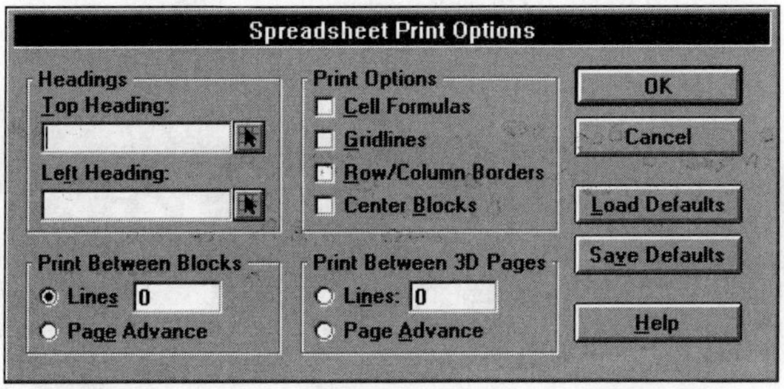

Figure 11-10: The Spreadsheet Print Options dialog box lets you adjust more settings.

Printing heading rows or columns on every page

If you have a lengthy multipage printout, you may want the top row or two (the heading rows or the rows that contain the field names), or even the entire left column, to print on every page, a technique especially useful for databases. By specifying that these rows or columns appear on every page of your printout, you make your report easier to read: you get the field names printed on each page, not just the first one.

To get a row or rows to appear on every page, go to the Top heading box and specify (or point to) the row(s) that you want to print on each page. To point from the dialog box, just click on the Top Heading text box and then select one or more rows in the worksheet.

To get a column or columns to appear on every page, go to the Left heading box and specify (or point to) the column(s) that you want to print on each page.

WARNING!

If you're printing only a block of cells (rather than the entire notebook), do not include the heading rows or columns in the print range you specify. If you do include them, they print twice on the first page. Everyone makes this mistake at least once, so don't feel bad if it happens to you.

REMEMBER

Don't confuse heading rows with page headers. They are different.

What to print

The Show box in the Page Setup dialog box gives you the following options for what you can print or ignore in your printout:

Cell formulas: As you know, Quattro Pro for Windows displays the results of a formula, not the formula itself. It also prints the results of formulas. If you ever want to print the actual formulas, check this box. This might be useful if you want to show it to the office spreadsheet genius to find out why your formulas aren't working right.

Gridlines: Normally, Quattro Pro for Windows doesn't print the gridlines that appear on-screen around each cell. If you like to see gridlines on your printout, however, just turn on this option.

Row/Column borders: Some people like to see row and column borders on their printouts because they then can tell the exact address of a cell. To have the borders appear on your printout, select this option.

Center blocks: If you want your printed output to be centered, check this. Normally, your printed output is aligned to the left margin.

Spacing things out

The bottom of the Spreadsheet Print Options dialog box lets you specify the spacing between pages or blocks printed. To skip to a new sheet of paper for each notebook page, click on the Page Advance option.

Printing charts, drawings, and other neat stuff

Printing charts and other graphic objects is no big deal. If charts or drawn objects are inserted in your notebook, they are simply printed along with everything else in the notebook.

Printers Du Jour

You should know what type of printer you have so that you can order supplies for it. If you didn't purchase the printer and are not sure what kind you are using, check the printer; most printers have a name printed somewhere on them. And if you have been around the different types of printers that are currently available, you usually can tell what type of printer you have by the quality of the output, called *resolution*.

Resolution refers to the number of dots per inch printed on the paper. If you look closely at something printed on a laser printer, you'll notice that the image is made up of many tiny dots. If you can't see the dots, try using a magnifying glass (or just take my word for it). The more dots there are per inch, the higher the resolution of your printer. For more information on resolution, read the sidebar, "You say you want a resolution," later in this chapter.

This section gives you a quick rundown of the pros and cons of each of the four general types of printers you may encounter.

Laser printers

No, you can't shoot anyone with them. But laser printers are the best because they are fast, quiet, easy to work with, and do great graphics. The street price of laser printers ranges from about $400 to several thousands of dollars. Laser printers differ in print speed, amount of memory, and maximum print resolution. A maximum resolution of 300 dots per inch is most common, but you also see printers that can print at 600 dots per inch. Laser printers are now considered the standard for office use, but many home computer users also choose laser printers.

Instead of using old-fashioned pin-feed paper, laser printers use normal single-sheet paper (and you can even use photocopier paper). Using regular paper makes laser printers much easier to work with because you don't have to worry about aligning the top of the page, tearing the pages apart, or ripping off the perforations along the side of the paper. However, the main disadvantage of a laser printer is that you can't print multipart forms with it. Keep this fact in mind when you purchase a printer.

Laser printers work by composing the image in their memory, which is separate from the computer's memory. When the image is fully composed, it is sent to the paper. This system of printing usually works very well; however, your laser printer may occasionally spit out the page without completing it (ahhhchooo!). If your printer is sneezing out incomplete pages, you can do one of the following tasks to correct the problem:

- Add more memory to your printer. (See your printer's manual for details — all printers handle this task differently.)
- Print at a lower resolution. (See the accompanying sidebar, "You say you want a resolution," for more information.)

Inkjet printers

Inkjet printers do their thing by spraying a very thin stream of ink on a page. They can handle both text and graphics, and some models even print in color. Because there is no physical contact with the paper, these printers are very quiet. An inkjet printer uses either tractor-feed paper or a single-sheet paper feeder.

The output from inkjet printers is very good — nearly as good as that from a laser printer (and they're usually cheaper, too). Because there is no physical contact with the paper, however, you can't use an inkjet printer to print multipart forms.

Dot-matrix printers

Dot-matrix printers come in a variety of styles and have price tags that range from very cheap to very expensive. Their output quality matches their price range — from very bad to pretty good, and most of them do a reasonably good job with graphics. The main advantage of having a dot-matrix printer is that it can print multipart forms (which lasers and inkjets can't handle). However, these printers can be very noisy, and some are dreadfully slow.

Daisywheel printers

You rarely see daisywheel printers anymore, except at garage sales. Because these printers don't even work with Windows, I won't bother discussing these dinosaurs. They do make superb paperweights, though.

You say you want a resolution

The quality of your laser printer output is a function of the resolution at which you're printing. As you read earlier, *resolution* refers to the number of dots per inch on the paper.

Printing at higher resolutions means that the printer needs more memory to compose the image before it puts the dots on the paper. Therefore, if your output is very complex (which means lots of graphics), your printer may not have enough memory to print the page at its maximum resolution. You can buy more memory for your printer, or you can change the resolution that your printer uses. Many laser printers offer a choice of 300, 150, or 75 dots per inch (dpi).

To adjust your printer's resolution setting directly from Quattro Pro for Windows, do the following:

1. **Choose the Print button on the Toolbar (or choose the File⇔Print command).**

    You'll get the Spreadsheet Print dialog box.

2. **Choose the Select Printer button.**

    You'll get a dialog box that lists all of the installed printers (there may be more than one).

3. **Choose the Setup button.**

    You get another dialog box, which looks different for each printer. The Setup dialog box for an HP LaserJet III laser printer is shown in the accompanying figure.

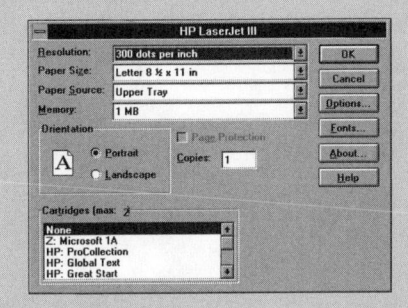

4. **Choose the Resolution drop-down listbox (if there is one) and select a lower resolution.**

    Not all printers let you change the resoluution.

5. **Choose OK to close the dialog box, and then select OK again to close the first dialog box.**

Now try printing your job again. You should be able to print the entire page (although it may not look as good as it does at a higher resolution).

If you change the resolution of your printer, these changes are in effect for all your Windows printing. So if you need higher resolution for another program that you use, you need to change the printer settings back.

Part III
How to Impress the Easily Impressed

The 5th Wave **By Rich Tennant**

"THIS 3D FLOATING BAR GRAPH IS REALLY GOING TO GIVE OUR PRESENTATION STYLE!"

In this part...

Welcome to Part III, in which you will learn some additional techniques to make you a more adept spreadsheet user. You'll discover how to apply fancy formatting to make your notebooks look better, how to create charts, ways to use all of the pages in a Quattro Pro for Windows notebook, and lots of other techniques that just may come in handy.

Chapter 12
Dressing Up Your Work

In This Chapter
▶ How to make your notebooks look great — or at least good
▶ The ins and outs of dealing with fonts — or, making sure WYS is really WYG
▶ All sorts of other formatting options, including drawing borders, changing cell colors, and adjusting cell alignment
▶ Some suggestions to keep you from going hog wild

When it comes to type fonts, sizes, and colors, many people are quite content to accept all of Quattro Pro for Windows' default settings. Using these defaults produces a perfectly acceptable — albeit boring — notebook. Not too many years ago, spreadsheet users didn't have a choice in these matters. Everything that spewed forth from the printer looked pretty much the same: all in one font, with no accoutrements such as borders and shading. Nowadays, even regular people like yourself can produce notebooks that look like they were prepared for a software ad.

If you want to add some pizzazz to your work (and give your creative juices a chance to flow — or trickle), this chapter will tell you all about the stylistic formatting options at your disposal.

What is Stylistic Formatting?

This chapter is mainly about aesthetics. In other words, you'll learn how to use the formatting commands that make your work look good and stand out in a crowd of pages. By formatting, I'm not talking about the *numeric* formatting you do with the numbers in cells. Instead, I'm talking about the following types of formatting (sometimes referred to as stylistic formatting):

- Changing the type font
- Changing the size of the type
- Changing the type attributes (bold, italic, underlined)

Part III: How to Impress the Easily Impressed

- Adding borders and lines
- Changing the colors (or shading) of the text and the background of cells
- Adjusting the alignment of cell contents

When Plain Old Text Won't Cut the Mustard

How something is presented can often have a major influence on how it's accepted. Consider this scenario: Both you and your counterpart (we'll call him Ned) at a competing company submit a proposal to a potential client. Ned's proposal uses plain Courier type (like a typewriter), and yours is nicely formatted with different type sizes, neat borders, and even some shading. Which proposal do *you* think the potential client will read first?

An attractive presentation demands more attention, is easier to read, and makes the reader think that you really care about your work (fooled 'em again!). Figure 12-1 shows an example of an unformatted report (produced by Ned). Figure 12-2 shows that same report after Ned wised up and applied some simple stylistic formatting. Which one do *you* prefer?

	A	B	C	D	E
1					
2		Accounts Receivable Report by City			
3		Montana	Helena	121455	
4		Montana	Cut Bank	90923	
5		Montana	Missoula	87233	
6		Montana	Bozeman	65477	
7		Total for Montana		365088	
8		Oregon	Medford	189221	
9		Oregon	Portland	177834	
10		Oregon	Corvallis	154677	
11		Oregon	Bend	132456	
12		Total for Oregon		654188	
13		Utah	Orem	54667	
14		Utah	Salt Lake City	23343	
15		Total for Utah		78010	
16		Washington	Seattle	533092	
17		Washington	Spokane	124435	
18		Washington	Redmond	45663	
19		Total for Washington		703190	
20					

Figure 12-1: An unformatted report.

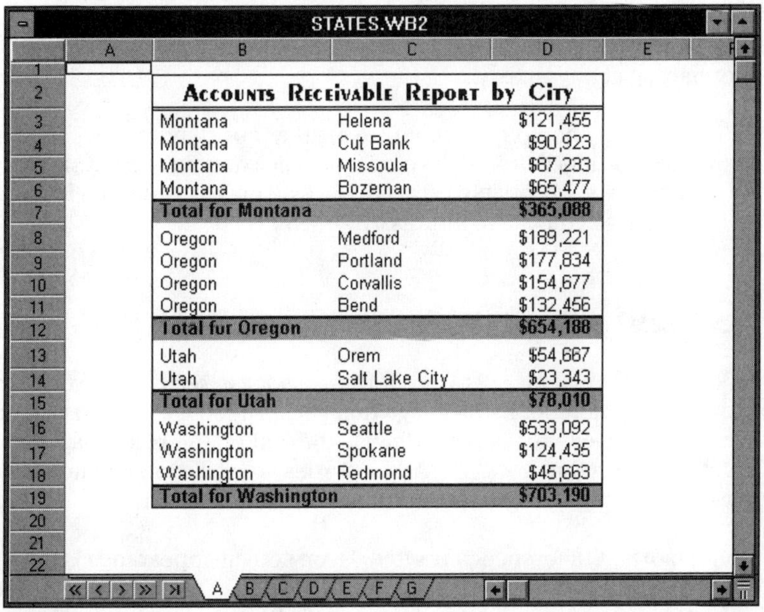

Chapter 12: Dressing Up Your Work *215*

Figure 12-2: A report with some simple formatting.

	A	B	C	D
1				
2		Accounts Receivable Report by City		
3		Montana	Helena	$121,455
4		Montana	Cut Bank	$90,923
5		Montana	Missoula	$87,233
6		Montana	Bozeman	$65,477
7		**Total for Montana**		**$365,088**
8		Oregon	Medford	$189,221
9		Oregon	Portland	$177,834
10		Oregon	Corvallis	$154,677
11		Oregon	Bend	$132,456
12		**Total for Oregon**		**$654,188**
13		Utah	Orem	$54,667
14		Utah	Salt Lake City	$23,343
15		**Total for Utah**		**$78,010**
16		Washington	Seattle	$533,092
17		Washington	Spokane	$124,435
18		Washington	Redmond	$45,663
19		**Total for Washington**		**$703,190**

The preceding scenario is not meant to imply that a nicely formatted notebook report can compensate for a lousy analysis. In most cases, you must have the content before you add the flair. But if you take the time to do some stylistic formatting, at least you won't have a lousy analysis *and* a lousy-looking report.

But there's one more reason to make time to format your work nicely: it's fun. In fact, you'll probably find that formatting your work is a lot more interesting than building formulas and copying ranges (I do).

General Principles of Formatting

Before we get too far into formatting, I'll offer a few general words of wisdom on this topic. Take it as gospel or with a grain of salt.

When to format

Some people like to format their notebooks as they develop them. Others prefer to save the formatting for the final step — after they're sure everything works the way it should. Neither of these approaches is better than the other. It's just a matter of individual preferences. Like everything else you do in Quattro Pro for Windows, nothing is carved in stone. So you can always change your formatting at any time.

By the way, it should go without saying that not all notebooks need to have fancy formatting. If you're developing a quick and dirty analysis for your own use only, there's probably no need to waste even one minute formatting it nicely (unless you like to impress yourself).

Screen vs. printer

One thing to remember is WYSIWYG — *what you see is what you get.* When you format your notebook, the image that gets printed will look very much like the image you see on the screen. Change the font on the screen, and your notebook will print with that new font. Add a border around a table of numbers, and the border will appear in the printout. And so on and so on.

An important difference in printed vs. on-screen appearance is color. Because most people don't have color printers, your on-screen colors get translated into shades of gray when you print your work. It's important to keep this difference in mind, because some color combinations look great on the screen, but they look terrible when they're printed. If you need to have something that looks good on paper *and* looks good on screen, the best approach is to experiment with various colors.

General formatting how-to

When it comes to stylistic formatting, Quattro Pro for Windows makes it pretty easy on you. In general, you select the range of cells that you want to format, and then you give an instruction that represents the type of formatting you want.

There are several choices at your disposal:

- Use the Toolbar tools for many of the formatting operations.
- Use the Property Band (below the Toolbar) for some formatting operations.
- Use the shortcut menu (right-click on your selection) and select Block Properties.
- Use automatic "SpeedFormats" (discussed later).
- Copy existing formats to other cells.

You'll learn all this fun stuff in this chapter, so don't go away.

Introducing the Format Toolbar

You can perform much of your notebook formatting using the Format Toolbar. Normally, this Toolbar doesn't appear, but it's easy to get to. Here's how:

1. **Choose the Toolbars pull-down on the Property Band (it probably says Main).**
2. **Choose Format from the pull-down list of Toolbars.**

This will replace the current Toolbar with the Format Toolbar, which is shown in Figure 12-3.

Figure 12-3: The Format Toolbar — your key to easy formatting.

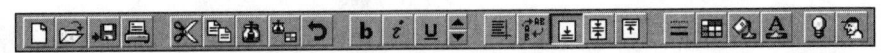

Table 12-1 gives a quick rundown on what these buttons can do for you. As always, these buttons operate on the current cell or selected block of cells.

Table 12-1	Buttons on the Format Toolbar
Button	What It Does
Cut	Cuts the selection and puts it on the Clipboard
Copy	Copies the selection and puts it on the Clipboard
Paste	Pastes the contents of the Clipboard
Paste Properties	Pastes only the properties from the Clipboard (not the Clipboard contents)
Undo/Redo	Reverses the last operation you performed (or reverses an undo)
Bold	Toggles bold on and off
Italic	Toggles italic on and off
Underline	Toggles character underlining on and off (but does not affect cell borders)

(continued)

Table 12-1 *(continued)*

Button		What It Does
	Font Size Arrows	Makes the font larger (up arrow) or smaller (down arrow)
	Word Wrap	Toggles cell word wrapping
	Orientation	Changes the text orientation
	Vertical Alignment: Bottom	Puts the text at the bottom of the cell (normal)
	Vertical Alignment: Center	Centers the text vertically in the cell
	Vertical Alignment: Top	Puts the text at the top of the cell
	Line Draw	Displays the Line Drawing dialog box to put borders around cells
	SpeedFormat	Brings up the SpeedFormat dialog box to quickly format a table
	Shading	Brings up the Shading dialog box to change the background color
	Text Color	Brings up the Text Color dialog box to change the color of text

You'll do yourself a favor by becoming familiar with these buttons.

Dealing with Fonts

One thing that can drastically change the look of your work is the font or fonts that you use. A *font* refers to the typeface that's used for text and numbers. The actual fonts that you can use depend on what fonts are installed in your computer system. There are many different fonts, and they come in many different sizes. Some are designed for ordinary work, and others can best be described as decorative.

Types of fonts

You can use only the fonts that are installed in your system. Actually, the fonts come in files and are installed in Windows itself, not in the individual programs you run.

Fonts come in two flavors:

- **Fixed-size fonts.** With these fonts, you need a separate font file installed for each size that you want to use. For example, you might have a 12-point Helvetica font and a 10-point Helvetica font. You can use either size, but you *can't* use 14-point Helvetica.

- **Scalable fonts.** These fonts are the most versatile. A scalable font can appear in virtually any size you want. If you have a scalable Helvetica font installed, you can use it any size. You can have a 6-point Helvetica footnote and a 20-point Helvetica title — and they both use the same installed font file.

Chances are, you already have access to some scalable fonts known as TrueType fonts. A few of these fonts are included with Windows. They have names like Arial, Times New Roman, and Courier New. You may have even more.

You may have noticed that fonts differ on another characteristic — their horizontal spacing. With some fonts, every character takes up the same amount of horizontal space. These are known as *monospaced* fonts. A common example of a monospaced font is Courier. Other fonts use different amounts of horizontal space for each character. For example, the letter *i* doesn't take up as much horizontal space as the letter *W*. Figure 12-4 shows the same text in both Courier (a monospaced font) and Times New Roman (a variable-spaced font).

But the good news is that most fonts use the same amount of horizontal space for the number characters, which means that the numbers you put in a column of cells will line up nicely regardless of what font you select.

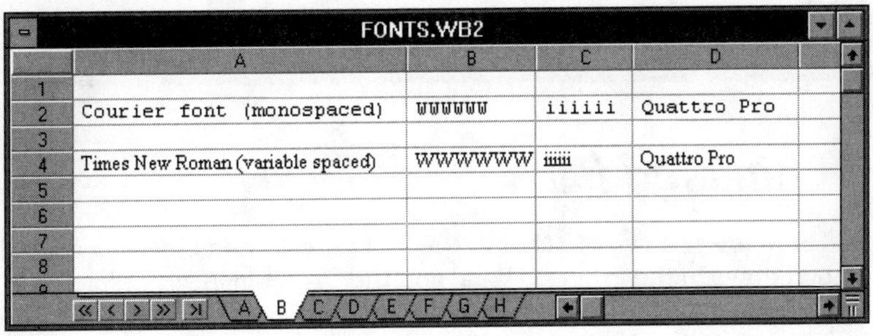

Figure 12-4: Fonts vary in the amount of horizontal space they use.

Got a case of font envy?

You may have seen some printed output from a colleague that used some great-looking fonts. Chances are, this person acquired some new TrueType fonts from one of many sources. The accompanying figure shows a sampling of some TrueType fonts that I have installed. As you can see in the following figure, there's a good variety — although not all of them are appropriate for a board report.

So where do you get these new fonts? Sometimes, when you install a new software program, the program adds some new fonts. You can also buy separate font collections and install them in Windows. And if you know where to look, you can get lots of new fonts for free. For example, you can download fonts from computer bulletin boards or on-line services such as America Online or CompuServe. And you can get collections of shareware or public domain fonts by mail order or in your local computer store (very cheaply, I might add).

Installing new fonts is done through the Windows Control Panel. After running Control Panel, click on the Fonts icon, and then choose the Add button. You'll need to tell the program where the new fonts are located (usually on a floppy disk). Consult your Windows manual (or your office font freak) if you need help. When you install new TrueType fonts, these fonts are automatically available in all your Windows programs.

```
                          FONTS.WB2
This font is Braggadocio
Carlson Open Face Font
This font is called Cricket
This font is Minstrel...
KEYSTROKE FONT
This font is named Kids - Wonder why?
Matura MT Script
This font is: Video Terminal Screen
This font is called Oz Handicraft. It is very narrow.
```

Changing fonts

There are two ways to change the font for cells and blocks of cells: the Font pull-down in the Property Band and the Object Inspector dialog box. There are advantages and disadvantages to both.

Chapter 12: Dressing Up Your Work **221**

Changing the font with the Property Band

The easiest way to change the font is to select the cells you want to change and then use the Font pull-down on the Property Band. Simply choose the font you want, and it will be applied to the selected cells. Figure 12-5 shows the Font pull-down in action.

Easy enough, eh? So why would you need to use the Object Inspector? The main disadvantage of using the Font pull-down on the Property Band is that you can't get a preview of the font. This is no big deal if you know what the font looks like. But if you're like I am, you have several dozen fonts installed, and you can't always remember what they look like.

Changing the font with the Object Inspector dialog box

Figure 12-6 shows the Object Inspector dialog box with the Font option selected. To refresh your memory, the Object Inspector dialog box appears when you right-click a cell or block and then choose Block Properties from the shortcut menu.

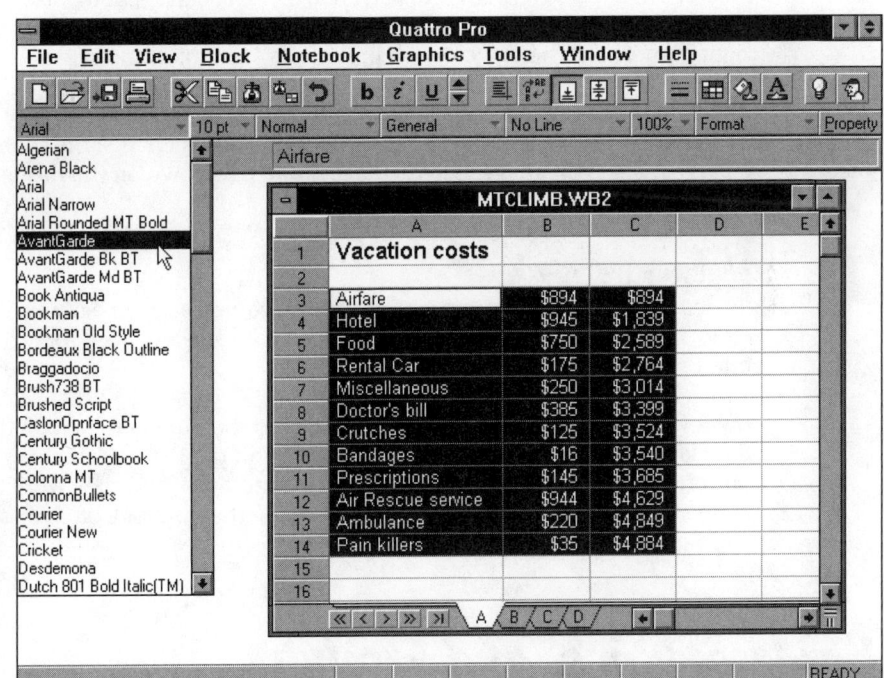

Figure 12-5: Here's the easiest way to change fonts.

Figure 12-6: The Object Inspector is your one-stop shopping place for formatting cells and ranges — although it may not be the most efficient way.

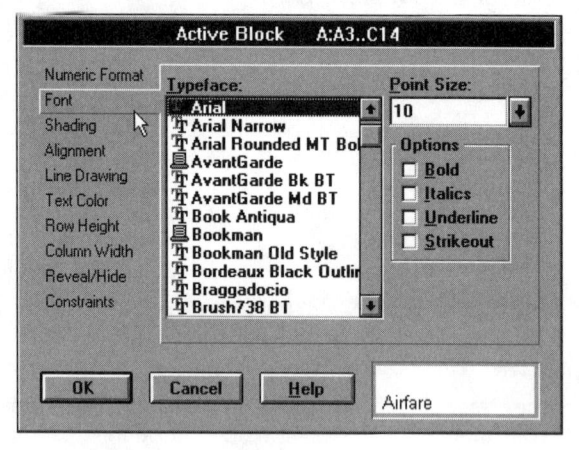

As you can see from this figure, you change the typeface, point size, and attributes such as bold and italic. Also notice the little sample box in the lower right corner. This box gives you a preview of the font at the selected size.

> If your notebook text is hard to read on-screen, you don't necessarily have to use a larger font to make it readable. You can always change the zoom factor to enlarge the screen image. Use the Page Zoom pull-down on the Property Band to do this.

Changing font attributes

If you use the Object Inspector to set a font, you can also specify that it be bold, italic, underlined, or strikethrough (I have yet to see any need for strikethrough, but it's there if you need it).

However, you've probably already discovered the Bold and Italic buttons on the Main Toolbar (these buttons also appear on the Format Toolbar). These buttons do just what you would expect them to do — and they work both ways. If the selected cells are already bold, choosing the Bold button makes them unbold (normal).

Borders, Lines, and Frames

The grid lines that normally appear on your screen make it easy for you to see where the cells are. Normally, you don't print the grid lines (although you can,

Chapter 12: Dressing Up Your Work

if you want). But Quattro Pro for Windows lets you add all kinds of other lines to your notebook — and you have plenty of control over how they look. Adding lines or borders can greatly enhance your notebook, as you can see in Figure 12-7. This figure shows an example of a range before and after adding some lines and borders.

Figure 12-7: Adding lines and borders can spruce up your work.

> **TIP**
>
> If you add lines and borders to your notebook, it's a good idea to turn off the cell grid display. This makes it easier to see the lines that you add. To get rid of the cell grid display, use the Inspect pull-down in the Property Band. Choose Active Page, and then select Display. Uncheck the Horizontal and Vertical options in the Gridlines box. As if by magic, the grid lines will disappear from the current notebook page.

Adding lines or borders

There are three ways to add lines and borders to your notebook. You can

- Use the Property Band (underlines only)
- Use the Object Inspector (any type of lines)
- Use the Line Draw button on the Format Toolbar (any type of lines)

Adding underlines using the Property Band

The Underline pull-down on the Property Band is a quick way to add a border to the *bottom* of a cell or selection. You can't use this method to add borders to the top of a cell, or to the left or right. In other words, it's a bit limited. You do, however, get a choice: thin line, double line, or thick line — plus no line (which removes any underlining).

Adding lines using the Object Inspector

For adding anything but underlines, you'll need to use the Object Inspector dialog box. As usual, start by selecting the cell or block that you want to work with; then right-click and select Block Properties. Choose the Line Drawing option, and you'll see the dialog box shown in Figure 12-8.

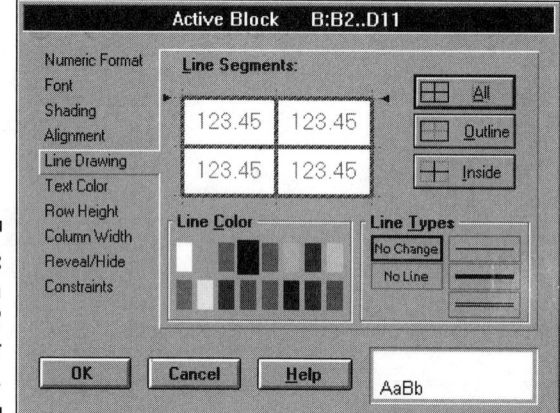

Figure 12-8: Need a border? Take your pick.

This part of the dialog box can be a bit intimidating. Let's break it down into its parts.

Line Segments: Lets you choose where in the selection you want the line to appear. Your choice is controlled by the three buttons to the right (although you can click in the Line Segments box to make your choice).

All: Applies the selected line type around every cell in the block. Choose this button and watch what happens to the Line Segments display.

Outline: Applies the selected line type around the block but not between cells. When you click on this button, the Line Segments display shows only an outline.

Inside: Applies the selected line type between cells but not around the perimeter of the block.

Line Types: Selects the type of line to draw. The No Line choice removes previously drawn lines, and the No Change choice cancels a change you make to a line.

Line Color: Selects the color of the line.

At the risk of copping out, the best way to learn how to draw lines is to try it. It's easier to draw borders than it is to explain how to use this dialog box.

Adding lines using the Line Draw button

The Line Draw button simply displays the part of the Object Inspector dialog box that appears when you select the Line Drawing option. This feature was all described previously, so I won't repeat myself.

Color, Color Everywhere

When I first started out in computing, a color monitor was considered a luxury item. And the color monitors that were available were pretty wimpy by today's standards. Nowadays, practically every system is equipped with a color monitor (except laptops and portables — but that's also rapidly changing). Color is great. It lets you make certain text stand out from the crowd, and coloring the background of a range makes it easy to remember that those cells belong together (not to mention the fact that it's easier on the eyes).

Quattro Pro for Windows lets you change the color of the text in the cells, as well as the background of the cells. I can't really demonstrate this effect with a screen shot because this book is strictly black and white. But suffice it to say that you can get some nice-looking notebooks — as well as some genuinely ugly notebooks — by changing the color of the text and background.

You change colors using Object Inspector. Choose Text Color to change the color of the text in the cells (Figure 12-9), or choose Shading to change the color of the cell background (Figure 12-10).

TIP
The Format Toolbar has tools that let you jump directly to the part of the Object Inspector dialog box that you need. Use the Text Color button to change the color of text and the Shading button to change the background color of cells.

The text in a cell can be any of 16 colors. You have many more choices, however, for the background. When you use the Shading option, you can actually choose two different colors to blend together (seven different blends are provided).

REMEMBER
When you print your notebook on a black-and-white printer, different colors appear as shades of gray. Some combinations of text colors and background colors that look great on the screen will look terrible when they are printed. And to make things even more unpredictable, the results you get depend on the printer you're using. All I can say here is to experiment and see what you get.

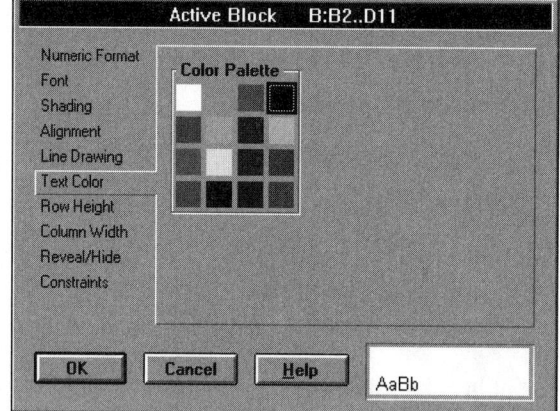

Figure 12-9: Here's where you change the color of the text in a cell or block.

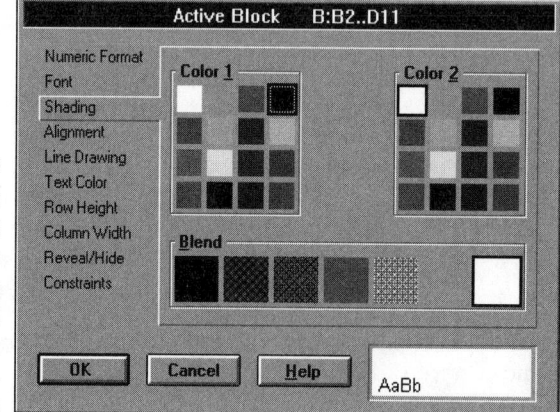

Figure 12-10: And here's where you change the background color of a cell or block.

Alignment and Misalignment

Alignment refers to how the text appears in the cell. There are two types: horizontal alignment refers to how the text lines up in a cell horizontally, and vertical alignment refers to how it lines up vertically.

Horizontal alignment

You probably already know about the common ways of aligning things in cells. You can either make the contents of a cell flush left, flush right, or centered. And the Align pull-down on the Property Band makes such alignment a one-click proposition.

But there are some other alignment options that you might find interesting in your stylistic pursuits. These choices are made in the Alignment section of the Object Inspector dialog box (Figure 12-11).

Figure 12-11: Quattro Pro for Windows gives you the full gamut of alignment options.

Vertical alignment

Normally, information that you enter into a cell sits at the bottom of the cell. Even if you make the row height very large, the cell contents still remain at the bottom of the cell. Quattro Pro for Windows also lets you adjust the alignment of cells in the vertical direction. For example, if you have a very tall row, you can make the text centered vertically within the cell.

Changing the vertical alignment is a good way to space information. If you want, you can make the row that contains the heading for a table of numbers fairly tall, and then center the text vertically (or align it to the top of the cell to add more space between the heading and the table).

Word wrap

One of my favorite things about Quattro Pro for Windows is its Wrap text option. This feature makes each cell formatted with this option work like a tiny word processor. In other words, when you type a long label into the cell, the words wrap around and the row height increases to accommodate the extra lines. Figure 12-12 shows an example of this wrapping. As you can see, it's great for the headings in tables.

Figure 12-12: Using the Wrap text alignment option makes long labels wrap around within a cell.

	A	B	C	D	E
1					
2		Amount Budgeted for 1994	Amount Actually Spent in 1994	Difference (Budget vs Actual) 1994	1995 Budgeted Amount
3	Personnel	784,000	754,988	29,012	825,000
4	Equipment	65,000	82,500	(17,500)	85,000
5	Outside Services	145,000	175,000	(30,000)	200,000
6	Other	90,000	15,670	74,330	20,000
7	Total	1,084,000	1,028,158	55,842	1,130,000

Centering across cells

Another handy feature lets you center a label across a group of cells. Figure 12-13 shows a label that's actually in cell B2, but it's centered across the range B2..G2. This is a good way to put titles across a multicolumn table of numbers. Back in the dark ages (1989), people used to add spaces to their labels (by trial and error) to get this effect.

Figure 12-13: The label is actually in cell B2 — but it's centered across several columns.

	A	B	C	D	E	F	G
1							
2			First Half Results				
3	Jan	71	550	271	814	831	479
4	Feb	13	608	499	387	504	500
5	Mar	491	598	850	188	69	384
6	Apr	725	449	801	882	446	24
7	May	502	209	880	772	402	831
8	Jun	722	691	489	798	306	375

To center a label across a group of columns, first enter the label in the left-most cell of the range you want the label in. Then select that cell and the cells to the right — enough to cover the entire area that you're centering across. Right-click and bring up the Object Inspector dialog box, choose Alignment, and select Center Across block. Voilà!

It's quicker to use the Alignment pull-down on the Property Band. Just select the cells and choose the Center Across Block option from the pull-down list.

Changing orientation

Another interesting feature lets you change how the text is oriented in a cell. You have only two choices, which you can select by choosing the Alignment option in the Object Inspector dialog box. Figure 12-14 shows an example of vertical orientation.

A faster way to change the orientation of the text in a cell is to select the Orientation button on the Format Toolbar.

Figure 12-14: For special cases, you may want to make the text in a cell have a vertical orientation.

	A	B	C	D	E	F	G
1							
2		J a n	F e b	M a r	A p r	M a y	J u n
3	Product A	71	13	491	725	502	722
4	Product B	550	608	598	449	209	691
5	Product C	271	499	850	801	880	489
6	Product D	814	387	188	882	772	798
7	Product E	831	504	69	446	402	306
8	Product F	479	500	384	24	831	375
9							

And Now, the E-Z Way to Format Tables

If you made it through the preceding sections of this chapter, you should have a pretty good handle on formatting your notebooks. Let's say you have a table of numbers in your notebook. You can use any or all of the techniques I previously discussed to make a pretty spiffy looking table. Doing so may take you a good 15 minutes or more. Or you can take the express route and have Quattro Pro for Windows do the work for you — in about 2 seconds.

To format a table of numbers automatically, first select the entire table. Then choose the SpeedFormat button on the Format Toolbar. Quattro Pro for Windows displays the dialog box shown in Figure 12-15. This box lets you select from a list of 21 formats and shows you an example of each as you scroll through the template list. For some reason, these formats are named for composers. Don't ask me...

When you find one you like, choose OK, and the formatting will be applied instantly.

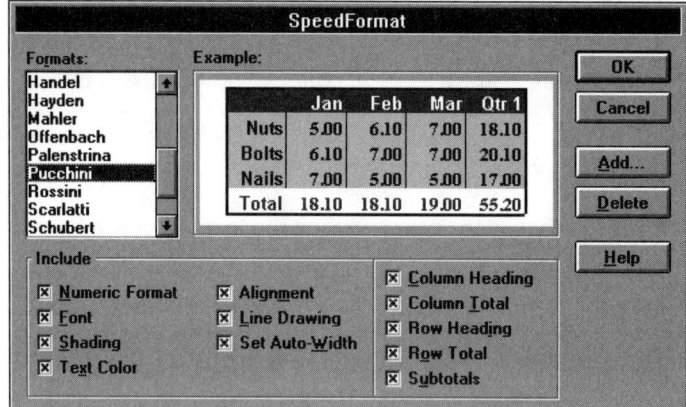

Figure 12-15: Here, you can select one of 21 canned styling formats.

The bottom part of this dialog box lets you turn off formatting features that you don't want. For example, if your table doesn't have column totals and row totals, you'll want to uncheck these choices in the SpeedFormat dialog box. Also, you may not want to have the column widths adjusted — so uncheck the Set Auto-Width checkbox.

Applying one of these SpeedFormats to a selected range can cause some drastic changes in the look of your notebook. For example, the column widths may change, the fonts and attributes may change, and you may get many new colors. If you don't like the looks of things after you close the dialog box, select Edit⇨Undo immediately to reverse the effects (or save your original file before applying a SpeedFormat). As an alternative to scrapping the whole formatting job, you can simply reformat the part of the table that you don't like.

If you don't like any of the canned SpeedFormat options, you can create your own. Start by formatting a table exactly as you like it. Select the table, choose the SpeedFormat button, and then select the Add button in the SpeedFormat dialog box. You give the format a name, and it will show up in the list the next time you use the SpeedFormat button.

Some Final Words

I've found that it's really easy to get carried away with formatting. Once you learn what you can do (and you can do a great deal), it's very tempting to waste too much time trying to get everything just perfect. You have to weigh the value of what you're doing against the value of your time. In other words, don't spend

Chapter 12: Dressing Up Your Work

three hours formatting a report that took you 15 minutes to develop — especially if no one will ever read it. Also, bad formatting is worse than no formatting. So don't go overboard with colors and lines.

If your system has dozens of fonts installed, go easy on them. Just because you have two dozen fonts available doesn't mean you need to use them all in a single notebook. As a general rule of thumb, you should not use more than two fonts in a document. If you want variety, it's often better to change the size of some of the text, or to make the text italic or bold.

And finally, remember that substance is what really counts. It's better to spend your time making sure your analysis is correct than making it look good. 'Nuff said.

Chapter 13
Presto Chango: Turning Numbers into Graphs

● ●

In This Chapter
▶ Transforming a block of common, everyday numbers into an attention-grabbing graph
▶ Converting your graph to the graph type you want
▶ Changing some of the graph parts
▶ Exploring some of the more interesting graph types you can create in Quattro Pro For Windows

● ●

*B*ecause people tend to be visual by nature (which is a polite way of saying we can't read), often we can grasp a concept better if it's in the form of a picture or diagram. Take a look at Figure 13-1. It shows a block of numbers on the left and the same numbers expressed as a graph on the right. Which tells the story better?

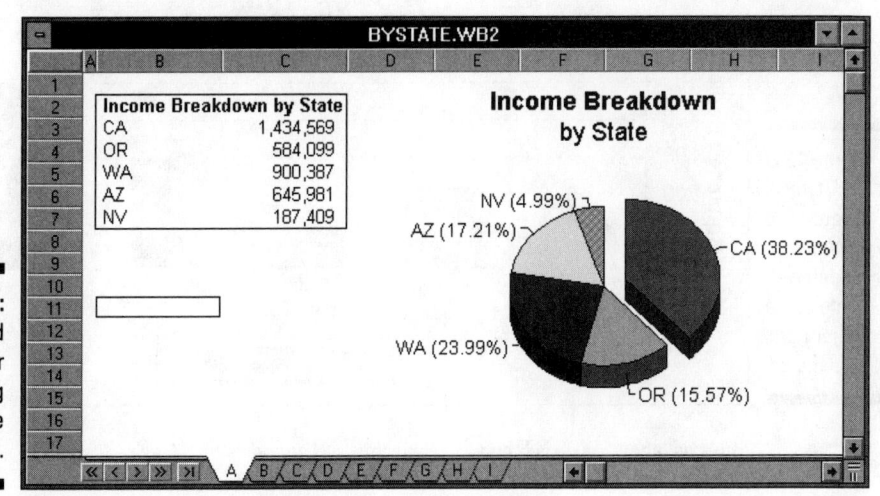

Figure 13-1: Boring old numbers or a titillating graph? Take your pick.

Quattro Pro for Windows has some great graphing capabilities, and, with them, you can create some awesome-looking graphs. It's easy to make a simple graph, and if you spend some time playing around, it won't take long to discover how to customize a graph to your liking and make it even better.

The Graph's Parts

Figure 13-2 shows a graph I created in Quattro Pro For Windows, with all the major parts labeled. Some of these parts are optional, and you can get rid of them if you don't want to see them. For example, when you're plotting only a single group of data, you probably don't want a legend. I'll be referring to the various parts of a graph throughout this chapter, so you may want to familiarize yourself with these terms.

Graphs typically display one or more series of numbers. A series of numbers is stored in the cells in your notebook. The series can be displayed as lines, bars (or columns), pie slices, and several other options. The example shown displays a company's income by month, depicted as bars. There are many types of graphs and many variations on each type. You'll learn much more about these issues throughout the chapter.

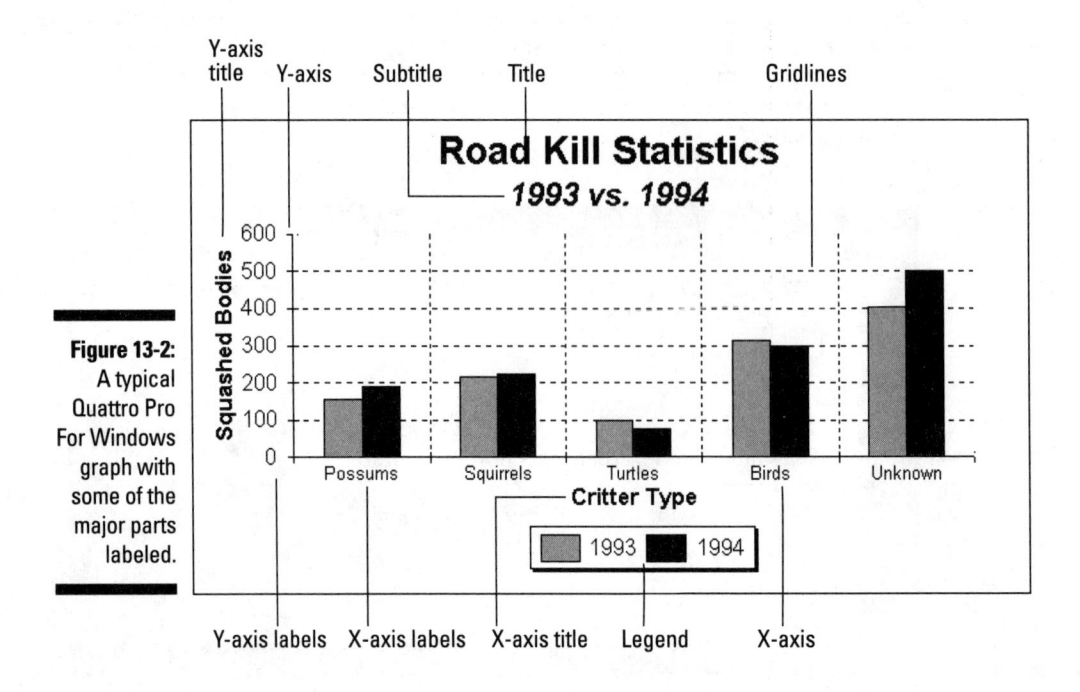

Figure 13-2: A typical Quattro Pro For Windows graph with some of the major parts labeled.

Graph Tidbits

Before you charge into this challenging graph chapter, take a few minutes to digest the following factoids:

- To create a graph, Quattro Pro For Windows uses numbers that are stored in a notebook. The numbers can be values or the results of formulas.
- When you change any of the numbers used by a graph, the graph automatically changes to reflect the new numbers.
- A Quattro Pro For Windows graph can show any number of number series in a single graph.
- You can choose from a long list of graph types: bar graphs, line graphs, pie graphs, and more. And a single graph can have both lines and bars, for example.
- You don't have to have a legend if you don't want one. A *legend* (like on a map — not the King Arthur type) explains what each color or line stands for.
- You have almost complete control over the graph's colors, hatch patterns, line widths, line markers, title and label fonts, and so on.
- Graphs live right on your notebook. This lets you print a graph along with the data it uses — and you also can move a graph and change its size.
- A notebook can have any number of graphs stored in it. And you can put as many as you want on a single page.

How to Create a Graph

OK, I've wasted enough pages with this preliminary graph chit-chat. Now it's time to get down to the nitty gritty.

Despite rumors you may have heard, creating a graph is very easy. Figure 13-3 shows a block of cells that's practically begging to be turned into a graph. Here's how to make a graph out of these numbers. If you want to follow along at home, take a minute to re-create this notebook first.

1. **Select the data that will make up your graph.**

    This includes the cells that hold labels and legends. For this example, select A1..C6.

Part III: How to Impress the Easily Impressed

Figure 13-3:
This information would make a very nice graph.

	A	B	C
1		Widgets	Sprockets
2	Jan	344	211
3	Feb	365	202
4	Mar	398	188
5	Apr	402	173
6	May	477	155

   2. **Choose the Graph button on the Main Toolbar (it has a picture of a graph on it).**

   The mouse pointer will turn into a small graph.

   3. **Click and drag the graph mouse pointer in your notebook.**

   The exact size or location isn't important. Make it approximately four cells wide by ten cells high. When you release the mouse button, Quattro Pro For Windows displays the graph in the area you outlined (see Figure 13-4).

That's all there is to it. After selecting the data, all it takes is a click of the Toolbar button and a bit of dragging in your notebook — and you have yourself a graph.

Quattro Pro for Windows analyzes the data in the selected block and tries to figure out which type of graph would be most appropriate (its guess is not always right). In this case, Quattro Pro For Windows chose a 2-D bar graph. If you don't like the graph type, it's easy enough to change it (more about this later).

Figure 13-4:
The graph appears with only a few mouse clicks.

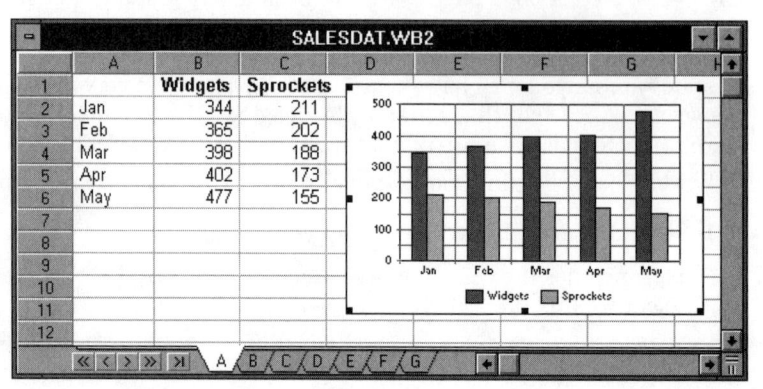

Notice the following things about this graph:

- It doesn't have a title (but we can easily add one).
- It realized that the first column had labels and used these for axis labels.
- It also figured out the names for the series (Widgets and Sprockets).

If you want to learn how to change some of these things, don't stop now. Keep reading.

REMEMBER: To create a graph, select the data (including labels), and then choose the Graph button on the Main Toolbar. Click and drag in the notebook to specify the graph's size and location. Quattro Pro for Windows will analyze your data and create a graph that it thinks will satisfy you.

Making a Graph Be Your Eternal Slave

After Quattro Pro for Windows draws a graph on your notebook, you have a great deal of control over it. You can change its graph type, move the graph around, change its size, print it, and even wipe it off the face of the planet if you don't like it. This section tells you how to do all of these things.

There are two ways to select a graph for modification:

- **Click it once.** This selects the graph and lets you make changes to the graph as a whole (big changes). For example, this lets you change the graph type.
- **Double-click it.** This lets you select individual elements in the graph for you to modify (and fine-tune). For example, double-clicking is the first step to take if you want to change the color of the bars in the graph. Double-clicking a graph also displays the Graph Toolbar, which has many goodies on it.

When you're finished working with a graph, just click anywhere in your notebook to de-select the graph.

I'll start out by discussing some simple changes you can make to a graph.

Part III: How to Impress the Easily Impressed

> ### Exploring the drawing tools on the Toolbars
>
> Double-clicking on a graph automatically displays the Graph Toolbar, which has many interesting buttons on it. Many of these buttons are tools that let you draw things directly in your graph. You can draw lines, arrows, geometric shapes, and even boxes that hold text. These options are often useful when you want to spiff up an otherwise boring graph.
>
> These drawing tools are also available on the Layout Toolbar — which you can select from the Toolbars pull-down on the Property Band. If you display the Layout Toolbar, you can draw things directly on your notebook (not just in a graph). These tools are easy to use and work just as you would expect them to. Once an object is drawn, you can right-click on it and adjust its properties. You can come up with some interesting doodles using these tools — a great way to pass the time when you're put on eternal hold on a phone call. The accompanying figure shows a sample of my idle doodling using the drawing tools.

Changing the graph type

Quattro Pro for Windows lets you choose from 48 graph types. You can customize each of these quite a bit, so you really have more flexibility than you'll ever need.

How do you know what type of graph to create? Don't ask me. There are no hard-and-fast rules on choosing graph types, but I do have some advice: use the graph type that gets your message across in the simplest way. To display quantities over time, a line, bar, or area graph is a good choice. To show percents of a total, use a pie graph.

Chapter 13: Presto Chango: Turning Numbers into Graphs

To change the graph type, first select the graph (click on it), and then choose the Graphics⇨Type command from the menu. You can also right-click on the graph and choose Type from the shortcut menu. Either way, you'll see the dialog box shown in Figure 13-5.

Figure 13-5: You change the graph type in the Graph Types dialog box.

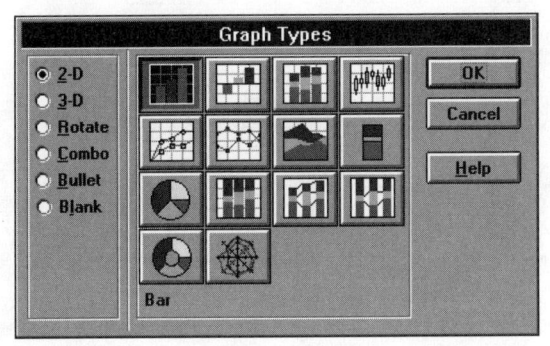

Choose one of the option buttons on the left to display a different set of graphs on the right. The Bullet and Blank options are for text charts and don't really apply to most of the graphs you'll make. Click on the image that looks good, and then select OK. Your graph will be transformed to the selected graph type.

If you don't like what you see, try again. Chances are, one of the four dozen graph types will suit your fancy.

Adding titles

When you first create a graph, it won't have a title. Normally, it's a good idea to give a title to a graph (sorry, "War and Peace" is already taken). Select the graph and choose the Graphics⇨Titles command from the menu (or right-click on it and select Titles). You'll get a dialog box that lets you enter a Main Title, a Subtitle, an X-Axis Title, and a Y1-Axis Title (two if your graph has two y axes — which it usually won't). Figure 13-6 shows a graph with all of the titles entered so that you can see where they go.

Changing the graph series

After you make a graph, you may want to change the data series — make it use more or fewer data points, for example. You *could* just redo the graph. But if you've made many changes to it, you'll have to repeat all those changes with your new graph. An easier way is to tell Quattro Pro for Windows to use different blocks of data for the graph.

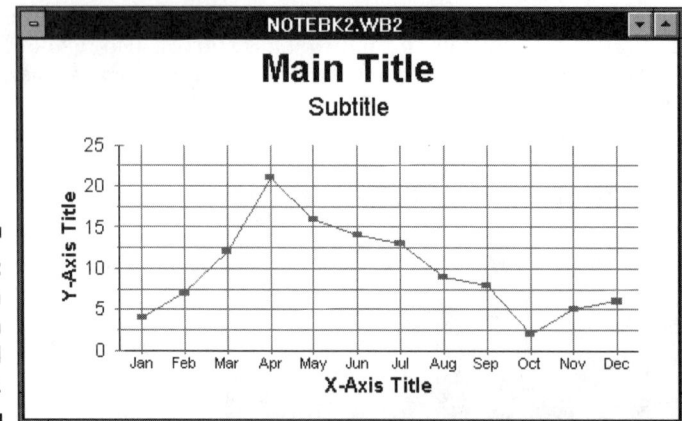

Figure 13-6: This graph has been customized with titles.

Psst. Want to make a really fancy graph?

Don't tell anybody, but it's very easy to create some truly stunning graphs in Quattro Pro for Windows — with virtually no effort on your part. The secret is the Graphics⇨Graph Gallery command. After you create a graph and select it, choose this command. You'll get a dialog box like the one shown in the accompanying figure.

This dialog box is fairly straightforward. Choose a graph category from the Category drop-down list. This list will display several styles in the Style section (use the scroll bar to see even more). When you find a style you like, choose it. Then move over to the drop-down list labeled Color Scheme, and choose one of the color schemes from the list. When you find something good, choose it. When you're satisfied with the sample shown, select OK and watch your mundane graph turn into a work of art. You can tell your coworkers that you spent all afternoon customizing your graph so the boss would like it.

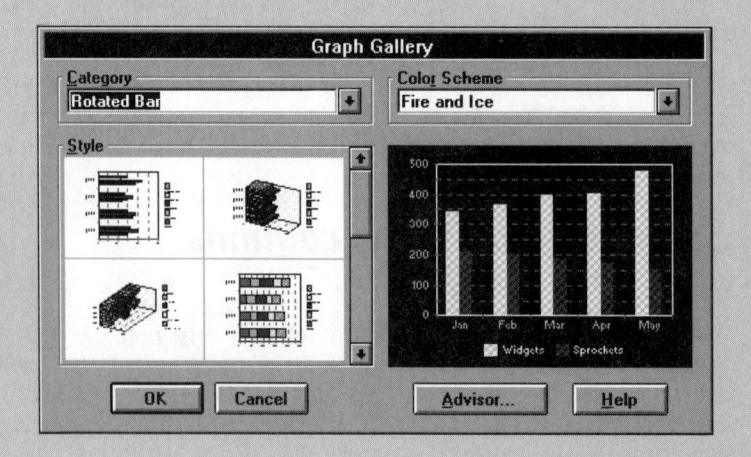

To change the graph series, choose the Graphics⇨Series command (or right-click and choose Series from the shortcut menu). You'll see a rather intimidating dialog box like the one shown in Figure 13-7.

Figure 13-7: The Graph Series dialog box lets you change the data used for the graph.

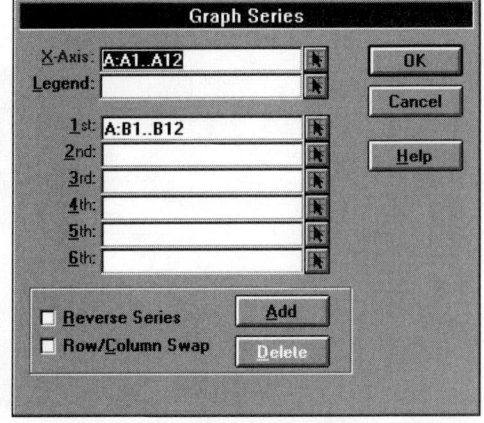

This dialog box shows you which blocks of cells are being used for the graph's parts: the X-Axis, the Legend, and each of the data series. To change the data series, just modify the cell references in the appropriate part of the dialog box.

Here's an example. Say your graph's data is in B1..B11 and its X-axis labels are in A1..A11. You added another data point in cell B12 (and a corresponding label in A12). To get this new information in your graph, just change the references for the X-Axis and the 1st Series. You can make the change by editing the text box, or select the text in the text box and point to the new range in the notebook. When you choose OK, your graph will be updated with the new data point.

Of course, you also can *reduce* the number of data points being plotted by changing the block references. You even can add a completely new data series by entering a block reference in the next available series slot.

Swapping rows and columns

Sometimes your graph won't look the way you thought it would. Take a look at Figure 13-8. This shows some data and the graph generated by Quattro Pro for Windows (I changed it to a 2-D bar graph). It's a perfectly good graph. You showed it around, and the office staff were drooling. When you showed it to your boss, she said that the month names should be in the legend. As you saunter back to your cubicle, you realize that you have two choices: Re-enter your data in the opposite orientation, or find the command that swaps the rows and columns in the graph.

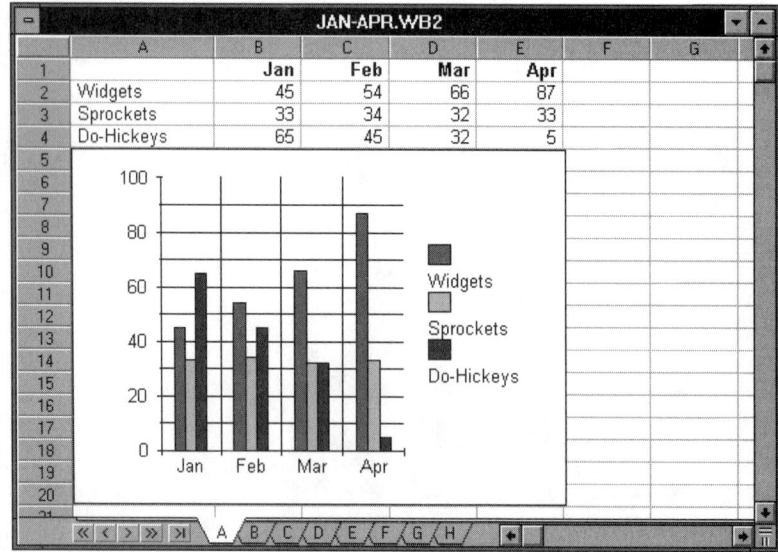

Figure 13-8: Nice graph, but your boss wanted the rows and columns swapped.

Re-entering a small amount of data is no big deal. But it *is* a big deal if your graph uses hundreds of cells. Because you could waste quite a bit of time looking for that *swap* command, I'll tell you where it is. Select the graph and choose Graphics⇨Series from the menu (or right-click on it and choose Series from the shortcut menu). There, at the bottom of the dialog box, is a checkbox labeled Row/column swap. Check this box, choose OK, and your graph will go through a dynamic dimensional transformation. In plain English, it'll swap the rows and columns. The new graph is shown in Figure 13-9 — same data, different view.

You'll have to admit that this modification makes it much more apparent that Widgets are doing great, Sprockets are holding their own, and the person responsible for Do-Hickey sales had better start looking for another job.

Moving and resizing a graph

To move a graph, click on it and drag it. The mouse pointer will turn into a hand when you can drag it. You also can use the Windows Clipboard to move graphs to places where you can't drag them. For example, if you want to move a graph from one notebook page to another, you can cut it with the Edit⇨Cut command and then paste it in another sheet with the Edit⇨Paste command.

To resize a graph, first select it. You'll notice that the graph has eight "handles." These guys are the little black dots at each corner and in the middle of each side. Click on any of these handles and drag it. You can make a graph as large or as small as you like.

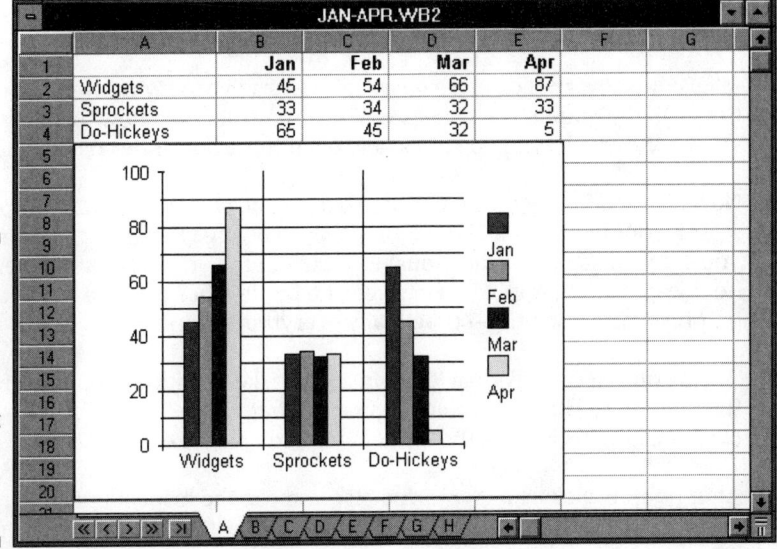

Figure 13-9: The same data as shown in the previous figure, but the rows and columns are reversed.

Graph annihilation techniques

To remove a graph from your notebook (and from the known universe), select it and issue the Edit⇨Clear command (or simply press Del).

Printing graphs

Graphs look best on the screen, because they show up in living color (assuming that you have a color monitor, of course). But, most of the time, you'll need to print a graph on paper so you can share it with someone who likes (or, unfortunately, demands) to see such things.

When a graph is inserted on your notebook, it will be printed along with all of the cell contents. It's that simple.

When using a laser printer, it's not uncommon to try to print several graphs on one page and discover that the entire page did not get printed. This means that your printer doesn't have enough memory to print the entire page. You have three choices: rearrange your notebook to print fewer graphs on one page, add more memory to your printer (usually an expensive proposition), or print at a lower resolution (see Chapter 11 for details).

Rearranging Your Graph's Furniture

Like almost everything else you do in Quattro Pro for Windows, you can change things in the graphs you generate. You already learned how to change some things: the graph type, the titles, and even the graph series data.

Now it's time for some fine-tuning. To fine-tune elements in your graph, always start by double-clicking the graph. This will change the graph's border, and you'll be able to select individual elements in the graph. For example, after double-clicking a graph, you can select a bar in a bar graph, a line in a line graph, an axis, the title — practically everything there is.

> **TIP:** When you select individual items in a graph, keep your eye on the left side of the input line. This tells you the name of what you selected. For example, if you click the graph's legend, the input line will display the word *Legend*.

> **TIP:** After double-clicking a graph, you also can use the Inspect pull-down on the Property band to choose a graph part to work with. For example, if you want to modify the legend, just choose Legend from the pull-down. This command will select it for you and display the Object Inspector dialog box for you.

> **TIP:** Double-clicking a graph also displays the Graph Toolbar for you. Oddly, most of the buttons on this Toolbar are for drawing, not working with graphs (the drawing buttons are also on the Layout Toolbar). One useful button is the Graph Gallery button, which lets you create some way-cool graphs without even trying.

You can make hundreds of changes to the elements in your graph. If you don't like the way something looks, change it. One way to change something in a graph is to right-click the part that you want to change. Choose xxx Properties from the shortcut menu (xxx will be replaced by the name of the item you right-clicked). You'll get an Object Inspector dialog box that's appropriate for what you selected. Choose the desired category from the list and make your changes.

Here's a list of some of the things you may want to change in a graph:

- **Colors.** You can change the color of anything in a graph — bars in a bar graph, lines in a line graph, the graph background, text, and so on.
- **Shading and patterns.** Besides color, you can control the shading and patterns used in a graph.
- **Scales.** A graph's scale is made up of the numbers used on the *y* axis. Usually, the scale chosen by Quattro Pro for Windows is just fine. Sometimes, however, you may want to change the scale to emphasize or de-emphasize changes in the data. Do this by selecting the axis and choosing the Scale option.

✔ **Gridlines.** You can remove gridlines, add gridlines, or change the way gridlines look. Select the axis and choose Major Grid Style or Minor Grid Style. To remove gridlines, click the <u>L</u>ine Style option button and select the upper left sample box.

After you double-click a graph, you have access to a new Toolbar called Palette; all you have to do is select it from the Toolbars pull-down in the Property band. This little gambit lets you quickly change the color of a selected object. Also, don't overlook the Color Scheme pull-down — which is available only after you double-click a graph. The color scheme pull-down lets you make massive changes to your graph's colors with a single click.

Hungry for More Graph Power?

There's much more you can do with graphs. But because this is a beginner's book, I'll have to stop now. Here's some advice, though: You'll learn much more by simply digging in and playing around than you will by reading instructions. And you'll be surprised at how easy it is. So just go for it, eh?

When you want to change something in a graph, just remember these three rules:

1. Right-click the graph, and look for the command you want in the shortcut menu.

2. If you can't find what you want in the shortcut menu, double-click the graph, and then right-click the element you want to modify. Chances are, you'll find what you want in the Object Inspector dialog box.

3. Keep your eye on the Toolbar and Property band. Both of them have some useful information when a graph is selected.

Gallery of Gorgeous Graphs

I'll close this chapter by filling the pages with some sample graphs that I created. These examples demonstrate some of the things you can do with graphs and may give you some ideas that you can adapt to your own situation.

An annotated line graph

This graph, in Figure 13-10, shows a line graph with some annotations added. I used the Text tool on the Graph Toolbar to add free-floating text. Then I used the Arrow tool to identify certain points on the graph.

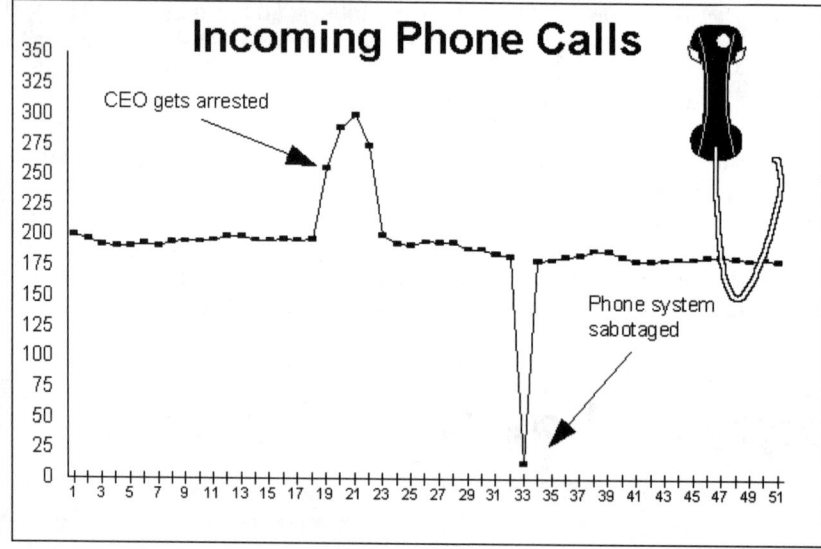

Figure 13-10: Sometimes it's useful to add comments to a graph using the drawing tools on the Graph Toolbar.

A combination graph

When is a bar graph not a bar graph? When it also includes lines. The graph in Figure 13-11 is called a combination graph (or a mixed graph). Notice that this graph has two different scales. The bars belong with the left Y-axis and show the monthly sales. The line goes with the right Y-axis and shows the percent of sales goal reached. If I had used the left scale for both series, the line would not have shown up because all of the values are less than 1.1 (110%).

This graph began life as an ordinary bar graph. Then I changed the second series to be shown as a line. To do this, double-click the graph, and then right-click the series you want to change. Choose Bar Series Properties from the shortcut menu. In the dialog box that comes up, you can change the series to whatever you want in the Override type box. Then assign the series to the Secondary Y-Axis.

A rotated bar graph

Bar graphs don't always have to start from the bottom and work their way up. The graph in Figure 13-12 shows a bar graph — but with the Horizontal orientation option chosen. This graph type is particularly useful when the X-axis labels are long. In this graph, I used the Text tool to add free-floating text (the survey question) right below the title. I also added data labels to the graph series — which make the values appear in the graph. You do this in the Bar Series dialog box.

Chapter 13: Presto Chango: Turning Numbers into Graphs   **247**

Figure 13-11: This combination graph features bars and a line (hence the name).

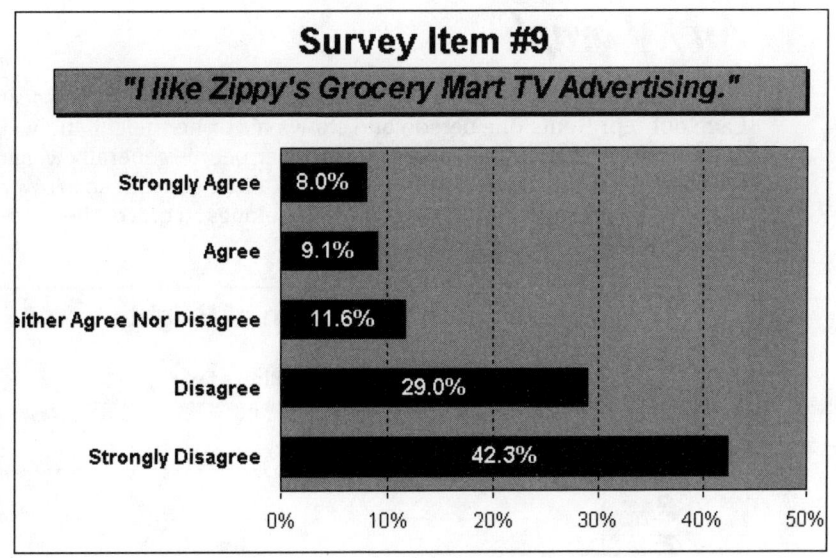

Sales Performance — bar chart showing Sales (Jan–Jun) with a Pct of Goal line overlay. Left axis: Sales 60,000–240,000. Right axis: Pct. of Sales Goal 85%–110%.

Figure 13-12: A rotated bar graph.

Survey Item #9 — "I like Zippy's Grocery Mart TV Advertising."
- Strongly Agree: 8.0%
- Agree: 9.1%
- Neither Agree Nor Disagree: 11.6%
- Disagree: 29.0%
- Strongly Disagree: 42.3%

Stacked bars

This graph (shown in Figure 13-13) compares two sets of data using a stacked bar graph. Another option would be to use one of the combination graph types (for example, two pies). Quattro Pro for Windows converted the values to percents.

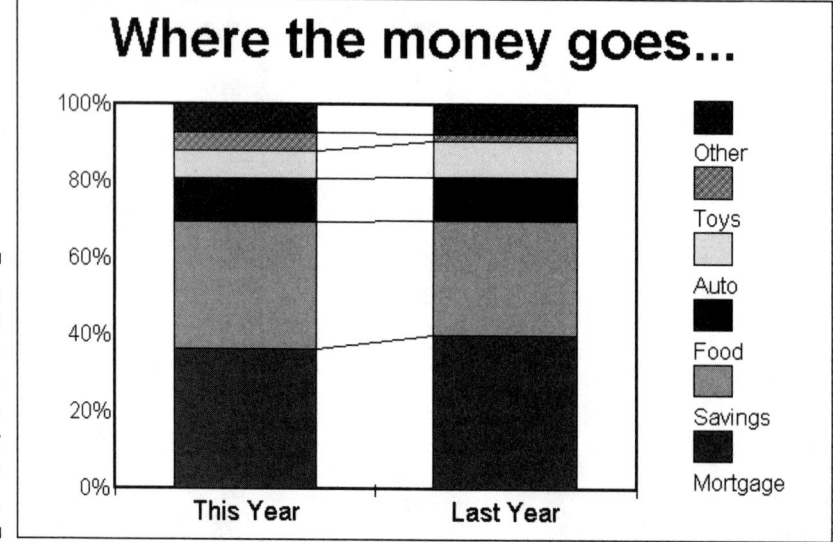

Figure 13-13: A stacked bar graph can substitute for two or more pie graphs.

An XY graph

The graph in Figure 13-14 is an XY graph (sometimes known as a scattergram). Each dot represents one person and shows his or her height and weight. As you can see, there's an upward linear trend: taller people generally weigh more than shorter folks. I also used the drawing tools (a text box and an arrow) to make a tasteless comment about the person who belongs to one of the dots.

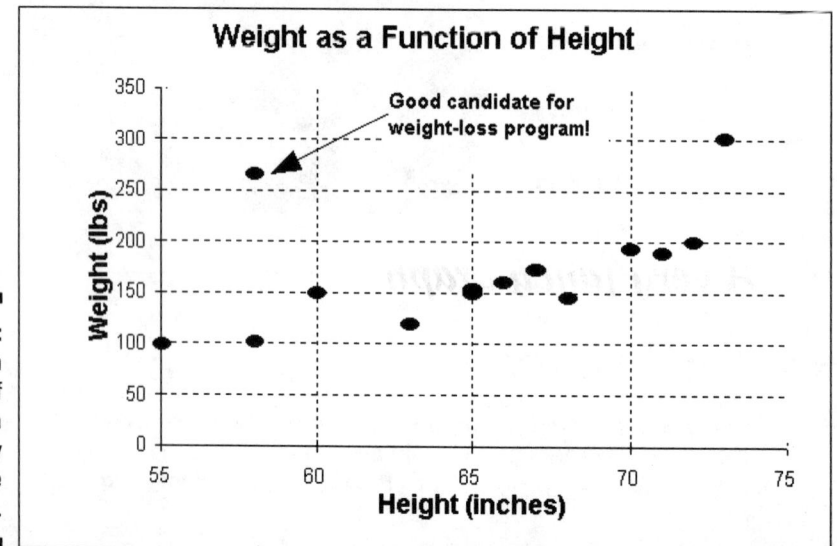

Figure 13-14: An XY graph can show if your data has any discernible trend.

A stock market graph

Stock market analysts get off on this sort of thing. The graph in Figure 13-15 shows stock performance over a period of time. For each day, the graph shows the daily high, the daily low, and the opening and closing prices. Each of these is a separate data series.

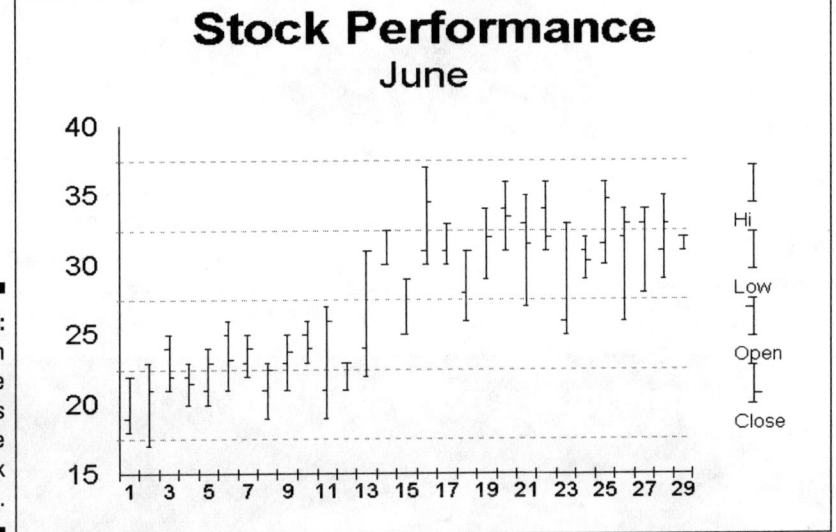

Figure 13-15: This graph shows the month's performance of this stock at a glance.

A doughnut graph

If your favorite restaurant is out of pie, you might order a doughnut. Quattro Pro for Windows can make pie graphs, so it stands to reason that it can also make doughnut graphs, right? A doughnut graph is just a pie graph with a hole in the middle. The example in Figure 13-16 shows a doughnut graph with one of the slices "exploded."

A very fancy graph

The example in Figure 13-17 demonstrates just how slick a Quattro Pro for Windows graph can be. This one is suitable for a boardroom presentation. I used the Graph Gallery dialog box to choose a background for the graph and then moved the graph around to fit nicely.

Part III: How to Impress the Easily Impressed

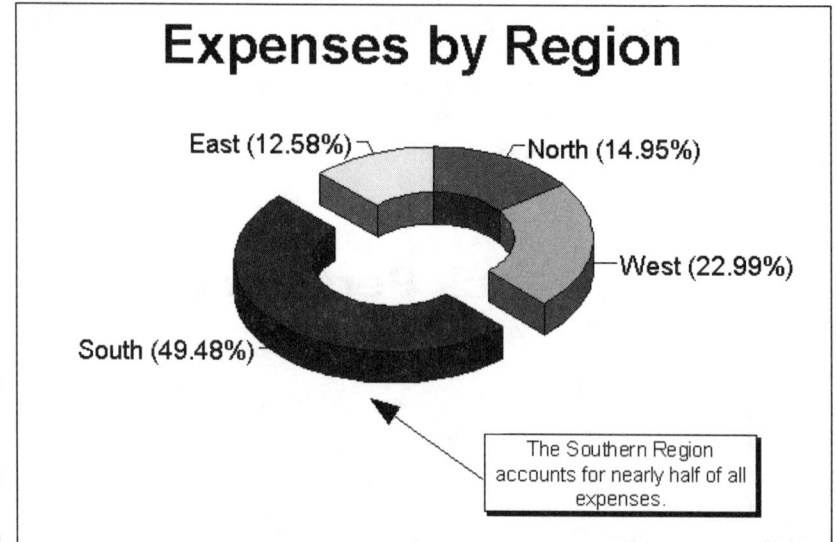

Expenses by Region

- East (12.58%)
- North (14.95%)
- West (22.99%)
- South (49.48%)

The Southern Region accounts for nearly half of all expenses.

Figure 13-16: A tasty doughnut graph.

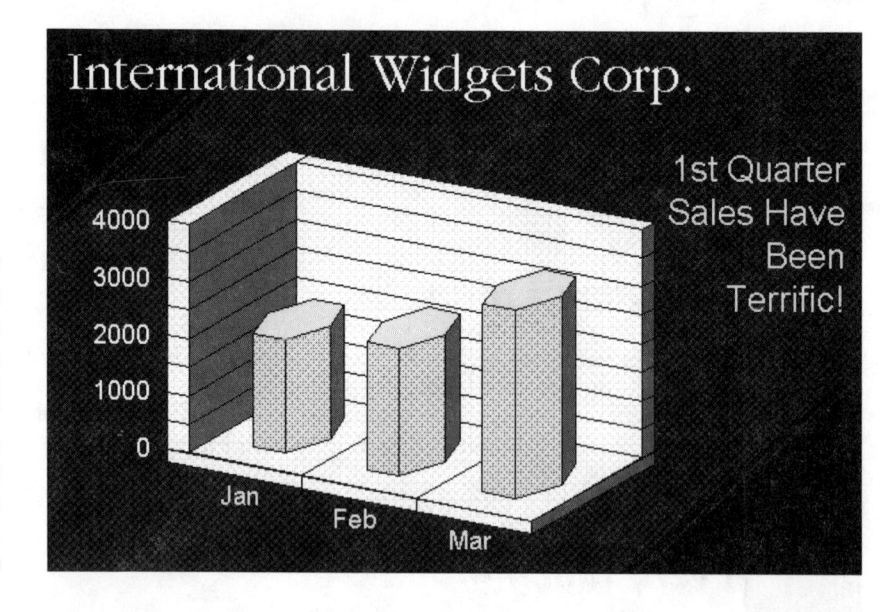

International Widgets Corp.

1st Quarter Sales Have Been Terrific!

Jan, Feb, Mar

Figure 13-17: Need to make a boardroom presentation? Quattro Pro for Windows won't let you down.

> **TIP:** Quattro Pro for Windows can display impressive on-screen slide shows using the graphs that you create. Consult your manual or the on-line help for more details. It's not difficult, but it's beyond the scope of this book (sorry).

A surface graph

Scientific types might be interested in the surface graph type (Figure 13-18 shows an example). Each ribbon in this surface is a separate graph series.

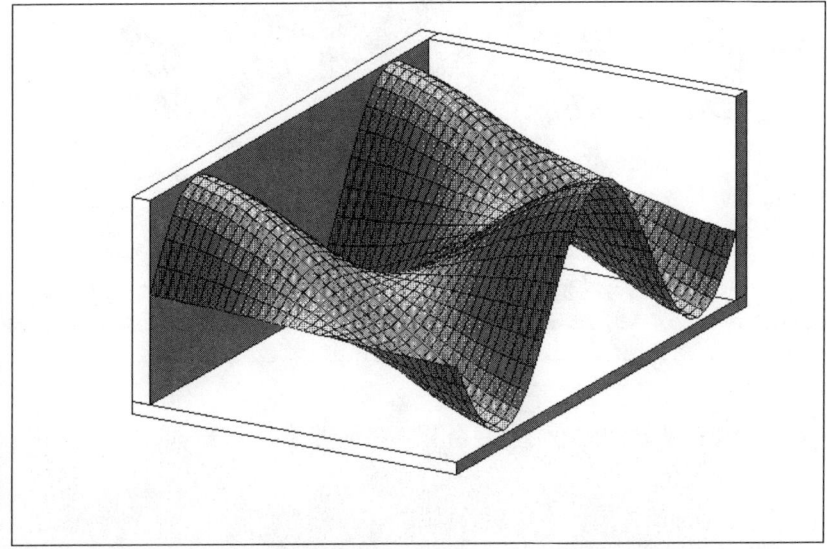

Figure 13-18: A surface graph is useful for some scientific applications.

Another XY graph

Figure 13-19 shows that you can have some fun (in an academic sort of way) with graphs. This XY graph plots data generated with formulas that use trigonometric functions (namely, the @SIN and @COS functions).

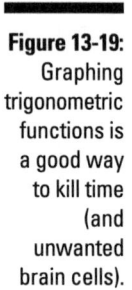

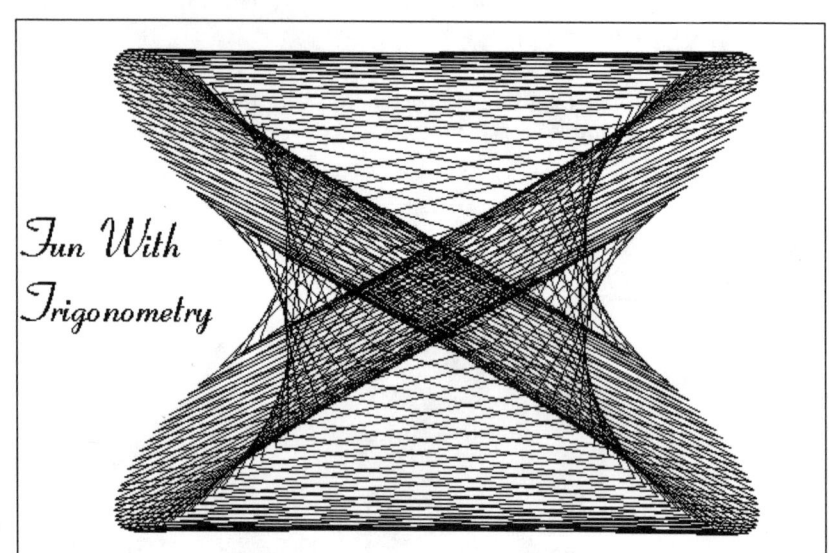

Figure 13-19:
Graphing trigonometric functions is a good way to kill time (and unwanted brain cells).

Chapter 14
Making the Most of Notebooks

In This Chapter
▶ Making the most of those 255 extra pages lurking around in every Quattro Pro for Windows file
▶ Understanding the basic 3-D notebook operations: naming the pages, seeing more than one at a time, moving them, and printing more than one at a time
▶ Navigating and selecting across multiple pages
▶ Formatting several pages at once in group mode

*Y*ou may already know that Quattro Pro for Windows, like all other Windows spreadsheets, lets you use many pages in a single file — 256 pages to be exact. Each of these pages has 8,192 rows and 256 columns. If you do your arithmetic, you see that the total works out to more than a half billion cells at your disposal. This chapter explains how to use this powerful feature for fun and profit — well, at least maybe for profit.

Why Use More Than One Page?

Jeepers, a half billion cells! Don't get too excited, however, because you can never use all these cells (as if you'd ever *want* to). You'd run out of memory long before you even got close to using all of these cells. The benefit of a 3-D notebook therefore is *not* in the number of cells you can access. Instead, using multiple notebook pages is a great way to organize your work and break it up into more manageable units.

Many spreadsheet projects can be broken down into distinct portions. For example, you may have a portion that holds your assumptions, several different portions that hold tables of values, a portion to store data for graphs, and so on. Before the days of 3-D notebooks, one of the most difficult aspects of dealing with large spreadsheets was figuring out where to put all the various portions. With a 3-D notebook, however, it's simple: put each portion on a separate page.

Figure 14-1 shows an example of a 3-D notebook being used for budget tracking. Notice that the name of each department appears on its tab; therefore, you can jump to a department's budget just by clicking the tab.

	A	B	C	D	E	F	G	H
1	Operations							
2		Jan	Feb	Mar	Apr	May	Jun	
3	Salaries	45,500	45,500	45,500	45,500	45,500	45,500	45,5
4	Benefits	9,555	9,555	9,555	9,555	9,555	9,555	9,5
5	Office	9,250	9,250	9,250	9,250	9,250	9,250	9,2
6	Computer	2,200	2,200	2,200	2,200	2,200	2,200	2,2
7	Transportation	3,000	3,000	3,000	7,500	3,000	3,000	3,0
8	Hotel	1,050	1,050	1,050	3,200	1,050	1,050	1,0
9	Meals	500	500	500	1,200	500	500	5
10	Computers	4,500	4,500	4,500	4,500	4,500	4,500	4,5
11	Copiers	1,100	1,100	1,100	1,100	1,100	1,100	1,1
12	Other	950	950	950	950	950	950	9
13	Lease	2,500	2,500	2,500	2,500	2,500	2,500	2,5

Figure 14-1: Using separate pages is ideal for budget applications.

Ideas for Using 3-D Notebooks, No Weird Glasses Needed

Before you get into the meat of 3-D notebooks, let me whet your appetite with a few ideas on how to put this 3-D notebook business to use. You may be able to use some of these ideas — or, better yet, you may come up with some new ideas on your own. (If so, let me know. I'm always looking to steal good ideas for future books!)

- **Store results for different time periods.** If you track information in a spreadsheet, such as sales, orders, or new customers, you may want to organize your work by time periods. For example, you can have a separate page for each month or quarter, enabling you to locate quickly what you want and still use formulas to get grand totals and summaries.

- **Use a 3-D notebook in place of separate files.** If you're working on a project that uses five different single-page notebooks, for example, you may find it more practical to keep them all in one 3-D notebook file (each on a separate page). That way, when you're ready to work on the project, you simply load the one notebook file, and everything you need is handy.

- **Document your work.** If you're working on a fairly complex notebook, you may want to use a separate page to make notes to remind yourself of what you did, why you did it, and how you did it. And, if you're really industrious, you even can keep a historical log that describes the changes you made to the notebook over time.

- **Put graphs on separate pages.** If your notebook file has several graphs, you can insert each graph onto a separate page and give each page a descriptive name. Then, when your boss barges in and wants to see the production chart for July, you simply click on the appropriate tab. She'll think that you're very organized and give you a raise.

- **Keep macros in a separate page.** If you're into macros, you may find that it makes sense to keep your macros on a separate page. This way, they are away from your data and easy to find when you need to make a change or try to figure out why a macro isn't working correctly.

- **Store different scenarios.** Many people use a spreadsheet to do what-if analyses, and 3-D notebooks make this process easier. For example, you can copy an entire page of a 3-D notebook to other pages. Then you just make some experimental changes in the assumptions for each copy and give the pages names such as *BestCase, WorstCase, LikelyCase, JoesScenario,* and so on.

Those extra notebooks have a great deal of other uses, too, but first you need to learn a few background ideas.

Things You Should Know about 3-D Notebooks (Things That Your Mother Never Told You)

Keep in mind the following concepts when you're working with more than one page in a Quattro Pro for Windows notebook file:

- The extra pages are in every file. You don't need to add them (and you can't get rid of them).

- The pages normally are labeled with letters, starting with page A and continuing through page IV (the 256th page in a file). This labeling method is the same as the one used for columns.

- You can change the page letters to names that are more meaningful to you and that reflect the contents of the page.

- You also can change the color of the tabs — handy for color-coding your work.

- When you refer to cells or ranges on another page, you must precede the cell reference with the page letter (or page name, if it has one). For example, C:A1 refers to the upper left cell on the third page (page C).

- Formulas that use range references can use ranges that span across pages. For example, @SUM(A:C:A1:C3) adds a 3 x 3 x 3 cube of cells starting with the upper left cell on the first page and extending through to the cell in the third row and third column of the third page (27 cells in all).

- You can format a group of pages in one fell swoop with group mode — a real time-saver when you want all your pages to look the same.

Fundamental Stuff

This section explains how to do some basic operations involving 3-D notebooks, including naming pages, displaying multiple pages at once, moving pages, and printing multiple pages.

Naming pages

It's a good idea to give a meaningful name to every page that you use. By naming the pages, you make it easy for you (or anyone else who may inherit the file) to identify what's on each page. After all, it's easier to remember that your boss's sales projections are on a page named *BOSS* than on a page named *R*. You also can use page names in formulas, which can make the formulas more understandable. Calculating a ratio with a formula such as +BOSS:A1/BOSS:A2 makes more sense than using +R:A1/R:A2, no?

To name a page, just double-click on the page's tab and then type in a name. Quattro Pro for Windows does not distinguish between uppercase and lowercase letters in names. Avoid using spaces, commas, semicolons, periods, or any other nonletter or nonnumber characters (but spaces are OK). And, finally, don't create page names that look like cell addresses (such as AB12); Quattro Pro for Windows may get confused.

You can continue to use the original page letter even if you give the page a name. For example, if you name the first page *IntroScreen,* you then can enter either a formula such as @SUM(INTROSCREEN:A1..A6), or a formula such as @SUM(A:A1..A6). The program recognizes both formulas as the same request for information, one using the page name and the other using the page letter. However, Quattro Pro for Windows always replaces a page letter reference that you enter with its name (if it has one).

Displaying more than one page at a time

Normally, you can see only one page at a time. But if you want to see or work with more than one page from a 3-D notebook, you can open another window (a new view) for the notebook as shown in Figure 14-2.

Chapter 14: Making the Most of Notebooks *257*

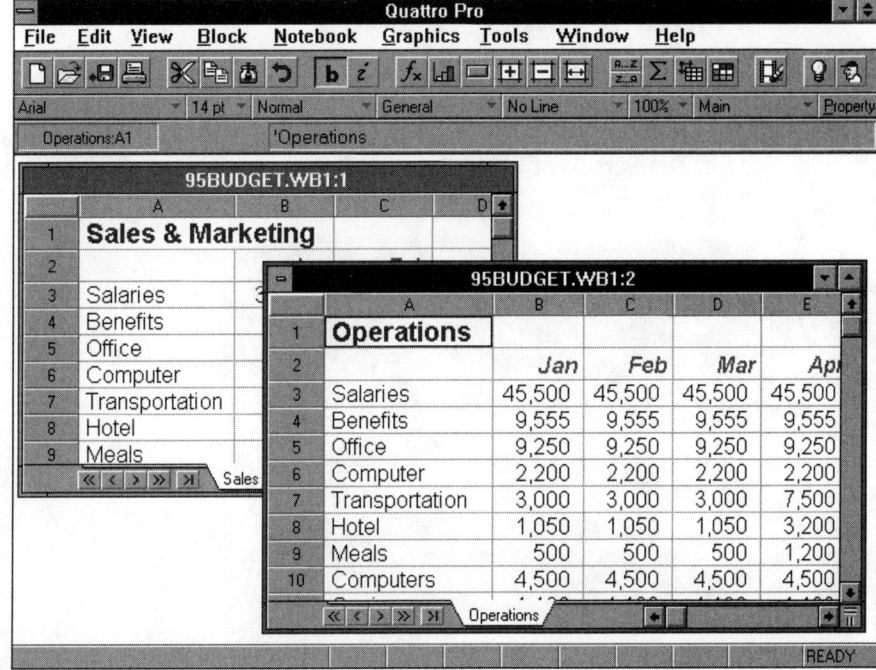

Figure 14-2: This notebook has two windows, so you can see two pages at once.

To open a new window for a notebook, choose the Window⇨New View command. The notebook title bars then will display a number (preceded by a colon) to indicate which view they are showing. You can arrange the windows any way you like. Selecting a different page in one window doesn't change the other. You can have as many views of one notebook as you like.

> **TIP**
> You can even drag cells or blocks from one window to another. If you need to move three cells from page A to page C, start by opening a new window. Then display page A in one window and page C in the other. To move the cells, select them, and when the mouse pointer turns into a hand, drag the selection to the other window.

Moving pages

If you want your notebook pages to be in a different order, you can move the pages around. To move a page, click on its tab and drag it to its new location. Painless, eh?

Printing multiple pages

If you read Chapter 11, you already know how to print — one page, a selection of cells, or the entire notebook. To refresh your memory, take a look at Figure 14-3. This is the dialog box that appears when you select the Print button in the Main Toolbar. To print all of the used pages, just choose the Notebook option.

Figure 14-3: The Spreadsheet Print dialog box has an option that lets you print all of the pages in a notebook.

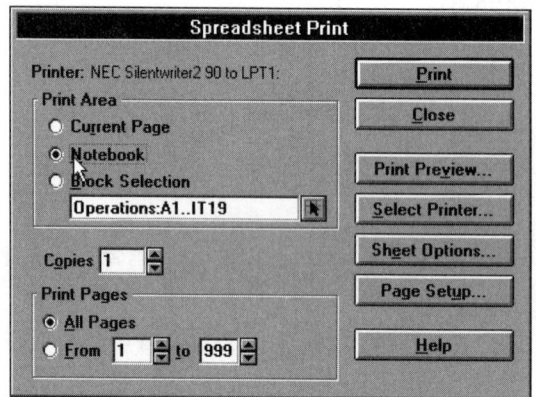

TIP: If you want each page to start on a new piece of paper, choose the Sh<u>e</u>et Options button in the Spreadsheet Print dialog box. You'll get another dialog box. Select the Page <u>a</u>dvance option in the box labeled "Print between 3D pages."

Navigating in the Third Dimension (without the Help of Captain Picard)

You already know how to navigate through one page of a notebook by using the arrow keys, mouse, scroll bars, and so on. Moving around in a 3-D notebook requires a bit more effort, however, because you have another dimension to be concerned about. But, again, learning to move around a 3-D notebook is fairly logical once you get the hang of it. It's kind of like driving on the Los Angeles freeway, only infinitely safer.

Activating other pages

Before you can scroll around on a page, you must activate, or display, it on-screen. The easiest way to activate a specific page in a 3-D notebook is to click on the tab with your mouse. If you have many pages or pages with long names, the tab you want may not appear. You can click on any of the four tab scrollers at the bottom left of your screen to scroll the tabs. These scrollers are shown in Figure 14-4.

Figure 14-4: Click on any of these arrows to scroll the tab display left or right.

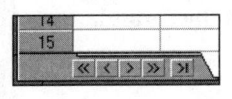

Sometimes, using the keyboard to activate a different page may be more efficient. Table 14-1 lists the keyboard combinations necessary to activate a page.

Table 14-1 Keyboard Combinations to Activate Pages

Key Combination	What It Does
Ctrl+PgDn	Activates the preceding page, unless you're on the first page. (Then it has no effect.)
Ctrl+PgUp	Activates the next page, unless you're on the last page. (Then it has no effect.)
Ctrl+Home	Activates the first page and moves the cell pointer to the upper left cell.
End, Ctrl+Home	Moves to the last cell that contains data on the last page that contains data.

TIP

A fast way to activate a far-off page is to press F5, the GoTo key. Quattro Pro for Windows asks you what address you want to go to. Enter a page letter followed by a colon, and you're there in a jiff. For example, if you want to activate page M, press F5, type **M:** and then press Enter. If the page has a name, you can enter the name followed by a colon. Wouldn't life be wonderful if we had GoTo buttons on our cars?

Selecting 3-D ranges

When you're building a formula that references information on more than one page, you can either enter the cell references manually or use pointing techniques similar to those used in a single page.

For example, assume that you are building a formula in cell A:A1 that adds up the figures in range B:A1 through F:A1, a common formula to consolidate the numbers in six pages. You can either type **@SUM(B..F:A1)** or simply point to the argument and let Quattro Pro for Windows create the range reference for you. Do so by performing the following steps:

1. **Move to cell A:A1 and type** @SUM(**to start the formula.**
2. **Press Ctrl+PgUp to move to the next page, and then move the cell pointer to cell B:A1, if it's not already there.**

   Watch the formula being built in the edit line.
3. **Press the period to anchor the first cell in the selection.**
4. **Press Ctrl+PgUp four more times until you get to page F, and move the cell pointer to cell F:A1, if it's not already there.**
5. **Type) and press Enter to finish the formula.**

Quattro Pro for Windows brings you back to the cell that holds the formula.

Instead of pressing Ctrl+PgUp to activate other pages while you're pointing, you can hold down Shift and click on a page tab with your mouse.

When you're formatting ranges that extend across different pages, you can select the entire 3-D range and do the formatting with a single command. (But, as you'll see later, group mode can simplify formatting all the pages.)

When you're dealing with a single page, just drag the mouse across the range to select it (or press Shift+arrow keys to preselect the range). Selecting across several pages is very similar: Just hold down Shift while you activate another page either by clicking a tab or by pressing Ctrl+PgUp or Ctrl+PgDn.

Group Mode

Before we put this chapter to bed, I want to discuss one more topic that's relevant and actually pretty useful at times — group mode. Group mode enables you to format several pages in a 3-D notebook file at once. After you're in group mode, any changes you make on one page affect all other pages in the group. For example, if you're in group mode and you change the font in cell A1 on page A, the program also changes the font in cell A1 on all the pages in the group.

Naming a group of pages

Before you can use a group you must define it. Choose the Notebook⇨Define Group command, and you'll get the dialog box shown in Figure 14-5.

Figure 14-5: The Define/Modify Group dialog box lets you define a group of pages to work with simultaneously.

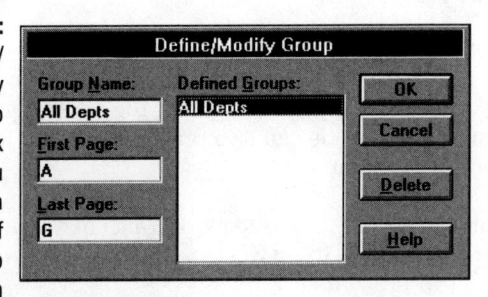

Enter a name for the group, and then specify the first and last page in the group. Choose OK. You can have as many named groups as you like.

Getting into group mode

After you define your group of pages, you get into group mode by choosing the View⇨Group Mode command. Actually, this command toggles group mode on and off. You can also press Alt+F5 to toggle group mode.

When you're in group mode, Quattro Pro for Windows displays a blue line below the page tabs in the group (this reminds you that you're in group mode and shows you which pages are in the group). Figure 14-6 shows a notebook in group mode. Notice that the page tabs for pages B – D are underlined. Pages B – D are the pages in the group.

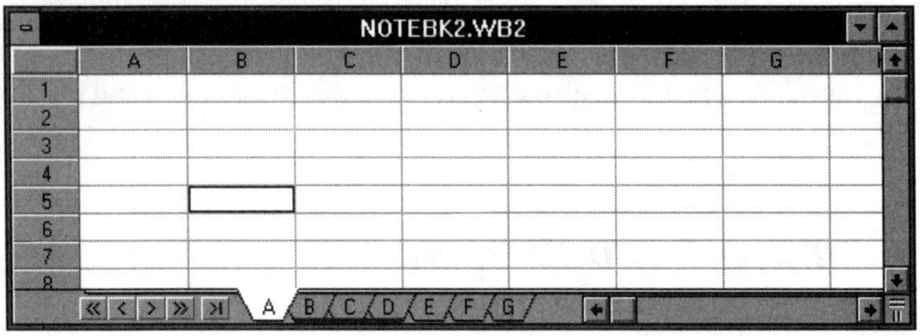

Figure 14-6: Pages B and D are in a defined group, and group mode is on.

Using group mode

Group mode can be very handy if you want a group of pages in your notebook to have exactly the same formatting. For example, after you change column widths or the formatting of cells in one page in a group, the other pages all follow suit. Obviously, using group mode can be a real time-saver — it also makes your work look more consistent.

If you enter something into a cell while in group mode, that entry only goes into the current page. In other words, formatting works when you're in group mode, but cell entries do not.

A Final Note

If life in the third dimension confuses you, don't despair. It's all very logical, and you'll get the hang of it after you start playing around with 3-D notebooks. Once you master it, you'll wonder how you ever got along without out. If you find yourself getting really frustrated, however, just stick with single-page notebooks. After all, people have been using only one page for more than a decade — and they get along just fine.

Chapter 15
Making Quattro Pro for Windows Your Slave

In This Chapter
▶ Adjusting how the screen looks by zooming in and out and by removing things you don't want to see
▶ Splitting a notebook window into panes
▶ Freezing rows or columns so that they always appear
▶ Avoiding embarrassing misspellings in your notebook

*1*f you're reading this book in sequence, you already have a great deal of nitty-gritty Quattro Pro for Windows knowledge — more than enough to do some meaningful work (or cause some serious damage). But, as you probably realize, you can do many creative things with Quattro Pro for Windows, too. This chapter is like the proverbial icing on the cake: you don't really have to know how to do the tasks explained here, but they can make your life easier — and they're sort of fun, too. Several of these topics show you how to make Quattro Pro for Windows work or look differently than it normally does.

You may not be interested in everything I discuss in this chapter, but, at the very least, I suggest that you glance through the pictures to see whether anything here strikes your fancy.

I don't go into a lot of detail in this chapter, because this material is all fairly straightforward. If you're interested in more information, play around with the software or check the manual (aarrrrgggh!) or on-line help.

Have It Your Way

Burger King used to use the slogan "Have it your way." When it comes to the appearance of Quattro Pro for Windows on-screen, you can have it your way there, too (as long as you don't want onions).

Hiding and showing things

As you know, the Quattro Pro for Windows screen is made up of many different parts, but sometimes you won't want to see all its parts at once. For example, when you want to see as much information on-screen as possible, you may want to remove the scroll bars and even the notebook frame from the screen.

Fortunately, you have a great deal of freedom to put exactly what you want on-screen at any particular time, and you can drastically change the way your Quattro Pro for Windows screen looks. The secret is in the View⇨Display command. After you select this command, you get the dialog box shown in Figure 15-1.

Figure 15-1: The Display dialog box, where you can change the on-screen appearance of Quattro Pro for Windows.

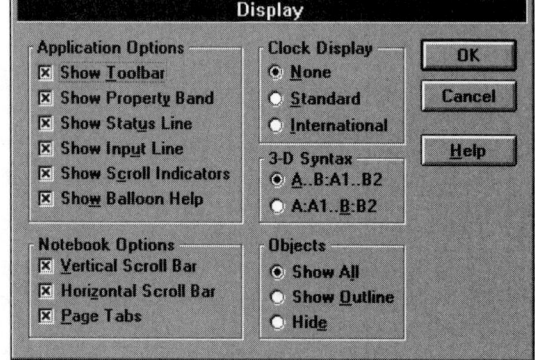

The Display dialog box is divided into five parts. The choices in the upper left part of the dialog box (Application Options) apply to the Quattro Pro for Windows window. Here you choose whether to display the Toolbar, Property Band, status line, input line, scroll bars, and balloon help (those pop-up yellow boxes that describe Toolbar buttons). By default, all of these objects are shown, but you can turn off one or more if you like.

Figure 15-2 shows what Quattro Pro for Windows looks like when all of these options are turned off. As you can see, you are left with pretty much of a blank slate, with only the menu bar remaining. Also, notice that after you turn off the edit line display, you have no idea where the cell pointer is at any given time, unless it's on-screen. You probably don't want your screen to be *this* naked, but turning off a few of these elements may do you some good in the right circumstances (if you get a thrill from a naked notebook).

> **TIP**
> If you're a prankster at heart, here's a suggestion. Next time weird Harold leaves his desk, sneak over and remove all of the parts from his Quattro Pro for Windows screen. He'll return to his desk, freak out, and yell for help. Then you can casually walk over and fix it up. He'll think you're a genius.

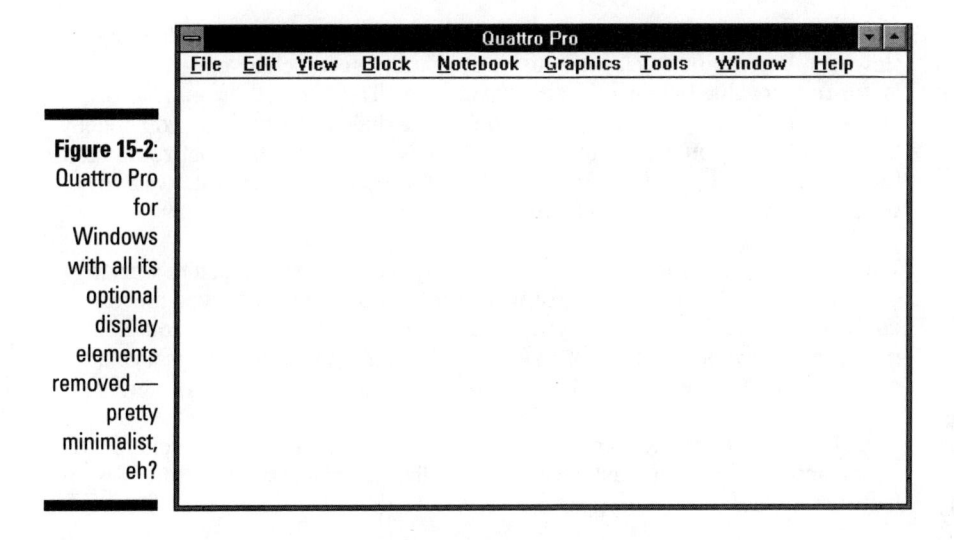

Figure 15-2: Quattro Pro for Windows with all its optional display elements removed — pretty minimalist, eh?

The choices in the Notebook Options section of the Display dialog box affect the current notebook. You can remove the scroll bars (either one) and hide the page tabs.

Other parts of the Display dialog box offer no surprises. If you like, you can display the current date and time in the left corner of the status bar, and you can select how objects (such as graphs and drawings) will appear — or not appear.

> **TIP**
>
> If you find that having graphs and drawings in your notebook slows down Quattro Pro for Windows, you can choose the Show Outline option. That way, you'll know where the objects are, but your computer won't waste time redrawing them.

> **TIP**
>
> You also can hide an entire notebook by using the Window⇨Hide command. The notebook is still loaded, but it's completely out of your way. Be careful with this command, because it's easy to forget about a notebook that you can't see. Rather than hide a notebook, you may want to just minimize it (turn it into an icon). To minimize a notebook, click the down arrow located at the right side of the notebook's title bar.

Zoom in, zoom out

If you have a video camera, it probably has a zoom lens. This lets you zoom in on your subject for a closer look (handy at your local nude beach) or zoom out to record the big picture (to fit all those large relatives into the scene). Quattro Pro for Windows isn't a video camera, but it does have a zooming feature.

Part III: How to Impress the Easily Impressed

Normally, Quattro Pro for Windows displays everything at 100 percent size. However, you're not stuck with this option, and you can change the zoom factor to any value between 10 and 400 percent. To change the zoom factor, choose the View⇨Zoom command. You'll get a dialog box that lets you specify the zoom factor you want. You also can specify whether to use that zoom factor for the current page or for all pages in the notebook. Figure 15-3 shows two windows with different zoom factors.

Why might you want to zoom in or out? Many reasons exist. If you're working on a graph or using some of the drawing tools, zooming in gives you more control over the details. And if you have a large notebook, you can zoom out to get a better idea of how the notebook is laid out. Zooming out also makes it easier to select large ranges with a mouse.

TIP

You also can use the Page Zoom pull-down on the Property Band to change the zoom factor — but you must choose from a list (it doesn't let you enter a zoom factor manually).

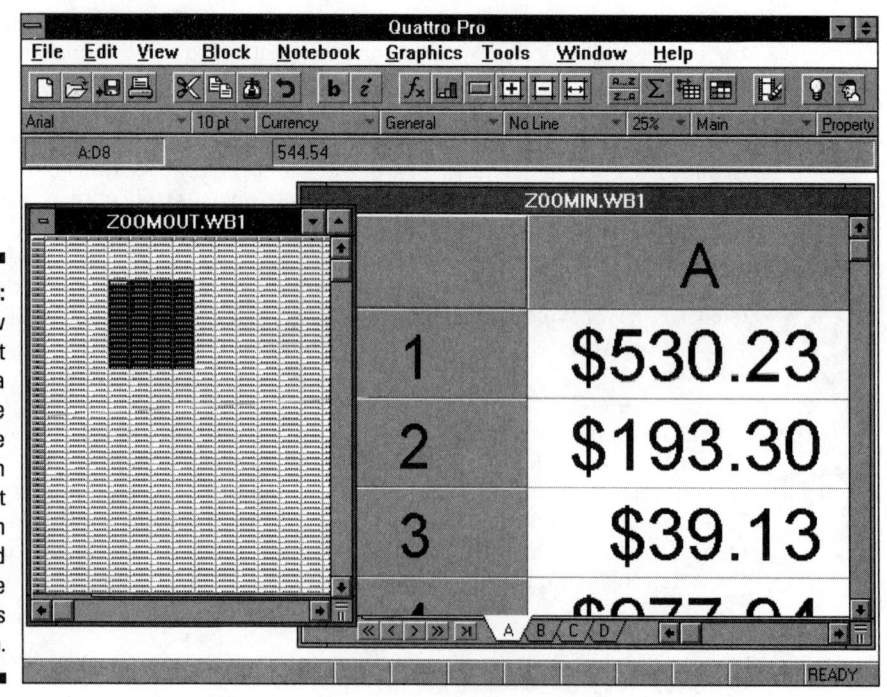

Figure 15-3: The window on the left shows a bird's eye view. The window on the right shows an enlarged view, legible from across the room.

The Paneful Way of Seeing More of Your Notebook

If you have a great deal of information in a notebook, scrolling through the notebook can get tedious when you're examining it. In Chapter 14, I mentioned the Window⇨New View command, which opens another window for the current notebook. This procedure lets you see two or more parts of your notebook on-screen without scrolling around. As you may recall, you can use this command multiple times to open as many new views as you like.

Another way to see different parts of your notebook — although it is a bit more limiting — is to split the notebook window into two *panes*. Figure 15-4 shows a window split into two vertical panes. Notice that this single window is showing two different parts of the notebook. Besides making it easy to see two parts of one notebook, the window pane option is also useful for copying cells and blocks across long distances, because you can jump back and forth between the panes.

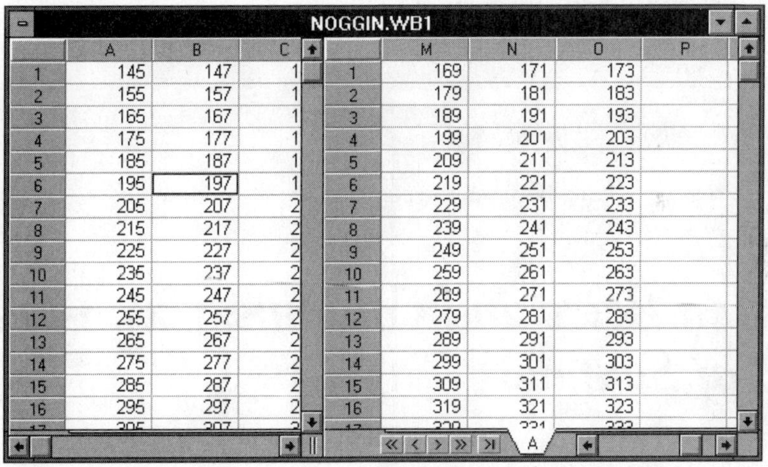

Figure 15-4: Splitting a window into two panes lets you see two different parts without scrolling.

One way to split a window is to use the View⇨Panes command. This command displays the dialog box shown in Figure 15-5 and gives you the choice of splitting the window vertically or horizontally. The window splits wherever the cell pointer is when you issue the command.

Figure 15-5: One way to split a window into two panes.

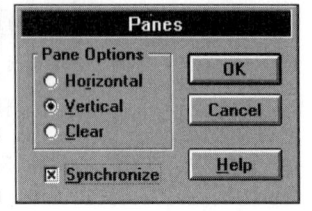

An easier way to split windows is to use the mouse to drag the window splitter to the place where you want to split the screen. Actually, two window splitters exist — one for vertical splitting and one for horizontal splitting. Figure 15-6 shows where you'll find the window splitter.

Figure 15-6: Click and drag up or to the left to split the window into two panes.

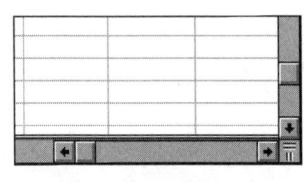

TIP

Press F6 to jump between the panes in a split window.

Freezing Rows and Columns (Even in the Dead of Summer)

Many notebooks have row and column labels that describe the cells. A standard budget is a good example. Typically, the top row has month names, and the left column has budget categories. However, after you start scrolling around through the notebook, the first row and first column often are no longer visible; it's easy to lose track of what a particular cell is. If you have difficulty remembering your cell labels, then you need to learn how to freeze rows and columns.

The View⇨Locked Titles command comes in handy and is worth your while to learn. To freeze (or lock) a row or column means that you arrange things so that one or more rows and/or columns always display on-screen, regardless of where the cell pointer is. Suppose that you want the first row and the first column in your notebook to appear on-screen at all times. To lock them in place, follow this procedure:

Chapter 15: Making Quattro Pro for Windows Your Slave 269

1. **Move the cell pointer to cell B2, and choose the View⇨Locked Titles command.**

   You get the dialog box shown in Figure 15-7.

2. **Because you want to lock both a row and a column, you choose the Both option.**

Figure 15-7: The Locked Titles dialog box enables you to tell Quattro Pro for Windows what to freeze.

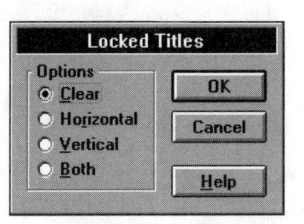

3. **Select OK.**

   After you close the dialog box, everything looks the same — until you start scrolling the window. You then discover that Quattro Pro for Windows always displays row 1 and column A.

   Figure 15-8 shows a notebook with the first row and first column locked in place. Notice that row 1 and column A are displayed at the same time that the cell pointer is far away from the upper left corner.

Figure 15-8: An example of a locked row and column.

To unfreeze (or thaw out?) the frozen rows or columns, choose the View⇨Locked Titles command and select the Clear option.

Chekking Your Speling

If you use a word processor, you are probably on friendly terms with its built-in spelling checker. Quattro Pro for Windows isn't a word processor, but it does have a spelling checker, which can save you a great deal of embarrassment (but, of course, good spelers lyke me don't nede sutch thingz).

You access this feature by selecting the Tools⇨Spell Check command. Quattro Pro for Windows then displays the dialog box shown in Figure 15-9.

Figure 15-9: Doing a spell check is a good idea before you print out important spreadsheets.

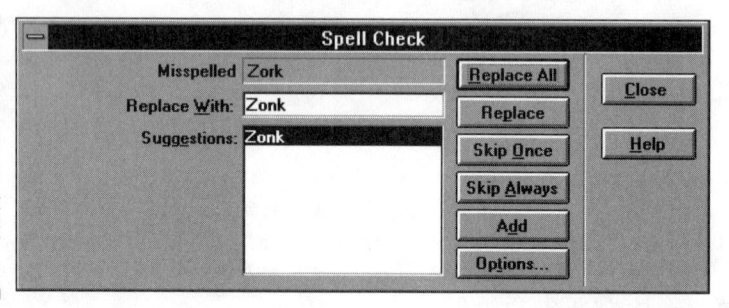

Choose Start to begin the spell check. Quattro Pro for Windows will display any words it doesn't recognize, and you can change them (by choosing from the list of suggestions or entering the correct spelling manually) or accept them (by clicking on Skip Once or Skip Always). Choose the Options button to specify additional spell-checking options.

The spelling checker isn't a substitute for a careful review of your notebook. The checker can't identify words that are spelled correctly but used incorrectly in a sentence. In the following example, all the italicized words are used incorrectly but are in the spelling checker as being correct (so the text passes the spelling checker with flying colors): I like *two* go to *sea* the *see inn* May *sew* that *eye* can drink *tee* at the golf *tea* while I try *too* get the little ball in the *whole*. Whew! This golfer needs my editor for sure.

Part IV
Faking It

The 5th Wave   **By Rich Tennant**

In this part...

Now we come to the part of the book that covers advanced features in Quattro Pro for Windows. We're talking databases, semicomplex formulas, macros, and more. Beginning users usually don't need to spend much time mastering these topics, but I'll give you the basics so you won't be completely in the dark.

Chapter 16
The Lowdown on Lists and Databases

In This Chapter
- Why Quattro Pro for Windows is good for keeping track of things
- What the difference between a simple list and a database means to a normal person like you
- How to keep track of information in lists, and how to set up and use databases

Chances are, you also use a word processing program on your computer. And you've probably used your word processor to store lists of things. Compared to spreadsheets, typical word processing programs are best classified as dumb. That is, most word processors don't let you use formulas to do calculations and require you to know about tab settings and other boring topics when working with tables and multicolumn lists.

Spreadsheets — including Quattro Pro for Windows — are great for dealing with lists, as you will find out in this chapter. Keep reading to learn how to use Quattro Pro for Windows to create and manage these lists and locate information quickly.

Lists and Databases

Before going any farther, let me give you two definitions:

- A *list* is a collection of items, each of which is stored in a separate row in a notebook. Each item may have more than one part (that is, use more than one column). The order of the items may or may not be important.
- A *database* is an organized collection of items. Each item is called a *record,* and each record has multiple parts called *fields.* Furthermore, each field has a designated *field name.*

A sample list

Figure 16-1 shows a list I developed in Quattro Pro for Windows. This particular list contains seven items. Each item has two parts (actually, one of the items includes a third part), and there's a blank line (row 8) in the middle of the list. Notice that the numeric formatting isn't the same for all items — typical of an informal list like this one. This notebook also happens to use a formula that calculates the total.

Making a list in Quattro Pro for Windows is a snap. Just start putting things in, change the column widths if necessary, insert new rows if you need them, and do anything else you can think of to make the list do what you want it to do. Feel free to move things around — do whatever makes you happy. The early chapters in this book tell you how to do all of these things. The only rule for this type of list is that there are no rules.

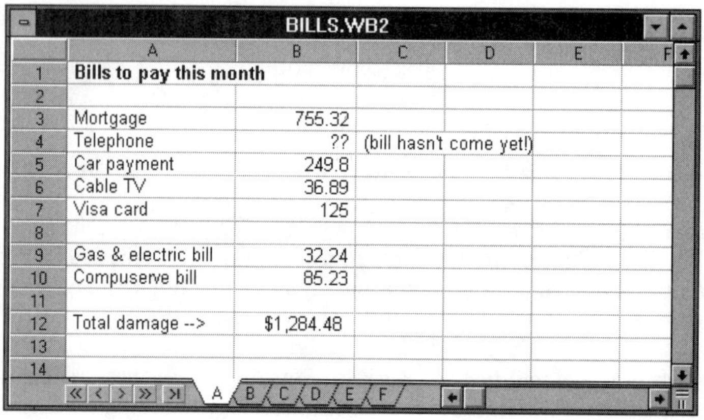

Figure 16-1: A simple list stored in Quattro Pro for Windows.

	A	B	C
1	Bills to pay this month		
2			
3	Mortgage	755.32	
4	Telephone	??	(bill hasn't come yet!)
5	Car payment	249.8	
6	Cable TV	36.89	
7	Visa card	125	
8			
9	Gas & electric bill	32.24	
10	Compuserve bill	85.23	
11			
12	Total damage -->	$1,284.48	

A sample database

Figure 16-2 shows a database I created in Quattro Pro for Windows. This particular database tracks items by date purchased, value, and reason purchased (that is, for business or personal use). This database has 16 records and four fields. Notice that the first row contains labels that list the field names; this row is not counted as a record.

At this point, the difference between a list and a database may seem fuzzy to you. To make a long story short, a database is basically just a more *organized* list. In the example shown, every record is laid out identically, with the same number of fields and numeric formats. Because of this added degree of organization, a database makes it easier to locate the exact information you want (as you'll see later). The tradeoff, however, is that it takes a bit more up-front work to set up a database, and the information you put into it has to conform to the fields that you define.

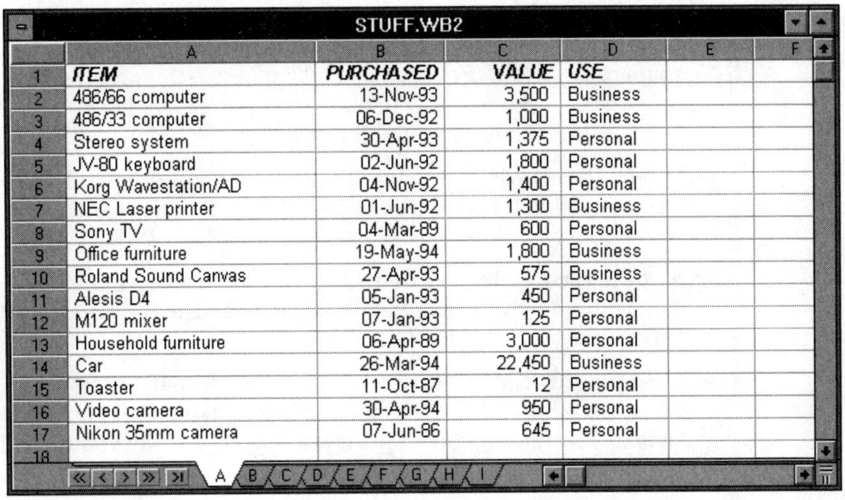

Figure 16-2:
A database stored in Quattro Pro for Windows.

	A	B	C	D
1	ITEM	PURCHASED	VALUE	USE
2	486/66 computer	13-Nov-93	3,500	Business
3	486/33 computer	06-Dec-92	1,000	Business
4	Stereo system	30-Apr-93	1,375	Personal
5	JV-80 keyboard	02-Jun-92	1,800	Personal
6	Korg Wavestation/AD	04-Nov-92	1,400	Personal
7	NEC Laser printer	01-Jun-92	1,300	Business
8	Sony TV	04-Mar-89	600	Personal
9	Office furniture	19-May-94	1,800	Business
10	Roland Sound Canvas	27-Apr-93	575	Business
11	Alesis D4	05-Jan-93	450	Personal
12	M120 mixer	07-Jan-93	125	Personal
13	Household furniture	06-Apr-89	3,000	Personal
14	Car	26-Mar-94	22,450	Business
15	Toaster	11-Oct-87	12	Personal
16	Video camera	30-Apr-94	950	Personal
17	Nikon 35mm camera	07-Jun-86	645	Personal

But, on the other hand, you can always modify a database after the fact. If you find that you no longer need to use a certain field, you can just delete it (along with all of the data). Or, if you find that you need to track other types of information, you can always add more fields to your database.

Because lists are pretty easy to handle (and there are no rules), I'll drop this subject for now. The remainder of this chapter focuses exclusively on databases.

What You Can Do with a Database

You can use a database to track and update customer information, account information, budget plans, sales figures, and myriad other important (and unimportant) data.

Because a database is more organized than a list, it allows you to do things that would be more difficult (or even impossible) with a simple list. For example, with a database you can

- **Extract all records that meet certain criteria and put them in another place.** This procedure is sometimes known as *querying* a database. In a customer database, you can easily find all of your customers who live in a certain state, those who have spent more than a specific amount of money with your company, those who haven't purchased anything in the past year, and so on (assuming, of course, that your database actually has fields that store the information about which you're querying).

Querying a database enables you to make a subset of the database that contains only the records of immediate interest. You may want to extract some records and use them in a mail merge letter created in your word processor. When you extract data, you don't have to extract all of the fields — just the ones you're interested in.

- **Delete all records that meet your criteria.** You can automatically trash records that you no longer need — and do it quickly and error-free (if you're lucky).

- **Sort the records by any field.** Actually, you can sort any block of data in a spreadsheet — it doesn't have to be a database. But sorting databases is very common.

- **Print nice-looking reports.** Because a database is an organized list of items, it's perfect for producing professional-quality reports. Everything lines up nicely, and your reports make you look like you really have a handle on your job.

- **Summarize data.** You can use Quattro Pro for Windows' database @functions to summarize information in a database. For example, you can write a formula that sums the Amount field in a database — but only for customers who live in Rhode Island.

Database Basics

Most of the work people do with databases involves searching for records that meet some criteria. Another word for search is *query;* database people use this term a lot. Quattro Pro for Windows has some very definite expectations regarding databases — and, to be successful, you have to do things the way the software expects them to be done (so what else is new?).

For starters, you need to know three concepts:

- **The database block.** This is the database itself, including the field names.

- **A criteria table.** This is a block of cells where you tell Quattro Pro for Windows what you want to find (that is, your search criteria).

- **An output block.** This is a block of cells where Quattro Pro for Windows copies the records from the database that meet your criteria. If you are only locating the records, you don't need to specify an output range.

If you're totally confused, don't despair. More detail is on the way.

The database block

Usually, the first step you take when doing searches on a database is to tell Quattro Pro for Windows where the database is. This step is necessary because you can have more than one database stored in a single notebook. Remember, a database consists of one row of field names followed directly by the rows of data — and each row of data is called a record.

A database can be as large as you want, but you're limited to the constraints of a notebook page. That is, a Quattro Pro for Windows database can have up to 8,191 records (because there are 8,192 rows in a notebook — one row must be used for the field names). And the maximum number of fields is 256 (because there are 256 columns in a notebook page). Chances are, your databases will be considerably smaller than this.

The criteria table

Many people find the concept of a criteria table confusing and avoid using databases altogether because they can't understand it. But the simple fact is that you need a criteria table if you want to search for data that meets some criteria that you specify. If you're just using a database to store data and will *never* search for anything, only then do you have no need for a criteria table.

But databases are most useful when you search them, so it's a good idea to learn about criteria tables. Actually, criteria tables are not all that difficult to understand. A criteria table is something that you set up ahead of time, and you use it to tell Quattro Pro for Windows what you're looking for in the database (remember, this software has its own way of doing things).

A criteria table is just a block of cells consisting of two parts. The first row of the criteria table holds field names from your database. The rows directly beneath this row hold special instructions to Quattro Pro for Windows that describe what you're searching for. To save time (and reduce errors), you can copy the field names from the database to the area of your notebook that you'll be using for the criteria block. Actually, the criteria table doesn't have to have *all* of the field names — only those that you'll be using in your search.

Figure 16-3 shows a criteria table set up for use with the database presented earlier in this chapter. The criteria table is highlighted and is in the block A21..D22.

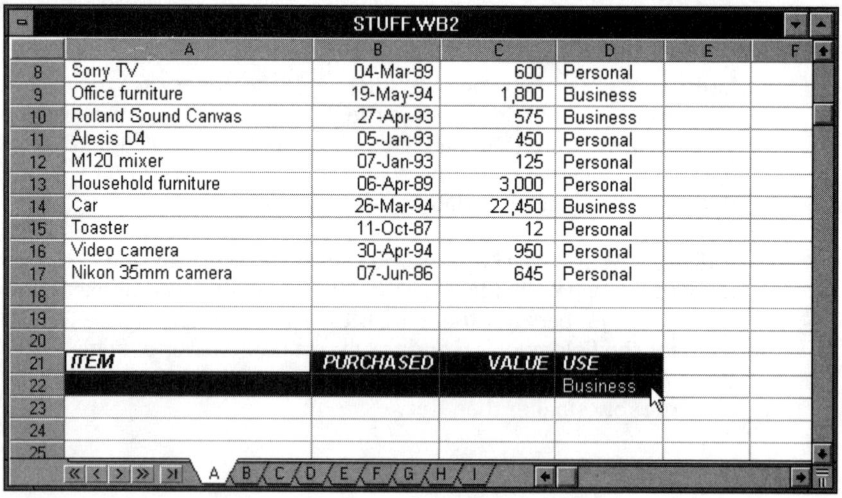

Figure 16-3:
Use a criteria table to tell Quattro Pro for Windows what to find in your database.

	A	B	C	D
8	Sony TV	04-Mar-89	600	Personal
9	Office furniture	19-May-94	1,800	Business
10	Roland Sound Canvas	27-Apr-93	575	Business
11	Alesis D4	05-Jan-93	450	Personal
12	M120 mixer	07-Jan-93	125	Personal
13	Household furniture	06-Apr-89	3,000	Personal
14	Car	26-Mar-94	22,450	Business
15	Toaster	11-Oct-87	12	Personal
16	Video camera	30-Apr-94	950	Personal
17	Nikon 35mm camera	07-Jun-86	645	Personal
18				
19				
20				
21	**ITEM**		**PURCHASED**	**VALUE**	**USE**
22					Business
23				
24				
25				

The output block

When you do operations on a database, you can either locate the records in the database (that is, just look at them), or you can instruct Quattro Pro for Windows to extract the records you're interested in and copy them to another area of the notebook called the *output block*. The output block is the area that holds copies of the found records.

An output block consists of the field names from your database — plus the blank rows below them that Quattro Pro for Windows will fill in for you. To save time (and reduce errors), you can copy the field names from the database to another area of your worksheet. If you don't need to see all of the fields of your database, set up the output block only with the fields you want.

Creating a Database

Now that you're somewhat knowledgeable about the key concepts of database block, criteria table, and output block, we can move on.

Setting up field names

As you already know, a database consists of a rectangular block of cells. The first row of this block has the field names, and all of the other rows contain the data (one row per record).

Learning the following rules pays off in the long run:

- Each field in the database must have a name, and no two names can be the same. Also, limit the field names to 15 characters, and don't use spaces.
- Don't leave blank rows between the field names and the actual data.
- Don't leave blank rows in your database.
- Use the same type of data in each column. In other words, give some thought to what kind of data each field holds; don't mix labels and values in a single column.

Entering data into a database

Entering your data is straightforward, because you use the data entry methods you already know. After you enter the field names at the top, just put the data into the cells below.

If you prefer, you can use a database form to help you enter the data. Figure 16-4 shows a notebook with field names entered for a database — but no data has been entered.

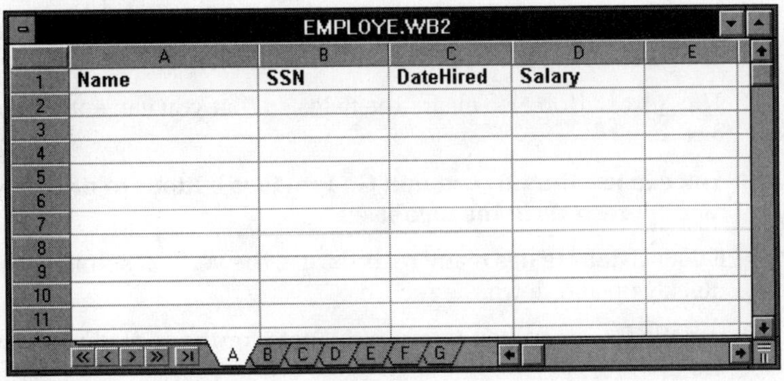

Figure 16-4: An empty database — just dying for some data.

One way to enter data is to select the field names plus one blank row beneath them, and then issue the Tools⇨Database Tools⇨Form command. For this example, start by selecting block A1..D2. Quattro Pro for Windows displays a small dialog box that asks you to confirm the input range (just choose OK). It then displays a dialog box like the one shown in Figure 16-5. This dialog box will correspond to the fields in your database. Because this database has four fields, the dialog box shows four fields.

Figure 16-5: Using a database form is an easy way to put data into a database.

You can enter your data into this dialog box. Here are a few pointers on using this type of dialog box:

1. **Press Tab to move to the next field; press Shift+Tab to move to the previous field.**

2. **When you've entered all of the data for the current record, use the Next button to insert the next data into the database.**

   The Next button also clears the fields so that you can enter data for the next record.

3. **You can use the Go Next and Go Previous buttons to display (and modify) records in the database.**

   If your database has many records, use the vertical scrollbar to move quickly up and down the records.

4. **Use the Revert button to erase the data for the record you're working on.**

   If you're changing a record that has already been entered, the Revert button puts it back to its original condition.

5. **When you're finished, select Close to close the dialog box.**

Using the database form feature in Quattro Pro for Windows is optional. You may find it easier to enter your database data directly into the notebook (I do).

An Example

The best way to explain how this database works is to use an example, so I'll run through an example. You can either read the words and try to digest the example, or duplicate the database and follow along on your own computer.

The database

Figure 16-6 shows a small database that might be set up by a real estate company to keep track of properties sold. This particular database consists of five fields:

Office: The office that sold the property. This real estate company has two offices.

Date: When the property was sold (month only). This database is for January and March.

Price: The amount the property sold for.

Area: Where the property was located. This field can be City, N. County, S. County, or Other.

Type: The type of property sold. Options are House, Condo, or Land.

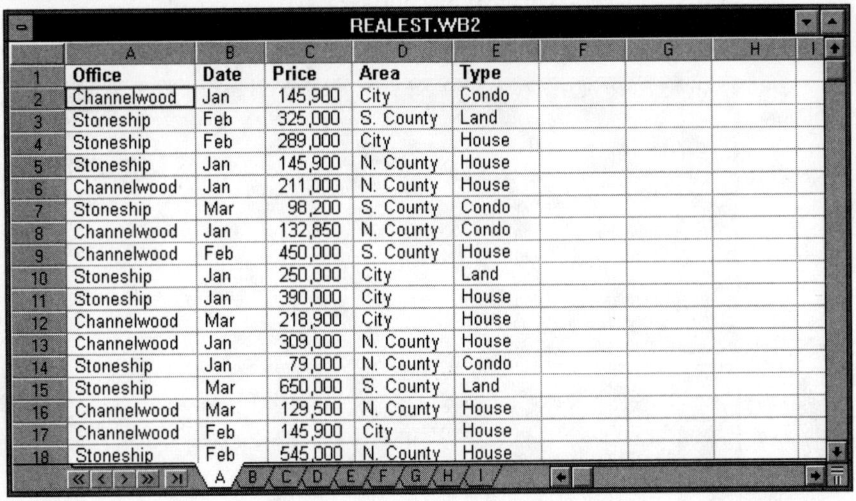

	A	B	C	D	E
1	Office	Date	Price	Area	Type
2	Channelwood	Jan	145,900	City	Condo
3	Stoneship	Feb	325,000	S. County	Land
4	Stoneship	Feb	289,000	City	House
5	Stoneship	Jan	145,900	N. County	House
6	Channelwood	Jan	211,000	N. County	House
7	Stoneship	Mar	98,200	S. County	Condo
8	Channelwood	Jan	132,850	N. County	Condo
9	Channelwood	Feb	450,000	S. County	House
10	Stoneship	Jan	250,000	City	Land
11	Stoneship	Jan	390,000	City	House
12	Channelwood	Mar	218,900	City	House
13	Channelwood	Jan	309,000	N. County	House
14	Stoneship	Jan	79,000	N. County	Condo
15	Stoneship	Mar	650,000	S. County	Land
16	Channelwood	Mar	129,500	N. County	House
17	Channelwood	Feb	145,900	City	House
18	Stoneship	Feb	545,000	N. County	House

Figure 16-6: A database used by a real estate company.

The database has 50 records and occupies the block A1:E51. This is fairly small, as databases go. Locating information in this small database isn't too difficult. But if this database had, say, 2,000 records, you can see how it might be difficult to locate all N. County condos that sold for more than $125,000 in March.

You'll notice that the data for this database were entered in no particular order.

The objective

OK, so we have the database all set up. Now we want to do something with it. For starters, we want to extract all records that meet the following criteria:

- Sold by the Channelwood office
- Selling price greater than or equal to $150,000

Setting up the criteria table

Now it's time to create a criteria table. Because we're searching on only two of the five fields in the database, the criteria table need only be two columns wide. We need to figure out where to put it. Column G is a good choice.

Figure 16-7 shows the criteria table I created.

Cell G2 contains the word *Channelwood*. Cell H2 contains the formula +Price>=150000. This formula appears as 0 in the cell.

Figure 16-7: A criteria table used to locate specific records.

	A	B	C	D	E	F	G	H
1	Office	Date	Price	Area	Type		Office	Price
2	Channelwood	Jan	145,900	City	Condo		Channelwood	0
3	Stoneship	Feb	325,000	S. County	Land			
4	Stoneship	Feb	289,000	City	House			
5	Stoneship	Jan	145,900	N. County	House			
6	Channelwood	Jan	211,000	N. County	House			
7	Stoneship	Mar	98,200	S. County	Condo			
8	Channelwood	Jan	132,850	N. County	Condo			
9	Channelwood	Feb	450,000	S. County	House			
10	Stoneship	Jan	250,000	City	Land			
11	Stoneship	Jan	390,000	City	House			
12	Channelwood	Mar	218,900	City	House			
13	Channelwood	Jan	309,000	N. County	House			
14	Stoneship	Jan	79,000	N. County	Condo			
15	Stoneship	Mar	650,000	S. County	Land			
16	Channelwood	Mar	129,500	N. County	House			
17	Channelwood	Feb	145,900	City	House			
18	Stoneship	Feb	545,000	N. County	House			

The gory details of creating a criteria table

Here are the general steps you'll go through to create a criteria table and enter your search criteria:

1. **Find an area to put the criteria table in.**

   Usually, the area directly to the right of the database is a good place. Or, if your database isn't going to be increasing in size, you can put it below the database (leaving at least one blank row).

2. **Enter the field names from the first row of your database block to the first row of the area you chose for your criteria block.**

3. **Directly below the field names in your criteria block, enter instructions that tell Quattro Pro for Windows what to look for.**

   For example, if you want to locate all records with *Condo* in the Type field, simply type **Condo** under the Use field in the criteria table.

Step 3 was admittedly rather vague. The instructions that you put under the field names in the criteria block can be one of two types:

- **An exact match.** Use a label or value. If you're looking for all records that have the label *City* in the Area field, simply put the label City under the Area field in the criteria block.

- **A condition.** Use a formula. If you're looking for all records that have a sales price value greater than or equal to $100,000, you can use a formula like +C2>=100000. Place this formula under the Price field name in the criteria block. The cell reference always refers to the first row of *data* (not the row with the field names).

You also can put instructions under more than one field name in the criteria block. For example, if you want to find all records that deal with condo sales *and* have a price greater than or equal to $100,000, you would put the label **Condo** under the Type field and **+C2>=100000** under the Price field name.

And there's more. You can use more than one line of instructions to perform *or* searches. For example, if you want to locate records that have a price less than or equal to $100,000, *or* that have a value greater than or equal to $400,000, you would use two formulas under the price field name (each in a separate row).

As you may expect, there's even more you can do when it comes to entering search instructions. If you don't need an exact match, you can use *wildcard* characters. Quattro Pro interprets *?* as "match any single character." Therefore, entering ?ig as a search instruction will locate records that have fig, big, dig, and so on in the field. When it sees *, it interprets it as "match any number of characters." Therefore, *ig will find records with twig, big, thingamajig — and anything else that ends in *ig*. Quattro Pro interprets ~ to mean "not." Therefore, if you want to locate all records except those that have *paid* in a field, enter ~paid as the search instruction.

If you're constantly changing the instructions in the criteria table to perform different database tasks, consider setting up more than one criteria table. Then, when you're ready to do a task, simply specify the appropriate criteria table. Specifying a criteria table is much easier if you give a descriptive name to each criteria table, because you can just type in the name rather than point out the block.

Setting up the extract block

Next, we need to identify a place to hold the records that are extracted. This can be anywhere you want, as long as there are plenty of blank rows below to hold the records that Quattro Pro for Windows will extract.

For this example, we'll put the extract block below the database starting in row 54. If the database will be increasing in size, it's not a good idea to put the extract block below it, because the database won't have any room to expand. But we'll assume that this database is as big as it's going to get.

Figure 16-8 shows the extract block. Notice that this is simply the field names from the database. (I copied them, rather than retype them.) In this case, we want the extract block to show all of the fields. But if we were not interested in, say, the month the property sold, we could have left that field out.

	A	B	C	D	E
45	Channelwood	Feb	256,000	N. County	Land
46	Channelwood	Feb	582,000	S. County	House
47	Stoneship	Jan	103,900	City	House
48	Stoneship	Mar	95,000	City	House
49	Channelwood	Mar	198,000	N. County	Condo
50	Channelwood	Feb	256,800	N. County	Condo
51	Stoneship	Feb	580,000	S. County	House
52					
53					
54	Office	Date	Price	Area	Type
55					

Figure 16-8: The extract block is where Quattro Pro for Windows copies the qualifying records.

Performing the query

Now it's time to actually do the query. Select the Tools⇨Database Tools⇨Query command. You'll get the dialog box shown in Figure 16-9.

This dialog box is asking for three pieces of information: the database block (A1..E51), the criteria table (G1..H2), and the output block (A54..E54). You can enter these block addresses manually or point to them in your notebook. Remember that the database block includes the row with the field names.

Chapter 16: The Lowdown on Lists and Databases

Figure 16-9:
The Data Query dialog box is where you specify the query criteria.

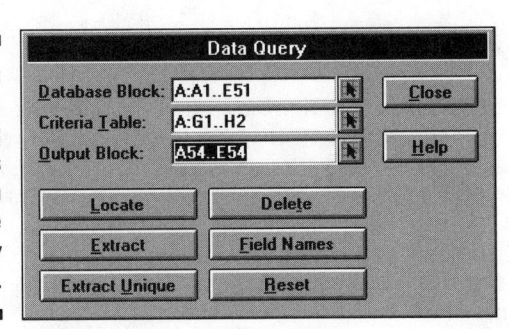

(Data Query dialog box showing:)
- Database Block: A:A1..E51
- Criteria Table: A:G1..H2
- Output Block: A54..E54
- Buttons: Close, Locate, Delete, Extract, Field Names, Extract Unique, Reset, Help

> **TIP:** If you select the database before you issue the Tools⇨Database Tools⇨Query command, the block address will appear in the Database Block range box.

Next, choose the Extract button. This tells Quattro Pro for Windows to copy the records from the database that meet our criteria into the output block. When you select this, nothing appears to happen, and the dialog box does not go away. Actually, Quattro Pro for Windows did its thing immediately. To get rid of the dialog box, choose Close.

Figure 16-10 shows the extracted records. As you can see, these records do indeed meet the criteria we specified: All were sold by the Channelwood office, and all have selling prices of $150,000 or more.

Figure 16-10:
The records that meet your criteria were copied by Quattro Pro for Windows to the extract block.

(Spreadsheet REALEST.WB2 showing:)

	A	B	C	D	E
50	Channelwood	Feb	256,800	N. County	Condo
51	Stoneship	Feb	580,000	S. County	House
52					
53					
54	Office	Date	Price	Area	Type
55	Channelwood	Jan	211,000	N. County	House
56	Channelwood	Feb	450,000	S. County	House
57	Channelwood	Mar	218,900	City	House
58	Channelwood	Jan	309,000	N. County	House
59	Channelwood	Jan	215,900	N. County	Condo
60	Channelwood	Feb	198,000	S. County	House
61	Channelwood	Feb	314,200	City	House
62	Channelwood	Mar	209,500	N. County	House
63	Channelwood	Feb	214,500	S. County	House
64	Channelwood	Mar	198,000	S. County	Condo
65	Channelwood	Feb	256,800	N. County	House
66	Channelwood	Feb	580,000	City	Land
67	Channelwood	Mar	159,000	City	Land

Locating records

Now you know how to extract information from a database and have Quattro Pro for Windows copy the desired records to another location. But what if you just want to see the qualifying records without copying them? Easy. Just use the Locate button in the Data Query dialog box.

When you choose the Locate button, the dialog box goes away, and Quattro Pro for Windows selects the first record in the database that qualifies. Figure 16-11 shows what this looks like.

Figure 16-11: Quattro Pro for Windows locates a qualifying record by selecting it for you.

	A	B	C	D	E	F	G	H	I
1	Office	Date	Price	Area	Type		Office	Price	
2	Channelwood	Jan	145,900	City	Condo		Channelwood	0	
3	Stoneship	Feb	325,000	S. County	Land				
4	Stoneship	Feb	289,000	City	House				
5	Stoneship	Jan	145,900	N. County	House				
6	Channelwood	Jan	211,000	N. County	House				
7	Stoneship	Mar	98,200	S. County	Condo				
8	Channelwood	Jan	132,850	N. County	Condo				
9	Channelwood	Feb	450,000	S. County	House				
10	Stoneship	Jan	250,000	City	Land				
11	Stoneship	Jan	390,000	City	House				
12	Channelwood	Mar	218,900	City	House				
13	Channelwood	Jan	309,000	N. County	House				
14	Stoneship	Jan	79,000	N. County	Condo				
15	Stoneship	Mar	650,000	S. County	Land				
16	Channelwood	Mar	129,500	N. County	House				
17	Channelwood	Feb	145,900	City	House				
18	Stoneship	Feb	545,000	N. County	House				

To see the next qualifying record, press the down-arrow key. Keep pressing the down-arrow, and Quattro Pro for Windows highlights each record that qualifies. You can also use up-arrow to locate a previous record in the database.

When you're finished viewing the records, press Enter, and you'll return to the Data Query dialog box. Then you can choose Close to get rid of that box.

Changing the criteria

If you want to locate or extract different records, you have two choices:

- ✔ Set up a different criteria table and specify it in the Data Query dialog box
- ✔ Change the current criteria table

Just for grins, we'll change the current criteria table to find all condos sold in January. Change the criteria table so that it looks like Figure 16-12.

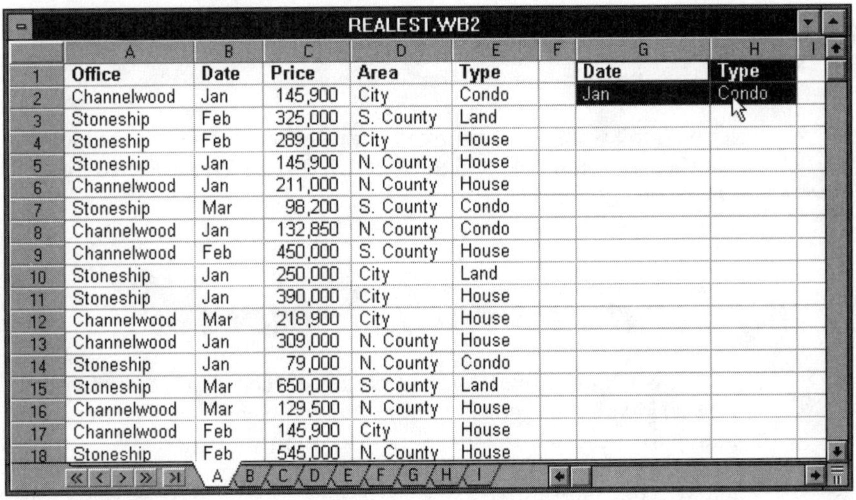

REALEST.WB2

	A	B	C	D	E	F	G	H
1	Office	Date	Price	Area	Type		Date	Type
2	Channelwood	Jan	145,900	City	Condo		Jan	Condo
3	Stoneship	Feb	325,000	S. County	Land			
4	Stoneship	Feb	289,000	City	House			
5	Stoneship	Jan	145,900	N. County	House			
6	Channelwood	Jan	211,000	N. County	House			
7	Stoneship	Mar	98,200	S. County	Condo			
8	Channelwood	Jan	132,850	N. County	Condo			
9	Channelwood	Feb	450,000	S. County	House			
10	Stoneship	Jan	250,000	City	Land			
11	Stoneship	Jan	390,000	City	House			
12	Channelwood	Mar	218,900	City	House			
13	Channelwood	Jan	309,000	N. County	House			
14	Stoneship	Jan	79,000	N. County	Condo			
15	Stoneship	Mar	650,000	S. County	Land			
16	Channelwood	Mar	129,500	N. County	House			
17	Channelwood	Feb	145,900	City	House			
18	Stoneship	Feb	545,000	N. County	House			

Figure 16-12: The criteria table, after changing it for a new query.

Select the <u>T</u>ools⇨Data<u>b</u>ase Tools⇨<u>Q</u>uery command again, and you'll see that Quattro Pro for Windows remembers the previous range addresses you entered. But, because the criteria table is changed, we'll get different records now. Select E<u>x</u>tract and then Close. The output block now looks like Figure 16-13.

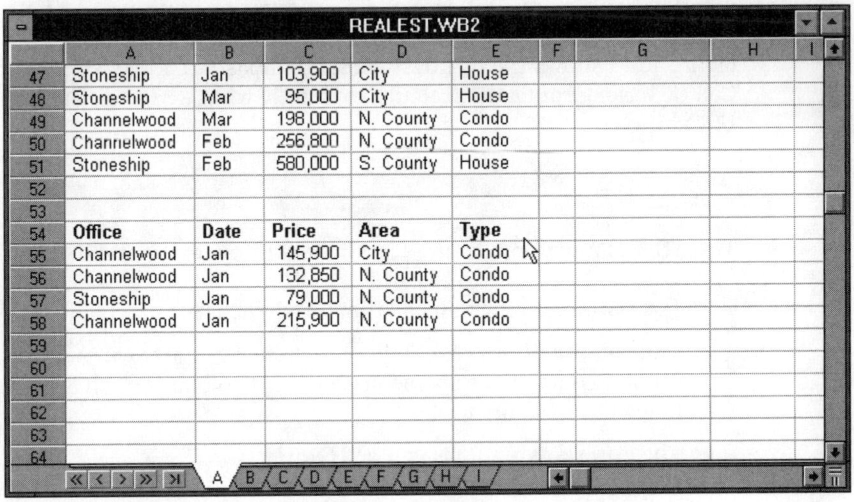

REALEST.WB2

	A	B	C	D	E
47	Stoneship	Jan	103,900	City	House
48	Stoneship	Mar	95,000	City	House
49	Channelwood	Mar	198,000	N. County	Condo
50	Channelwood	Feb	256,800	N. County	Condo
51	Stoneship	Feb	580,000	S. County	House
52					
53					
54	Office	Date	Price	Area	Type
55	Channelwood	Jan	145,900	City	Condo
56	Channelwood	Jan	132,850	N. County	Condo
57	Stoneship	Jan	79,000	N. County	Condo
58	Channelwood	Jan	215,900	N. County	Condo
59					
60					
61					
62					
63					
64					

Figure 16-13: The output block now contains the records that match the new criteria.

Part IV: Faking It

> **TIP:** There's no need to delete the old extracted records from the output block. Quattro Pro for Windows will automatically delete the old information and replace it with the new extracted records.

> **TIP:** If you don't want to lose the old information in the output block, just set up another output block, and tell Quattro Pro for Windows where it is in the Data Query dialog box.

Using Formulas with Databases

So far, you know how to extract database records that meet your criteria and how to locate the records right in the database. Now I'll discuss a way to summarize information in a database using @functions.

Quattro Pro for Windows has a special category of @functions called database @functions. These functions are designed specifically to work with databases like those you've seen in this chapter.

So what can you do with database @functions? Glad you asked. These functions provide an easy way to summarize information in a database. Using the previous example, let's say you need to find the total January sales by the Channelwood office. One approach is to use the techniques you already know: extract the qualifying records to an extract block, and then use an @SUM function to obtain the totals. Not a bad approach, but there's a better way.

Figure 16-14 shows the by-now familiar database example with one key addition. Cell G6 has a formula that calculates exactly what we need. The formula in cell G6 is:

```
@DSUM(A1..E51,2,G1..H2)
```

The @DSUM function has three arguments that correspond to

- **The database block.** Recall that the database is in A1..E51.
- **The column of interest.** Column numbering starts with 0, so using 2 as the second argument really means the third column, which is the field that holds the sales prices.
- **The criteria table.** This is block G1..H2.

The nice thing about these database @functions is that they work without having to extract information. If you want the formula to calculate the total sales of houses, just change Condo to House in the criteria table, and the formula will recalculate instantly to show the new answer.

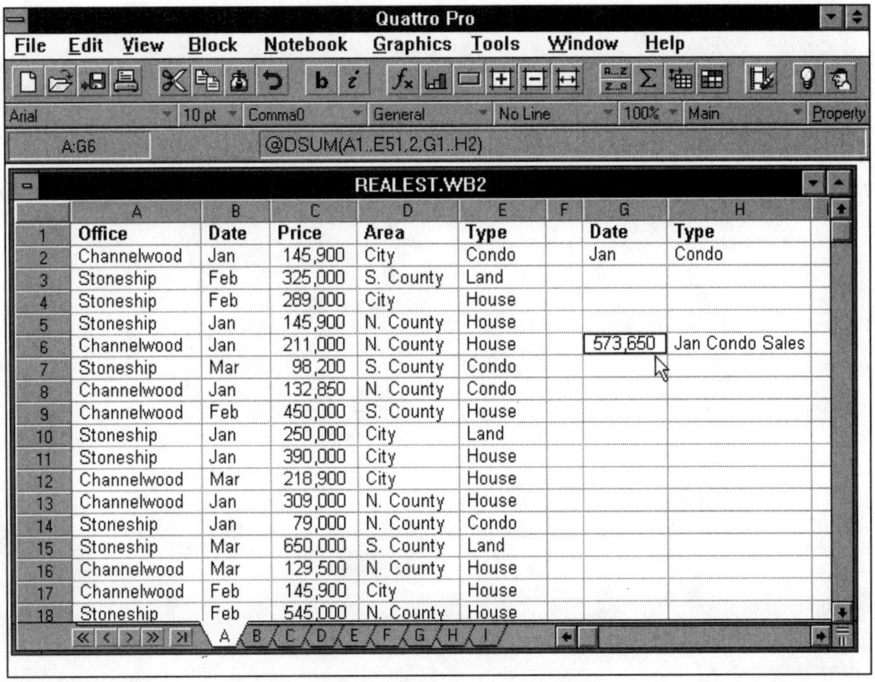

Chapter 16: The Lowdown on Lists and Databases 289

Figure 16-14: The @DSUM function calculates the total condo sales for January.

Quattro Pro for Windows provides several other database @functions for your dining and dancing pleasure. Some of the more useful ones are @DCOUNT (counts the number of qualifying records) and @DAVG (computes the average of the qualifying records).

Figure 16-15 shows more examples. Here, I created a nifty summary table that shows the total sales for each office categorized by property type. The formulas in the table's six cells are identical — except for the third argument of the @DSUM function. Notice that I had to set up a separate criteria table for each formula. This process gets kind of messy (and can be confusing), but it certainly makes it easy to summarize information.

Just so you can see what's going on, I've listed the actual formulas in these cells. As you can see, they are indeed identical (except for the criteria table references).

H15: @DSUM(A1..E51,2,G1..H2)
H16: @DSUM(A1..E51,2,G7..H8)
I15: @DSUM(A1..E51,2,G3..H4)
I16: @DSUM(A1..E51,2,G9..H10)
J15: @DSUM(A1..E51,2,G5..H6)
J16: @DSUM(A1..E51,2,G11..H12)

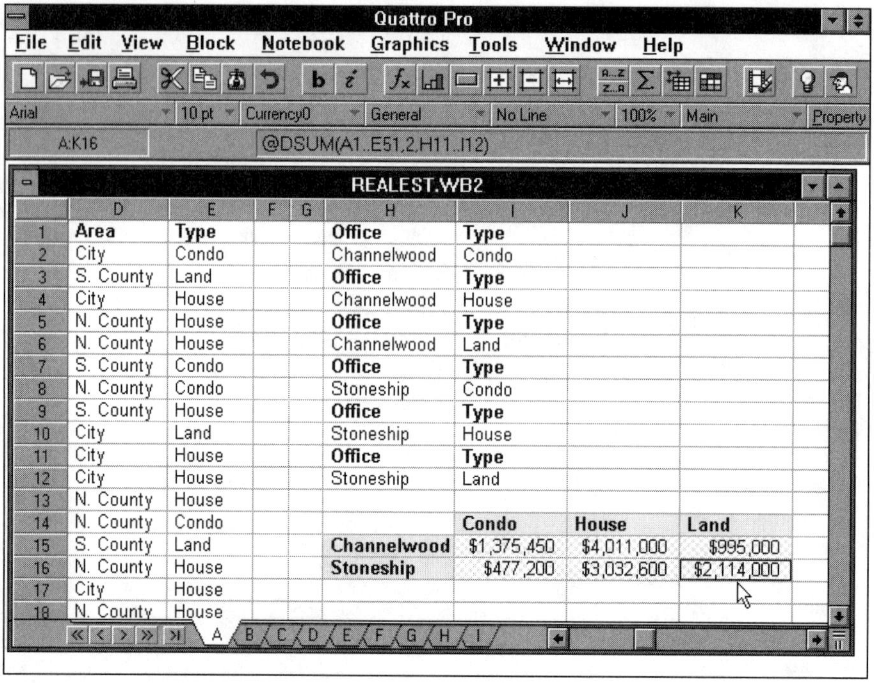

Figure 16-15:
The @DSUM function is used six times to create this summary table.

Printing Databases

If you want to print your database, you don't have to do anything special. Just use the knowledge you gained from Chapter 11. Printing a database is no different from printing any other notebook.

If you want to print only those records that meet certain criteria, use the information in this chapter to extract them to an extract block, and then specify the extract block as your print block.

Chapter 17
Cool Formulas You Can Steal

In This Chapter
▶ Common formulas that you can find many uses for
▶ Mathematical formulas that let you do slick things with numbers
▶ Formulas that let you manipulate text
▶ Formulas that let you do things with dates

I've found that people who use spreadsheets tend to want to do the same general kinds of tasks. Many of these procedures are built right into the spreadsheet in the form of menu commands or @functions. But many other popular spreadsheet actions require formulas (and you thought you were finished with this topic in Chapter 8!).

I can't develop formulas for you (unless the price is right...). However, I *can* share with you some formulas that I find useful. Most of these formulas use @functions, so this chapter serves double-duty by also demonstrating some realistic uses of these functions. You might find one or two that are just what you need to get that report out on time. Or seeing a formula here may give you an idea for a similar formula you can create. Or, you may not care about this material at all and decide to close the book right now.

In any case, feel free to do what you want with these formulas: study them diligently, ignore them completely, or do anything in between.

Read This First

The formulas in this chapter use names for @function arguments, which means that you cannot simply enter the formulas into a notebook and expect them to work. You have to make some minor changes to adapt the arguments to your own needs. When you incorporate these formulas into your notebooks, you must do one of the following:

- ✔ Substitute the appropriate cell or block reference for the block name I use. For example, the formula @SUM(expenses) uses a block named *expenses*. If you want to sum the values in block A12..A36, substitute that block reference for *expenses*. Therefore, your adapted formula would be @SUM(A12..A36).
- ✔ Name cells or blocks on your notebook to correspond to the block names used in the formulas. Following the previous example, you could simply use the Block⇨Names command to assign the name *expenses* to the block A12..A36.
- ✔ Use your own block names, and make the appropriate changes in the formulas. If your notebook has nothing to do with tracking expenses, define a name that applies.

Common, Everyday Formulas

The formulas in this section are relatively simple (and perhaps even trivial). But they show up again and again in spreadsheets all over the world.

Calculating a sum

To calculate the sum of a block named *expenses*, use the following formula:

```
@SUM(expenses)
```

TIP

The SpeedSum button on the Main Toolbar can write a formula like this for you automatically. Just move the cell pointer to the cell that you want the @SUM formula to be, and choose the SpeedSum button (it's the one with the Greek sigma). Quattro Pro for Windows will insert the formula in a jiffy.

Computing an average

To calculate the average (also known as the arithmetic mean) of a block named *expenses*, use the following formula:

```
@AVG(expenses)
```

WARNING!

If the block that you're averaging includes labels, @AVG will give you the wrong answer, because it treats labels as zeros.

Quattro Pro for Windows also provides the @MEDIAN function, which returns the median value of a block. If you rank all the values in the block, the median is the value that's in the middle of the ranked values (half of the values are greater than the median, and half are less than the median). Statistical freaks may also be interested in the @MODE function, which returns the most common value in the block.

Calculating a percentage change

If you want to calculate the percentage change between the value in a cell named *old* and the value in a cell named *new,* use the following formula:

```
+(new-old)/old
```

If *old* is greater than *new,* the percentage change value is positive. Otherwise, the value is negative. You'll probably want to format this cell to appear as a percentage.

If there's a chance that *old* will be equal to 0, use the following formula instead:

```
@IF(old=0,@NA,(new-old)/old)
```

This revised formula displays NA rather than ERR, which shows up if you attempt to divide by zero (division by zero is against the law on this planet).

Finding the minimum and maximum in a block

To find the largest number in a block named *scores,* use the following formula:

```
@MAX(scores)
```

To find the smallest number in a block named *scores,* use the following formula:

```
@MIN(scores)
```

Quattro Pro for Windows considers labels to have a value of 0. Therefore, if the block argument for @MAX and @MIN has labels in it, the function may not return what you want.

Part IV: Faking It

> **TIP:** Another @function, @LARGEST, tells you the *n*th largest number in a block. For example, to get the second-highest value in the block *scores,* use the following formula:
>
> ```
> @LARGEST(score,2)
> ```

As you might expect, there's also an @SMALLEST function that returns the *n*th smallest number in a block.

Calculating a loan payment

You can rely on your bank to figure your monthly loan payment amount — or you can do it yourself using Quattro Pro for Windows. This example assumes that you have cells named *amount* (which is the loan amount), *term* (which is the length of the loan in months), and *rate* (which is the annual interest rate). The following formula returns the monthly payment amount:

```
@PMT(amount,rate/12,term)
```

Notice that this formula divides the annual interest rate (*rate*) by 12. This produces a monthly interest rate. If you are making payments every other month, divide *rate* by 6.

> **TIP:** If you want to determine the amount of a loan payment that's applied to the principal, use the @PPAYMT function. To determine the amount that's applied to interest, use the @IPAYMNT function. These functions are demonstrated in Figure 17-1. Cell B5 contains the payment number (from 1 to 48 in this case). The amount allocated to principal and interest varies with the payment number — more goes to interest earlier in the loan.

Figure 17-1: @functions calculate the portions of a loan payment that are applied to principal and interest.

	A	B	C
5	Payment #	3	
6	To Interest	138.98	<-- @IPAYMT(B2/12,B5,B3,-B1)
7	To Principal	252.35	<-- @PPAYMT(B2/12,B5,B3,-B1)
8	Total Payment	391.34	<-- @SUM(B6..B7)
10	Total Payment	391.34	<-- @PMT(B1,B2/12,B3)

Mathematical Formulas

These formulas have to do with mathematical operations: square roots, cube roots, random numbers, and so on.

Finding a square root

The square root of a number is the number that, when multiplied by itself, gives you the original number. For example, 4 is the square root of 16, because 4 x 4 = 16. To calculate the square root of a cell named *value,* use the following function:

```
@SQRT(value)
```

Finding a cube (or other) root

Besides square roots, there are other roots (like carrots and potatoes). The cube root of a number is the number that, when multiplied by itself twice, results in the original number. For example, 4 is the cube root of 64, because 4 x 4 x 4 = 64. You can also calculate 4th roots, 5th roots, and so on. To get the cube root of a number in a cell named *value,* use the following formula:

```
+value^(1/3)
```

The fourth root is calculated as

```
+value^(1/4)
```

Calculate other roots in a similar manner by changing the denominator of the fraction.

Checking for even or odd values

To determine whether the value in a cell named *cointoss* is odd or even, use the following formula:

```
@MOD(cointoss,2)
```

This formula returns 1 if *cointoss* is odd and 0 if it's even.

For an even fancier formula that returns words rather than numbers, use this formula:

```
@IF(@MOD(cointoss,2)=1,"ODD","EVEN")
```

The @MOD function, by the way, returns the remainder when the first argument is divided by the second argument. So in the first example, the value in *cointoss* is divided by 2, and the @MOD function returns the remainder of this division operation.

Generating a random number

Spreadsheet users often use random numbers to simulate real events. For example, if you're trying to predict next year's sales, you might want to add some random numbers to this year's sales.

To get a random number between 0 and 1, use the following formula, which displays a new random number every time the notebook is recalculated or every time you make a change to a cell:

```
@RAND
```

If you need a random integer (a whole number) that falls in a specific range, the formula gets a bit trickier. The following formula returns a random integer between two integers stored in *low* and *high*. For example, if *low* contains 7 and *high* contains 12, the formula returns a random number between (and including) 7 and 12. The formula reads:

```
@INT(@RAND*(high-low))+low
```

Rounding numbers

To round a number in a cell named *amount* to the nearest whole number, use the following formula:

```
@ROUND(amount,0)
```

To round the number to two decimal places, substitute a 2 for the 0 in the formula. In fact, you can round the number to any number of decimal places by changing the value of the second argument.

The value returned by the @ROUND function is the actual rounded value of its argument. If you merely want to change the number of decimal places displayed in a cell, you can change the numeric formatting using the Object Inspector dialog box (select the cell, right-click, and choose Block Properties). In other words, @ROUND affects not only how the value is displayed but also the value itself.

Label Formulas

As you know, Quattro Pro for Windows can deal with text (or *labels*) as well as numbers. Here are a few formulas that let you manipulate labels.

"Adding" labels

Joining two strings is called *concatenation*. Assume the cell named *first* contains the label *Miles* and the cell named *last* contains *Davis*. The following formula concatenates these strings into a single name:

```
+first&" "&last
```

The ampersand (&) is the concatenation operator. Note that I concatenated a space character to separate the two names (otherwise the result would be *MilesDavis,* not *Miles Davis*). You can concatenate a label with a label but not a label with a value. However, you can get around this restriction, as shown in the following examples.

Working with labels and values

If you want to concatenate a label with a value, you must first convert the value to a label. In this example, the cell named *word* holds the label "AMOUNT:". The cell named *answer* holds the value 125. The formula below displays the label and the value in a single cell.

```
+word&" "&@STRING(answer,0)
```

The @STRING command converts a value to a label, and the second argument for the @STRING function gives the number of decimal places to be displayed (in this case, none).

The result of this formula is

```
AMOUNT: 125
```

Here's another example. Assume that you have a block of cells named *scores*. The following formula displays a label and the maximum value in *scores* in one cell:

```
+"Largest: "&@STRING(@MAX(scores),0)
```

If the largest value in scores were 95, this formula would display:

```
Largest: 95
```

The @STRING function converts the value returned by the @MAX function into a label. This label is then concatenated with the string "Largest: ". Pretty neat, huh?

Date Formulas

Here are a few formulas that deal with dates.

WARNING! The date and time @functions get their information from your computer's clock. If you rely on any of these functions for serious work, make sure that the date and time are set properly in your computer. Procedures for setting computer clocks vary, so consult your system manual for instructions.

Finding out what day it is

If you would like a cell in your notebook to display the current date, enter the following formula into any cell:

```
@TODAY
```

This formula returns a date serial number, so you need to format it as a date (the Style pull-down on the property band is the easy way to do this). You may also have to make the column wider so that the date shows up properly.

Determining the day of the week

The following formula returns the current day of the week:

```
@CHOOSE(@WKDAY(@TODAY),"Sat","Sun","Mon","Tue","Wed","Thu","Fri")
```

You can replace @TODAY in the preceding formula with a reference to a cell that has a date serial number in it to get the day of the week for any date.

Determining the last day of the month

In business situations, it's often necessary to know the last day of the month — the day that you have to produce the monthly reports. The following formula returns the last day of the current month:

```
@EMNTH(@TODAY)
```

To figure out the last day of the month for any date serial number, substitute a reference to a cell that has a date for @TODAY.

Quattro Pro for Windows has many more @functions that deal with dates. If you tend to work often with dates, you should check them out. Chances are you'll find one or two that are perfect for what you're trying to do.

Miscellaneous Formulas

Here are a few more miscellaneous formulas for your computing pleasure.

Displaying the notebook name

The formula below returns the name of the notebook that it's in. This might be useful if you want the filename to appear in your printouts. By the way, you can substitute any cell reference for A1 — it will always return the name of the notebook.

```
@CELL("Notebookname",A1)
```

Looking up a corresponding value

Many spreadsheets need to look up a value in a table that is based on another value. Examples include parts lists and income tax tables: you need to look up the tax rate from a table, and the rate is based on a person's taxable income.

Figure 17-2 shows an example of a small lookup table. In this notebook, the user can enter a part number into cell B3, which is named *partnum*. The formulas in cells B4 and B5 return the corresponding price and discount. The lookup table is in block D2..F11 and has the name *partlist*. The values in the first column of any lookup table must be in ascending order (smallest to largest).

	A	B	C	D	E	F
1				Part No.	Price	Discount
2				101	$114.50	5.00%
3	Partnum:	109		102	$98.75	5.00%
4	Price:	$22.44		103	$45.00	5.00%
5	Discount:	10.00%		104	$32.44	10.00%
6				105	$111.59	5.00%
7				106	$32.12	5.00%
8				108	$5.01	10.00%
9				109	$22.44	10.00%
10				110	$9.31	5.00%
11				111	$89.30	15.00%

Figure 17-2: Looking up a value in a table.

The formula in cell B4, which displays the price, is

`@VLOOKUP(partnum,partlist,1)`

The formula in cell B5, which displays the discount, is

`@VLOOKUP(partnum,partlist,2)`

The @VLOOKUP function looks for the first argument (here, *partnum*) in the first column of the block specified by the second argument (here, *partlist*). It then returns the value in the column represented by the third argument (0 corresponds to the first column in the table, 1 to the second column, 2 to the third column, and so on). If the formula doesn't find an exact match, it simply uses the first row that's not greater than what it's looking for. In some cases this is okay, but in others it can be a problem.

Converting measurements

I'll wrap up this chapter by discussing one of the most useful @functions available: @CONVERT. This one can convert between two measurement systems. Assume the cell named *inches* contains the value 15 (which is in inches). To convert this to feet, use the following formula:

```
@CONVERT(inches,"in","ft")
```

This formula will return 1.25 — which means that 15 inches equals 1.25 feet.

The first argument of the CONVERT function refers to the cell that has the value to convert. The second argument is the *from* units, and the third argument is the *to* units. In this case, the formula converts the value in the *inches* cell from inches to feet.

Here's another example. To convert five days into minutes, enter this formula:

```
@CONVERT(5,"day","mn")
```

This formula returns 7,200 — because there are 7,200 minutes in five days.

The @CONVERT function is very versatile. Table 17-1 lists some of the more common measurement units (and their abbreviations) that it can deal with.

Table 17-1 Some of the Measurement Units Recognized by @CONVERT

Measurement Unit	Abbreviation
Distance	
Meter	m
Statute mile	mi
Nautical mile	nmi
Inch	in
Foot	ft
Yard	yd
Angstrom	ang
Time	
Year	yr
Day	day
Hour	hr
Minute	mn
Second	sec

(continued)

Table 17-1 (continued)

Measurement Unit	Abbreviation
Liquid	
Teaspoon	tsp
Tablespoon	tbs
Fluid ounce	oz
Cup	cup
Pint	pt
Quart	qt
Gallon	gal
Liter	lt

The 5th Wave By Rich Tennant

"KEVIN HERE HEADS OUR WINDOWS SOFTWARE DEVELOPMENT TEAM. RIGHT NOW HE'S WORKING ON A SPREADSHEET PROGRAM THAT'S SORT OF A COMBINATION QUATTRO PRO 6-STREET FIGHTER II."

Chapter 18
Just Enough about Macros to Get By

In This Chapter
- An introduction to macros
- How to create simple macros — and why you may want to do so
- How to use macros that other people created
- Examples that will help clarify this topic
- Even more about macros that you probably can safely ignore

Somewhere along the line, you may have heard that computers are supposed to make your life easier and save time. The time-saving spreadsheet feature most often mentioned by the studio audience of TV's *Family Feud* is macros. Learning about macros is not essential to using Quattro Pro for Windows (and you certainly won't win any lovely parting gifts). In fact, most spreadsheet users wouldn't know a macro from a mango. But you owe it to yourself to at least learn what macros can do so that you'll know what you're missing out on.

What Is a Macro?

Imagine that you have a spreadsheet set up, and you need to enter the name of your company in several places throughout the notebook. You can type the company name each time you need it, or you can enter the company once and then copy it to the other locations. Another way is to create a macro to type the company name for you automatically upon command.

If your company's name is Star-Spangled Widgets Corporation of America, you can assign these letters to a key combination such as Ctrl+S. Then, whenever you press Ctrl+S, Quattro Pro for Windows spits out this text instantly (and, as a bonus, always spells it correctly).

> ### Why "macro"?
>
> Contrary to popular belief, MACRO does *not* stand for Messy And Confusing Repeatable Operation. Actually, I don't know why they use this term. The dictionary tells me that *macro* means large and is the opposite of *micro*. My guess is that they call these things macros because you can perform a large operation by making a small effort. If anyone knows the real answer, please let me in on it.

And — believe it or not — it gets even better. You also can create macros that execute a series of commands. Suppose that you like to apply specific formatting such as bold, red text, and a thick border. You can assign all of these commands to a key combination such as Ctrl+F. Pressing Ctrl+F then executes these commands in the blink of an eye.

So there you have it. A macro is simply a shortcut way of typing text, numbers, or even commands. The only hitch is that you have to create the macro before you use it.

More about Macros

Before we get too far into macros, there are a few things you should know about Quattro Pro for Windows' macros:

- A macro can play back predefined keystrokes. Playing back the predefined keystrokes is called *running the macro* or *executing the macro*. As you'll see later, there are a number of ways to run a macro.
- Every macro should have a name.
- You usually store your macros in the notebook that you plan to use them with. Actually, macros are just labels — labels that have a special meaning to Quattro Pro for Windows.
- You must create the macro before you can use it, and there are two ways to create a macro: manually, and by recording your keystrokes.
- You can use a macro as many times as you want, and the macro always does exactly the same thing — day after day, week after week.

Your First Macro

Ready to give it a try? You'll create a macro that types your name into a cell and then moves the cell selector to the cell directly below. You will assign the macro to the Ctrl+N key combination. When you're finished, you'll be able to go to any cell in the notebook and press Ctrl+N to have Quattro Pro for Windows enter the text you specified and move the cell selector down to the cell below. Ready?

Creating the macro

1. **Start with a blank notebook page.**
2. **Select cell A1, and type your name in the cell followed by a tilde (~).**

   For example, if your name happens to be Bill Clinton, type **Bill Clinton~**.
3. **Move the cell selector to cell A2 and type {DOWN}.**
4. **Move the cell selector back to cell A1, right-click and choose Names from the shortcut menu.**
5. **Enter \n, click Add, and then click Close.**

   This step assigns the name \n to cell A1 (the first cell of the macro). This lets you run the macro by pressing Ctrl+N.

That's it. Your notebook should look like Figure 18-1 (although the name in cell A1 will be different unless your name is really Bill Clinton). This macro consists of two labels, and it's named \n.

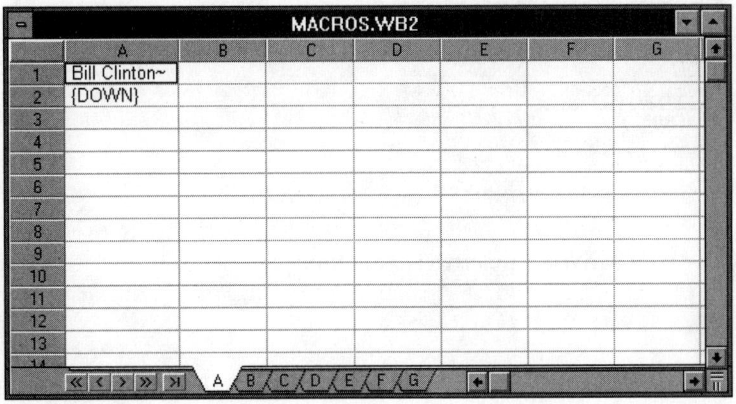

Figure 18-1:
A simple macro that types your name on command.

Running the macro

You now can play back (or execute) the macro in one of two ways. You can use the macro's key combination (Ctrl+N in this example), or you can use the Tools⇨Macro⇨Play command and select \n from the list of macros displayed (there is only one in this case). The following are step-by-step instructions for each method.

With the key combination

1. **Move the cell selector to any blank cell in the notebook.**
2. **Press Ctrl+N.**

The macro types your name and then moves the cell selector down one cell. You can move all over the notebook (even to different pages) and press Ctrl+N until your fingers are numb. You'll see your name show up each time you execute this macro.

If the macro doesn't do what it's supposed to do, the source of the problem is probably the name. Cell A1 must be named \n. You used the Block Names dialog box to do this. If it doesn't work, go back and try again.

With the Tools⇨Macro⇨Play command

Earlier in this chapter, I told you that all macros must have a name. I lied. Although it makes them easier to work with, macros don't *need* to have a name. You can run a macro that doesn't have a name by using the Tools⇨Macro⇨Play command (or its Alt+F2 shortcut). After you issue this command, Quattro Pro for Windows responds with the dialog box shown in Figure 18-2.

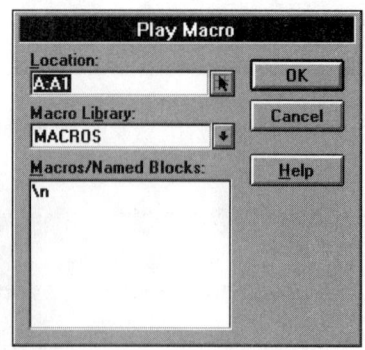

Figure 18-2: The Macro Play dialog box.

In the box labeled Location, you can enter the cell address for the first cell of the macro. In this case, it's A1. If the macro has a name, you can select it from the list at the bottom. Choose OK, and the macro will be executed.

How it works

This simple two-cell macro does two things: it types your name and it moves the cell selector down one cell. When you press Ctrl+N, Quattro Pro for Windows goes through the following artificial thought process:

1. **Hmmm. This user just pressed Ctrl+N.**
2. **Is there a macro named \n?**

   If not, I'll open a new workbook (the normal action for Ctrl+N).
3. **Hey, there is a macro named \n.**

   That means I'll have to execute it.
4. **The first cell is just a bunch of letters.**

   I'll stick them in the cell where the cell selector is. There's a tilde at the end of the letters, so I'll press Enter.
5. **There's another cell below, so I'll take a look at it.**
6. **This cell has a command that tells me to move the cell selector down. Okay.**
7. **Because there's nothing below this macro command, my job's over for now.**

You probably noticed a few things about this two-cell macro. The tilde character after your name represents the Enter key. When Quattro Pro for Windows encounters a tilde, it's just like you pressed Enter. The {DOWN} part of the macro is responsible for moving the cell selector. {DOWN} is a macro command. Quattro Pro for Windows has quite a few macro commands, which are always enclosed in curly brackets. If this command were not in brackets, Quattro Pro for Windows simply types the letters *D, O, W,* and *N.* As you might expect, you can use other commands, such as {UP}, {LEFT}, and {RIGHT}, to move the cell selector around.

If you assign a macro to a key combination that already does something, the macro will take precedence. In this example, Ctrl+N normally opens a new workbook. But since there's a macro by that name, Quattro Pro for Windows executes the macro instead.

Modifying the macro

Now, modify the macro so that it does even more (add the first line of your address):

1. **Move to cell A3 (the cell directly below the end of the existing macro), and enter the first line of your address.**

   You're adding on to the existing macro to make it type an address.
2. **Move to the cell below (A4) and type** {UP}.

   This macro command tells Quattro Pro for Windows to move the cell selector up. Therefore, when you execute the macro, the cell selector returns to the spot where you started.

Figure 18-3 shows how this modified macro will look.

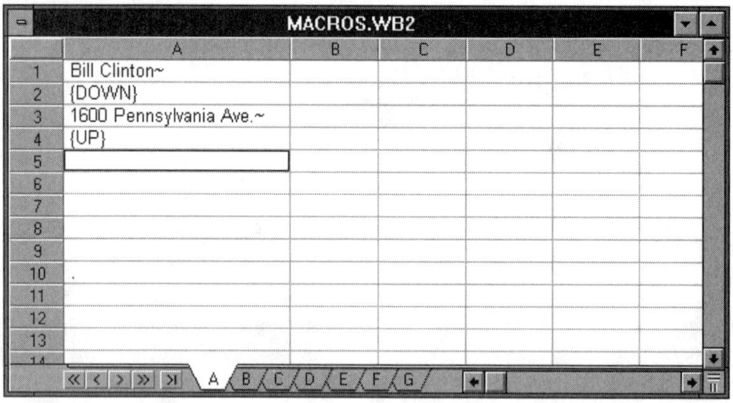

Figure 18-3: The macro after making some modifications.

This modified macro types your name, moves down, types your address, and then moves up a cell. Move to a blank cell, and press Ctrl+N. Quattro Pro for Windows executes this slightly more complex macro just as it should. You might be surprised at how fast it types.

Notice that you don't have to rename this macro if you make any changes. The original name (\n) still applies to the first cell of the macro.

Some macro rules

With this minor bit of macro experience under your belt, you're ready for some rules of the game:

- A macro simply consists of labels made up of text and special macro commands enclosed in brackets.
- A macro is stored in one or more cells in a single column. A blank cell signals the end of the macro.
- You can edit the text that makes up a macro command just as you would edit any other cell.
- Quattro Pro for Windows plays back the labels and executes the commands in order, starting at the top and working down the column, until it hits a blank cell.
- If you want to execute the macro using the Ctrl key, the first cell of the macro must have a name that starts with a backslash and has one additional character. This additional character is used with the Ctrl key to execute the macro.

- You can put any number of macro commands into one cell (but you make it easier on yourself if you use only one command per cell).
- You can enter macros directly, or you use the macro recorder to record your keystrokes (explained next).

The Macro Recorder

Quattro Pro for Windows has a special built-in feature that's capable of analyzing your actions and creating a macro out of them. This feature works much as a tape recorder works: turn recording mode on, do your thing, turn recording mode off, and then play it back as many times as you want. And the nice thing about it is that you never have to buy blank tapes.

Recording and Executing a Macro

Ready to record a macro? Ready or not, that's what this section does. At the risk of being bored to tears, you'll record a macro that does the same thing as before: type your name and address.

Recording it

Start with a blank notebook (not necessary, but it makes the process easier for me to describe), and then do the following:

1. **Start with the cell selector in cell A1.**
2. **Select the Tools⇨Macro⇨Record command.**

    You'll get a dialog box that lets you choose a location for the macro. You'll begin the macro in cell A1 (which already appears in the Location box), so just click OK to accept it.

    From this point on, everything you do is being recorded for posterity.

3. **Move the cell selector to cell E1 (you don't want to enter things in the block that the macro is being recorded to).**
4. **Enter your name into the current cell (E1).**
5. **Move down to cell E2, and enter your address (start it with one single-quote character to make it a label).**

6. **Move the cell selector back up to cell E1.**

7. **Select the Tools⇨Macro⇨Stop Record command to turn off the macro recorder.**

Your screen should look something like Figure 18-4.

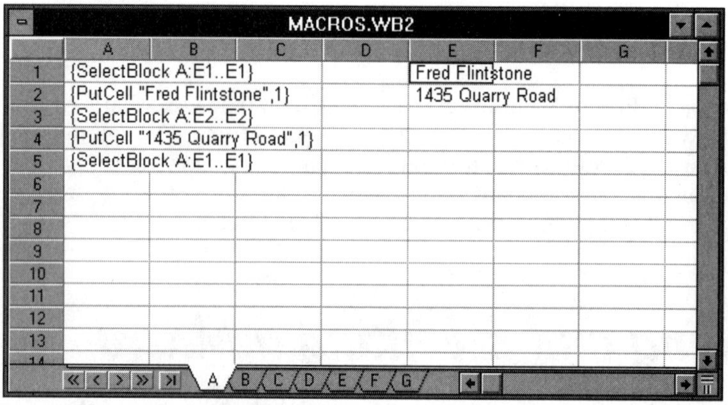

```
            MACROS.WB2
      A              B           C     D       E           F       G
1  {SelectBlock A:E1..E1}                   Fred Flintstone
2  {PutCell "Fred Flintstone",1}            1435 Quarry Road
3  {SelectBlock A:E2..E2}
4  {PutCell "1435 Quarry Road",1}
5  {SelectBlock A:E1..E1}
6
7
8
9
10
11
12
13
```

Figure 18-4: Your first recorded macro.

As you were typing, undoubtedly you noticed that Quattro Pro for Windows was spitting out the macro while you typed, beginning in cell A1. You also probably noticed that it looks very strange — but more about this strangeness later.

Naming it

Now, move the cell selector to cell A1, right-click, and select Names. Give this macro the name \n. As before, this step will let you execute the macro by pressing Ctrl+N.

Playing it

Try the new macro by moving to a blank cell in the notebook and pressing Ctrl+N. If you did everything right, you will notice that the macro doesn't work. Actually, it *does* work — but it doesn't do what you were expecting. Every time this macro is executed, it starts playing back cell E1 — which is where you were when you recorded it.

What's wrong? Well, actually you recorded this macro using Quattro Pro for Windows' default recording mode — absolute. This means that absolute cell references get recorded. Since the first action was to move the cell selector to cell E1, that exact cell was recorded into the macro. Sometimes this is what you want, but in this case you want the macro to play back at the *current* cell position. Don't worry, you'll just record it again.

Fixing it

We'll try again, but this time we'll record the macro in relative mode.

1. **Delete everything on the sheet to start with a clean slate.**
2. **Move the cell selector to cell E1.**
3. **Choose Tools⇨Macro⇨Options.**

   You'll see the dialog box shown in Figure 18-5.

Figure 18-5: This dialog box lets you choose between relative and absolute mode.

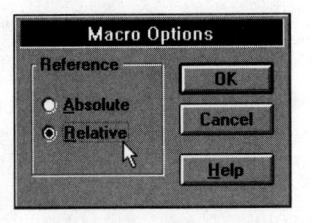

4. **Select the Relative option, and choose OK.**
5. **Choose the Tools⇨Macro⇨Record command.**

   Enter **A1** in the Location box and select OK. As before, start recording the macro in cell A1.
6. **With the cell selector still in E1, enter your name.**
7. **Move down one cell, and enter your address.**
8. **Move back up to cell E1.**
9. **Choose the Tools⇨Macro⇨Stop Record command to turn off the macro recorder.**

   Your screen should look something like Figure 18-6.

Because cell A1 is still named \n from the previous macro (which you erased), there's no need to name the macro again. Move to a blank cell, and press Ctrl+N. The macro will immediately type your name, move down a cell, type your address, and then go back to the original cell.

The recorded macro may look very strange to you. Not what you expected, huh? Some parts of it don't look anything like the keys you pressed when you recorded it. Quattro Pro for Windows doesn't record keystrokes literally. Rather, it interprets them into commands. For example, it uses the {PutCell}

Figure 18-6: Your second recorded macro. This one will do what you want.

```
                    MACROS.WB2
      A              B           C        D      E         F       G
1  {PutCell "Fred Flintstone",1}               Fred Flintstone
2  {SelectBlock C(0)R(1)..C(0)R(1)}            1435 Quarry Road
3  {PutCell "1435 Quarry Road",1}
4  {SelectBlock C(0)R(-1)..C(0)R(-1)}
```

macro command to insert things into a cell, and it uses the {SelectBlock} macro command to move the cell selector. You don't have to know what all of these weird commands mean — as long as the macro does what you want it to do.

REMEMBER You can record a macro in two modes: absolute (the default) or relative. Record in absolute mode when you always want exactly the same thing to happen when you play the macro. Use relative mode when you want the macro to do things relative to the current cell. This may sound confusing, but after you record a few macros, it will all become semicrystal clear.

Getting More Advanced

So far, the macros you've developed have been pretty wimpy — simply typing your name and address is useful, but it won't save you all that much time. Now you'll record a macro that actually does something constructive.

The macro you create will apply an attractive format to the selected cells — suitable for a fancy heading. The finished macro will convert the block B2..E2 in the notebook shown in Figure 18-7 so that it looks like B4..E4 — all with a single keystroke.

Next, you'll record the macro that does this formatting. For simplicity, start with a blank notebook.

1. **Type** This is a Fancy Table Heading **in cell B2.**

    This is just a dummy label to give us something to start with. Keep the cell selector in this cell.

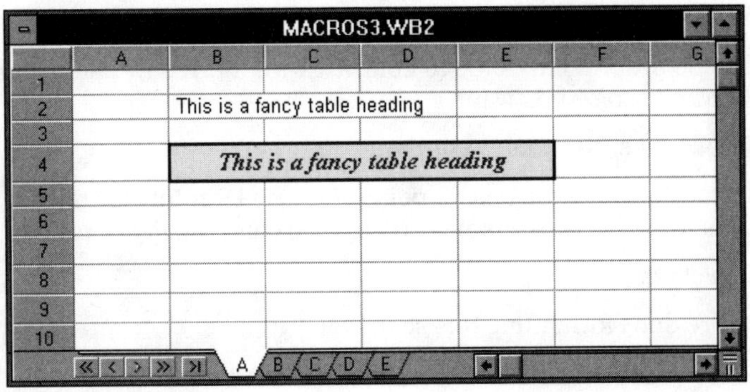

Figure 18-7:
Before running the macro (top) and after running the macro (bottom).

2. **Select the Range B2..E2.**

    Because this macro will center the text across a block of cells, we'll start with a block of cells selected.

3. **Select the Tools⇔Macro⇔Options command, and make sure the recording mode is Relative.**

    We want this macro to work for the current selection — not for a specific block of cells.

4. **Choose the Tools⇔Macro⇔Record command.**

5. **In the Record Macro dialog box, enter G1 in the Location box.**

    We'll use this location to keep the recorded macro out of the way of what we're doing. Choose OK to begin recording.

6. **Right-click and choose Block Properties from the shortcut menu.**

    This brings up the familiar Object Inspector dialog box.

7. **Select the Font option, and choose a font for the text.**

    I chose Times New Roman, but you can pick anything you like. Make the Point Size 12, and select the Bold and Italics check boxes.

8. **Next, select the Shading option, and choose a shading you like.**

    I used bright yellow for the cell background.

9. **Choose the Alignment option.**

    For Horizontal Alignment, select the Center across block option. For Vertical Alignment, select the Center option.

10. **Choose the Line Drawing option.**

    Click the Outside button, and then select the thick line choice.

Part IV: Faking It

11. **Select the Text Color option.**

    I made the text dark blue to contrast with the yellow background. Choose whatever color you want.

12. **Choose the Row Height option.**

    Because I made the text 12 points, I chose 18 points for the row height. This will give the text some room to be centered in the row.

13. **Select OK.**

    We're done formatting this selection.

14. **Choose Tools⇨Macro⇨Stop Record to turn off recording mode.**

15. **Finally, select cell G1 (the first cell of the macro), and name this cell \f.**

    At this point, the recorded macro will look something like Figure 18-8.

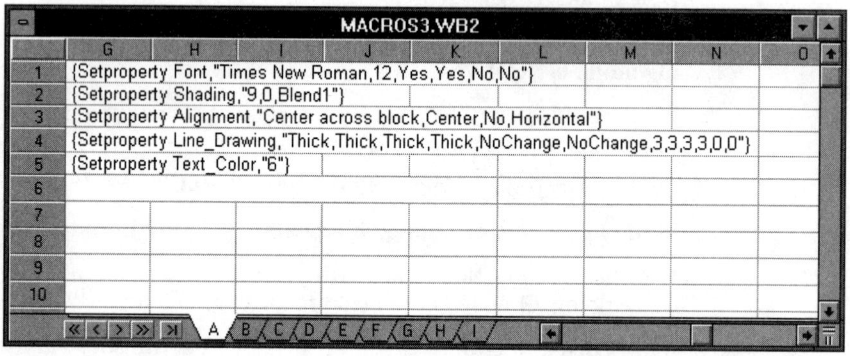

Figure 18-8: A formatting macro, recorded by Quattro Pro for Windows.

	G	H	I	J	K	L	M	N	O
1	{Setproperty Font,"Times New Roman,12,Yes,Yes,No,No"}								
2	{Setproperty Shading,"9,0,Blend1"}								
3	{Setproperty Alignment,"Center across block,Center,No,Horizontal"}								
4	{Setproperty Line_Drawing,"Thick,Thick,Thick,Thick,NoChange,NoChange,3,3,3,3,0,0"}								
5	{Setproperty Text_Color,"6"}								

Move to a blank cell, such as B6, and enter a label (**Yet Another Fancy Label**, for example). Select the block B6..F6. Press Ctrl+F; Quattro Pro for Windows executes the macro. In a flash, the selected cells are formatted according to your recorded specifications.

Enter a few more labels, and try it again. It's much faster than doing all that formatting manually, wouldn't you agree? And it's an easy way to make your headings look consistent.

Using Other People's Macros

At some point in your career, you may receive a notebook from someone who actually knows what he's doing. This notebook may have one or more macros on it, and you've been told that these macros make the spreadsheet do something useful. In fact, this scenario isn't all that unusual. Some people take great pride in developing macros that do useful things.

If you're lucky, the notebook will have instructions that tell you what to do. For example, it may say something like "To print this notebook, press Ctrl+P" or "Press Ctrl+U to update the monthly sales figures."

The person who created such a notebook was simply trying to make things easier for you or anyone else who uses the spreadsheet. The macros may do quite a bit behind the scenes — more than you care to do or know how to do. In this case, running a macro is much like issuing a command.

You don't have to know what the macro is doing in order to use it. Just press the appropriate key combination, and sit back and relax while Quattro Pro for Windows follows the orders in the macro.

What Next?

The nice thing about macros is that you can use them at whatever level you want. This chapter explained how to record simple macros. Knowing how to do this is enough for most people. And if you understand this, you can count yourself among the Quattro Pro for Windows elite.

Some people really enjoy playing around with macros (author included), and they end up writing some extremely complicated macros that do amazing things. Refer back to Chapter 1, and take a look at Figure 1-4 for an example that uses some heavy-duty macros to simulate a video poker machine.

If you find that you could use macros in your work, just take it slowly. Eventually things will start to come together, and your macros will get better and more powerful. The on-line help explains it all pretty well, but you'll learn the most by experimenting.

Chapter 19
How Do I...

In This Chapter
▶ A quick reference that tells you how to perform common — and some not so common — Quattro Pro for Windows operations
▶ Things that aren't covered in other chapters

Here's where you go when you need to do something in Quattro Pro for Windows, but you can't quite remember how to do it. Besides steering you to the right menu command, I also tell you what you need to look out for, and I even list the shortcut keys you can use. (What a guy!)

The chapter is arranged somewhat logically, grouped by classifications such as editing, formatting, graphing, and so on. And, of course, don't overlook the catch-all Miscellaneous section at the end.

Editing

These procedures involve modifications you make to a notebook. For additional details on these procedures, see Chapters 5 and 10.

Changing the contents of a cell

If you have something in a cell and you want to put something else there, you simply enter the new value, label, or formula, and Quattro Pro for Windows will replace what's already there.

If you just need to make a small change, you're probably better off editing the cell. Move the cell selector to the cell you want to edit, and press F2 (or double-click the cell). The editing takes place directly in the cell. Use the left-arrow and right-arrow keys to move the insertion point to the part of the cell you want to change. You can use Del to delete the next character and Backspace to delete the preceding character. To add new characters, just type them — everything will be pushed to the right to accommodate the new text.

Another way to change a cell is to click in the input line. If you use this method, the editing takes place on the input line rather than in the cell.

Selecting a block of cells

Selecting a block of cells is a common thing to do, because you generally select cells before you do anything with them. There are several ways to select a block of cells:

- Click and drag the mouse over the cells you want to select.
- Press Shift, and use the arrow keys to select cells.
- Click one or more row or column borders to select entire rows or columns.
- Click the little gray button at the upper left corner of the notebook (where the row and column borders intersect). This action selects every cell on the notebook page.

Copying a block of cells

Again, there are several ways to copy a block of cells. Take your pick:

1. **Select the block, hold down Ctrl, and wait until the mouse pointer turns into a hand with a plus sign.**

   Drag the block to where you want to copy it.

2. **Select the block, right-click, and choose Copy from the shortcut menu.**

   Then select the upper left cell of the block where you want the cells to be copied. Right-click again, and choose Paste from the shortcut menu.

3. **Select the block, and choose Edit⇨Copy from the menu.**

   Select the upper left cell of the block where you want the cells to be copied, and choose Edit⇨Paste from the menu.

Copying between notebooks

Copying a cell or block from one notebook to another is really no different from copying within a single notebook — but both notebooks have to be open. To make it easier, arrange your window so you can see both notebooks. Refer to the preceding section for how to copy blocks.

Copying a cell or block, but not its formats

Select the cell or block, right-click, and choose Copy from the Shortcut menu. Select the cell where you want to copy it (or the upper left cell of the block), and choose Edit⇨Paste Special from the menu (this command isn't on the shortcut menu). Remove the checkmark from the Properties checkbox, and choose OK.

Copying only the formats from a cell or block

Select the cell or block, right-click, and choose Copy from the Shortcut menu. Select the cell where you want to copy it (or the upper left cell of the block), and choose Edit⇨Paste Special from the menu (this command isn't on the shortcut menu). Remove the checkmark from all of the checkboxes *except* the Properties checkbox, and choose OK.

Moving a block of cells

There are several ways to move a block of cells:

1. **Select the block, and wait until the mouse pointer turns into a hand.**

    Drag the block to where you want to move it.

2. **Select the block, right-click, and choose Cut from the shortcut menu.**

    Select the upper left cell of the block where you want to move it. Right-click again, and choose Paste from the shortcut menu.

3. **Select the block, and choose Edit⇨Cut from the menu.**

    Select the upper left cell of the block where you want the cells to be copied, and choose Edit⇨Paste from the menu.

Deleting a cell or block

Select the cell or block, and press Del. This deletes the contents, but *not* the formatting. To remove the contents and the formatting, select the cell or block, right-click, and choose Clear from the shortcut menu.

Reversing the effects of a command

If you do something that royally messes up your notebook, there's an excellent chance that you can undo it. Simply select the Edit➪Undo command immediately (or use the Ctrl+Z shortcut key combination).

In order for this to work, you must have Undo enabled. To find out whether undo is enabled or disabled (or to change from one to the other), select the Inspect pull-down on the property band, and choose Application. Then select the General option in the Application dialog box. If Undo Enabled is checked, that means Undo is turned on.

Inserting a new column

There are two ways to insert a column:

- Click on the column heading to select an entire column. Right-click and choose Block Insert from the shortcut menu. To insert more than one new column, just select additional columns before you perform this operation.
- Move the cell selector to any cell in the column, and choose the Block➪Insert command from the menu. In the Dimension box, select the Columns option, and choose OK.

Inserting a new row

There are two ways to insert a row:

- Click on the row heading to select an entire row. Right-click and choose Insert from the shortcut menu. To insert more than one new row, just select additional rows before you perform this operation.
- Move the cell selector to any cell in the row, and choose the Block➪Insert command from the menu. In the Dimension box, select the Rows option, and choose OK.

Entering dates

To enter a date, just make sure it is in one of the following formats:

DD-MMM-YY (04-Jul-94)

DD-MMM   (04-Jul, assumes current year)

MMM-YY   (Jul-94, assumes first day of the month)

MM/DD/YY (07/04/94)

MM/DD   (07/04, assumes current year)

Your entry will be converted to a serial number date. See Chapter 9 for more details.

Sorting a block

To sort a block of data, first select the entire block you want to sort. Then use the Block➪Sort command. You can specify up to five sort keys if you want to perform a sort within a sort to handle ties. You can also specify whether to sort in ascending or descending order.

Converting formulas to values

If you have one or more formulas that never change (that is, *always* return the same answer), you can convert the formulas. Converting formulas to values makes your notebook less complicated and makes it recalculate faster. Just be absolutely sure that you only convert formulas that always return the same answer; otherwise, you could cause yourself some problems.

Start by selecting the cell or block that has the formulas. Right-click and choose Copy from the shortcut menu. Then select Edit➪Paste Special from the menu, and choose the Paste formulas as values option. Select OK to do the conversion.

You can also convert a formula to a value before it even goes into a cell. Enter the formula in the input bar, but press F9 before you press Enter. The formula disappears, and in its place is its result. Press Enter to store the result in the cell.

Converting vertical data into horizontal data (and vice versa)

If you enter some data vertically (down a column) and you discover that you should have entered it horizontally (across a row), you don't have to re-enter it. Rather, go for the Block⇨Transpose command. This command copies the source block to a different block and changes the orientation in the process. You can then go back and delete the source block. Be careful, however, because transposing cells that have formulas will change the formulas (they won't refer to the same cells after being transposed).

Searching and replacing

Most word processor users are familiar with the concepts of searching and replacing. Quattro Pro for Windows has a similar feature. Rather than pound on the keyboard trying to find something that may be hundreds of rows and columns away, use the Edit⇨Find and Replace command. This command also lets you replace a particular text string with something else — either globally or selectively in a block.

Formatting

The procedures in this section involve changing how things look on your notebook. See Chapter 12 for more details.

Quattro Pro for Windows couldn't make it any easier on you when it comes to formatting. Just follow these rules:

1. **Select the cell or cells that you want to format.**
2. **Check the Toolbar.**

   There could be a button that does what you need. For example, if you want to make the selection bold, choose the Bold button.

3. **If your formatting choice doesn't appear on the Toolbar, try the property band.**

   This has pull-downs for many common formatting tasks.

4. **When all else fails, right-click and choose the Block Properties command from the shortcut menu.**

   The resulting dialog box has every formatting option known to man. Make your choices and select OK.

Graphing

This section deals with — you guessed it — commands you can use with graphs. Chapter 13 tells even more about graphing.

Making a graph

The easiest way to create a graph is to select the block that contains the data to be graphed (including the labels). Then click the Graph button on the Main Toolbar. The mouse pointer will turn into a miniature graph. Click and drag in your notebook to specify the location and size of the graph. Quattro Pro for Windows creates a graph in a flash.

Changing the graph type

Right-click on the graph, and choose the Type command on the shortcut menu. You'll get a dialog box that lets you choose from a slew of graph types. You can also select the graph and choose the Graphics⇨Graph Gallery command. This gives you a different dialog box with some fancier options.

Adding things to a graph

You can customize a graph by adding text, arrows, clip art, and other things. Start by double-clicking the graph. This action also displays the Graph Toolbar — which has all kinds of drawing tools on it. Click a tool and then drag in the graph. For example, to add an arrow, click the Arrow button, and then drag in the graph where you want the arrow to be. After it's placed, you can select it, move it, or resize it.

Making changes to elements in a graph

You can change just about any part of a graph — colors, fonts, line styles, background, you name it. Start by double-clicking the graph. Then, right-click on the graph part that you want to change. Choose *xxx* Properties from the shortcut menu (where *xxx* corresponds to the object you right-clicked on). You'll get a dialog box that lets you change what you want to. Rather than right-clicking, you can use the Inspect pull-down on the property band and select the object from a list; you'll go right to the Object Inspector dialog box.

Moving or resizing a graph

To move a graph, click it and wait until the mouse pointer turns into a hand. Then drag it to its new location. To change the size of a graph, click it and drag any of the eight "handles" until it's the size you want.

To move a graph to a different notebook page, use the Edit⇨Cut and Edit⇨Paste menu commands.

Printing

Care to guess the topic of this section? If you need a hint, check out Chapter 11 — where you'll learn even more.

Printing the current notebook page

To print the current notebook page, choose the Print button on the Main Toolbar, and then press Enter (or select the Print button in the Spreadsheet Print dialog box).

Printing part of a notebook page

To print part of a notebook (that is, just a block of cells), start by selecting the block you want to print. Then choose the Print button on the Main Toolbar. This step displays the Spreadsheet Print dialog box, with the Selection option already chosen. Verify that the Selection box is showing the block you want, and then choose the Print button.

Printing all used pages in a notebook

To print all pages in a notebook that have something in them, choose the Print button on the Main Toolbar to get to the Spreadsheet Print dialog box. Select the Notebook option, and choose the Print button.

Previewing your work

To get a sneak preview of what your work will look like when it comes out of the printer, choose the Print button on the Main Toolbar. Then select the Print Preview button in the Spreadsheet Print dialog box. Your screen will display the first page of your printed output. Use the controls at the top of the screen to zoom in, switch pages, or actually print the job.

Adding a page header or a footer

If you want something to appear at the top or bottom of each printed page, start by choosing the Print button on the Main Toolbar. Then select the Page Setup button to get to the Spreadsheet Page Setup dialog box. Choose the Header/Footer option, and enter the text for the header and/or footer.

Printing page numbers

You can put page numbers on your printed output in either a header or a footer (see the previous section). The code to print a page number is #p. See Chapter 11 for a list of other useful (and nonuseful) codes that you can put in headers and footers.

Files and Notebook Windows

The following procedures cover files and windows that contains notebooks. You can refer to Chapter 7 for more information on these topics.

Opening a notebook

Use the Open Notebook button on the Main Toolbar to bring up the Open File dialog box. If the file you need is not displayed, change to the appropriate directory. When you find the notebook file you want, double-click it to open it. The notebook you're currently working on (if any) will not be affected.

Saving a notebook

Use the Save Notebook button on the Main Toolbar to save your work. If your notebook hasn't been saved, Quattro Pro for Windows will prompt you for a filename first. If you want to give the notebook file a different name or save it to a different disk or directory, use the File⇨Save As command.

Activating a particular notebook

If you have more than one notebook open, you can activate the one you want to work with by choosing the Window command on the menu. A list of all open notebook windows appears in the drop-down menu. Choose the one you want. You can also press Ctrl+F6 to cycle through all the open notebooks.

Seeing more than one notebook

If you have more than one notebook loaded, you can view them all at once in two different styles. The Window⇨Tile command arranges all the notebook windows in a tiled pattern on your screen. The Window⇨Cascade command stacks the windows neatly, one behind another. If you want to get a full-screen view, activate the notebook window you want, and then click the upward-pointing arrow on the right side of the window's title bar.

Moving a window

The easiest way to move a notebook window to another location on your screen is to click the window's title bar and then drag the window to where you want it.

Resizing a window

The easiest way to change the size of a notebook window is to click on a border and then drag. If you click on one of the corners, you can change both height and width at once.

Splitting a window

Every notebook window can be split into two panes — either horizontally or vertically. Splitting windows comes in handy when you want to look at two parts of a notebook that are not near each other.

To split a window vertically, move the mouse pointer to the window splitter at the bottom right corner of the notebook window. When the mouse pointer shows two arrows pointing left and right, click and drag to the left. To split a window horizontally, do the same thing — but when the mouse pointer shows two arrows pointing up and down, drag up.

Miscellaneous

I couldn't find a place to put this material, so I created a catch-all category.

Switching to another program (temporarily)

If you ever need to do something in another program — such as write a memo in your word processor — you don't have to close Quattro Pro for Windows. Just press Ctrl+Esc to get to the Windows Task Manager. If the program you want is listed, double-click it. If it's not listed, select Program Manager from the list. Then run the desired program from Program Manager. When you're ready to return to Quattro Pro for Windows, press Ctrl+Esc again, and double-click the Quattro Pro choice.

Finding a circular reference

If you have a formula that refers to itself (either directly or indirectly), Quattro Pro for Windows displays CIRC in the status line. Normally, this is a sign that something is wrong with one or more of your formulas. To find out which cell is causing the problem, use the Inspect pull-down of the Property Band, and choose Active Notebook. Then select the Recalc Settings option. The dialog box will tell you which cell is causing the circular reference.

Changing the clock display

Quattro Pro for Windows can display the current date and time at the bottom of the screen (left side of the status bar). You can turn this on or off by selecting the Application option on the Inspect pull-down of the Property Band. Select the Display option, and choose None, Standard, or International.

Saving your notebook automatically

If you're the forgetful type, you may want to turn on Quattro Pro for Windows automatic file save option. Select the Application option on the Inspect pull-down of the Property Band. Then select the File Options choice. Here, you can specify the number of minutes between file saves. Make sure you turn on the Activate checkbox to enable this feature.

Leaving Quattro Pro for Windows

There are three ways to exit Quattro Pro for Windows (they make it very easy to quit!). You can get out of the program by using the File⇒Exit command, by pressing Ctrl+Q, or by pressing Alt+F4. If you have any unsaved work, Quattro Pro for Windows lets you know.

Part V
The Part of Tens

The 5th Wave — By Rich Tennant

"OOPS - HERE'S THE PROBLEM. SOMETHING'S CAUSING SHORTS IN THE MAINFRAME."

In this part...

For reasons that are mainly historical, all the books in the ...*For Dummies* series have chapters with lists in them. Because I'm a sucker for tradition, I went along with this convention and prepared a few top-ten lists. In this part, you'll find a list of desirable habits, a list of handy shortcut keys, a list of things every Quattro Pro for Windows user (including you) should understand, and even The Ten Commandments of Quattro Pro for Windows.

Chapter 20
Ten Good Habits You Should Acquire

You've probably heard from your parents or some other authority figure that the habits you form early on will stick with you over the years. All Quattro Pro for Windows users should try to develop the following ten habits as they learn to use the program:

Use the SpeedBar buttons and Property Band

Many people completely ignore all the ease-of-use features that spreadsheet designers work so hard to include (and their ad agencies charge so much to promote). Using dialog boxes for routine things like aligning the contents of a cell is not only slower, it also increases the chance that you will make mistakes.

Don't save your worksheet files only to a floppy disk

Always use your hard disk as your primary file storage place, because file saves and retrieves are faster, and hard disks are less likely to go bad than floppy disks. However, you *should* use floppies to store backup copies of all your important files.

Take advantage of multiple worksheet files

If you have experience using an old spreadsheet program, such as Lotus 1-2-3 Release 2, that does not have 3-D capability, you may have a tendency to ignore the extra pages that are available in every Quattro Pro for Windows notebook. Using these extra pages is a great way to organize your work, and it provides a quick way to jump to a particular part of your notebook by simply clicking a tab.

Use cell and block names whenever possible

If you have some cells or blocks of cells that are used a great deal in formulas, you should take a few minutes to give them names with the Block➪Names command. By naming the frequently used cells or blocks, you can use their names in formulas (rather than obscure addresses) so that the formulas are easier to read and understand. A side benefit is that you can use F5 (the GoTo key) to jump directly to a named cell or block. And on the off-chance that you'll be writing macros, named cells and ranges make macro writing much easier (and safer).

Don't forget that you can work with more than one program at a time

When you're working away in your spreadsheet and need to do something else (like compose a memo in your word processor), you do not need to close Quattro Pro for Windows. Just press Ctrl+Esc to access the Windows Task List, select Program Manager, and execute the program you need. Quattro Pro for Windows remains in the background, ready to be called back to action.

Take advantage of the on-line help in Quattro Pro for Windows

Great as this book is, it doesn't tell you *everything* about Quattro Pro for Windows. If you get stuck, your first line of attack should be to press F1 and see what the on-line help has to say. You can often solve your problem by going no further than that.

Don't be afraid to try new things

As you know, dozens of weird commands lurk within the bowels of the Quattro Pro for Windows menu system and dialog boxes. Don't be afraid to try out these unfamiliar commands to see what happens. But to be on the safe side, use an unimportant notebook for your experimentation. And don't forget to use Edit➪Undo if the command messes things up.

Don't waste time printing drafts

All too often, people print draft after draft of their worksheets, making only minor changes before each printing. A better approach is to use the Print Preview feature, which shows you exactly how your printed output will look. You even can zoom in to examine parts more closely.

Don't go overboard with fancy formatting

I know that it's very tempting to spend hours trying to get your worksheet to look perfect; it's actually kind of fun to experiment with fonts, type sizes, colors, borders, and the like. But the final product may not be worth that much attention. Unless you have lots of time on your hands, focus on the content of your notebook rather than on its appearance.

Don't be afraid of macros

After you get comfortable with using the basic features of Quattro Pro for Windows, you may want to explore the world of macros. Even a rudimentary knowledge of macros can save you a great deal of time when you're doing repetitive tasks.

Chapter 21
Top Ten (Or So) Shortcut Keys

*O*K, OK. This chapter lists a lot more than ten shortcut keys. There are just so many that I found it impossible to choose the top ten. So sue me.

Key (or Key Combination)	Function
Ctrl+N	Creates a new (empty) notebook
Ctrl+O	Opens an existing notebook
Ctrl+W	Closes the current notebook
Ctrl+S	Saves the current notebook to disk
Ctrl+Q	Quits Quattro Pro for Windows
Ctrl+Z	Reverses the effect of the last command
Ctrl+X	Cuts the selection and puts it on the Clipboard
Ctrl+C	Copies the selection to the Clipboard
Ctrl+V	Pastes the contents of the Clipboard
Ctrl+B	Clears the values from the selected cells (but leaves the formatting)
Delete	Erases the contents (but not the formatting) of the selected cells
Ctrl+PgDn	Moves to the preceding page in the notebook
Ctrl+PgUp	Moves to the next page in the notebook
F1	Brings up the on-line Help system
F2	Lets you edit the contents of a cell
Ctrl+F3	Lets you give a name to the selected cell or block
Alt+F4	Quits Quattro Pro for Windows
Ctrl+F4	Closes a notebook window
F5	Moves the cell selector to a specified cell

(continued)

Key (or Key Combination)	Function
Alt+F5	Switches Group mode on and off
F6	If the window is split into two panes, jumps to the other pane
Ctrl+F6	Cycles among all open notebook windows
F9	Recalculates the notebook
F10	Activates the menu bar (useful for selecting commands from the keyboard)
F12	Displays the Object Inspector dialog box for the selected object (same as right-clicking)

Chapter 22

Top Ten Concepts Every Quattro Pro for Windows User Should Understand

If you use Quattro Pro for Windows, you should definitely know about these things.

There are lots of versions of Quattro Pro out there

When someone talks about using Quattro Pro, there's no reason to believe that they're talking about the same version that you use. Generally, the versions are *very* different from each other. So someone who knows how to use Quattro Pro for Windows Version 6 doesn't necessarily know how to use Quattro Pro for DOS Version 4. Different Quattro Pro versions also use different file formats. So if someone asks you to send them a Quattro Pro file, make sure you know which file format they want (your choices are WB1, WB2, WQ1, and WQ2). Quattro Pro for Windows Version 6 uses WB2 files, but you can save your work in any of the other formats using the File⇨Save As command.

Quattro Pro for Windows works well with other Windows applications

You should know that you can run more than one Windows program at a time and switch among them. Furthermore, you can easily copy information between different programs using the Windows Clipboard. Therefore, you can copy a range of cells from Quattro Pro for Windows and paste it into your Windows word processor. You can also copy and paste graphics in the same manner. The Clipboard is one of the most useful features of Windows, so don't ignore it!

The Quattro Pro for Windows window has other windows

Many users don't really understand this obvious concept. Each program that you run, including Quattro Pro for Windows, has its own window. And you can resize, move, minimize, or maximize these program windows within the Windows environment. By the same token, each notebook has its own window, and you can resize, move, minimize, or maximize *these* windows within the Quattro Pro for Windows window.

There are many different ways to select ranges

For a small range that doesn't extend beyond the current screen, dragging the mouse over the range may be the fastest way. But usually, the keyboard is more efficient. You can select a range by pressing Shift and then using the navigation keys. You can also combine pressing Shift with pressing the End key, followed by an arrow key. And don't forget that you can select an entire row or column by clicking the row number or column letter in the notebook frame.

You have lots and lots of command options

Quattro Pro for Windows is a flexible program that usually offers several ways to do the same thing. You can perform most operations by making a selection and then right-clicking. The shortcut menu that appears usually has the command you want. Often, using a Toolbar button or the Property Band is even faster. And don't forget about drag and drop. For simple copy and move operations, dragging and dropping can't be beat.

You can preselect a range to simplify data entry

If you have to enter a bunch of numbers in a range, you'll soon get weary of using the arrow keys to move to the next cell. A better approach is to select the range first. Then you can press Enter to end each entry, and the cell pointer automatically moves to the next cell. This method is not only faster but saves plenty of wear and tear on your arrow keys.

There are more @functions than you'll ever need

If you ever have a few spare minutes (like when you're put on hold during a telephone call), you may find it interesting to browse through the @function list. I guarantee that you'll find something that you can use. The little @ icon on the input line is one of the handiest tools in Quattro Pro for Windows. This icon can lead you right to the @function you need — and even type it for you. The Help button tells you everything you need to know about an @function and its arguments.

The on-line help system is very comprehensive

If you are stuck, your first course of action should be to press F1, the express route to the on-line help system. Unlike some of the previous versions of Quattro Pro, Version 6's on-line help has a great deal of information and plenty of examples. And don't overlook the Help⇨Interactive Tutors command — it's a good way to kill some time and maybe even learn something in the process.

Hard disks crash for no apparent reason

Every computer user needs to know about hard disk crashes. They happen thousands of times a day. You turn on your computer, and DOS reports that it can't recognize the hard disk. In other words, everything stored on your hard disk is gone. You can reinstall the software, but all of your data files (including your Quattro Pro for Windows notebooks) will be gone — unless you take the advice I offer in several places throughout this book and make a backup copy of your notebook files on a floppy disk.

The more you use Quattro Pro for Windows, the easier it gets

It's only understandable that new users may be overwhelmed and intimidated by this program — it can do a lot of things and has tons of commands. But the fact is, you'll soon be very comfortable with the commands you use frequently. And as your comfort level increases, you'll find yourself wondering what some of those other commands do. That is how you progress from a beginner to an expert. It just takes time. Trust me. It's true. Really. I'm not kidding.

"A STORY ABOUT A SOFTWARE COMPANY THAT SHIPS BUG-FREE PROGRAMS ON TIME, WITH TOLL-FREE SUPPORT, AND FREE UPGRADES? NAAAH – TOO WEIRD."

Chapter 23
The Ten Commandments of Quattro Pro for Windows

Here, direct from a sold-out engagement at beautiful Mount Sinai, are the Ten Commandments of Quattro Pro for Windows.

I: Thou shalt always maketh backup copies

Make backup copies, on a floppy disk, of every important file and store the disks in a safe place.

II: Thou shalt check thy work carefully

Check (and then double-check) your work before making decisions based on a Quattro Pro for Windows notebook. Computers don't make mistakes — but you may. It's tempting to put too much trust into something that comes out of a computer. But you probably know that one incorrect formula can mess up hundreds of other cells.

III: Remember thy right mouse button

The right-mouse button is invaluable and can save you many trips to the menu. Keep it holy, dude!

IV: Thou shalt not take the name of Philippe Kahn in vain

Although Philippe Kahn, the CEO of Borland International, no longer has anything to do with Quattro Pro for Windows, he and his company are responsible for it — and they did a superb job. Let's just hope its new owner takes proper care of it.

V: Honor thy toolbar buttons and shortcut keys

Without these time-saving wonders, you'd be forced to spend more time at the office fiddling around with menus and dialog boxes.

VI: Thou shalt not copyeth the program from others

Get your own, licensed copy of Quattro Pro for Windows. (It's cheap!) You'll be privy to insider information, an attractive box to grace your bookshelf, and the gripping and poetic user's guide. And you'll be able to sleep at night.

VII: Save thy file before taking drastic measures

Remember that it only takes a few seconds to save your notebook file but hours and hours to recreate it if something goes awry.

VIII: Thou shalt enable undo and forgeteth not that it exists

The Edit⇨Undo command can reverse the effects of about any action you take in Quattro Pro for Windows. To make sure that Undo is enabled, right-click Quattro Pro for Windows' title bar, then click the General option in the Application dialog box.

IX: Thou shalt consult thy local guru with matters of importance

Don't be afraid to ask someone else — hopefully someone well versed in Quattro Pro for Windows. Chances are, if you have a problem, someone else has had that same problem and can help you.

X: Feareth not to experiment

This is the best way to master Quattro Pro for Windows — but don't forget about Commandment VII.

Appendix A
If You Gotta Install It Yourself

Before you can use Quattro Pro for Windows — or any software, for that matter — you must install the program on your computer. When you install software, you simply copy files from floppy disks to your hard disk in a way that the software works when you execute it. Most software (including Quattro Pro for Windows) includes a special Install utility that automatically installs the program for you.

If you're lucky, Quattro Pro for Windows is already installed on the computer that you are using. (In most large companies, whole departments full of computer wizards specialize in these types of magical tasks.) In smaller companies, you're often on your own. But you can usually find some sort of computer guru who is happy to help you out (and at the same time, demonstrate just how smart he or she is).

For Do-It-Yourself Types

If you're sitting at your computer and holding a shrink-wrapped box that contains Quattro Pro for Windows, you're probably going to have to install the sucker yourself. If you've never installed a program before, don't be afraid to ask for help from someone more experienced. However, installing Quattro Pro for Windows is not a difficult process, if you can follow simple instructions and know how to insert a floppy disk into a disk drive (skills that most 20th-century people have). If Quattro Pro for Windows is already installed, you can skip this appendix — unless you thrive on redundancy redundancy redundancy.

Preflight Checkout

If someone has assured you that your machine is ready for Quattro Pro for Windows to be installed, you can skip this section. Otherwise, check out the following details before you install Quattro Pro for Windows:

- **Make sure that Microsoft Windows is installed on your system.** Quattro Pro for Windows needs Microsoft Windows 3.1 or later. Windows is a separate software program that is *not* included in your Quattro Pro for Windows package. You must purchase Microsoft Windows separately, and it must be installed on your computer before you attempt to install Quattro Pro for Windows.

  TIP: To see if Windows is installed on your system, type **WIN** at the DOS prompt. If you see a colorful Windows logo screen, you're in luck. If DOS returns the message `Bad command or file name`, Windows is not installed (sorry 'bout that).

- **Make sure that you have the right equipment.** Quattro Pro for Windows requires a fairly fast computer. A system with an 80386, 80486, or Pentium processor is best. If your system uses an 80286 processor and it can run Windows, you can still install Quattro Pro for Windows (but I hope you have a great deal of patience). You also need at least four megabytes of random access memory (RAM) — but a system with eight megabytes is recommended. If your system is capable of running Microsoft Windows (and you have enough RAM), it can run Quattro Pro for Windows. You also need a mouse to operate Quattro Pro for Windows.

- **Make sure that you have the correct disk drive needed to handle the Quattro Pro for Windows disks.** Your box will contain either 3 1/2-inch disks or 5 1/4-inch disks. Make sure that you have a disk drive that can handle the disks in your Quattro Pro for Windows box.

- **Make sure that you have enough room on your hard disk to hold the program and its files.** It's a good idea to have at least 20 – 30MB free. If you don't have enough free disk space, the Install program will tell you.

TIP: If you get a warning that you don't have enough free disk space, I strongly suggest that you find someone to help you delete some unnecessary files from your disk.

Installing Quattro Pro for Windows

To install Quattro Pro for Windows, follow these steps:

1. **Turn on your computer.**
2. **If your computer does not start Microsoft Windows automatically, type** WIN **at the DOS prompt.**

Appendix A: If You Gotta Install It Yourself

The Windows Program Manager screen appears. If your system is set up to run some other third-party Windows menu program instead of Program Manager, you'll need to consult the documentation for that program to determine how to execute the Install program from a floppy disk.

3. **Tear the shrink wrap off the Quattro Pro for Windows box, and open the box.**

   Dig around until you find the disks. Tear the shrink wrap off the disks (software companies just love shrink wrap), and find the disk labeled *Disk 1 Install*.

4. **Insert Disk 1 in your disk drive.**
5. **From the Windows Program Manager menu, select the File command.**
6. **Select Run on the File menu.**

   The dialog box in Figure A-1 appears.

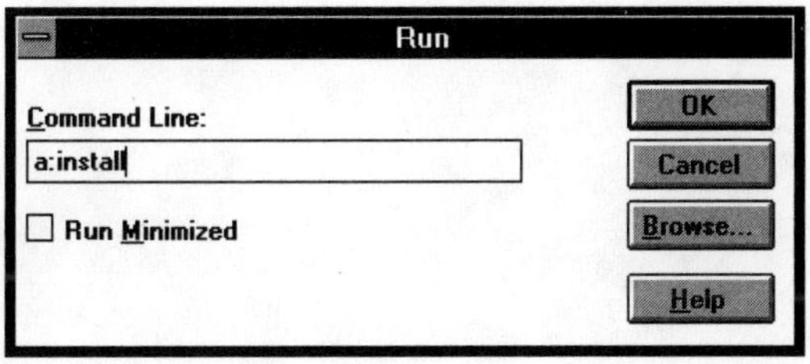

Figure A-1: The Run dialog box, where you enter the program name that you want to run.

7. **Type a:install if you're installing the program from drive A (or type b:install if you're using drive B).**
8. **Press Enter (or select OK).**

After a few moments, the screen displays a box with three choices: Default, Minimum, and Custom. If you're installing it on a system that has very little free disk space, you can choose the Minimum option. Otherwise, choose Default. The Custom option lets you pick and choose what to install (this option is for people who know what they're doing).

You'll be asked to enter your name and your company's name. Next, you'll be asked to specify a directory to which Quattro Pro for Windows will be installed. The best approach is to accept the default directory. In fact, just accept the defaults for all the subsequent prompts.

If you find the installation instructions confusing, refer to the Quattro Pro for Windows manual. It tells you everything that you need to know (and more). Or you can recruit your favorite computer guru, who will happily install the program for you.

After the installation is complete, you are returned to the Program Manager screen. Chapter 2 explains how to start Quattro Pro for Windows. But I suggest that you actually begin with Chapter 1 for some background information.

Appendix B
Glossary

This glossary contains terms that you may encounter while using Quattro Pro for Windows, reading this book, thumbing through magazines, or listening to people talk about computers. Although it does not substitute for a real computer dictionary (try *The Illustrated Computer Dictionary For Dummies*), you may find that it contains enough terms for you to hold your own at the water cooler.

A

@function

A special process (preceded by an "at" sign) that performs some calculation for you in a formula. Quattro Pro for Windows has hundreds of @functions — some that are very useful to real people and others that are designed for scientists and mathematicians. Most @functions use arguments. (Also see *formula*.)

absolute cell reference

A cell reference in a *formula* that always refers to a specific cell (as opposed to a *relative cell reference*). After the formula is copied to another cell, it still refers to the original cell. Use dollar signs to specify an absolute cell reference (for example, $A$1). (Also see *relative cell reference*.)

active cell

The *cell* in a *notebook* that's ready to receive input from you. The contents of the active cell also appear in the *input line*.

active notebook

The *notebook* file that you're currently working on. You can have several notebook files open in Quattro Pro for Windows, but only one of them can be the active notebook file. The active notebook's title bar is a different color than the title bar in the other windows.

address

The way you refer to a *cell*. Every cell has its own address (some are on the wrong side of the tracks). An address consists of a page letter, a colon, a column letter, and a row number (the page letter is optional — if you omit it, also leave out the colon). Here are some examples of addresses: A:C4, C:Z12, A1, and K9 — also known as the dog cell. (Also see *cell reference*.)

arguments

The information you provide that gives the details for a particular @*function*. The arguments are in parentheses, separated by commas.

ASCII file

See *text file*.

B

backup

An extra copy of a *file*, which is usually stored on some other *disk*. It's a good idea to make a backup copy of every important file and to keep the backup copy on a floppy disk. That way, if you turn on your computer and discover that your hard disk died during the night, it won't ruin your whole day (just your morning).

block

A group of cells. Other spreadsheets refer to a group of cells as a range, but Quattro Pro for Windows calls it a block. (Also see *cellblock*.)

borders

The different type of lines that you can put around a *cell* or *range*. You have a good choice of border types, and you can even specify different colors and thicknesses.

Borland, Al

Tim (the Toolman) Taylor's plaid-clad assistant on TV's "Home Improvement." If Al used a spreadsheet, it would probably be Quattro Pro for Windows.

Borland International

The software company that invented Quattro Pro, Quattro Pro for Windows, and several programming languages and database products. In 1994, Borland sold its spreadsheet business to Novell.

bug

To bother or pester. This is what you do to the office *guru* when you need his or her help. This term also refers to an error in software programs that causes strange things to happen; it can *crash* your system.

button

A rectangular box, usually found in a *dialog box*, that causes something to happen after you click it with your *mouse*. Buttons are also found on *Toolbars*.

byte

The amount of *memory* or disk space needed to store one character, such as a letter or number. (Also see *memory*.)

C

callipygian

Having nicely proportioned buttocks.

CD-ROM

An acronym for compact disk read-only memory. It is rapidly gaining popularity as a method to store information. This technology requires a special drive, and it uses disks that look exactly like audio CDs. These disks can hold massive amounts of information — the equivalent of about 300,000 typewritten pages (a stack three stories tall). Unlike hard and floppy disks, however, you cannot write information to CDs. Once you buy one, you cannot change anything on it. Also, CD-ROM access times are *much* slower than those for hard disks.

cell

The basic building block of life. Also, the intersection of a *row* and a *column* in a notebook. A cell can hold a *value,* a *label,* a *formula,* a prisoner, or nothing at all.

cellblock

The living unit in a prison.

cell selector

A heavy outline that lets you know which cell in the notebook is the *active cell.* You can move the cell pointer by pressing the cursor movement keys or by clicking another cell with your *mouse.*

cell reference

Identifies a *cell* by giving its column letter and row number. For example, C5 refers to the cell at the intersection of column C and row 5. If you refer to a cell on a different notebook page, you need to tack on a page letter before the cell reference. For example, B:C5 refers to the cell at the intersection of column C and row 5 on the second page (B). You can have *relative cell references* (more common) or *absolute cell references.*

central processing unit

Your computer's brain. Also known as the CPU, it is located on the motherboard and determines how fast and powerful your computer is. Your CPU may be made by Intel and labeled 80386, 80486, or Pentium. (Also see *motherboard.*)

cereal port

The wharf where Cheerios, Cap'n Crunch, and Wheaties are unloaded. (OK, so it's probably called a *serial port.*)

chart

See *graph.*

check box

In a *dialog box,* an option that can be turned on or off by clicking the mouse (not the same as a radio or *option button*). You can activate more than one check box at a time.

Cheetos

Bits of a puffed-up orange processed cheese-like food that are effective bribes for getting computer gurus to help you do things. If Cheetos don't work, splurge for a large pepperoni pizza (with extra cheese).

circular reference

An error condition in which the result of a *formula* depends on the formula itself (either directly or indirectly). For example, if you put @SUM(A1..A10) in cell A10, the formula refers to its own cell — a circular reference. If your notebook has a formula with a circular reference, you see CIRC displayed in the status bar.

click

To press and release the left mouse button. (Also see *right-click*.)

clip art

A graphic image stored in a *file* that can be used by various programs (including Quattro Pro for Windows). There are thousands of clipart files available for you to use freely in your work.

Clipboard

An area of *memory* managed by Windows that stores information (usually to be pasted somewhere else). You can put information on the Clipboard with the Edit⇨Copy or the Edit⇨Paste command.

column

A vertical group of 8192 *cells* in a notebook. Columns are identified by letters from A to IV. (Also see *row*.)

command

What your wish is to me. Also, an order that you give to Quattro Pro for Windows by using the *menu* system, a *Toolbar* button, or a *shortcut key*.

crash

What happens when your computer stops working for no apparent reason. If you're running *Windows,* you'll get a message that tells you there's been a serious error, and asks you if you want to continue or ignore it. Ignoring it rarely does any good, so you may as well kiss your work good-bye. This is a good reason to save your work often. A system crash is usually the result of a software bug or trying to run too many programs at one time.

criteria block

A block of cells that contains specifications for a database *query*. The first row of the criteria block consists of field names from the database.

cursor movement keys

The keys on your keyboard that cause the *cell selector* to move, such as the arrow keys and the Home, End, PgUp, and PgDn keys.

D

database

An organized list made up of records (*rows*) and fields within records (*columns*). You can work with a database by performing a *query* or by *sorting*. You can store a database in a Quattro Pro for Windows notebook or in a separate file. (Also see *list*.)

database block

The *block* of cells that contains a database stored in a notebook. The first row of the database block contains the field names.

default

Settings that come automatically with a computer program. They are designed to include the popular choices of most users. If you don't specify some options, your work looks the way it does because of the default settings. (For example, the default type size may be 10 points.) When something goes wrong, you can always say, "It's not my fault. It's default of the software."

dialog box

A box that pops up after you have chosen a *command* and lets you make even more choices. After you make the choices, you close the dialog box by selecting the OK button. If you change your mind or if you want to undo any change you make in the dialog box, simply choose the Cancel button.

disks

Media used to store information. Every computer has at least one disk drive. Most computers have at least two, and many computers have three. There are two main types of disks: *hard* disks and *floppy* disks. Both types store information as a series of magnetic impulses. (Also see *hard disk* and *floppy disk*.)

double-click

To click the left mouse button twice in rapid succession.

Dove soap

See *mouse*.

drag-and-drop

To use the *mouse* to grab an object, move it, and drop it somewhere else. You can use drag-and-drop to move a *cell,* a *block,* or a *graphic object.*

draw layer

The invisible layer on top of every Quattro Pro for Windows notebook that holds charts and drawn objects.

drawing tools

Buttons found on the Draw *Toolbar* that let you draw or manipulate *graphic objects* on the *draw layer*.

drop-down listbox

In a *dialog box,* a listbox that normally shows only one option but has an arrow next to it, indicating that there are more options available. If you click the arrow, the listbox drops down to show more options.

dummy

An affectionate name given to readers of this book. Actually, the author prefers the more politically correct term — *technologically challenged.* But *Quattro Pro for Windows for the Technologically Challenged* doesn't quite make it as a book title.

E

endless loop

See *infinite loop.*

Enya

A female singer/musician from Ireland. Practically everyone likes her music, and it sounds particularly good when you're writing computer books. Unfortunately, her albums appear only at three-year intervals.

expansion cards

The cards that stick out of the back of your computer and often have jacks into which you plug wires and cords. Your computer probably has several of these cards. Some expansion cards are necessary for the computer to operate (for example, video cards), and some give it added power (such as sound cards). You probably have at least one expansion card that supplies your system with *serial* and *parallel ports* to connect a *modem,* a printer, or some other device.

extension

The part of a filename that follows the period. For a file named BUDGET.WB2, the WB2 is the extension. Usually, a filename's extension tells you what type of a file it is (files created by Quattro Pro for Windows have a WB2 extension).

extract block

The block of cells that holds the results of a database *query.*

F

field

In a database, this is a column that holds a particular part of a *record.* In the country, this is a bunch of dirt with crops coming out of it where animals roam around.

file

An entity stored on a *disk.* A Quattro Pro for Windows *notebook,* for example, is stored in a file that has a WB2 *extension* on the filename. This is also used to help prisoners escape from a *cellblock.*

floppy disk

Removable disks, used for memory storage, that come in two sizes: 3½-inch and 5¼-inch. You might think that makers of 3½-inch disks are lying to you; they have a sturdy (very unfloppy) plastic case. However, if you were to break the case of a 3½-inch disk (which I must advise against), you would find a very floppy disk inside. The smaller floppies can store either 720K (double density) or 1.44MB (high density), and the larger ones store either 360K (double density) or 1.2MB (high density). Your primary floppy disk drive is known as drive A. If you have another floppy drive, it's called drive B.

font

The combination of a typeface and a type size.

formatting

The process of changing the way your information looks — usually (but not always) resulting in a more attractive look. You can have two general types of formatting: *numeric* and *stylistic*.

formula

Information that you put into a *cell* that performs a calculation. A formula can use the results of other cells in its calculation, and it can also use *@functions*.

frozen titles

See *locked titles*.

function

See *@function*.

G

graph

A graphic representation of a *block* of *values* in a notebook. Graphs (that is, charts) are stored on the *draw layer* of a notebook. Quattro Pro for Windows has many different chart types — probably more than you'll ever need.

graphic object

Something that you draw on the *draw layer* of a notebook using the *drawing tools*. You can move and resize these graphic objects.

group mode

Setting things up so that when you format one *page* in a *notebook*, all the other pages in the group get formatted at the same time — making your pages look the same. You turn group mode on and off by pressing Alt+F5.

guru

Someone who appears to know everything there is to know about computers and software. (Also see *Cheetos*.)

H

hamster

See *mouse*.

handles

The little square objects at the corners and on the sides of graphic objects. You can drag handles with a mouse to change the size of the object. Also, the names that truck drivers give to themselves when they talk on CB radios.

hard disk

A device, usually fixed inside your computer, that can store a large amount of information and transfer the information quickly. Hard disks come in a variety of sizes, from 40MB up to a gigabyte (1000MB) or more. Your hard disk is usually known as drive C. You can have more than one hard disk in a PC, and a single hard disk can be partitioned so that it appears as more than one disk. (Don't worry if that sounds confusing.)

I

IBM

If you've never heard of IBM, you probably just arrived from the planet *Zordox*. IBM has always been known as *the* computer company. They started out by making big, expensive mainframe computers and then developed the IBM PC. Other companies soon copied their PC, and many people think the clones are better than the original. In practically every case, clones are much cheaper than real IBMs.

IDG Books Worldwide

Currently the most successful computer book publisher in the world. You're reading one of its products right now.

infinite loop

See *endless loop*.

input line

The line at the top of the Quattro Pro for Windows screen (just below the *property band*) that shows the address of the *active cell*. The contents of the active cell also appear in the edit line.

insertion point

The position where new text is inserted when you're editing the contents of a *cell*. You can tell the insertion point, because here the cursor looks like a vertical bar.

installation

The process of copying the files needed by Quattro Pro for Windows from floppy disks to your hard disk. (See Appendix A.)

J

jerk

A name for the person who kicks your PC's power cord out of the wall just before you realize you haven't saved your file in the past six hours.

K

keyboard

The device through which you give commands and information to your software. There are a number of different keyboard layouts available, and most people don't really give much thought to which one they choose. Various keyboards feel different; some people prefer clicky keys, while others like a more mushy feel. Pianos also have keyboards, but most of them don't have a Ctrl key.

kilobyte

The definition of 1000 bytes, normally abbreviated Kbyte or K. It is used to measure storage capacity of disks and memory. One K of memory stores about 1,024 characters. (Also see *memory*.)

L

label

A group of letters (and even numbers) that you put into a cell to provide information about your notebook or other cells. A label is not a *value* or a *formula,* but it's handy to have in your notebook for clarity.

lagniappe

A special little bonus thrown in for good measure.

laptop computers

Small computers whose diminutive size sets them apart from standard desktop computers and makes them convenient for people who travel a great deal. Also called notebook computers, they usually run on batteries, and people on airplanes like to show them off. Although laptops (or notebooks) have become very powerful over the years, they're much more expensive than equally powerful desktop models. (This usage of *notebook* has nothing in common with Quattro Pro for Windows notebooks.)

lawsuit

A common activity among lawyers at many large software companies. This gives them something to do in order to justify their six-figure salaries.

list

A collection of items, each of which is stored in a separate *row*. Each item may have more than one part (that is, use more than one *column*). The order of the items may or may not be important. (Also see *database*.)

listbox

Something you find in a *dialog box* that lets you choose an option by displaying a list of options.

locked titles

Certain top *rows* or left *columns* that are always displayed, no matter where the *cell pointer* is. You can freeze (lock) titles by using the View⇨Locked Titles command.

Lotus Development Corporation

The company that makes the program 1-2-3 — another spreadsheet product that competes with Quattro Pro for Windows. Lotus used to be completely focused on spreadsheets, but now the company has diversified and makes several other types of software products.

M

macro

A series of special commands that Quattro Pro for Windows can process automatically upon command. You can write macro commands directly, or you can record them with the macro recorder that comes with Quattro Pro for Windows.

math coprocessor

A computer chip, located on the motherboard, that speeds up mathematical operations. The chip can make Quattro Pro for Windows spreadsheets recalculate their results faster than lightning (reducing your coffee break time considerably). If your computer has an 80486 or a Pentium processor, a math coprocessor is built into the *central processing unit*. If you find yourself waiting excessively for large spreadsheets to recalculate, you might consider popping one of these puppies into your PC. (Also see *motherboard*.)

Maximize button

The up-arrow button on the *title bar* of a *window* that makes the window as large as it can be after you click it with your mouse. If the window is already maximized, this button is replaced with a different button (a *Restore button*), which will return the window to its previous size. (Also see *Minimize button*).

Appendix B: Glossary

memory

The temporary area of your computer that gets wiped out every time you turn the unit off. Every computer has memory, which usually ranges from 640K to 16 or more megabytes. A memory of 640K is roughly equivalent to 640,000 characters and is not enough to run Quattro Pro for Windows. Your computer should have 4MB of memory to run most Windows applications, although you may be able to get by with less. Similarly, 16MB works out to about 16 million characters.

menu bar

The collection of words at the top of the Quattro Pro for Windows screen (File, Edit, and so on). After you select one of these words, the menu drops down to display commands.

Microsoft

The mother of all software companies. They make MS-DOS, Windows, Excel, Word for Windows, and many other popular software programs. Some people think Microsoft has an unfair advantage because they created DOS and Windows — which almost everyone has to use to develop new software.

Minimize button

The down-arrow button on the *title bar* of a *window* that turns the window into an icon after you click it with your mouse. (Also see *Maximize button*.)

mode indicator

The word at the right end of the *status bar* that tells you what mode Quattro Pro for Windows is currently in (READY, EDIT, and so on).

Ks, megs, and gbytes

You can't be around computers for long without learning new measurement units. Computer memory and disk storage come in different capacities. Here's the lowdown:

Table B-1 Computer Memory Terms

Unit	What It Means
Bit	The smallest unit of computer measurement. A bit is either on (1) or off (0).
Byte	8 bits
Kilobyte (K)	1000 bytes
Megabyte (MB)	A million bytes, or 1000K
Gigabyte (GB)	A billion bytes, or 1000MB

modem

The device used to communicate directly with other computers. A modem connects your PC (via a *serial port*) to a normal phone line and (if you're lucky) makes a connection with another computer that has a modem. If you want to call computer bulletin board systems, connect to on-line services such as CompuServe or America Online, or send and receive faxes, you need a modem.

monitor

The hardware device that displays information that your software wants you to see. There are many types and sizes of monitors, and they vary in *resolution*. Your monitor works in conjunction with your video card, and the combination determines how the information looks on-screen. Today, the standard monitor is VGA (640 pixels wide x 480 pixels high), although 800 x 600 and 1024 x 768 are quite common, also.

mouse

The device that probably looks like a bar of Dove soap that's connected to your computer. Some computers use a trackball, which is a good low-calorie mouse substitute.

mouse pointer

A representation of the *mouse* on-screen. Normally, the mouse pointer is an arrow, but it often changes to other shapes to let you know that you can do certain things.

motherboard

A printed circuit board with a bunch of electronic gizmos that sits at the bottom of the inside of your computer. It contains all the circuitry that makes a computer a computer. The motherboard also contains chips that hold your computer's memory and a number of slots. Some of these slots should hold *expansion cards*, and some should be empty. (Also see *central processing unit* and *expansion cards*.)

N

named block

A *block* of cells (or even a single cell) that has been given a meaningful name. Naming cells and ranges makes them easier to use in formulas and makes the formulas more readable. Use the Block⇨Names command to assign a name to a cell or block.

notebook

Where your *cells* are stored. A notebook appears in a *window* and is stored in a *file*. Small computers that fit in a briefcase are also called notebook computers.

Novell

The company that owns Quattro Pro for Windows, after buying it from Borland International. They also own the WordPerfect word processor.

numeric formatting

The process of changing the way a number looks when it's displayed in a cell (for example, displaying a number with a percent sign). Changing the numeric formatting does not affect the value in any way — it just affects its appearance.

O

operator

A symbol in a formula that specifies certain operations. For example, the plus sign (+) is the operator for addition, the asterisk (*) is the operator for multiplication, and so on.

option button

A button that may be chosen from a *dialog box* (also known as a radio button).

P

page tab

See *tab*.

pain

That unpleasant sensation you experience when Howard, your clumsy coworker, drops the laser printer on your foot. It is frequently accompanied by loud screams and profanities.

pane

One of two parts of a notebook *window* that has been split with the View⇨Panes command. Splitting a window into panes lets you see and work with two different parts of a notebook without having to do a great deal of scrolling around.

parallel port

A part of your computer that sends and receives information in several different (parallel) streams. This process permits faster communication. Printers usually use parallel ports. (Also see *port* and *serial port*.)

parallel universe

See *Twilight Zone*.

paste

To copy an item that has been stored on the Windows *Clipboard* into a notebook or graph. You can paste a *cell*, a *range*, a *graph*, or a *graphics object* (but it must be copied to the Clipboard first).

pointing

The process of selecting a *block* by using either the keyboard or the mouse. When you need to indicate a cell or block address, you can enter it directly, or you can point to it by selecting cells with your mouse or by highlighting cells using the keyboard.

port

The device by which computers communicate with external devices (such as printers, modems, and mice). There are two types of ports: *serial* and *parallel*.

preview

To see on-screen how your notebook will look after it's printed. Also, what movie theaters force you to sit through so you'll buy more popcorn.

printer

That device that spits out paper with black stuff on it.

Program Manager

The Windows program that lets you run other Windows programs — it's the one with all the cute icons. Normally, Program Manager appears when you start Microsoft Windows.

Property Band

Located directly below the *Toolbar* in Quattro Pro for Windows, this contains pull-down lists of items that speed up formatting and do lots of other things. Learning what's available on the property band will make you more efficient.

Property Inspector

The person who looks over the house you're about to purchase. Also, the *dialog box* that appears when you right-click an object and choose *xxx* Properties from the *shortcut menu* (where *xxx* is the name of the object selected). Property Inspector dialog boxes have several parts, which you access by clicking an option on the left side.

Q

query

The process of locating specific *records* in a *database*. You can specify the exact criteria that you want.

R

radio button

See *option button*.

random access memory (RAM)

A type of *memory* that can be written to and read from. This commonly refers to the internal memory of your computer. The *random* means that any one location can be read at any time; it's not necessary to read all of the memory to find one location.

range

See *block*.

recalculation

The process of evaluating all the *formulas* in a notebook. Normally, this is all done automatically. But if your notebook is in manual recalc mode, you have to specify when to recalculate (by pressing F9).

record

One unit (*row*) of a *database* that's comprised of *fields* (*columns*). It is also an obsolete (albeit nostalgic) method of storing music.

relative cell reference

A normal *cell reference* in a *formula*. If the formula is copied to another cell, the cell references adjust automatically to refer to cells in their new surroundings. (Also see *absolute cell reference*.)

relative cell preference

The decision you must make on visiting day at San Quentin. Should you go see Uncle Ned or Cousin Chuck?

resolution

What you make on New Year's Eve and forget about by January 3. This term also refers to the number of pixels in a *monitor*. The more pixels, the higher the resolution, and the higher the resolution, the better the picture.

Restore button

On a *maximized* window, the dual-arrow button on the title bar that returns the window to its previous size.

right-click

To press and release the right mouse button. In Quattro Pro for Windows, right-clicking displays a *shortcut menu* that's relevant to whatever you have selected at the time. Some people refer to this as squeezing the mouse's right ear.

row

A horizontal group of 256 *cells*. Rows are identified by numbers. (Also see *column*.)

S

scroll bar

Not your neighborhood pub, but one of two bars on the notebook window that enables you to scroll quickly through the notebook by using the mouse. The bar along the right side of the window is called the *vertical scroll bar;* the one at the bottom of the window is the *horizontal scroll bar*.

selection

The *cell*, *block*, *graph*, or *graphic object* that is affected by the *command* you choose.

serial port

A device that sends and receives information in a single stream of bits. These ports are sometimes known as COM ports. Modems, mice, and some printers use serial ports. (Also see *port* and *parallel port*.)

shortcut key

A Ctrl+key combination (such as Ctrl+C) that is a shortcut for a *command*.

shortcut menu

The menu that appears when you *right-click* the mouse after an item is selected. Most of the time, you find the *command* that you need here.

sorting

The process of rearranging the *rows* of a *block* by using one or more *columns* in the block as the sort key. Use the Block⇨Sort command.

sound cards

A device that is inserted into a slot on your *motherboard*. It is capable of generating much better sound than the normal tinny speaker.

spreadsheet

The generic word for a notebook *file* or for a program such as Quattro Pro for Windows.

status bar

The line at the bottom of the Quattro Pro for Windows screen that shows the status of several items in the program or on-screen.

stylistic formatting

The process of changing the appearance of cells and blocks, which involves changing colors, modifying type sizes and fonts, and adding borders.

T

tab

What you hope your friend picks up when you go out to dinner. In a *notebook,* it's the item that displays the page letter (or the name you gave to the sheet by double-clicking it). To activate another page, click its tab. Tab is also the name of one of the keys on the keyboard.

text box

In a *dialog box,* a small box in which you type letters or words.

Appendix B: Glossary 363

text file

A generic computer file that holds information, but no special formatting commands. Most programs (including Quattro Pro for Windows) can read and write text files.

title bar

The colored bar at the top of every *window*. You can move a nonmaximized window by dragging its title bar with the mouse.

toolbar

The row of colorful buttons directly below the *menu bar*. Clicking a Toolbar button is usually a faster substitute for a menu command.

Twilight Zone

The state of mind you enter after spending eight hours working on a Quattro Pro for Windows notebook — and don't try calling Rod Serling for help.

U

undo

To reverse the effects of the last command. Use the Edit⇨Undo command (or press Ctrl+Z).

V

value

A number entered into a cell.

W

Walkenbach, John

The author of this book. (Also see *guru*.)

window

Where a *notebook* is displayed or held. Quattro Pro for Windows is also a window — a window that holds other windows. (Also see *Windows*.)

Windows

The software product made by Microsoft. You must have Windows installed on your computer to run Quattro Pro for Windows.

WITTGOOHOT

An acronym for "Whatever it takes to get out of here on time." People often use this term when it's getting close to quitting time.

wrap

A property of a cell that causes lengthy text to use more than one line.

WYSIWYG

An acronym for "What you see is what you get." This saying refers to the fact that the formatting you perform and see on-screen also applies to what gets printed.

X

X-rated

The only word I could think of that starts with *x*. Don't worry; Quattro Pro for Windows is suitable for the whole family.

Z

zoom

The process of changing the size of the information displayed in a notebook. You can zoom in or out with the View⇨Zoom command.

Zordox

See *IBM*.

Index

Numbers and Symbols

@button, 154
@functions, 347. *See also* functions
@function dialog box, 154, 156
3-D notebooks, 253–255
  3-D ranges, 260–261
  basics, 256–258
  concepts, 255–256
  documenting work, 255
  graphs, 255
  group mode, 260–262
  in place of separate files, 254
  macros, 255
  multiple pages, 256–258
  navigation, 258–260
  pages, 256–257, 259
  results for different time periods, 254
  scenarios, 255

• A •

absolute cell references, 139–143, 176, 310, 347
  reasons to use, 141–142
actions, undoing, 169
Active Block dialog box, 179, 182
active cell, 45–46, 347
active notebook, 347
Active Page dialog box, 180
active window, 111
addresses, 347
Align pull-down list, 79
ampersand (&) concatenation operator, 297
annotated
  formula, 134
  line graph, 245
Application dialog box, 320
arguments, 348

arrow keys
  end of numbers and labels, 81
  only giving numbers, 48
ASCII files, 348
asterisks, 58
AUTOEXEC.BAT file, 25
automatic recalculation, 144
averages, 148, 292–293
@AVG function, 67, 145, 148, 292

• B •

backups, 52, 109, 121–126, 341, 348
  DOS, 125
  File Manager, 123–125
  Quattro Pro for Windows, 122–123
  storing, 52
Bar Series dialog box, 246
Beginning of Notebook (Ctrl+Home) key combination, 48
Beginning of Page (Home) key, 48
binary system, 44
Block Delete command, 186
Block Insert command, 185
Block menu, 93
Block Names
  Ctrl+F3 key combination, 165
  dialog box, 165
Block Properties command, 75
block reference, 150
block selection boxes, 98
Block➪Insert command, 320
Block➪Move command, 98
Block➪Names command, 96, 164, 292, 332
Block➪Sort command, 190–191, 321
Block➪Transpose command, 187, 322
blocks, 149–151, 348
  copying cells to, 175
  copying formats from, 319
  copying to block, 175

copying without formats, 319
cutting and pasting, 172
deleting, 319
erasing, 183
minimum and maximum, 293–294
moving, 172–173, 319
naming, 163–165, 292, 332
noncontiguous, 151
references, 150
sorting, 189–191, 321
spacing between while printing, 206
bold column headings, 55
Bold button, 63, 222
borders, 222–225, 348
Borland, Al, 348
Borland International, 348
bugs, 348
built-in functions, 59, 145. *See also* functions
buttons, 96, 348
bytes, 348

• C •

Calc (F9) function key, 144, 321, 336
CALC indicator, 144
callipygian, 349
Cancel button, 95
cascading menu, 91
CD (DOS) command, 125
CD-ROMs, 349
@CELL function, 299
cell grid display, 223
cell pointer movement, 45–49
  keyboard movement, 46–48
  left or right one screen, 47
  mouse movement, 46
  one cell at a time, 47
  up or down one full screen, 47
  which cell it is in, 54
cell reference, 349
cell selector, 40, 349
cellblock, 349
cells, 12, 43, 149–151, 349
  absolute references, 139–143, 176, 347
  active, 45, 347
  adding to pages to references, 151
  addresses, 44–45, 54
  alignment and misalignment, 226–229
  blank, 72–73
  centering text across, 228
  completely clearing, 83
  copying, 175, 318–319
  cutting and pasting, 171
  default style, 76
  deleting, 319
  editing, 81–83, 317–318
  erasing, 183
  external references, 138
  formatting, 13
  formulas, 72–73
  going directly to, 48
  horizontal alignment, 226–227
  inserting, 83
  labels, 72–73, 76–77
  limitations, 44
  mixed references, 142–143
  moving, 172–173, 319
  naming, 163–165, 332
  numbers, 72–74
  overwriting, 81, 83
  referring to in another notebook, 138
  reformatting, 67
  relative references, 139–143, 361
  selecting block, 318
  sorting blocks, 189–191
  text orientation, 229
  types of information, 72
  vertical alignment, 227
  word wrap, 227
central processing unit (CPU), 349
cereal port, 349
charts, 349. *See also* graphs
  printing, 206
check boxes, 96–97, 349
Cheetos, 350
@CHOOSE function, 299
circular reference, 350
  finding, 327

Index

Clear Value (Ctrl+B) key combination, 335
clicking, 47, 350
clip art, 350
Clipboard, 169–170, 174, 350
Clipboard Viewer, 170
clock, changing display, 327
Close Notebook (Ctrl+W) key combination, 335
Close Window (Ctrl+F4) key combination, 335
Coaches, 34
color, 225
columns, 12, 43, 350
   adding, 184–185
   asterisks, 58
   bold headings, 55
   border, 40
   default size, 78, 178
   deleting, 184–186
   dragging width, 180–181
   freezing, 268–270
   global widths, 180
   headings, 54
   inserting, 320
   menu width adjustments, 179
   nonadjacent, 179
   resizing, 56, 178–181
   transposing with rows, 186–187
combination graph, 246
commands, 350
   Block Properties, 75
   Block⇨Insert, 320
   Block⇨Move, 98
   Block⇨Names, 96, 164, 292, 332
   Block⇨Sort, 190–191, 321
   Block⇨Transpose, 187, 322
   CD (DOS), 125
   COPY (DOS), 125
   dimmed, 91
   Edit⇨Clear, 83, 183, 243
   Edit⇨Copy, 170, 174–175, 318
   Edit⇨Cut, 91, 170–172, 183, 242, 319, 324
   Edit⇨Find and Replace, 168, 188, 322
   Edit⇨Paste, 170–175, 242, 318–319, 324
   Edit⇨Paste Special, 319, 321
   Edit⇨Undo, 169, 183, 230, 320, 332
   ellipsis (…), 91
   File⇨Close, 117, 119
   File⇨Copy, 124
   File⇨Exit, 28–29, 52, 118, 122, 125, 327
   File⇨New, 113–114, 119
   File⇨Open, 115–118, 123
   File⇨Page Setup, 97
   File⇨Print, 99
   File⇨Save, 115–116, 119–120, 124
   File⇨Save As, 52, 110, 116, 122, 325, 337
   File⇨Workspace, 117–118
   File⇨Workspace⇨Restore, 118
   File⇨Workspace⇨Save, 118
   Graphics⇨Graph Gallery, 240, 323
   Graphics⇨Series, 241–242
   Graphics⇨Titles, 239
   Graphics⇨Type, 239
   Help Always on Top, 34
   Help⇨About, 15
   Help⇨How to Use Help, 34
   Help⇨Interactive Tutors, 339
   Help⇨Search, 32
   issuing, 86
   key combinations, 91
   Notebook⇨Define Group, 261
   options, 338
   reversing effect, 320
   Tools⇨Database Tools⇨Form, 279
   Tools⇨Database Tools⇨Query, 284, 287
   Tools⇨Macro⇨Options, 311, 313
   Tools⇨Macro⇨Play, 306–307
   Tools⇨Macro⇨Record, 309, 311, 313
   Tools⇨Macro⇨Stop Record, 310–311, 314
   Tools⇨Spell Check, 81, 270
   Tools⇨User Setup, 173
   undoing, 342
   View⇨Display, 96, 264
   View⇨Group Mode, 261
   View⇨Locked Titles, 268, 270
   View⇨Panes, 267
   View⇨Zoom, 90, 96, 266

WIN, 25
WIN QPW, 25
Window, 111
Window⇨Cascade, 112, 326
Window⇨Hide, 265
Window⇨New View, 257, 267
Window⇨Tile, 112, 326
computers
  avoiding damage, 52
  turning off or leaving running, 30, 52
concatenation, 297
Control menu, 89
Control Panel, installing fonts, 220
controls, 95–100
@CONVERT function, 301
converting measurements, 301–302
Copy (Ctrl+C) key combination, 170, 175, 335
COPY (DOS) command, 125
Copy (F8) function key, 124
copying
  block to block, 175
  cell to block, 175
  drag-and-drop feature, 177
  formulas, 176
  reasons to, 174
@CORREL function, 138
@COS function, 251
@COUNT function, 61
crashes, 350
criteria block, 350
criteria table, 276–277, 282–283
cube (or other) root, 295
Currency style, 58, 62
cursor movement keys, 46–48, 350
Cut (Ctrl+X) key combination, 91, 170–172, 335
cutting and pasting, 169–173
  blocks, 172
  cells, 171
  drag-and-drop feature, 172–173
  formulas, 172
  reasons for, 171
Cycle (Ctrl+F6) key combination, 111, 325, 336
Cycle Active Programs (Alt+Tab) key combination, 28

• D •

daisywheel printers, 208
data entry, 57
Data Query dialog box, 286
database block, 276–277, 351
database functions, 288–289
databases, 66–67, 273–275, 351
  basics, 276–278
  changing criteria, 286–288
  creation, 278–280
  criteria table, 276–277, 282–283
  database block, 276–277
  entering data, 279–280
  external, 20
  extract block, 284
  field names, 278–279
  fields, 273
  formulas, 288–289
  location, 277
  managing, 19–20
  objective, 282
  output block, 276, 278
  printing, 290
  querying, 275–276, 284–285
  records, 273, 275–276, 286
  reports, 276
  sample, 281–288
  searching, 277
  size limitations, 277
  summarizing data, 276
  what you can do with, 275–276
date formulas, 298–299
@DATE function, 159
date functions, 159
dates, 159
  day of week, 299
  entering, 320–321
  formats, 160
  last day of month, 299
  printing, 203
  today's, 298
@DAVG function, 289
@DCOUNT function, 289

Index

default, 351
Delete button, 186
Delete key, 83, 183, 243, 317, 319, 335
dialog boxes, 94–102, 351
  block selection boxes, 98
  buttons, 96
  Cancel button, 95
  check boxes, 96–97
  controls, 95–100
  Help button, 95
  key combinations, 101
  keyboard movement, 101–102
  list boxes, 97
  mouse movement, 101
  Object Inspector, 98
  OK button, 95
  option buttons, 96
  parts, 94–95
  sample box, 100
  spinner controls, 99
  text boxes, 100
  title bar, 95
disks, 108, 351
Display dialog box, 264–265
documents, 43
DOS
  backups from, 125
  starting Quattro Pro for Windows, 25
dot-matrix printers, 208
double-clicking, 47, 351
doughnut graph, 249
Dove soap, 351
{DOWN} macro command, 307
down-arrow key, 57
drag-and-drop feature, 351
  copying, 177
  cutting and pasting, 172–173
dragging, 47
draw layer, 351
drawing tools, 351
drop-down listbox, 352
@DSUM function, 288–289
dummy, 352

• E •

Edit (F2) function key, 82, 153–154, 317, 335
Edit menu, 92
Edit mode, 82
Edit⇨Clear command, 83, 183, 243
Edit⇨Copy command, 170, 174–175, 318
Edit⇨Cut command, 91, 170–172, 183, 242, 319, 324
Edit⇨Find and Replace command, 168, 188, 322
editing, 317–322
  changing cell contents, 317–318
  converting formulas to values, 321
  copying, 318–319
  deleting cells or blocks, 319
  entering dates, 320–321
  inserting columns or rows, 320
  moving block of cells, 319
  reversing command effect, 320
  searching and replacing, 322
  selecting block of cells, 318
  sorting blocks, 321
  vertical data conversion to horizontal, 322
Edit⇨Paste command, 170–172, 174–175, 242, 318–319, 324
Edit⇨Paste Special command, 319, 321
Edit⇨Undo command, 169, 183, 230, 320, 332
@EMNTH function, 299
empty cell formatting, 76
endless loop, 352
Enya, 352
even or odd values, 295–296
Exit (Alt+F4) key combination, 29, 52, 65, 118, 327, 335
expansion cards, 352
extension, 352
external cell references, 138
external databases, 20
extract block, 284, 352

• F •

fields, 273, 352
  field names, 273, 278–279
File (Alt+F) hot keys, 110
File Manager, backups from, 123–125
File menu, 28, 92, 110–119
  listing last four notebook files, 66
File⇨Close command, 117, 119
File⇨Copy command, 124
File⇨Exit command, 28–29, 52, 118, 122, 125, 327
File⇨New command, 113–114, 119
File⇨Open command, 115–118, 123
File⇨Page Setup command, 97
File⇨Print command, 99
File⇨Save As command, 52, 110, 116, 122, 325, 337
File⇨Save command, 115–116, 119–120, 124
File⇨Workspace command, 117–118
File⇨Workspace⇨Restore command, 118
File⇨Workspace⇨Save command, 118
filenames, 116
files, 43, 109–112, 325–326, 352
  automatically saving, 109
  backups, 52, 109, 121–126
  closing, 117, 119
  deleting, 52
  different format, 116
  exiting, 118
  formats, 117
  naming, 110, 116
  notebooks, 109
  opening, 65–66, 115–118, 123
  protecting, 107–109
  saving, 27, 52, 110, 115–116, 119, 331, 342
  step-by-step usage, 119–121
Fit button, 181
fixed-size fonts, 219
floppy disks, 52, 353
fonts, 218–222, 353
  attribute changes, 222
  changing, 220–222
  fixed-size, 219
  installing, 220
  monospaced, 219
  Object Inspector dialog box, 221–222
  scalable, 219
  sources for, 220
  TrueType, 219–220
  types, 219–220
footers
  codes, 201–202
  printing, 200–203, 325
foreign files, 117
Format (\f) macro, 312–314
Format Toolbar, 217–218, 225
  buttons, 217–218
  Orientation button, 229
  SpeedFormat button, 229
formatting, 322, 353. *See also* stylistic formatting
  dollar amounts, 57–58
  empty cells, 76
  numbers, 74–76
formulas, 12, 59–62, 72–73, 127–145, 291–302, 353
  absolute references, 139–143
  actions they perform, 137
  ambiguity, 131–132
  annotated, 134
  averages, 292–293
  block minimum and maximum, 293–294
  calculating sum, 292
  calculating total amount spent, 61–62
  cell addresses, 128
  combined functions, 161–163
  complexity, 138–139
  controlling recalculation, 143–144
  converting measurements, 301–302
  converting to values, 321
  copying, 176
  cube (or other) root, 295
  cutting and pasting, 172
  databases, 288–289
  date, 298–299
  day of week, 299

Index 371

definition of, 128–130
displaying notebook name, 299
entering, 60, 135–138
even or odd values, 295–296
external cell references, 138
functions, 145, 147–165
labels, 297–298
last day of month, 299
loan payment calculation, 294
logical, 145
looking up corresponding value, 300
matching parentheses, 133
mathematical, 295–297
meaningful names in, 134
mixed cell references, 142–143
nesting, 133
operators, 130–134
order of precedence, 131
parentheses, 131–139
percentage change, 293
pointing, 135–136
random number, 296
relative references, 139–143
returning ERR, 137
rounding numbers, 296–297
square root, 295
text, 145
today's date, 298
two answers, 131
types, 145
viewing, 61, 128
where to put, 59
frames, 222–225
frozen titles, 353
function keys
  F1 (Help), 30, 90, 94, 335
  F2 (Edit), 82, 153–154, 317, 335
  F5 (Goto), 48, 165, 259, 332
  F5 (Move Cell Selector), 335
  F6 (Next Pane), 336
  F8 (Copy), 124
  F9 (Calc), 144, 321, 336
  F10 (Menu Bar), 336
  F12 (Object Inspector), 336

functions, 59, 145, 147–165, 339, 347, 353
  @AVG, 67, 145, 148, 292
  @CELL, 299
  @CHOOSE, 299
  @CONVERT, 301
  @CORREL, 138
  @COS, 251
  @COUNT, 61
  @DATE, 159
  @DAVG, 289
  @DCOUNT, 289
  @DSUM, 288–289
  @EMNTH, 299
  @IF, 162–163, 293, 296
  @INT, 296
  @IPAYMNT, 294
  @LARGEST, 294
  @MAX, 157, 293, 298
  @MEDIAN, 293
  @MIN, 158, 293
  @MOD, 295
  @MODE, 293
  @NOW, 203
  @PMT, 148, 294
  @PPAYMT, 294
  @RAND, 296
  @ROUND, 158–159, 162, 296
  @SIN, 251
  @SMALLEST, 294
  @SQRT, 145, 148, 158, 295
  @STRING, 297
  @SUM, 61, 145, 149, 292
  @TIME, 160–161
  @TODAY, 160, 298–299
  @VLOOKUP, 300
  @WKDAY, 299
  adding pages to cell references, 151
  arguments, 149, 152–153
  at sign (@), 148
  blocks, 149–151
  categories, 156
  cells, 149–151
  combined in formulas, 161–163
  database, 288–289

dates and times, 159
entering, 151–156
example, 148–149
listing, 154–156
nested, 156, 162
numeric, 157–159
pointing, 152
testing conditions, 162–163
what they are, 148

• G •

Goto
  dialog box, 48
  F5 function key, 48, 165, 259, 332
Graph button, 236
Graph Gallery dialog box, 249
Graph Toolbar, 237–238, 244, 323
  Text tool, 245
graphic objects, 353
graphics, printing, 206
Graphics menu, 93
Graphics⇨Graph Gallery command, 240, 323
Graphics⇨Series command, 241–242
Graphics⇨Titles command, 239
Graphics⇨Type command, 239
graphs, 17, 233–251, 323–324, 353
  adding things, 323
  annotated line, 245
  block references, 241
  changing data series, 239–241
  changing elements, 323
  changing type, 238–239, 323
  colors, 244
  combination, 246
  creation, 235–237, 323
  deleting, 243
  double-clicking, 244
  doughnut, 249
  facts, 235
  fancy, 240, 249–250
  gridlines, 245
  learning how to use, 245
  modifying, 237–245
  moving and resizing, 242, 324
  parts, 234
  printing, 243
  rotated bar, 246
  scale, 244
  selecting, 237
  selecting data, 235
  shading and patterns, 244
  stacked bar, 247
  stock market, 249
  storing, 43
  surface, 251
  swapping rows and columns, 241–242
  titles, 239
  XY, 248, 251
group mode, 260–262, 353
  Alt+F5 key combination, 261, 336
  getting into, 261–262
  naming group of pages, 261
guru, 354

• H •

hamster, 354
handles, 354
hard disks, 354
  crashing, 339
headers
  codes, 201–202
  printing, 200–203, 325
help, 30–34, 339
  backing up topics, 33
  help with, 34
  on-line, 332
  pointers, 33–34
  searching with, 32–33
Help (F1) function key, 30, 90, 94, 335
Help⇨About command, 15
Help Always on Top command, 34
Help button, 67, 95
Help menu, 32, 94
Help window, 33
  Alt+Tab key combination, 33
Help⇨How to Use Help command, 34
Help⇨Interactive Tutors command, 339

Help⇨Search command, 32
Home key, 62
hot keys, 7
   Alt+F (File), 110
   Alt+V (View), 90
How Do I...
   editing, 317–322
   files, 325–326
   formatting, 322
   graphs, 323–324
   notebook windows, 325–326
   printing, 324–325

• I •

IBM, 354
icons, 7–8
IDG Books Worldwide, 354
@IF function, 162–163, 293, 296
infinite loop, 354
inkjet printers, 208
input line, 39, 54, 354
   @ button, 154
Insert button, 185
insertion point, 82, 354
installation, 355
installing Quattro Pro for Windows, 343–346
   correct disk drive size, 344
   do-it-yourself types, 343
   enough room on hard disk, 344
   hardware and software requirements, 344
   Microsoft Windows is installed, 344
   pre-flight checkout, 343–344
@INT function, 296
@IPAYMNT function, 294
Italic button, 222

• J •

jerk, 355

• K •

Kahn, Philippe, 341
key combinations, 6

activating pages, 259
Alt+F2 (Run Macro), 306
Alt+F4 (Exit), 29, 52, 65, 118, 327, 335
Alt+F5 (Group Mode), 261, 336
Alt+F6 (Cycle Window), 111
Alt+Tab (Help Window), 33
commands, 91
Ctrl+B (Clear Value), 335
Ctrl+C (Copy), 170, 175, 335
Ctrl+Esc (Task List), 27, 124–125, 327, 332
Ctrl+F3 (Names), 165, 335
Ctrl+F4 (Close Window), 335
Ctrl+F6 (Cycle), 325, 336
Ctrl+Home (Beginning of Notebook), 48
Ctrl+left-arrow (Left One Page), 47
Ctrl+N (New Notebook), 335
Ctrl+O (Open), 335
Ctrl+PgDn (Next Page), 47, 136, 335
Ctrl+PgUp (Previous Page), 47, 136, 335
Ctrl+Q (Quit), 118, 327, 335
Ctrl+right-arrow (Right One Page), 47
Ctrl+S (Save), 335
Ctrl+V (Paste), 170–172, 175, 335
Ctrl+W (Close Notebook), 335
Ctrl+X (Cut), 91, 170–172, 335
Ctrl+Z (Undo), 169, 320, 335
dialog boxes, 101
macros, 306
navigation, 49
top ten, 335–336
keyboard, 6–7, 355
   accessing menus, 90
   dialog box movement, 101–102
   moving cell pointer, 46–48
   navigation key combinations, 49
keys
   Delete, 83, 183, 243, 317, 319, 335
   down-arrow, 57
   Home, 48, 62
   left-arrow, 57
   NumLock, 48
   PgDn, 47
   PgUp, 47
   right-arrow, 54, 57

kilobyte (K), 355

• L •

labels, 72–73, 76–79, 355
  adding, 297
  aligning, 79–80
  concatenation, 297
  formulas, 297–298
  prefixes, 77, 79–80
  values and, 297–298
  will not fit in cell, 78–79
lagniappe, 355
landscape orientation, 200
laptop computers, 355
@LARGEST function, 294
laser printers, 207–208
lawsuit, 356
Layout Toolbar, 238
{LEFT} macro command, 307
Left One Page (Ctrl+left-arrow) key
    combination, 47
left-arrow key, 57
Line Draw button, 225
Line Drawing option, 313
lines, 222–225
list boxes, 97, 356
lists, 273–275, 356
  managing, 18–19
loans, monthly payment, 148, 294
locked titles, 356
logical formulas, 145
lookup tables, 300
Lotus Development Corporation, 356

• M •

macro commands
  {DOWN}, 307
  {LEFT}, 307
  {PutCell}, 311
  {RIGHT}, 307
  {SelectBlock}, 312
  {UP}, 307
Macro Recorder, 309
macros, 20, 303–315, 333, 356
  \f (Format), 312–314
  \n (Name), 305–309, 310
  absolute cell references, 310
  absolute or relative recording, 312
  advanced, 312–314
  definition of, 303–304
  editing, 311–312
  executing, 304
  facts, 304
  how they got their name, 304
  key combinations, 306
  Macro Recorder, 309
  modifying, 307–308
  names, 304, 310
  playing, 310
  recording, 309–310
  rules, 308–309
  running, 304, 306–307
  storing, 304
  tilde (~) character, 307
  using other people's, 314–315
main menu bar, 87
Main Toolbar, 42, 103
  Bold button, 222
  Graph button, 236, 323
  Italic button, 222
  Open Notebook button, 325
  Print button, 194, 258, 324–325
  Save Notebook button, 325
  SpeedSum button, 292
manual recalculation, 144
margins and printing, 203
math coprocessor, 356
mathematical formulas, 295–297
@MAX function, 157, 293, 298
Maximize button, 356
maximum number, 157
@MEDIAN function, 293
memory, 108, 357
menu bar, 39, 41, 357
  activating, 90
  F10 function key, 336
menus, 86–87, 92–94
  Block, 93

Index

cascading, 91
characteristics, 90–91
Control, 89
Edit, 92
File, 92
Graphics, 93
Help, 94
horizontal lines, 91
keyboard access, 90
main menu bar, 87
mouse access, 88
Notebook, 93
SpeedMenus, 87
Tools, 93
View, 93
viewing, 41–42
Window, 93
Microsoft, 357
@MIN function, 158, 293
Minimize button, 357
minimum number, 158
mixed cell references, 142–143
@MOD function, 295
@MODE function, 293
mode indicator, 71, 357
modems, 358
monitors, 358
monospaced fonts, 219
motherboard, 358
mouse, 6–7, 358
  accessing menus, 88
  active cell, 46
  clicking, 47
  dialog box movement, 101
  double-clicking, 47
  dragging, 47
  how to use, 47
  moving cell pointer, 46
  moving cells or blocks, 172–173
  page activation, 46
  right button, 341
  right-clicking, 47
  scroll bars, 46
  SpeedMenu access, 88

mouse pointer, 358
Move Cell Selector (F5) function key, 335
multiple worksheet files, 331
Music notebook, 52–53
  adding recordings, 64
  bold column headings, 55
  calculating total amount spent, 61–62
  column headings, 54
  column widths, 56
  entering data, 57
  first steps, 53–56
  formatting dollar amounts, 57–58
  formulas, 59–62
  inserting rows, 60
  planning, 53
  possible additions, 67
  saving, 63–65
  titles, 62–63

• N •

Name (\n) macro, 305–309, 310
  editing, 311–312
  how it works, 307
  modifying, 307–308
  playing, 310
  running, 306–307
Name (Ctrl+F3) key combination, 335
named block, 358
nested function, 156, 162
New Notebook (Ctrl+N) key combination, 335
New Notebook button, 115
Next Page (Ctrl+PgDn) key combination, 47, 136, 335
Next Pane (F6) function key, 336
nonadjacent columns, 179
nonadjacent rows, 182
noncontiguous block, 151
Norton Commander, 125
Norton Desktop, 125
notebook, 39
Notebook menu, 93
notebook windows, 40, 325–326
Notebook⇨Define Group command, 261

notebooks, 40–41, 43, 109, 253–262, 358
  activating, 325
  active, 347
  active cell, 45
  automatically saving, 327
  beginning, 48
  blank, 71
  bold column headings, 55
  cells, 43–45
  changing, 168–169
  closing, 117, 119
  columns, 43, 54, 56
  copying between, 318
  copying items, 173–177
  cutting and pasting, 169–173
  different file format, 116
  displaying name, 299
  entering data, 57
  exiting, 118
  formatting dollar amounts, 57–58
  formulas, 59–62
  hiding, 265
  listing last four files, 66
  maximum size, 111
  minimizing, 265
  modifying, 317–322
  moving between pages, 111
  Music, 52–53
  naming, 63, 110, 114, 119
  new, 113–114, 119
  next page, 47
  Objects page, 43
  opening, 65–66, 115–118, 123, 325
  organizing projects, 40
  pages, 43–44
  previous page, 47
  printing, 324
  referring to cell in another, 138
  rows, 43, 60
  saving, 52, 63–65, 110, 115–116, 119, 325
  saving printing settings with, 199
  storing, 41
  titles, 62–63
  undoing changes, 169
  using more than one page, 253–254
  viewing multiple, 326
  zooming, 90, 265–266
Novell, 358
@NOW function, 203
numbers, 72–74
  adding, 148–149
  aligning, 79–80
  averages, 148
  crunching, 16–17
  entering, 73
  formatting, 74–76, 359
  maximum, 157
  minimum, 158
  previewing formatting, 75
  rounding, 158–159, 296–297
  scientific notation, 74
  square root, 148, 158
  VALUE mode, 74
numeric functions, 157–159
NumLock key, 48

• O •

Object Inspector dialog box, 75, 98, 244
  aligning numbers and labels, 79
  Alignment option, 313
  centering text across cells, 228
  changing fonts, 221–222
  color, 225
  F12 function key, 336
  File Options, 109
  Font option, 313
  horizontal text alignment, 227
  Line Drawing option, 313
  lines, 224–225
  Row Height option, 314
  Shading option, 313
  Text Color option, 314
  text orientation, 229
Objects page, 43
OK button, 95
on-line help system, 67
Open (Ctrl+O) key combination, 335
Open File dialog box, 65, 115, 119, 121, 325

Index 377

Open Notebook button, 65, 115
operators, 130–134, 359
　order of precedence, 131
option buttons, 96, 359
output block, 276, 278
overwrite mode, 83

• p •

page numbers, 203
　printing, 325
Page Setup dialog box, 206
page tabs, 40, 111, 359
pages, 43–44
　adding to cell references, 151
　heading rows or columns, 205–206
　letter, 44
　limitations, 43
　mouse activation, 46
　moving between, 111
　naming, 44
　next, 47
　number of columns, 43
　previous, 47
　printing, 194, 206, 324
　scrolling, 46
pain, 359
Palette Toolbar, 245
panes, 267–268, 359
paper size and orientation, 200
parallel port, 359
parallel universe, 359
Paste (Ctrl+V) key combination, 170–172, 175, 335
pasting, 359
PC Tools, 125
PgDn key, 47
PgUp key, 47
@PMT function, 148, 294
POINT mode, 136
pointing, 359
portrait orientation, 200
ports, 360
@PPAYMT function, 294
preview, 360

Previous Page (Ctrl+PgUp) key combination, 47, 136, 335
Print button, 194
print preview, 196–197, 324
　buttons, 197
Print Toolbar button, 197
printers, 193–194, 207–208, 360
　daisywheel, 208
　dot-matrix, 208
　inkjet, 208
　laser, 207–208
　resolution, 207
printing, 193–208, 324–325
　basics, 194–195
　charts, 206
　current notebook page, 324
　databases, 290
　dates, 203
　entire notebook, 324
　graphics, 206
　graphs, 243
　headers and footers, 200–203, 325
　heading rows or columns, 205–206
　landscape orientation, 200
　margins, 203
　multiple copies, 199
　multiple pages, 258
　naming print settings, 204–205
　options, 197–206
　page numbers, 203, 325
　Page Setup options, 199–205
　pages, 194
　paper size and orientation, 200
　part of page, 324
　portrait orientation, 200
　print preview, 196–197, 324
　printers, 207–208
　scaling printout, 203–204
　selecting what gets printed, 198–199
　spacing between blocks or pages, 206
　time, 203
　wasting time with drafts, 333
　Windows, 195
printouts, scaling, 203–204

Quattro Pro 6 For Windows For Dummies

program group icons, 24
Program Manager, 360
   File Run command, 345
   starting Quattro Pro for Windows, 24–25
programs
   Clipboard Viewer, 170
   multiple, 26, 332
   Norton Commander, 125
   Norton Desktop, 125
   PC Tools, 125
   switching to another, 327
   XTree, 125
Property Band, 39, 42, 76, 104–105, 331, 338, 360
   Active Notebook, 327
   Align pull-down, 226, 228
   changing fonts, 221
   Color Scheme pull-down, 245
   Inspect pull-down, 223, 244, 327
   Page Zoom pull-down, 222, 266
   Property pull-down, 144
   pull-down lists, 105
   Size pull-down, 62
   Style pull-down, 58
   Toolbars pull-down, 217, 238, 245
   underlines, 223
Property Inspector, 360
protecting work
   automatic backup feature, 109
   backup copy of files, 109
   saving work to disk frequently, 108
{PutCell} macro command, 311

• Q •

Quattro Pro for Windows
   backups from, 122–123
   Coaches, 34
   competition, 15
   customizing, 263–266
   exiting, 52, 118, 327
   external databases, 20
   fun stuff, 20
   getting easier to use, 339

   graphs, 17
   hiding and showing things, 264–265
   how it got its name, 14–15
   installing, 343–346
   not copying, 342
   primary uses, 16–21
   quitting, 28–30, 65
   right way to exit, 28–29
   starting, 24–25
   switching out of, 26–28
   top ten concepts, 337–339
   versions, 15, 337
   what it can't do, 21–22
   windows, 338
   working with other applications, 337
   wrong way to exit, 29
querying, 284–285, 360
Quick Templates, 113–114, 119
Quit (Ctrl+Q) key combination, 118, 327, 335

• R •

radio buttons, 96, 360
@RAND function, 296
random access memory (RAM), 108, 360
random number, 296
ranges, 361
   adding, 145
   adding values, 61
   counting number of nonblank cells, 59–61
   preselecting, 338
   selecting, 55
READY mode, 71, 73-74
recalculation, 361
   automatic and manual, 144
   controlling, 143–144
Record Macro dialog box, 313
records, 273, 361
   locating, 286
relative cell preference, 361
relative cell references, 139–143, 361
   reasons to use, 139
resolution, 361

Index

Restore button, 361
{RIGHT} macro command, 307
Right One Page (Ctrl+right-arrow) key combination, 47
right-arrow key, 54, 57
right-clicking, 47, 361
ripple effect, 137
rotated bar graph, 246
@ROUND function, 158–159, 162, 296
rounding numbers, 158–159, 296–297
rows, 12, 43, 361
  adding, 184–185
  border, 40
  deleting, 184–186
  freezing, 268–270
  heights, 182–183
  inserting, 60, 320
  nonadjacent, 182
  transposing with columns, 186–187
Run Macro (Alt+F2) key combination, 306

• S •

sample box, 100
Save (Ctrl+S) key combination, 335
Save As dialog box, 116, 120, 122
Save Notebook button, 63–64, 116, 124
scalable fonts, 219
scattergram, 248
scientific notation, 74
screen
  display resolutions, 37
  input line, 39
  menu bar, 39
  notebook, 39
  property band, 39
  status bar, 39
  title bar, 39
  toolbar, 39
scroll bar, 361
  list boxes, 97
  mouse, 46
  notebook window, 40
Select-All button, 40
{SelectBlock} macro command, 312

selection, 362
serial port, 362
sheets, 43
shortcut keys. See key combinations
shortcut menu, 75, 338, 362
  Bar Series Properties, 246
  Block Delete, 186
  Block Insert, 185, 320
  Block Properties, 179, 182, 313
  Clear, 319
  Copy, 318–319, 321
  Cut, 319
  Insert, 320
  Names, 165
  Series, 241–242
  Type, 239, 323
  xxx Properties, 244, 323
@SIN function, 251
Size pull-down menu, 62
@SMALLEST function, 294
Sort dialog box, 190
sorting, 189–191, 362
  reasons to, 189
  what to watch out for, 189
sound cards, 362
Speed tab button, 40
SpeedBar buttons, 331
SpeedFormat dialog box, 230
SpeedMenus, 87
  accessing, 87
  mouse access, 88
SpeedSum button, 149
spelling checker, 81, 270
spinner controls, 99
Spreadsheet Page Setup dialog box, 199–205
  Named Settings option, 204
  Page Setup button, 325
  Paper Type option, 200
  Print Margins option, 203
  Print Scaling option, 204
Spreadsheet Print dialog box, 194, 197, 205–206, 324
  Print button, 324

Print Preview button, 196, 324
selecting what gets printed, 198–199
Sheet Options button, 258
Spreadsheet Print Options dialog box, 205–206
spreadsheets, 43, 362. *See also* notebooks
  basics, 11–14
  definition of, 12–13
  maximum size, 13
  putting together, 22
@SQRT function, 145, 148, 158, 295
square root, 145, 148, 158, 295
stacked bar graph, 247
status bar, 39, 362
status line, 71
stock market graph, 249
string, 78
@STRING function, 297
Style pull-down list, 58, 76
stylistic formatting, 213–231, 362
  borders, lines, and frames, 222–225
  cell alignment and misalignment, 226–229
  choices for performing, 216
  color, 225
  fonts, 218–222
  Format Toolbar, 217–218
  general principles, 215–216
  screen vs. printer, 216
  when to format, 215–216
@SUM function, 61, 145, 149, 292
surface graph, 251

• T •

tab, 362
tab scrollers, 40, 259
tables, formatting, 229–230
Task List (Ctrl+Esc) key combination, 27, 123–124, 327, 332
ten commandments
  backups, 341
  checking work, 341
  experiment, 342
  local guru, 342
  not copying Quattro Pro for Windows, 342
  right mouse button, 341
  saving files, 342
  toolbar buttons and shortcut keys, 342
  undoing commands, 342
ten good habits, 331–333
  cell and block names, 332
  don't waste time printing drafts, 333
  fancy formatting, 333
  macros, 333
  multiple worksheet files, 331
  on-line help, 332
  Property Band, 331
  saving files to hard disk, 331
  SpeedBar buttons, 331
  try new things, 332
  working with multiple programs, 332
terminology, 43–45
text, 78
  alignment, 226–229
  centering across cells, 228
  changing orientation, 229
  enlarging, 62
  finding and replacing, 188, 322
  word wrap, 227
text boxes, 100, 362
Text Color option, 314
text files, 363
text formulas, 145
text strings, finding and replacing, 188
tilde (~) character, 307
time, 160–161
  functions, 159
  printing, 203
@TIME function, 160–161
title bar, 39, 363
  describing items, 90
  dialog boxes, 95
  notebook window, 40
titles, 62–63
  graphs, 239
@TODAY function, 160, 298–299
Toolbars, 39, 42, 102–104, 338, 363
  Bold button, 63
  bold column headings, 55
  buttons, 67, 103–104
  Coaches button, 34
  Delete button, 186

facts, 102
Fit button, 181
Help button, 67
Insert button, 60, 185
Main, 42, 103
New Notebook button, 115
Open Notebook button, 65, 114
Save Notebook button, 63, 116, 123
SpeedSum button, 149
Tools menu, 91, 93
Tools⇨Database Tools⇨Form command, 279
Tools⇨Database Tools⇨Query command, 284, 287
Tools⇨Macro⇨Options command, 311, 313
Tools⇨Macro⇨Play command, 306–307
Tools⇨Macro⇨Record command, 309, 311, 313
Tools⇨Macro⇨Stop Record command, 310–311, 314
Tools⇨Spell Check command, 81, 270
Tools⇨User Setup command, 173
top ten key combinations, 335–336
TrueType fonts, 219–220
Twilight Zone, 363

• U •

underlines, 223
undo, 363
  Ctrl+Z key combination, 169, 320, 335
{UP} macro command, 307

• V •

VALUE mode, 74
values, 363
  labels and, 297–298
vertical data converting to horizontal, 322
View (Alt+V) hot keys, 90
View menu, 93
View⇨Display command, 96, 264
View⇨Group Mode command, 261
View⇨Locked Titles command, 268, 270
View⇨Panes command, 267
View⇨Zoom command, 90, 96, 266
@VLOOKUP function, 300

• W •

Walkenbach, John, 363
WB2 file extension, 110
wildcard characters, 283
WIN command, 25
WIN QPW command, 25
Window command, 111
Window menu, 93
window splitter, 40
Window⇨Cascade command, 112, 326
Window⇨Hide command, 265
Window⇨New View command, 257, 267
Window⇨Tile command, 112, 326
Windows, 363
  Clipboard, 170
  printing, 195
windows, 110–112, 338, 363
  activating different, 111
  active, 111
  cascading, 112
  maximizing, 111–112
  minimizing, 112
  moving, 326
  panes, 267–268
  resizing, 326
  saving multiple configuration, 117–118
  splitting, 326
  tiling, 112
WITTGOOHOT, 363
@WKDAY function, 299
word wrap, 227, 364
words, 78
WSB file extension, 118
WYSIWYG, 216, 364

• X •

X-rated, 364
XTree, 125
XY graph, 248, 251

• Z •

zoom, 364
Zordox, 364

Notes

Notes

Notes

Database add names F9

Computer frozen   ALT/ctrl/delete

IDG BOOKS' ... FOR DUMMIES™ SERIES

Find out why over 6 million computer users love IDG'S ...FOR DUMMIES BOOKS!

"I laughed and learned..."
Arlene J. Peterson, Rapid City, South Dakota

DOS FOR DUMMIES,™ 2nd EDITION
by Dan Gookin

This fun and easy DOS primer has taught millions of readers how to learn DOS! A #1 bestseller for over 56 weeks!

ISBN: 1-878058-75-4
$16.95 USA/$21.95 Canada
£14.99 UK and Eire

INTERNATIONAL BESTSELLER!

WINDOWS FOR DUMMIES™
by Andy Rathbone

Learn the Windows interface with this bestselling reference.

ISBN: 1-878058-61-4
$16.95 USA/$21.95 Canada
£14.99 UK and Eire

#1 BESTSELLER!

THE INTERNET FOR DUMMIES™
by John Levine

Surf the Internet with this simple reference to command, service and linking basics. For DOS, Windows, UNIX, and Mac users.

ISBN: 1-56884-024-1
$19.95 USA/$26.95 Canada
£17.99 UK and Eire

NATIONAL BESTSELLER!

PCs FOR DUMMIES,™ 2nd EDITION
by Dan Gookin & Andy Rathbone

This #1 bestselling reference is the perfect companion for the computer phobic.

ISBN: 1-56884-078-0
$16.95 USA/$21.95 Canada
£14.99 UK and Eire

NATIONAL BESTSELLER!

MACs FOR DUMMIES,™ 2nd Edition
by David Pogue

The #1 Mac book, totally revised and updated. Get the most from your Mac!

ISBN: 1-56884-051-9
$19.95 USA/$26.95 Canada
£17.99 UK and Eire

#1 MAC BOOK

WORDPERFECT FOR DUMMIES™
by Dan Gookin

Bestseller Dan Gookin teaches all the basics in this fun reference that covers WordPerfect 4.2 - 5.1.

ISBN: 1-878058-52-5
$16.95 USA/$21.95 Canada/£14.99 UK and Eire

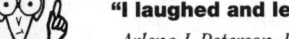

NATIONAL BESTSELLER!

UPGRADING AND FIXING PCs FOR DUMMIES™
by Andy Rathbone

Here's the complete, easy-to-follow reference for upgrading and repairing PCs yourself.

ISBN: 1-56884-002-0
$19.95 USA/$26.95 Canada

NATIONAL BESTSELLER!

WORD FOR WINDOWS FOR DUMMIES™
by Dan Gookin

Learn Word for Windows basics the fun and easy way. Covers Version 2.

ISBN: 1-878058-86-X
$16.95 USA/$21.95 Canada
£14.99 UK and Eire

NATIONAL BESTSELLER!

WORDPERFECT 6 FOR DUMMIES™
by Dan Gookin

WordPerfect 6 commands and functions, presented in the friendly ...*For Dummies* style.

ISBN: 1-878058-77-0
$16.95 USA/$21.95 Canada
£14.99 UK and Eire

NATIONAL BESTSELLER!

1-2-3 FOR DUMMIES™
by Greg Harvey

Spreadsheet guru Greg Harvey's fast and friendly reference covers 1-2-3 Releases 2 - 2.4.

ISBN: 1-878058-60-6
$16.95 USA/$21.95 Canada
£14.99 UK and Eire

NATIONAL BESTSELLER!

EXCEL FOR DUMMIES,™ 2nd EDITION
by Greg Harvey

Updated, expanded—The easy-to-use reference to Excel 5 features and commands.

ISBN: 1-56884-050-0
$16.95 USA/$21.95 Canada
£14.99 UK and Eire

NATIONAL BESTSELLER!

UNIX FOR DUMMIES™
by John R. Levine & Margaret Levine Young

This enjoyable reference gets novice UNIX users up and running—fast.

ISBN: 1-878058-58-4
$19.95 USA/$26.95 Canada/   £17.99 UK and Eire

NATIONAL BESTSELLER!

For more information or to order by mail, call 1-800-762-2974. Call for a free catalog! For volume discounts and special orders, please call Tony Real, Special Sales, at 415-312-0644. For International sales and distribution information, please call our authorized distributors:

CANADA Macmillan Canada
416-293-8141

UNITED KINGDOM Transworld
44-81-231-6661

AUSTRALIA Woodslane Pty Ltd.
61-2-979-5944

IDG BOOKS' ... FOR DUMMIES™ SERIES

"DOS For Dummies is the ideal book for anyone who's just bought a PC and is too shy to ask friends stupid questions."

MTV, Computer Book of the Year,
United Kingdom

"This book allows me to get the answers to questions I am too embarrassed to ask."

Amanda Kelly, Doylestown, PA on Gookin and Rathbone's PCs For Dummies

"If it wasn't for this book, I would have turned in my computer for a stereo."

Experanza Andrade, Enfield, CT

CORELDRAW! FOR DUMMIES™
by Deke McClelland

This bestselling author leads designers through the drawing features of Versions 3 & 4.

ISBN: 1-56884-042-X
$19.95 USA/$26.95 Canada/17.99 UK & Eire

QUICKEN FOR WINDOWS FOR DUMMIES™
by Steve Nelson

Manage finances like a pro with Steve Nelson's friendly help. Covers Version 3.

ISBN: 1-56884-005-5
$16.95 USA/$21.95 Canada
£14.99 UK & Eire

NATIONAL BESTSELLER!

QUATTRO PRO FOR DOS FOR DUMMIES™
by John Walkenbach

This friendly guide makes Quattro Pro fun and easy and covers the basics of Version 5.

ISBN: 1-56884-023-3
$16.95 USA/$21.95 Canada/14.99 UK & Eire

MODEMS FOR DUMMIES™
by Tina Rathbone

Learn how to communicate with and get the most out of your modem — includes basics for DOS, Windows, and Mac users.

ISBN: 1-56884-001-2
$19.95 USA/$26.95 Canada
14.99 UK & Eire

1-2-3 FOR WINDOWS FOR DUMMIES™
by John Walkenbach

Learn the basics of 1-2-3 for Windows from this spreadsheet expert (covers release 4).

ISBN: 1-56884-052-7
$16.95 USA/$21.95 Canada/14.99 UK & Eire

NETWARE FOR DUMMIES™
by Ed Tittel & Denni Connor

Learn to install, use, and manage a NetWare network with this straightforward reference.

ISBN: 1-56884-003-9
$19.95 USA/$26.95 Canada/17.99 UK & Eire

OS/2 FOR DUMMIES™
by Andy Rathbone

This fun and easy OS/2 survival guide is perfect for beginning and intermediate users.

ISBN: 1-878058-76-2
$19.95 USA/$26.95 Canada/17.99 UK & Eire

QUICKEN FOR DOS FOR DUMMIES™
by Steve Nelson

Manage your own finances with this enjoyable reference that covers Version 7.

ISBN: 1-56884-006-3
$16.95 USA/$21.95 Canada/14.99 UK & Eire

WORD 6 FOR DOS FOR DUMMIES™
by Beth Slick

This friendly reference teaches novice Word users all the basics of Word 6 for DOS

ISBN: 1-56884-000-4
$16.95 USA/$21.95 Canada/14.99 UK & Eire

AMI PRO FOR DUMMIES™
by Jim Meade

Learn Ami Pro Version 3 with this friendly reference to the popular Lotus word processor.

ISBN: 1-56884-049-7
$19.95 USA/$26.95 Canada/17.99 UK & Eire

WORDPERFECT FOR WINDOWS FOR DUMMIES™
by Margaret Levine Young

Here's a fun and friendly reference that teaches novice users features and commands of WordPerfect For Windows Version 6.

ISBN: 1-56884-032-2
$16.95 USA/$21.95 Canada/14.99 UK & Eire

For more information or to order by mail, call 1-800-762-2974. Call for a free catalog! For volume discounts and special orders, please call Tony Real, Special Sales, at 415-312-0644. For International sales and distribution information, please call our authorized distributors:

CANADA Macmillan Canada	UNITED KINGDOM Transworld	AUSTRALIA Woodslane Pty Ltd.
416-293-8141	44-81-231-6661	61-2-979-5944

IDG BOOKS' ...FOR DUMMIES QUICK REFERENCE SERIES

IDG's bestselling ...For Dummies Quick Reference Series provides a quick and simple way to remember software commands and functions, written in our down-to-earth, plain English style that guides beginners and experts alike through important commands and hidden troublespots.

Fun, Fast & Cheap!

"Thanks for coming up with the simplest idea ever, a reference that you really can use and understand."
Allison J. O'Neill, Edison, NJ

WORDPERFECT FOR DOS FOR DUMMIES™ QUICK REFERENCE
by Greg Harvey

With this guide you'll never have to worry about deciphering cryptic WordPerfect commands again!

ISBN: 1-56884-009-8
$8.95 USA/$11.95 Canada
£7.99 UK & Eire

WORD FOR WINDOWS FOR DUMMIES™ QUICK REFERENCE
by George Lynch

End your stress over style sheets, mail merge, and other pesky Word features with this quick reference. Covers Word 2.

ISBN: 1-56884-029-2
$8.95 USA/$11.95 Canada

ILLUSTRATED COMPUTER DICTIONARY FOR DUMMIES™
by Dan Gookin, Wally Wang, & Chris Van Buren

This plain English guide to computer jargon helps with even the most techie terms.

ISBN: 1-56884-004-7
$12.95 USA/$16.95 Canada
£11.99 UK & Eire

1-2-3 FOR DUMMIES™ QUICK REFERENCE
by John Walkenbach

Keep this quick and easy reference by your desk and you'll never have to worry about forgetting tricky 1-2-3 commands again!

ISBN: 1-56884-027-6
$8.95 USA/$11.95 Canada
£7.99 UK & Eire

WINDOWS FOR DUMMIES™ QUICK REFERENCE
by Greg Harvey

The quick and friendly way to remember Windows tasks & features.

ISBN: 1-56884-008-X
$8.95 USA/$11.95 Canada
£7.99 UK & Eire

EXCEL FOR DUMMIES™ QUICK REFERENCE
by John Walkenbach

A fast, fun and cheap way to remember bothersome Excel commands.

ISBN: 1-56884-028-4
$8.95 USA/$11.95 Canada
£7.99 UK & Eire

DOS FOR DUMMIES™ QUICK REFERENCE
by Greg Harvey

A fast, fun, and cheap way to remember DOS commands.

ISBN: 1-56884-007-1
$8.95 USA/$11.95 Canada
£7.99 UK & Eire

WORDPERFECT FOR WINDOWS FOR DUMMIES™ QUICK REFERENCE
by Greg Harvey

The quick and friendly "look-it-up" guide to the leading Windows word processor.

ISBN: 1-56884-039-X
$8.95 USA/$11.95 Canada/£7.99 UK & Eire

For more information or to order by mail, call 1-800-762-2974. Call for a free catalog! For volume discounts and special orders, please call Tony Real, Special Sales, at 415-312-0644. For International sales and distribution information, please call our authorized distributors:

CANADA Macmillan Canada
416-293-8141

UNITED KINGDOM Transworld
44-81-231-6661

AUSTRALIA Woodslane Pty Ltd.
61-2-979-5944

IDG BOOKS' PC WORLD SERIES

"I rely on your publication extensively to help me over stumbling blocks that are created by my lack of experience."

Fred Carney, Louisville, KY on
PC World DOS 6 Handbook

PC WORLD MICROSOFT ACCESS BIBLE
by Cary N. Prague & Michael R. Irwin

Easy-to-understand reference that covers the ins and outs of Access features and provides hundreds of tips, secrets and shortcuts for fast database development. Complete with disk of Access templates. Covers versions 1.0 & 1.1.

ISBN: 1-878058-81-9
$39.95 USA/$52.95 Canada
£35.99 incl. VAT UK & Eire

PC WORLD WORD FOR WINDOWS 6 HANDBOOK
by Brent Heslop & David Angell

Details all the features of Word for Windows 6, from formatting to desktop publishing and graphics. A 3-in-1 value (tutorial, reference, and software) for users of all levels.

ISBN: 1-56884-054-3
$34.95 USA/$44.95 Canada
£29.99 incl. VAT UK & Eire

PC WORLD DOS 6 COMMAND REFERENCE AND PROBLEM SOLVER
by John Socha & Devra Hall

The only book that combines a DOS 6 Command Reference with a comprehensive Problem Solving Guide. Shows when, why and how to use the key features of DOS 6/6.2.

ISBN: 1-56884-055-1
$24.95 USA/$32.95 Canada
£22.99 UK & Eire

QUARKXPRESS FOR WINDOWS DESIGNER HANDBOOK
by Barbara Assadi & Galen Gruman

ISBN: 1-878058-45-2
$29.95 USA/$39.95 Canada/£26.99 UK & Eire

PC WORLD WORDPERFECT 6 HANDBOOK
by Greg Harvey, author of IDG's bestselling 1-2-3 For Dummies

Here's the ultimate WordPerfect 6 tutorial and reference. Complete with handy templates, macros, and tools.

ISBN: 1-878058-80-0
$34.95 USA/$44.95 Canada
£29.99 incl. VAT UK & Eire

PC WORLD EXCEL 5 FOR WINDOWS HANDBOOK, 2nd EDITION
by John Walkenbach & Dave Maguiness

Covers all the latest Excel features, plus contains disk with examples of the spreadsheets referenced in the book, custom ToolBars, hot macros, and demos.

ISBN: 1-56884-056-X
$34.95 USA/$44.95 Canada /£29.99 incl. VAT UK & Eire

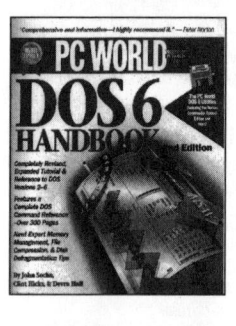

PC WORLD DOS 6 HANDBOOK, 2nd EDITION
by John Socha, Clint Hicks & Devra Hall

Includes the exciting new features of DOS 6, a 300+ page DOS command reference, plus a bonus disk of the Norton Commander Special Edition, and over a dozen DOS utilities.

ISBN: 1-878058-79-7
$34.95 USA/$44.95 Canada/£29.99 incl. VAT UK & Eire

OFFICIAL XTREE COMPANION, 3RD EDITION
by Beth Slick

ISBN: 1-878058-57-6
$19.95 USA/$26.95 Canada/£17.99 UK & Eire

For more information or to order by mail, call 1-800-762-2974. Call for a free catalog! For volume discounts and special orders, please call Tony Real, Special Sales, at 415-312-0644. For International sales and distribution information, please call our authorized distributors:

CANADA Macmillan Canada
416-293-8141

UNITED KINGDOM Transworld
44-81-231-6661

AUSTRALIA Woodslane Pty Ltd.
61-2-979-5944

IDG BOOKS' INFOWORLD SECRETS™ SERIES

...SECRETS

"Livingston is a Windows consultant, and it is hard to imagine any tricks or tips he has omitted from these 990 pages. True to the name, there are lots of undocumented hints that can make life easier for the intermediate and advanced user."

Peter H. Lewis, New York Times *on Brian Livingston's* Windows 3.1 SECRETS

"Brian Livingston has worked his magic once again. *More Windows 3.1 SECRETS* is well worth any serious Windows user's time and money."

Stewart Alsop, Editor in Chief, InfoWorld

"...Probably the most valuable book on computers I've ever seen, and I work in a library."

Jacques Bourgeios, Longueuil, Quebec, on Brian Livingston's Windows 3.1 SECRETS

"David Vaskevitch knows where client/server is going and he tells it all."

Dr. Robert Metcalfe, Publisher/CEO, InfoWorld, on David Vaskevitch's Client/Server Strategies

Over 750,000 SECRETS Books In Prints

WORDPERFECT 6 SECRETS™
by Roger C. Parker and David A. Holzgang

Bestselling desktop publishing wizard Roger C. Parker shows how to create great-looking documents with WordPerfect 6. Includes 2 disks with Bitstream fonts, clip art, and custom macros.

ISBN: 1-56884-040-3; $39.95 USA/
$52.95 Canada/£ 35.99 incl. VAT UK & Eire

DOS 6 SECRETS™
by Robert D. Ainsbury

Unleash the power of DOS 6 with secret work-arounds and hands-on solutions. Features "Bob's Better Than DOS" shareware collection with over 25 programs.

ISBN: 1-878058-70-3; $39.95 USA/
$52.95 Canada/£ 35.99 incl. VAT UK & Eire

PC SECRETS™ — BESTSELLER!
by Caroline M. Halliday

IDG's technical support expert shows you how to optimize your PC's performance. Includes two disks full of valuable utilities.

ISBN: 1-878058-49-5; $39.95 USA/
$52.95 Canada/£ 35.99 incl. VAT UK & Eire

HARD DISK SECRETS™
by John M. Goodman, Ph.D.

Prevent hard disk problems altogether with the insider's guide. Covers DOS 6 and SpinRite 3.1. Includes a disk of hard disk tune-up software.

ISBN: 1-878058-64-9; $39.95 USA/
$52.95 Canada/£ 37.99 incl. VAT UK & Eire

NETWORK SECURITY SECRETS™
by David Stang & Sylvia Moon

Top computer security experts show today's network administrators how to protect their valuable data from theft and destruction by hackers, viruses, corporate spies, and more!

ISBN: 1-56884-021-7;
$49.95 USA/$64.95 Canada
£ 44.99 incl. VAT UK & Eire

MORE WINDOWS 3.1 SECRETS™ — BESTSELLER!
by Brian Livingston

IDG's Windows guru, Brian Livingston, reveals a host of valuable, previously undocumented, and hard-to-find Windows features in this sequel to the #1 bestseller.

ISBN: 1-56884-019-5
$39.95 USA/$52.95 Canada
£ 35.99 incl. VAT UK & Eire

WINDOWS 3.1 SECRETS™ — BESTSELLER!
by Brian Livingston

The #1 bestselling Windows book/disk by the renowned *InfoWorld* and *Windows Magazine* columnist. Over 250,000 in print! A must-have!

ISBN: 1-878058-43-6
$39.95 USA/$52.95 Canada
£35.99 incl. VAT UK & Eire

WINDOWS GIZMOS™ — BESTSELLER!
by Brian Livingston and Margie Livingston

The best Windows utilities, applications, and games—over 30 programs on 4 disks!

ISBN: 1-878058-66-5
$39.95 USA/$52.95 Canada
£35.99 incl. VAT UK & Eire

CLIENT/SERVER STRATEGIES: A SURVIVAL GUIDE FOR CORPORATE REENGINEERS
by David Vaskevitch

An essential read for anyone trying to understand the data highways that will drive successful businesses through the '90s and beyond.

ISBN: 1-56884-064-0; $29.95 USA/$39.95 Canada
£ 26.99 incl. VAT UK & Eire

For more information or to order by mail, call 1-800-762-2974. Call for a free catalog! For volume discounts and special orders, please call Tony Real, Special Sales, at 415-312-0644. For International sales and distribution information, please call our authorized distributors:

CANADA Macmillan Canada
416-293-8141

UNITED KINGDOM Transworld
44-81-231-6661

AUSTRALIA Woodslane Pty Ltd.
61-2-979-5944

IDG BOOKS

Order Form

Order Center: (800) 762-2974 (8 a.m.-5 p.m., PST, weekdays) or (415) 312-0650

For Fastest Service: Photocopy This Order Form and FAX it to: (415) 358-1260

Quantity	ISBN	Title	Price	Total

Shipping & Handling Charges

Subtotal	U.S.	Canada & International	International Air Mail
Up to $20.00	Add $3.00	Add $4.00	Add $10.00
$20.01-40.00	$4.00	$5.00	$20.00
$40.01-60.00	$5.00	$6.00	$25.00
$60.01-80.00	$6.00	$8.00	$35.00
Over $80.00	$7.00	$10.00	$50.00

In U.S. and Canada, shipping is UPS ground or equivalent.
For Rush shipping call (800) 762-2974.

Subtotal _____
CA residents add applicable sales tax _____
IN and MA residents add 5% sales tax _____
IL residents add 6.25% sales tax _____
RI residents add 7% sales tax _____
Shipping _____
Total _____

Ship to:

Name _____
Company _____
Address _____
City/State/Zip _____
Daytime Phone _____

Payment: ❏ Check to IDG Books (US Funds Only) ❏ Visa ❏ Mastercard ❏ American Express

Card# _____ Exp. _____ Signature _____

Please send this order form to: IDG Books, 155 Bovet Road, Suite 310, San Mateo, CA 94402.
Allow up to 3 weeks for delivery. Thank you!

IDG BOOKS WORLDWIDE REGISTRATION CARD

RETURN THIS REGISTRATION CARD FOR FREE CATALOG

Title of this book: Quattro Pro 6 For Windows For Dummies

My overall rating of this book: ❏ Very good [1] ❏ Good [2] ❏ Satisfactory [3] ❏ Fair [4] ❏ Poor [5]

How I first heard about this book:

❏ Found in bookstore; name: [6] _____ ❏ Book review: [7]
❏ Advertisement: [8] _____ ❏ Catalog: [9]
❏ Word of mouth; heard about book from friend, co-worker, etc.: [10] ❏ Other: [11]

What I liked most about this book:
_____
_____

What I would change, add, delete, etc., in future editions of this book:
_____
_____

Other comments:
_____

Number of computer books I purchase in a year: ❏ 1 [12] ❏ 2-5 [13] ❏ 6-10 [14] ❏ More than 10 [15]

I would characterize my computer skills as: ❏ Beginner [16] ❏ Intermediate [17] ❏ Advanced [18] ❏ Professional [19]

I use ❏ DOS [20] ❏ Windows [21] ❏ OS/2 [22] ❏ Unix [23] ❏ Macintosh [24] ❏ Other: [25] _____
(please specify)

I would be interested in new books on the following subjects:
(please check all that apply, and use the spaces provided to identify specific software)

❏ Word processing: [26] ❏ Spreadsheets: [27]
❏ Data bases: [28] ❏ Desktop publishing: [29]
❏ File Utilities: [30] ❏ Money management: [31]
❏ Networking: [32] ❏ Programming languages: [33]
❏ Other: [34]

I use a PC at (please check all that apply): ❏ home [35] ❏ work [36] ❏ school [37] ❏ other: [38] _____

The disks I prefer to use are ❏ 5.25 [39] ❏ 3.5 [40] ❏ other: [41] _____

I have a CD ROM: ❏ yes [42] ❏ no [43]

I plan to buy or upgrade computer hardware this year: ❏ yes [44] ❏ no [45]

I plan to buy or upgrade computer software this year: ❏ yes [46] ❏ no [47]

Name: _____ Business title: [48] _____ Type of Business: [49] _____

Address (❏ home [50] ❏ work [51] /Company name: _____)

Street/Suite# _____

City [52] /State [53] /Zipcode [54]: _____ Country [55] _____

❏ **I liked this book!** You may quote me by name in future IDG Books Worldwide promotional materials.

My daytime phone number is _____

IDG BOOKS
THE WORLD OF COMPUTER KNOWLEDGE

❏ **YES!**
Please keep me informed about IDG's World of Computer Knowledge. Send me the latest IDG Books catalog.

BUSINESS REPLY MAIL
FIRST CLASS MAIL   PERMIT NO. 2605   SAN MATEO, CALIFORNIA

NO POSTAGE NECESSARY IF MAILED IN THE UNITED STATES

IDG Books Worldwide
155 Bovet Road
San Mateo, CA 94402-9833